Route 66

A Journey Around the Football Grounds of Yorkshire

M J Mowbray

Blackline|Press

First Published in 2012 by Blackline Press
This Second Edition was published in 2013

ISBN 978-0-9563238-8-0

www.blacklinepress.com
Blackline Press 15 Lister Road IPSWICH IP1 5EQ
info@blacklinepress.com

Blackline|Press

For Andy Hurrell. So young to be battling Motor Neurone Disease. Marching on together mate.

@MowbrayRoute66

www.clubroute66.co.uk

Foreword

At first glance, it could look strange that a Manchester born cricketer is writing the foreword for a book about football in Yorkshire. Like Michael, I can't claim to be true Yorkshireman, despite my family moving to Sheffield when I was just 9 years old. I probably would have preferred to be a footballer if I had been good enough, but my knees would never have lasted! Instead, I got into cricket, playing firstly for my school and then club cricket. My career with Yorkshire began whilst watching them play in Sheffield after I managed to catch the eye of their coach Doug Padgett during the tea break. Despite his interest, the club then had a strict policy of only playing lads that were born in the county, but eventually the rule was removed and I was selected. I ended my playing career whilst playing for Yorkshire in 2009. Some may say I have done my bit for this fine county but, even then, I was hugely flattered when Sheffield awarding me the freedom of the city in 2005.

I have had a busy life with cricket taking me around the world, but I still always manage to find time for my own team, Sheffield Wednesday. I enjoyed reading chapter 57 and strongly endorse Michael's view that Hillsborough is an amazing stadium. This sleeping giant is indeed awakening and I have high hopes for Wednesday getting back into the top flight where they belong. Despite my clear bias toward the Owls, what I like most about this book is how it highlights just how many football clubs there are on our doorstep. Yorkshire is a diverse county, but our love of football unites us and, sometimes of course, it divides us too. It is very evident from some of Michael's visits into the Non League that this love can result in an amazing level of commitment from supporters to keep their clubs afloat. In the current tough economic climate it is amazing that fans still manage to find the cash to support their team. The clubs are really feeling the pinch, so I hope that Route 66 will help to promote Yorkshire football and ultimately result in more fans coming through the turnstiles.

As football fans, we often talk about relegation and losing a derby as being devastating events. I still remember how it felt going to school the morning after Sheffield United had beaten Wednesday 3-1 at home in 1992. However, when you take time to understand what people with Motor Neurone Disease (MND) and their families are going through, it puts all those footballing, and life's other little dramas, into perspective. We must remember that taking part in, and enjoying, sport really is a luxury for some. My thoughts are with those suffering from MND.

Enjoy the book and I hope it inspires you to explore some of these grounds!

Thanks

Michael

Michael Vaughan OBE

Introduction

***Midlife crisis** is a term coined in 1965 by Elliott Jaques and used in Western societies to describe a period of dramatic self-doubt that is felt by some individuals in the "middle years" or middle age of life, as a result of sensing the passing of their own youth and the imminence of their old age. Sometimes, a crisis can be triggered by transitions experienced in these years, such as extramarital affairs, andropause or menopause, the death of parents or other causes of grief, unemployment or underemployment, realizing that a job or career is hated but not knowing how else to earn an equivalent living, or children leaving home. The result may be a desire to make significant changes in core aspects of day-to-day life or situation, such as in career, work-life balance, marriage, romantic relationships, large expenditures, or physical appearance.*
Source: Wikipedia

Although I'm fast approaching 40, surely I'm a bit too young to be in my 'middle years'?! I'm a married man with two young children, George aged 6 and Lucas 3. I am what I like to call 'new Yorkshire' which, I have convinced myself, is superior to being a real Yorkshire man. After all, I chose to live here so must be better qualified to appreciate its immense beauty and diversity than those who had no choice in where they were born. I live in the town of Ilkley, a prosperous bubble removed from the 'real' world which is both a good and bad example of Yorkshire life. I wear a suit to work, have a big sales target in the worst recession in my lifetime but manage to make just about enough to live by a busy road and park my car in the street.

That's all there is to say about me really, except that I am someone who likes football. Well perhaps 'likes' is not a suitable description and certainly not the word my poor wife, brain washed sons or a doctor would use to describe my passion with our national game. To most people, a home season ticket holder of a top flight club with a

Sky Sports subscription is a keen football fan. I have gone beyond this level and I'm probably now beyond help. It is, of course, possible that writing this book will act as therapy, will help me to see that I have gone too far and then realise that spending Tuesday nights in front of the TV is what normal people do. I do hope not.

Before I relocated to Yorkshire 6 years ago I had moved around a bit, always watching football in whichever Midlands town or city I lived in. I had a fling with a couple of teams and, at the time, confused lust with love until I found my sole-mate Leeds United. After a couple of visits to Elland Road with my former neighbour Steve whilst living in Worcestershire, a home season ticket became my priority once I became a West Yorkshire resident. Away games naturally followed, which were usually eventful and certainly not dull when Leeds were in town. I now know that my current football club relationship is true love, the real thing and will be with me until death. Trips to places like Millwall, Carlisle and Huddersfield often put this to the test a little earlier than planned.

I eventually discovered other likeminded individuals in existence locally and quickly joined the Ilkley Whites to improve the quality of my away days and give my liver something to think about. I owe my ability to have beer for breakfast, or at a time before I would usually be awake, to these fine people.

I eventually earned enough loyalty points to apply for an away season ticket and won one in a ballot. This is a similar concept to winning an overpriced item on e-Bay when you are blinded by the fact you are a winner. The away match tickets would then just appear through my letter box and my diary revolved around the fixture list. The club profited with their 'admin fee' and the stress of small ticket allocations in League One were replaced with the problem of deciding what type of cans to pack. Everyone was a winner.

Following Leeds United became fully imbedded in my life, but I still felt the need for a further football fix. The problem I had was that

Leeds didn't play every Tuesday night, but Tuesday's had become 'me time' since my oldest son got a season ticket, which resulted in less beer but more trips to the toilet for 50% of my matches. Saturday away games on the coach were a release although perhaps too dependent on alcohol. In a moment of maturity I came to the conclusion that sometimes I needed to be sober to fully appreciate the cities and grounds I was visiting. Arriving with seconds to spare before kickoff, despite leaving the house at 5am, became the norm.

The solution was found in a trip to Nethermoor, the home of Guiseley AFC, where I discovered non-league football. Admission was cheap in comparison to my regular destinations and visiting new grounds, fields on some occasions, became highly addictive as someone on twitter warned me. The experience was also surprisingly child friendly, which enabled me to keep everyone at home happy. In fact, some of the best quality time with my 3 year old son has been at a non-league ground. Matches had a unique atmosphere of their own. The banter was still there, my hobby of people watching took a new dimension and a goal was a goal at any level. Up until now, my geography of England was established on cities, but there I was travelling to unknown towns – places that I would surely not visit without my desire to bag another ground. Has visiting the towns of Ashington or Nostell enriched my life? In my opinion, yes. Travel, whatever form it takes, broadens the mind.

On one dark day I decided to count how many grounds I had visited, which seemed a perfectly reasonable thing to do. It was worryingly easy to recall the last 30 years of my life and my healthy hobby turned into a number crunching exercise. Soon the male gene to collect something took over. Yes, I had started to collect football grounds and last season saw my total leap from 77 to 104. Trips to clubs such as Barnoldswick Town or Bedlington Terriers became the norm and ground number 100 was achieved back in Worcestershire. An eventful weekend with Steve included seeing a ghost, a pub crawl where we were offered 'drugs or beer' like a bag of crisps and a fine Guiseley win at St George's Lane in the heat. I even got a mention in the Worcester City programme which, I suppose, was fame. I warned them of my milestone visit because I had hoped it might get me in for free – too much time with the Yorkshire people!

Clearly I had too much time on my hands and also volunteered to start coaching my son's Under 6's team. This leap into the unknown completed my induction of the grass roots game but created a diary management problem that would keep most prime ministers awake at night. I had an impressive football CV that would surely benefit the children of Ilkley. Then just as I was starting to get into my stride I ran out of time as the close season arrived.

A break from football was almost a relief, but it also fuelled my planning to become a "professional" ground hopper. The 92 Club was an obvious challenge to finish. However, first I wanted to look at what was on my doorstep. After a couple of nights with my non-league pyramid poster and google maps I calculated that there were 66 football grounds in Yorkshire. A couple of days later I purchased The Non League Directory which would have made this task a lot easier to begin with, but at least came up with the same number. I didn't go beyond Step 7 of the pyramid, known as 'other leagues'; that would have been just silly. Visiting pub teams would have surely ended in a straight jacket replacing my parker. 66 was a good number and with my track record of obsessive behaviour there really was only one option - to visit all of them in one season. I had ticked a few off to date but bagging the lot in one continuous hit was becoming more appealing by the second. It would be inconceivable to abandon my basic football loyalties, so this crusade would be in addition to following Leeds United around the country; a demanding job and demanding on the commitments of a family that I wanted to keep in my life.

There is no doubt that this would be a challenge, but it was an opportunity to discover the real Yorkshire. This trip will be an adventure that goes beyond a game of football. Each club is part of their community and the vast county of Yorkshire has a diverse range of communities. The people who watch their teams will create a story of their own. I am now writing a travel journal and children in years to come will read my book in their history classes. After all in my opinion the answer to everything in life can be found at a football match. I hope that my book will tempt others to make that giant leap beyond their Premiership or Football League comfort zone into the non-leagues. It could change your life!

This is the diary of a ground hopper aged 39 ¾. From Eccleshill United to Leeds United. My journey begins in pre-season and will finish as the season closes in the Championship.

June 2011

Ups and downs

Nothing stands still in football, not even for a fantastic book title. First I discovered that Route 66 had become Highway 67 thanks to Bradford based club Albion Sports joining the Northern Counties East Division. We were soon back to 66 though with the unfortunate news that Brodsworth Welfare had resigned from their league. The final twist was harder to see coming. Sheffield Parramore moved a few miles out of Yorkshire to Nottinghamshire to become Worksop Parramore.
So we are at 65... for now!

July 2011

I

The eagle has landed

Eccleshill United FC v Scarborough Athletic FC

The Rapid Solicitors Stadium

Pre Season Friendly

Saturday 9th July 2011. Kick off 3pm

To attend 65 games in one season would be easy based on my track record but only if I didn't follow a football team already. Ditching my Leeds United was not an option so I felt that it would be wise to extend the time by starting in the pre season. This would not only give me a valuable extra month but allow me to examine a now important part of our football calendar. A 'friendly' is a lovely term, but, in reality, is a game between 2 teams with absolutely nothing at stake, played by players who are unfit and probably wishing that they were still on a beach, or, in non-league circles, stuffing their faces in front of the telly. Who actually pays good money to attend these games? I do, but as this book will prove I have an unhealthy interest in football that my mother would say 'will end in tears'. Fans are excused for attending a home friendly game against a glamour club who they would not usually play. If Real Madrid were touring West Yorkshire it would be understandable if the entire village of Eccleshill fled to Kingsway to drool over Ronaldo strutting his stuff. Scarborough Athletic are the big boys at step 5 of the Northern Counties East Premier today, but, in reality, only one season apart in league status. Eccleshill play in the Northern Counties East Division One.

I have personally used Leeds United friendlies to indoctrinate my children. My oldest son was taken to an Elland Road friendly in 2009 against Blackburn Rovers to prove his maturity to me. He fidgeted enough to delay a season ticket by 12 months and we missed their late equaliser whilst in the toilet. I let him think we won, but in all honesty he was more interested in whether he had enough sweets left for the journey home. Two years later, his first away game is being built up as a 'European trip' when we enter foreign soil at Motherwell next weekend. We will be extending the 90 minutes of football by camping, buying a 'special' badge for his scarf and eating yet more sweets to make this seem like a lifestyle worth considering. Why break a winning formula? My youngest son will be next and making his long awaited home debut sometime after his 4th birthday. He will no doubt be a complete nightmare, but when the dust settles and I am safely back on the sofa with a cold beer I will brag that it was a complete success. The eventual reward will be that father and son quality time that you just can't get from weighing vegetables in Tesco on a Saturday afternoon.

For most fans attending a non-league game, let alone a non-league friendly, is something they just wouldn't consider. Therefore an away game of this type would be beyond comprehension, so how would Jo Public view the Scarborough fans travelling to West Yorkshire today? If Margaret Thatcher was still in power she would surely have made attending football games illegal by now. These away fans would tick all the boxes of any charge sheet and be forced into hiding. "An away game sir, non-league, a friendly too?... come this way to make your one phone call".

Eccleshill United's ground can apparently hold 2,225 but I anticipate that I may be able to count the attendance myself today. I will no doubt annoy my readers throughout my book when I actually do this on a regular basis. I recall that I was part of a 35 strong army of Guiseley fans at Worcester last April. I had been concerned by our poor support when I originally counted 34 until I discovered one gentleman who had a weak bladder that afternoon. It would really help me if supporters could keep still.

I discover from the Eccleshill website that the club actually play in Wrose which doesn't mean a lot to me other than it is somewhere in the large unexplored strip between Leeds and Bradford which I will soon be very familiar with. Eccleshill is so similar to the word Ecclescake that it sounded like a nice place to visit; Wrose somehow didn't feel so inviting. I have enough material to attempt a joke about Jonathan Ross in a West Yorkshire florists, but decide to avoid trying comedy in my first book. I contacted the club out of courtesy and received a kind email from Chairman Adrian Benson who informed me that 'I would be made very welcome' and to introduce myself on arrival. I am now feeling like a journalist which actually feels good, despite the current phone hacking scandal. I enjoy the moment as I pack my notepad, camera and refreshments for the short trip to Wrose.

The drive over the tops from Ilkley is particularly enjoyable today due to the clear sky. Once I get through the parade of pushchairs and balloons of the Baildon carnival I am soon climbing the hill from Shipley. The view of Salts Mill from the top of Carr Lane is worth the drive alone and I am now in high spirits. The anticipation and excitement of finding a new ground has returned as I drive around a housing estate looking for the sight of a floodlight. This moment always make me feel like a child again which could explain my ground hunting exploits. Despite my slow approach, I still manage to miss the entrance so obtain directions from a grumpy man who needed the services of a good dentist. He informs me that I 'can't miss it' which clearly is untrue.

I arrive to the sight of a very large 'Eccleshill United Football Club' sign which I shouldn't have missed as the bad teeth man had said. I will make a note to pass on my dentist's home number to the kind old man. The entrance resembles a garden centre and the bumpy drive leads to a large open area that could easily be the setting for a scrap yard. We are in the middle of housing estate, so the neighbours are no doubt pleased that beyond the potholes and lock up garages is a rather tidy football ground. The view from the overspill car park provides me with my first view of the green grass of a pre season pitch. It is a welcome sight and my first impression is good. I head for the club house, order a pint and boldly ask the barmaid if Adrian

Benson is around. Adrian appears before she can answer and immediately shows me that his friendly email is an accurate reflection of the football club I have entered.

Adrian is a middle aged man whose 'other job' I discover is in carpet manufacturing. I have no idea if he owns the factory or drives the van, but it doesn't matter as a mutual love of football is always a great leveller. I immediately feel very welcome and I'm introduced to more people than I can write in my blank notebook. I am then led through the clubhouse, avoiding the need for paying at the turnstile, to meet a younger man armed with my complimentary programme. Nick Hird is the Groundsman which, I soon discover, covers a range of duties far beyond gutting the grass, such as providing the referee with a half time drink and retrieving footballs. In fact, everyone retrieves balls. Even Adrian appears throughout the afternoon carrying balls under his arms. Balls in non league football are money, so a precious commodity! Nick likes his day job as a landscape gardener at Bradford Council but is devoted to Eccleshill United Football Club. He has been doing it for 20 years and has an impressive 33 year association with the club, from the juniors through to the first team. He looks much younger than my maths tell me he is, so a passion for football must agree with his health. I now hope that my doctor does read this book.

Nick spends over half an hour with me as we sit in the sun discussing the ground, the history of the club and his hopes for the future. The glint in his eye as he describes how he would love to build banked terracing on either side of the main stand will stay with me for a long time. I am delighted to learn that the blue seats in this stand were purchased from Chesterfield FC when they moved into their new stadium. I am currently reading Stuart Basson's fine book, 'Saltergate Sunset' and have fond memories of visiting their previous home. The white seats on the other side of the stand are from the Headingley cricket ground to form the blue and white stripes of their shirts, although today the team are wearing their yellow away stripe. The former 'John Butler Stadium' has been renamed thanks to a new sponsor that will raise more funds than the savings achieved from not losing the balls to the neighbours. The club colours originate from being formed by a Huddersfield Town fan. Their badge displays an eagle, hence being known as the eagles, and, Nick informs me, is from the Saxon roots of the town. This is exactly what I wanted to hear and, more importantly, it is delivered with the pride of a supporter.

Today's visitors are a high profile club in non league terms based on their large following and tragic past. In fact, I could write an entire book on their troubled history, but will save the challenge of summarising this for my visit to Bridlington! The sun is hot, but I fear that the vast majority of my 65 games will not be played in such a tropical climate. Nick had stated earlier that their average crowd is around 40 and clearly there is a lot more in attendance today. I estimate that as many as two thirds present are here to cheer on Scarborough Athletic. Crowds usually rise to the 85-95 level depending on the away support. It is incredible to think that a coach full of visiting supporters would double the attendance. This ground would have felt very crowded when over 2,000 supporters turned up for a friendly against Bradford City 2 years ago.

The game has a lively first half. There is plenty of effort from both sets of players with Scarborough having the edge in the final third. The away side are also the better finishers and soon take a 2 goal lead thanks to Ryan Blott and Matt Draper. The celebrating cheers confirmed that the majority of fans are supporting the Seadogs. Adrian offers me some 'corporate hospitality' at half time which I accept. I do feel a little guilty on the back of not paying at the turnstile, but hope that I can repay their generosity by telling others through my book of my fine afternoon in Wrose. I am led through the club house by Adrian to a small room at the back. I enjoy a cup of tea, complete with saucer, and I am told to help myself to the buffet. Around me is a who's who of the club, but feel it not a good time to scribble in my notepad. Unfortunately, most of their names escape me except for their Director of Football Mark Ellis who once played for Bradford City. I joke with Mark about whether there are any internal battles with the manager concerning selection policy. We discuss my experience to date of non league football and their ambitious plans to improve their junior development. I can't speak highly enough of how welcome they have all made me feel, which is appreciated by this mere ground hopper. I wonder if Ken Bates will offer me an egg sandwich next April?

I return to the match. The second half is played at a much slower pace to remind me that this is a pre season warm up. Eccleshill do pull a goal back with a strike by Andrew Howland but Scarborough then quickly add a third goal thanks to James Webb's clean finish. The final score of 3-1 is a fair result and most spectators leave the touchline happy. I decide as my parting gesture, before thanking the chairman in person, to remove a very large weed from the main stand. It would be inappropriate to show this fine specimen to Nick after the time he had spent with me. My twitter followers are treated to a photo before I make a very poor attempt at pulling it up with its roots.

Adrian's final words to me as I head to my car, which I almost expect to find valeted, is that today's attendance was an impressive 135. It dawns on me that I had missed the point of non-league friendlies. They generate much needed income! I, for one, have thoroughly enjoyed my afternoon. I am conscious that Eccleshill United may have set a very dangerous precedent for the other 64 clubs. I couldn't agree more with the statement in my complimentary match day programme that Eccleshill United 'has built up a reputation as one of the most hospitable clubs in the area'. I will definitely return to Wrose and perhaps next time will actually visit the village of Eccleshill too.

Eccleshill United 1 Scarborough Athletic 3

Attendance 135
Admission price Free (£5 normally)

Ground Address Kingsway, Wrose, Bradford, W Yorkshire, BD2 1PN
Club website www.pitchero.com/clubs/eccleshillunitedfc
Twitter None found

2

#doncasterisgreat

Armthorpe Welfare FC v Matlock Town

The Welfare Ground
Pre Season Friendly
Tuesday 12th July 2011. Kick off 7.30pm

I had a meeting this afternoon in Worksop with my day job, so a village on the outskirts of Doncaster is perfect for my second ground. This is a luxury that will diminish as the season progresses so I enjoy the moment as I enter the car park of Morrisons at 5.30pm. I am early, but thanks to the power of twitter opening doors I have some pre match entertainment (or rather I am it) in an hour or so in Doncaster. I want to find the ground, explore the bright lights of Armthorpe and then head into Doncaster without a mad rush. The ground doesn't take any finding. Before I can remove my seatbelt, I can see the floodlights and fine looking ones they are too. Although, they don't all match, they are chunky and some have a crow's nest fit for a pirate should there be any in South Yorkshire. A couple of photos and a duck wrap later I am back in my car.

There appears to be only one entrance to the ground. This is down a lane next to a scruffy looking health studio which doesn't make me want to commit to a monthly £35 direct debit, although a workout will be welcome for residents as opposite stands the Golden Cod serving 'Award Winning Fish & Chips'. I do wonder what the awards ceremony would be like and I am surprised Sky haven't purchased the rights to show subscribers the drama of winning the golden fish cake award. Yes, I am bored. Interestingly, I didn't think I had been to Armthorpe before, but soon realise that my car broke down 5 years ago in the car park of the Wheatsheaf pub next to the chip shop. I am genuinely not being rude, but can safely say that Armthorpe is instantly forgettable. I am living proof that it is!

My next stop is Sine FM in the centre of Doncaster where I had been invited to discuss my book live on the 'Doncaster is great' show. I had seen the hash tag on twitter and presenter Andrew Isaacs would retweet anything with it on. A challenge I may put to the test on a Friday night in October when they play Leeds. I am just a humble ground hopper, so this is a new experience that is both exciting and daunting as I drive the short distance from Armthorpe. The recording studio is not quite what I was expecting, more of a rundown newsagent but without the big window and magazines. There are certainly no DJs or loose women in sight. Not even a fast car, although I have heard the TDI engine of the blue Touran parked in the reserved space performs well on the open road. I follow the signs to the back door, ring the bell and I am in without even getting frisked. Inside, I find a dentist style waiting room where we can all see and hear the presenters performing from within their booth. It feels a bit surreal as the others in the room all take it in turns to laugh out loud at Andrew's jokes and a guest's various impressions of farmyard animals. I am not sure where my football adventure will fit in.

I am soon called in and I feel honoured to be following the Stone Roses but surprised by the lack of preparation. I am given a chair, shown a large microphone and we are on as the last beats of Waterfall fade out. Andrew is a real life Alan Partridge, which I do mean in the nicest possible way. Not just because I am indeed a huge fan of Radio Norwich but he oozes personality. I feel instantly at ease and even his robot socks don't distract me as we chat about my book for over 10 minutes. I am not embarrassed for the sake of entertainment, I'm taken seriously and manage to avoid commenting on whether I watch much of Leeds United despite his best efforts to trap me. "I am a fan of 65 teams this year" is my story. I whisper goodbye as the show continues, open the door and tiptoe outside to my car. Ten minutes later I am driving around in circles in Armthorpe trying to park my car without blocking a heavily pregnant lady's drive, or obstructing someone with an urge for a pizza rather than a fishcake.

The club was formed in 1926 as part of the Colliery Social Welfare scheme, but limited success resulted in their disbandment in 1974. The lack of senior football in the village was soon recognised, so the club was reformed in 1976. Since their glory days in the early 80's, winning the league and 3 cups, they have maintained their place in the Northern Countries East Premier Division (step 5) since 1985. There hasn't been any silverware in this period, but they could have gained promotion in 2010 if not for a late drop in form to finish third. Today's opponents, Matlock Town, play in the Northern Premier League Premier division, which is above Armthorpe in the dizzy heights of Step 3. In return for £4, I am inside the ground with 20 minutes to spare. After talking to Martin Turner, the Match Day Secretary, for a couple of minutes, the teams run onto the pitch earlier than I was expecting. I am informed that the kick off is in fact 7.30pm so that "hopefully we won't need the lights on". The pull of the main stand in the evening sun is just too strong for me to even consider any further interviews tonight. I need one of those benches to slow down the pace of my busy day after all of that media attention.

The pitch is bumpy and the colour of the grass suggests it needs a good watering; not the dark green carpet I had witnessed in Eccleshill 3 days earlier. Perhaps the 'sunny donny' catch phrase is not a myth after all and the pitch is living proof that it doesn't rain in these parts, unlike the rest of Yorkshire. It has certainly turned into a glorious evening and I am perfectly positioned to feel the warmth of the sun on my legs from the bench I am spread out on. I relax as the sun slowly sets in the distance and there is just the sound of 22 players calling to each other in the distance. This is the 'me time' I seek and I quickly become quite removed from the game of football that is happening in front of me. It feels like being on holiday, your children have found some other kids with a football and you watch them playing safely in the distance as you lie in the sun.

I feel the need to concentrate more on the game after the silence is broken by the laughter of the crowd as a Welfare player misses a free header, which he may not find as funny. I start to notice the others in my stand and, in particular, the amount of women present. A young girl, probably around 18, who is nearest to me does stand out. She is well dressed - I wasn't expecting to see turquoise nail varnish and pearl earrings tonight - and is clutching some white football socks. It then dawns upon me that I am sat with the player's Wives And Girlfriends (WAGS). The girl in question appears to be watching every move of the Armitage number 2 even when he isn't near the ball. The game has a burst of activity just before half time with 3 good chances for Matlock Town, one of which came after her man gave away a corner. He shakes his head, she yawns and the teams leave the pitch with the score level at 0-0. I always go for a wander at half time and continue the habit tonight in the confidence that my space on the bench will not be taken in the rush. However, unusually, the only penny I can spend is in the gents. Some retail therapy is not on offer and there isn't a shop wanting to sell me a souvenir pin badge. There isn't even a snack bar open to tempt me as the cabin, closed tonight, looks like it could have been shut for several decades. Upon reflection, too many badges will turn me into an anorak and I certainly don't need the calories of a juicy pie.

The second half gets under way as the girl returns with the socks. The noise has increased and the warm sun is disappearing with the tranquillity. The players' yells, the usual phrases such as "hold it" and "stay with him", are growing in volume almost as if their voice boxes are returning to full match fitness. Even the baby of one of the WAGS, who I hadn't even noticed in the first half, is starting to stir. As four women cluck over the baby, the game is improving, but I am not sure who to watch most. WAGS do exist in non-league football and watching them is just as entertaining as if Posh Spice was holding David's socks. Just as I am juggling between the match and watching the women, three teenagers arrive and one lad asks me if it is the first half or second?! I kindly update them and they then abuse my generosity by playing dance music on their mobile phones. I wanted to introduce them to some headphones, or even the back of my hand, in my darkest moment of grumpiness but then remember that I am 39 and not 69.

Matlock eventually take the lead with a goal by Nathan Joynes to remind me why I am actually here tonight. I need to be watching because, despite counting at least 2 away fans in the ground earlier, and surely 11 enthusiastic players, the goal doesn't even generate a clap. The Armthorpe back four break the silence with a range of swear words aimed at the linesman which echoes around the neighbours' back gardens. The away side then start to look the better team. One particular player, without a number on his back, is showing more desire than the other 21 put together. His finishing is verging on comical, but he is at least getting in the positions to fluff it in the first place. Just as the game has finally grabbed my attention, the man next to me starts to make calls on his mobile. He appears to be ordering sausage rolls and eventually does a deal to collect 200 first thing in the morning. The sausage roll is undoubtedly the ideal way to start any day so, clearly, #doncasterisgreat for a healthy breakfast.

The game is coming to an end and darkness is falling a little too quickly for the man with the floodlight switch to enjoy the remaining minutes. I decide it would be fun to count the attendance and arrive at 62. I tweet this to my followers and, interestingly the club reply with the figure of 65. I wonder if they counted the baby, who I decide would need to be awake for at least 50% of the game to be included, or those noise polluting late arrivals. Just as I am planning my route home in my head, up pops the Armthorpe player Craig Fletcher to score a goal that finally produces a cheer, but thankfully not enough to wake the baby. I decide that a draw is a good result for the home side but then hear a fan tell his returning friend that the score is 2-1. Sorry 2-1?! How can that be?!! Who to? I am completely flabbergasted as the final whistle blows. This mystery needs solving, so I quietly ask a passing fan the details of the final score, using the 'I had just nipped to the gents' line which he will know is a complete lie if he has also spent most of the evening watching other people rather than the game. Apparently Matlock's Joynes scored his second just before Armthorpe got their goal. A silent goal whilst I was counting is a little unfair and results in me slipping away with my tail between my legs. Oh well, a defeat, but a great sunset and I have reached a decision that perhaps a radio commentary career is not for me. Not if it requires any concentration anyway!

Armthorpe Welfare 1 Matlock Town 2

Attendance 65
Admission £4
Ground Address Church Street, Armthorpe, Doncaster, South Yorkshire, DN3 3AG
Club website www.pitchero.com/clubs/armthorpewelfare
Twitter @thewelfare

3

Free child places

Silsden AFC v Thackley AFC

The Asda Foundation Stadium
Pre Season Friendly
Saturday 23rd July 2011. Kick off 3pm

The age old question for football supporters with children is what age can you start taking them to matches? It depends of course on the sort of child you have and the game you take them to. If your 5 year old son is generally scared at birthday parties of balloons bursting, clowns and loud music then Millwall away on a Tuesday night may traumatise him for most of his school years. It's a tricky balance because it is likely that your first trip will always be 'too soon'. Children can't adjust to new surroundings until they are introduced to them. That first meal out with your toddler is hardly the dining experience of a lifetime, but eventually, after many attempts, using caffeine or alcohol to keep you sane, you eventually get there.

Today, I am taking my 3 year old son Lucas to Silsden AFC who play in the North West Counties Premier league, which is at Step 5 of the pyramid. Silsden are the only team from Yorkshire in the league so they no doubt get a lovely reception on their endless trips to Lancashire and Merseyside. It would make sense to me to move them sideways to the Northern Counties East Premier where they could make the short trip to today's opponents Thackley every year. It is obviously not that simple and you can find many teams stranded in leagues that don't appear to make sense. Silsden is what I would call a proper Yorkshire town, surrounded by amazing countryside with rows and rows of stone terraces. Lots of 'normal shops' that don't cost the earth, pubs (not bars) and, importantly to the Mowbray household, a very good Chinese Takeaway for which we will happily leave the city walls of Ilkley on a regular basis.

I discovered last season that non-league football is very child, and even dog, friendly but only if your expectations are realistic. If your enjoyment of football relies heavily on concentrating on every pass, reading the programme from cover to cover whilst sipping your pint and generally chilling out on the touchline, then please continue to go on your own or with other grown-ups. So, why would anyone want to change their football experience when trips have been running smoothly for all these years? Of course life changes when children arrive, but, in my opinion, children should, to a certain degree, fit around how you live your life. Easier said than done, although most will agree how important it is to do activities with your children. Whether that be pony trekking, fly fishing or, in my case, ground hopping, my boys like spending time with their father away from the home. Football grounds are big open spaces, full of interesting people and offer them an opportunity to do something that is viewed as 'grown up'. Convinced? Well help is at hand and I will explain the basic rules for you to follow if you are brave enough to introduce young children to football.

Rule 1- Equipment. You will need to pack a bag; yes, a bag is essential! This fact alone could make this idea a non-starter for many free spirited supporters who haven't even managed the concept of wearing a coat yet, even in sub zero temperatures. In addition to the usual supplies you tend to carry around on a daily basis, there are two important items of kit to purchase in advance. Firstly, a packet of sweets, which is one of the main perks of going to football matches and could make this a winner for your offspring without a ball even being kicked. Today we have gone for some Mr Men sweets at supermarket prices as I have learned not to rely on clubs to stock a range of novelty confectionary. Secondly, a new toy is a very wise investment. This morning we bought Lucas a small motorcycle which, at £2.99 (less than a pound anywhere other than Ilkley) will increase your enjoyment of the game.

Rule 2 – Route Planning. It is essential that you do not arrive at the ground too early. If you do they risk getting bored before the teams have even kicked off. By half time he will be begging you to go home. Silsden are the nearest football club to our house at only 6.1 miles in distance and 10 minutes journey time according to the AA Route Finder. Being the shortest trip of the 65 grounds it is obviously easy to get this right, assuming there aren't any jugganauts jack knived around Addingham today. At 2.30pm we both jump in the car and park our car in the nearby industrial estate at 2.43pm. No problems finding a space, no charge to park and comforted in the knowledge that we will just walk through the turnstiles without expensive pre-booked tickets. I look in my mirror and realise I have probably been talking to myself for most of the journey as my football companion is now fast asleep. Cars have that amazing power, but today this isn't good. A little sleep can perform miracles in deciding what type of boy I will have for the rest of the day, but I don't have a great deal of time to play with. I decide on leaving him for 10 minutes and then a dash to the ground which, after all, is just a few strides away.

When carrying a sleeping child it is amazing how far those few strides feel. I wonder if scientists have ever compared the weight of humans when awake to when we are asleep. At least I get to steal a few cuddles, which I have to admit is nice when your son is a mummy's boy. I hadn't really given the admission price any thought, but am pleasantly surprised when I discover it is only £2 for adults. I am sure I have paid more to enter a village fete, but don't think I will be able to buy a prize Victoria Sponge today, let alone enter the longest stinging nettle competition (which I did win once). Under 5's are free, but I wouldn't have minded paying the concessionary price of £1. The match day programme is only 40p and even at 10p a page offers excellent value for money, although I was hoping for a brief history of Silsden rather than Thackley. I will file that one away for later in the season. On the way to the stand we pass a very busy club house, but the ground looks like I have arrived on the wrong day. I count 9 spectators as we select a bench (so much better than getting your children to master tip up seats) at the back of the stand. We unpack our bag to set up camp as Robbie Williams pumps out of the speakers. The players soon appear to Simply Red's, 'Moneys Too Tight To Mention'. This does seem very appropriate for a non-league side who played in red shirts.

Rule 3 – Don't disturb a contented child. The game gets underway which prompts most to leave the bar and take their place in the warm sunshine. I have a sleepy boy who is very content to sit quietly and eat his sweets. His silence is only broken with the excitement of finding a Mr Happy sweet, which he proudly tells me is yellow just like the (Thackley) goalkeeper. I would never have made that connection without him. Another boy of a similar age arrives and sits in front of us with his young mother. A couple of minutes later his granddad persuades him to go for a walk. A school boy error in my opinion, you leave him alone until he tells you he is fed up sitting still. She could have got a good 20 minutes out of him before allowing him to be dragged off to do a few circuits of the pitch. Five minutes later the mum is cursing Granddad as the little boy returns on his own. 'Did you run away from Granddad?' she asks him and then tells her friend 'he wouldn't have been watching him you know'. The game wasn't great but this was still a possibility.

At 3.20pm my son is still sat happily watching the game and the various Mr Men as they appear from the bag. I am conscious that this will not continue, so am pleased that the other boy is starting to make eye contact with us, our sweets and one expensive plastic toy. We are in the early stages of a friendship forming and even Thackley's poor attempts at set pieces are not spoiling the mood of optimism. A tractor is spotted in the distance which wins the battle for his attention. If Carlsberg made child friendly matches they would parade various zoo animals around the outside of the pitch at regular intervals. At 3.23pm the last sweet is eaten, which is quite impressive as it was a large bag. It is time for a motorbike to go for a spin and the farmer knows that his moment of fame has passed. Just as the bike is starting to be thrown around, two dogs arrive which I knew would buy me a bit more time in our big grown up stand. I am convinced that neither team will score if they play all week, but I am enjoying the increasing pace of the game. Thackley do come close to scoring, which draws attention to the fact that there are five away fans in our stand, or relatives of the players perhaps.

Rule 4 – Be prepared to be distracted from the match. To bring me back to earth my little man decides to drink my water whilst I am actually watching the game, which I am soon trying to mop up off the bench with my one tissue. Whilst I am on my knees, five others jump up with a cheer and yes I had missed the opening goal. Thackley are ahead thanks to a goal from Liam Robinson. The stand is in the shade so, as I'm not confident that our seats will dry, I make a mental note to find a different vantage point in the second half. It is just an accident I tell him and if we don't cry over spilt milk we are certainly not going to let Highland Spring spoil our afternoon. The lack of tissues is definitely an error in my preparation. What will I wipe his always snotty nose with now! The other boy enviously tells his mother whilst watching us that 'we haven't brought anything to drive'. Indeed you bad parent and our race track now has puddles to drive through. Without any introduction the boys start to play together. Bingo and I can enjoy the final 5 minutes of the second half with the comforting sounds of 2 small boys roaring at each other and discussing whether they wanted the red or white team to win today.

Rule 5 – Make the most of half time. The whistle blows for half time and despite things going very well I know that it is wise to use this time for a wander and that all important toilet stop. We head to the clubhouse with everyone else including one of the Silsden players. Lucas asks me the question, "why is there a footballer in here daddy?" I explain that they are only human so get thirsty too. The next ten minutes are the most costly part of a very cheap afternoon out and I become £3.69 lighter. We order an apple juice, but end up with orange which does at least come with a straw and an amazing price of only 70p. I am driving so don't feel the need for a single pint or the constant 'are you nearly finished' cross examining every 30 seconds. After all, I get to drink the orange juice which is no longer required. It is a shame that I can't have a few beers because at these prices I think that I could give the goalkeeper a good run for that Mr Happy tag. The big TV screen is impressive, but half time scores from friendly matches don't quite have the same appeal. I now know how my twitter followers must feel when I am reporting on meaningless throw ins. Then the wheels literally fall off our trip when our once proud motorcycle becomes a unicycle and our £2.99 investment is written off. We must have been using the wrong wet tyres that didn't suit the terrain of a dry clubhouse dance floor. We forget the toilet stop, but do at least find granddad who looks quite happy that they don't stock apple juice. We head back to our seats hoping that we may pass a toy shop.

I sit down and suddenly remember something important as my jeans soak up the still mineral water. The boys carry on where they left off and are now taking it in turns to show off. They are starting to get a bit silly, but the mother takes charge to calm them down; a role I am happy to pass on and give the game more attention. Thackley are playing some good football and I forget that it is a meaningless friendly. For some reason I find myself willing on Thackley to get a second goal. I also forget my parental responsibilities and realise that the boys have moved to the far end of the stand. The mother has followed them but I now need to keep more of an eye on them. I gather my things and move to where they are, but she uses this distraction as an opportunity to move her loved one to the nearby stand. My boy follows them, so I follow him and the four of us are soon together again in our new stand. This time it is a very bouncy, and noisy, metal terrace which, luckily, nobody else has chosen this afternoon. After about 10 minutes of bouncing, our new friends decide that enough is enough and leave us for a convenient walk. We look at each other and both know that following them is pointless, even if I didn't have these wet trousers on to weigh me down.

Rule 6 – Balls can be dangerous. The ball struck the side of the stand with a bang that made us all jump. Perhaps we were all watching the farmer, but this did remind me that when bringing your children to football you need to watch the ball at all times. It's not like sitting in the upper tier of a 40,000 capacity Premiership stadium when you may see a ball every tenth season. A flying ball would undoubtedly hurt a 3 year old boy and probably make the prospect of a return visit a lot less appealing. Players at this level do have the habit of booting the ball out at close range where perhaps Xavi would have let the ball run out for a throw in.

Rule 7 – Every goal you see is a bonus. Just as I am wishing I had that pint in my hand (I seem to be the only one in the stand without one) Silsden do the unthinkable by equalising. It was a lovely bit of skill and a fine finish by Matthew Kershaw. The home side should really be dead and buried, but it's now game on. The Silsden players grow in confidence and get the ball forward a lot quicker. The words 'daddy I need a wee wee' remind me that we hadn't gone at half time and back to the club house we head. We slow down our walk as Thackley start to attack again at that end of the ground, but eventually run out of touchline. I joke to one of the fans that I bet we miss a goal as we go in. We nod to granddad as we pass the bar and are soon back at the pitch side. Scoreboards are rare in non-league football and you don't hear the 'roar' of the crowd from the toilets, so I check immediately with a fan if it is still 1-1. Of course not, we have missed another goal and Thackley are now leading 2-1 thanks to that mystery man, Robinson, again. I don't need any further information, knowing it was a 40 yard screamer wouldn't help. We return to our seats as I remind myself that the goal we did see was a fine one. We both head back to the car upon the whistle, yellow with happiness.

Some may say why bother going to a match when you can't watch it all? I could reply with news that we saw a cricket match, a river, a scull and cross bones car sticker and a funny looking white cat on the way back to our car. You would even be excused thinking my son could have been anywhere this afternoon, but he definitely took it all in. Lucas announces to his mother upon arrival home that he had seen a goal, got his hands dirty, made a friend and even saw a pirate's car. He did indeed and his father enjoyed some quality time with his little boy. Going to a match doesn't always mean taking time away from the family. I enjoyed ground number 3 for different reasons than I will hopefully enjoy ground number 4. And the Chinese takeaway later tonight will taste good after all that fresh air. Perhaps the chef is a pirate who drives a Vauxhall Astra?

Silsden 1 Thackley 2

Attendance Not recorded
Admission £2
Ground Address Keighley Road, Silsden, Keighley, West Yorkshire. BD20 0EH
Club website www.silsdenafc.net
Twitter @SilsdenAFC

4

Let it snow

Stocksbridge Park Steels FC v Rotherham United FC

The Look Local Stadium

Pre Season Friendly

Tuesday 26th July 2011. Kick off 7.45pm

I have been looking forward to this trip despite not knowing where Stocksbridge was until a couple of days ago. Few clubs have a better sounding name for my discovery of the 'industrial north'. In fact, the town lies only 7 miles from junction 35 of the M1, which I pass every week. It looks lovely from the map, almost being shaded in with the green of the Peak District. Their website also grabbed my attention with some impressive photos of the ground. As I drive on the A616, it soon becomes apparent that the town ahead set in the valley is Stocksbridge. It looks inviting in the bright sun. My approach down into the centre passes the steel works whose huge presence is immediately felt. The centre is narrow with attractive stone buildings either side of the road, though they may look very different on a wet February morning. I take a sharp right turn where the road climbs slowly and steeply uphill until, eventually, I arrive at the ground, which is surrounded by open space. The views from the top are spectacular and do hope that the locals don't take this for granted.

I have recently made a new friend on Twitter who has kindly arranged for someone to 'look after me' tonight. Tweeter 'PukkaMatt', Matthew Twigg of family run business Eric Twigg Foods, is sponsoring tonight's game, which they do regularly at Rotherham United. Matt is a Millers fan and his company supply Pukka pies, amongst other products, to customers that include many football clubs. Unfortunately, Matt could not make tonight's game, but has kindly arranged for his friend, Andy Horsley, to show me around. I am looking forward to meeting Andy on the back of such a good day at Eccleshill United under similar circumstances. I had enjoyed the solitude of The Welfare Ground and the time with my son in Silsden, but tonight I'm very happy to get an introduction to this football club. It is only 6.30pm when I head into the ground with both senior and junior players also arriving. Andy Horsley makes a good first impression. He is friendly, a down to earth man and is clearly popular based on our walk into the ground. My attention immediately focuses towards the pitch which looks stunning. It resembles more a bowling green than the bumpy pitches I have seen recently. I can't recall a better quality surface at this level and we both admire it under the evening sun from the height of the club house. Andy is a committee member of the football club, but also Chairman of the Stocksbridge Sports & Social club and Bracken Moor club house. I am not completely sure how these 3 come together, but there is no doubt that he lives and breathes Stocksbridge Park Steels. Firstly, we chat about the ground and how it has been improved over the years to ensure that promotion could be achieved to the Northern Premier League Premier. In 1990, the floodlights were installed at a cost of £17,000. I hope I will see them on tonight. There is no better sight even when you are 39! Getting to step 3 involved building a covered terrace behind the goal in 1994, which proved to be a good investment when promotion was approved the following year. The impressive main stand had ensured that they already met the number of seats criteria. These seats were once in the North Stand at Hillsborough, which is appropriate for a town, he informs me, is full of Wednesday fans. Sheffield Wednesday is located in the north of the city, so the nearest league club to Stocksbridge. The ground capacity of 2,200 was almost achieved when the owls once visited for a friendly when 'Carboni came to town'. Tonight the far touchline is open, but they have had to spend £20,000 on a fence to maintain their league status. It is taken down in the summer for the cricket season and can stay down for tonight's friendly match which creates a very spacious feel to the ground.

We move down to the playing surface which is a great experience with the Rotherham United players training around us. I feel like a small child, but hide my excitement and continue to fire off questions. I discover that the club is now in its 25th year after being established in 1986 from the merger of Oxley Parks with Stockbridge Works, who had occupied this ground since the 1920s. 'One had the team and the other had the ground' Andy tells me, so it made perfect sense to form Stocksbridge Park Steels FC. Around the turn of the millennium the club became self funding after they purchased the land from Corus, whose only connection now is sponsoring their main stand. The steel works are clearly still in existence, but 'not like the good old days when they had cash to spare'. This change in ownership also created the need for a new groundsman who was previously full time and paid by the steelworks. The current secretary now has this role and is not doing a bad job at all!

We then turn our conversation onto the future, but Andy is not confident that the team can progress to the next level with average attendances of only 150-200. In times of increased wages and signing on fees even in this league, viewed as 'madness', it is a constant challenge to attract fans to watch them. On an evening like tonight, I struggle to see why even the sternest Wednesdayite living in the town would not come to Bracken Moor when they were not watching their first love play. He is looking forward to the visit of FC United and Chester this season when their large away following will boost the gate. Promotion to the Conference North is viewed as too much of a big step without the finances to sustain this level. The club had once given the parents of the junior team free season tickets, now priced at £90, but even this gesture didn't improve attendances. They are currently offering fans a ticket for £49 that could get you into any 10 games during the season. Normal admission is £7, but tonight's friendly is reduced to £5.

After taking advantage of being on the pitch and getting some more photos, when I really just wanted to steal a ball and toe punt it into the open net, I am introduced to Philip Burkinshaw. Philip is the club's Press Officer, a printer by day, with responsibility for the club's website and match day programme. I sense that his duties extended beyond this and he jokes how Andy visits the ground every day. I doubt he is alone. If I had the keys to this ground I may be tempted to make sure I was passing most days. I remark again on the fine weather, but they both tell me that a ball wasn't kicked last December due to the snow. The pitch is high up so probably has a separate climate, but I find the stories of snow in May and June a little harder to believe.

The kick off is fast approaching, but I can't refuse the offer of a guided tour of the changing rooms. These are the first football changing rooms I have been inside seen and, luckily I don't see any bare bottoms tonight. The large baths are no longer in use due to the new rules on hygiene. The crazy world of health & safety has even reached grass roots football. It is good to hear the story of when the Daily Star published a photo of the players in the bath with local celebratory, topless model Kirsty Palmer. Andy recalls how all the married players were at the back with the young single lads getting a bit cosier.

I find time to visit the clubhouse for a quick pint of Brown Cow whilst I study the programme. Pie man Matt had warned me last week that the Rotherham players on show tonight would be their 'kids' due to only returning yesterday from their training in Portugal. I have to admit, as I study the teams, that I am not familiar with the names in front of me, but I am looking forward to the match regardless of who is playing. I am feeling a bit peckish and there really is only one thing to eat tonight. I queue for over 5 minutes, but, despite my new found pie network, they have actually run out of Pukka Pies on the night Eric Twigg Foods are in town. My sausage roll and I find a good spot on the steep terrace high up behind the goal which appears to be the away end tonight; well I am surrounded by 5 Rotherham fans. I ask the lad next to me, as he eats his pie, if they have any first team players here tonight. 'Six and one on the bench' I am told, so it is surprising that more Rotherham fans have not made the short journey to Stocksbridge. The players kick off, but with no names on the shirts I don't know who is a first teamer and who is a reserve.

The game is played at a decent pace, but isn't grabbing me tonight. It has too much of that pre-season feel, which, in both teams' defence, is exactly what it is. The handful of Rotherham fans are not providing that 'big league team visiting small local minnow' feel I had hoped for. My "creative" writing skills will surely be tested tonight and I am in need of some goals. The home side miss a penalty after half an hour and I am as disappointed as anyone as the ball strikes the post. Two minutes later Dominic Riordan must have read my thoughts as he gives Stocksbridge the lead. To my relief, an announcement on the tannoy follows the goal - they must have heard of my record of missing goals. After ten minutes the game looks very one sided as the home side go 3-0 up thanks to an own goal by Mark Bradley and a fine finish by Matt Telling. The League One side now look very ordinary and only the woodwork denies Stocksbridge a fourth goal as the half time whistle saves them any further embarrassment. A female Rotherham fan beside me informs us that it was in fact the linesman's fault, after halting several United attacks with his flag, and suggests that he should 'get to chuffing spec savers' as he leaves the pitch. This somehow starts an argument with another fan who claims to be the cousin of the linesman which is the reason for his presence. I am rescued by Andy and invited for some refreshments inside. Writing notes as two people argue may draw attention to myself I and certainly didn't want to get on the wrong side of this 'lady'. I enjoy my cup of tea, even if it comes with milk as standard, and get introduced to Eric of Eric Twigg Foods. I don't mention my struggles to find a pie, but we both appear to be communicating match updates to his son, Matt. The trip to Portugal, or the 3 training sessions a day without any matches, is blamed for Rotherham's collapse and we both hope for better things as the players return.

The lady in red is still there and advises me that there have been no "bloody changes" to her team. Someone bravely informs her that this isn't the case and I just resist telling her to visit a high street chain of opticians. She then boldly tells everyone that she has been 'robbed' in reference to the £5 entrance fee. I then notice 3 police officers arrive, so perhaps someone has reported this crime at half time. Thankfully, there isn't an investigation and they appear to be here to play with their mobile phones. There is an opportunity to help by clearing the cricket wicket from children, but thanks to a couple of announcements normal texting resumes. The away side have improved, so no doubt have adjusted to the Yorkshire air. The floodlights are turned on and the second half becomes as instantly forgettable as my sausage roll. The game is now too even and is very scrappy. It is turning cold now that the sun has disappeared and the final whistle arrives just as I am starting to worry whether I will get back to Ilkley in the snow. The vast majority of the fans here have witnessed their team convincingly beat a league side 3-0 so have in my humble opinion got value for their fiver. I have had a great evening, which proves that sometimes the 90 minutes of football can be a tiny detail of why we come to matches. I make a point of finding Andy to thank him and, indeed, I have been 'looked after'. My waistline didn't need a pie anyway and I will definitely return one day to Bracken Moore. If its winter I'll be sure to bring a hat and a snow shovel.

Stocksbridge Park Steels 3 Rotherham United 0

Attendance 255

Admission Free (£5)

Ground Address Bracken Moor Lane, Stocksbridge, Sheffield. Club **website** www.stocksbridgeps.com

Twitter @StocksbridgePS @SPSSupporters

5

Smart casual for the spa town derby

Harrogate Railway Athletic FC v Harrogate Town

Station View

John Smith's Cup

Saturday 30th July 2011. Kick off 3pm

Today, in the beautiful spa town of Harrogate, there is a big derby game which the world of football can be excused for overlooking. Every season we switch on our TVs to witness the high drama, now in HD and 3D, of the Old Firm between Rangers and Celtic, a Manchester Derby when United battle with their millionaire neighbours City or the glamour of Barcelona against Real Madrid. Supporters located in places like North London, Merseyside, Sheffield, Nottingham and Bristol will argue that it is, in fact, their derby which is the most important match in the football calendar. The majority of football fans probably don't even know that this North Yorkshire town has 2 football clubs, but this afternoon they face each other for their first opportunity to win a trophy this season. Harrogate Railway play at Step 4 in the Northern Premier League Division One North which is 2 steps below the Conference North where Harrogate Town currently stand.

Harrogate Railway Athletic were formed in 1935 by workers at the Starbeck London & North Eastern Railway depot. They borrowed £1,500 from the LNER and more than 300 workers contributed one old penny per week to repay the loan. This money secured ownership of the current Station View site. Sadly, the loco sheds closed in 1959, subsequently affecting finances as many of the workers, and players, had to leave the area. The club have remained in the suburb of Starbeck, but, as the crow flies, is not that far from Town's CGU

Stadium. The weather is hot and my air conditioning is working hard as I drive out of Harrogate towards Knaresborough. I have a rough idea where the ground is without the need for a map and a clear sign directs me to take a left turn. Within a couple of minutes of driving through a quiet residential area I can see the 8 slim floodlights in the distance. I find a large playing field which is used as a car park on match days. Without the need to part with any money once again, I find some shade and watch, from my now climate controlled car, the supporters crossing the open space towards the ground. Quite a few fans are wearing black and yellow scarves of Town, which does make me smile in the scorching hot sun. The ground is surrounded by a high corrugated iron fence painted green which is just about tall enough to hide what is waiting for me inside. As I approach the turnstile I hear a train pass, which reminds me why their home is called Station View. If I only knew where to look I could admire this view, but feel the need to watch where I am stepping as soon discover what this grass is used for on non match days.

Entrance into the ground is gained for just £5 plus £1.50 for a very glossy looking programme. I enquire if they sell pin badges and am pleasantly surprised to be told to visit the 'club shop'. I soon find an old portakabin with the words 'club shop' on the door. The inside space is a little cramped, but well stocked with goodies. I am served by a friendly elderly man and I buy three (social services may be interested that I have actively encouraged my children to collect football badges). After I politely remark that I have spent more here than at the turnstile, he reaches into a box on the floor and gives me 2 free programmes. I am told to show my children how many star players were listed inside. It was a very kind gesture, but I couldn't help feeling a little guilty. I didn't mean anything by my comments; if anything it was a compliment of the low admission cost. £3 is the going rate and these golden beaver badges are the best example of a golden beaver we have in our collection. On closer inspection, I have the programme for the 2nd round FA Cup home tie against Bristol City on Sunday 8th December 2002. I actually watched this game on TV, so was very interested to look at this. Railway lost, but the then second division leaders were made to fight after Steve Davey netted with 17 minutes to go. City scored in injury time to win 3-1, but as the programme editor had stated then, this was 'the biggest game in the club's 67 year existence'. Temporary stands were erected and the attendance that day was over 3,000. Unfortunately arguments over bonus payments clouded the day for the club.

As at most non league grounds, I have the choice of the entire touchline, but getting out of the hot sun is my priority. The seated stand behind the far goal looks perfect and I wander over with my travelling souvenir shop. From my seat, the slope of the pitch strikes me instantly. The ground around me looks patched up with nothing matching. If I wanted a symmetrical stadium I wouldn't be spending so much time in the lower depths of non league football. Probably the smallest stand in the world stands proudly behind the dugouts which is not quite wide enough for the full title of the club. This would make a very good family stand, i.e. it holds no more than an average family. Today, nine people have made this area their home and cosy they look too as the players run out. The teams form a line, which I hadn't seen at any games so far in the non leagues. This scene would look at home at the Camp Nou as they are encouraged to shake hands before battle commences. Well it would if a giant beaver was not shaking hands with them too. Railway are wearing their usual bright red shirts, green shorts and red socks. Town are in their away kit of white shirts, black shorts and white socks.

The game kicks off briskly whilst I am still deciding if I am in the home end or not as both sets of supporters are on display in addition to the usual Leeds United, Chelsea and Manchester United shirts. There is also an entire junior football team on the front row from neighbouring Knaresborough Celtic which, as a coach myself, I think is very brave. Town fans appear to be showing their colours more, I suppose like any 'away' fans do, and are scattered around the ground. Within the first minute Town almost take the lead and the pace increases as a result. After only five minutes the home side are awarded a penalty at the other end, which looks like it was for shirt pulling from where I am sat. Ex Town player Jon Maloney calmly steps up to give Railway the lead. Only a fraction of those in our stand cheer, so I know immediately that most of the Town fans are sat here, or we are all lonely ground hoppers. A small group of away fans are stood at the front and start to bang the advertising hoardings with chants of "come on you Town". That derby atmosphere I am seeking has arrived and the players respond with some fierce tackles. The game is quick with end to end action and does feel different from the previous four games. This is a cup tie after all and to those present today the result does actually matter. I am not suggesting that if the score stays 1-0 town fans will go back to their loved ones, smash up the BBQ and announce that summer is over... but they have paid their money to see their rivals get beaten.

After 22 minutes a Town shot hit our stand so hard a bit falls off (I am sure it can be patched up in the morning) which results in that very English cheer, like when some poor barmaid drops a tray of glasses in a pub. The away side are starting to get the edge with most chances falling to them. An equaliser does look on the cards. As the half hour mark approaches there is a clear handball by one of the Railway defenders, but to everyone's surprise a penalty isn't given. The resulting corner almost produces the equaliser and a further three chances are missed, which keep a group of young Railway fans busy chasing the balls behind the stand. As half time approaches, the tempo is starting to slow down which isn't really surprising in the hot sun with the 22 players not yet fully match fit. Town find the time to waste 2 further chances, which surely on any other day would hit the back of the net, and the home side somehow manage to finish the half a goal ahead.

I use the interval to enjoy some sun, but somehow end up returning to my seat with some chips. I am starting to think that this 65 ground marathon will do some real damage to my health. I did at least learn something from my visit to the refreshment stand. A plaque told me that the floodlights were officially switched on in March 1991 with the visit of Sheffield United. I also saw the plans on the wall for developing the ground, but even without the help of an architect it didn't look like a three tier stand with boxes. I have a quick flick through the programme as the teams come back out. This tells me the club is waiting for planning permission for a new Clubhouse, Changing Rooms and 3G pitches. I return to my stand, which has emptied, and there is now a long line of Town fans at the opposite end following the switch of ends at half time. Seven minutes from the restart the new away end is celebrating an equaliser. Trialist Craig Radcliffe strikes the post, but the rebound hit a Railway player for an own goal. My stand sits in silence which allows me to hear that Town are now singing. This doesn't happen very often in non league football. Both sets of players respond. The tackles start to fly in and I sit back to enjoy my secret derby. We are treated to few good chances for both sides and then someone flicks the 'back to meaningless friendly' switch and things slow down for the final half an hour. During this period we do see some good chances, mainly for the away side, but the goals don't follow.

Town are more physical and do look fitter in the final stages of the match, but miss a header in the last ten minutes that produces a wave of laughter at our end. Railway also have an opportunity to score a winner in the final seconds, but the young striker has too much time to think about his one on one with the keeper. His shot resembles more of a back pass, but gives us all something to sigh about as the whistle blows at 1-1. It strikes me as I am leaving my seat that I am alone. I soon catch on that we have a penalty shoot out to decide a winner. I love penalty shoot outs, unless they involve my own team or country, so am very happy with this. I didn't even have to change ends as the high drama is going to take place at this goal. There is no flashing score board or commentary today so we are left to good old counting. The maths are easy; Town missed two whilst Railway put all of theirs away as if it was Germany playing England. The home fans celebrate the 4-2 triumph and there appears to be a gathering of players for some kind of trophy presentation. It is hot and I know that traffic in Harrogate, shoppers rather than the 239 here today, would not be as enjoyable as today's finale. It does occur to me as I make my way back to the car park that this derby was in fact unique. It is a very middle class derby. The collection of cars in front of me, the use of smart casual clothes (that sweater over the shoulders is not the norm on a match day) and people just look 'comfortable'. Complete rubbish and outrageous stereotyping? Perhaps. This observation is not intended as a compliment or a criticism, but I know that the people of Glasgow, Liverpool or North London could not compete on this level. This gave me a lot to think about as I left Harrogate and I almost forgot my previous brain teaser – why a beaver?!

(I later discover it originates from the Railway Workers as it symbols a hard working industrious animal).

Harrogate Railway Athletic 1 Harrogate Town 1

(Railway win 4-2 on penalties)

Attendance Not recorded
Admission £5
Ground Address Starbeck, Harrogate, North Yorkshire. HG2 7JA
Club website www.pitchero.com/clubs/harrogaterailwayathletic
Twitter @THERAILFC

6

A square meal

Thackley AFC v Guiseley FC

Dennyfield

Pre-season friendly

Tuesday 2nd August 2011. Kick off 7.45pm

Tonight I want to be a supporter again. My local Non-League side Guiseley, where this entire ground hopping madness all started, are the visitors to Dennyfield. It's the first time I have seen them play since I left Telford last May. On that historic Sunday afternoon Guiseley were only 11 minutes away from Conference football, but left the New Bucks Stadium to the sound of the home fans celebrating promotion. I want to see if there is still life after 'Wally' (last season's top scorer James Walshaw moved to Darlington last month) and hopefully go home full of optimism following a good performance. I arrive in Thackley with an hour to spare and follow the clear, but wonky, sign to the ground. I approach Dennyfield down a long narrow country lane and park in the almost empty car park.

Once again, I am early and the only other people arriving appear to be the players. I still haven't adjusted to the lower leagues where you can just turn up with a few minutes to spare, although it is quite nice to relax and explore each location, particularly when it is such a pleasant evening. Tonight, I am in search of food. I have had a busy day at work, I'm a bit stressed and in need of something really nice to eat. I am in the sort of mood that I would quite happily replace food with a lot of beer, which would take the edge off my appetite, but unfortunately I'm in my car. I hope I can travel by train to some of my games and combine my visit with some decent pubs; for research purposes only of course. Thackley AFC were founded in 1930 by the younger members of Thackley Wesleyan Methodist Church who would have probably disapproved of my desire to drink real ale.

The club progressed by way of the Bradford Mutual Sunday School League and now play their football in the Northern Counties Eastern League Premier. Guiseley are currently 3 Steps above Thackley in the Non-League pyramid, playing their football in the Conference North.

I feel the need for a quick peep over the wall before my stomach is put in charge. I can see a very green pitch and catch a glimpse of the words 'Thackley Football Club' on the main, and only, stand. The ground isn't going anywhere so I start my walk back up the lane in search of a feast. As I leave the car park, it does feel like I am in the middle of the countryside, yet I know that we are not far from the busy main road to Shipley. I pass a riding school and no fewer than five people walking their dogs. It was the time of the day when their owners had returned home full of guilt and needed to go through this daily ritual to avoid the RSPCA visiting. Tonight, it is at least a good evening, but in all honesty I am not a dog person. I am not going to criticise people for running their lives around what I view as a one way inconvenience when my 'hobby' to them is no doubt on the same level as a train spotter; and I don't mean the risk taking fashionable youngsters in that brilliant film set in Edinburgh.

I haven't eaten much today although I have drunk a lot of coffee, so need to find a toilet. I wasn't confident I would find one so get carried away with all this open space. I do find a hedge, which wasn't difficult, but almost get caught by a group of teenage BMX bandits. The jog, the type usually done just after tripping over in the street, only sharpens my appetite. I can see a Chinese takeaway in the distance, which feels like spotting a lake in the desert. I have a weakness for oriental food and enter the Hou Hing in a reckless mood with a pocket full of money. I order some salt and pepper spare ribs and, within no time at all, I am proudly standing outside with my carrier bag. The problem I now have is where to consume these beauties.

I had, previously, loosely arranged to meet someone tonight, so I send a text whilst I am deciding my next move. Through Twitter, I have been communicating with Dan who, with the help of a couple of people produces the excellent Leeds United fanzine and podcast, The Square Ball. I am a huge fan of their work, so I am flattered that I have been given a double spread in every issue this season to feature my travels. I select a lovely spot in the evening sun to eat my ribs whilst waiting for Dan. I have excellent facilities, a bench next to a bin to pop the bones in after munching on each rib and I can even hear the music from the ground. What is that smell though? Oh dear, the detective in me discovers a very large, in fact three large, dog poos that are staring up at me. This is not helping to create the eating experience I was hoping for, so decide to move; a little jog again in case anyone is watching. I can see a man walking towards me with two huge dogs, well they could well be black sheep, but provided he has eaten I hope this is Dan. Otherwise, I am in trouble as he is now looking towards me and I didn't opt for the set meal for four. It is indeed Dan who I warm to instantly. His dogs also take an instant like to me and they both drool over my ribs. This does create a surreal moment as we chat about my book, his magazine and of course Leeds United, which always includes a certain bearded gentleman. I am having so much fun I am surprised to discover that it is 7.40pm. I drag myself away from this al fresco dinner party, which is a relief to Dan as his dogs are starting to misbehave; the usual climbing into other peoples cars, scaring the timid dogs (and owners) and running around in front of the arriving traffic.

I pay at the turnstile, but there isn't a programme tonight to tempt me. I am informed that there is a team sheet in circulation, but I am not given any clues on where to find this. This should not be a problem for someone who can find a Chinese takeaway and solve a foul smelling country air mystery. I have arrived as both sets of players are warming up in the evening sun and take my place by the nearest corner flag. My wild mood is spreading, so I choose a new position to watch the game from tonight. A couple of Guiseley fans move beside me which suggests that 'we' must be kicking this way. Isn't football at this level great in how you are given the freedom to swap ends at halftime? The ribs have actually made me hungrier and also very thirsty.

Play starts, which rescues me from searching for more food. The Dennyboys are wearing their usual red shirts with white sleeves, white shorts and red socks to give them that old Arsenal look. Guiseley are in their familiar white shirts, blue shorts and white socks and also, familiarly, start the game brightly. They have two half chances within the opening minutes and look the better side immediately. Lee Ellington almost scores with a glancing header, but in the 5th minute, as I am still trying to get a piece of meat from my tooth, his strike partner, Joe O'Niell, scores with a clean finish under the diving Thackley keeper. Straight from the restart Guiseley continue to attack and are playing some lovely football. The away side are putting some clinical through balls to the forwards and already the game is looking very one sided.

I assume that the far touchline behind the dugouts is terraced, either that or those fans are particularly tall. Despite their height, they don't appear to have the best of views in the glaring sun, which may help their enjoyment of the game if they follow Thackley. Eventually, I give in to my hunger and go in search of a pie which, of course, they don't sell. I order a burger and just as I am putting on the ketchup I see the Guiseley players celebrating. They have taken a two goal lead in the first 14 minutes and I am informed that the scorer was Danny Boshell. I over hear someone commenting on the "difference in quality" between the two sides which is very apparent to me, even from behind a cheese burger.

My stomach has at least led me to the team sheet, which is a hand written piece of paper pinned to a board next to the catering stand. I love how personal it is, but unfortunately can't read it. It must of been produced by the club doctor. I return to my corner flag to find a large brown dog wearing a Guiseley scarf who then prefers to watch me eating, every single chew, rather than his team. I hadn't given in with my ribs but he has a sporting chance with a very below par burger. It always amazes me how football grounds all sell burgers yet finding a decent one is so difficult. I am not asking grounds to cook me a Dover sole and scallops but can we at least start by buying burgers made from meat?

Guiseley continue to attack and it's no surprise when they score again in the 24th minute. A well worked free kicked ends with a fine strike from Gavin Rothery. The home fans are not impressed with their players who do appear to be showing Guiseley a bit too much respect on the ball. The cries of "tackle", "get your foot on the ball' and "wake up" say it all. This game is effectively over with only a third of the match played. The rest of the half is not as eventful, which silences the supporters to create a tranquil atmosphere. There is just the sound of the ball being kicked, so again it feels like we are in the middle of the open countryside. I need to see an aerial photograph as I know we must be near a built up area despite there being no traffic noise at all. The whistle blows to end a very slick half for Guiseley.

I make a visit to the club house for a quick pint and I am pleased to find that classic environment. There is the usual furniture that doesn't match, loads of team photos on the walls and a trophy cabinet which houses some treasures. There is also a room at the far end serving cups of tea and sandwiches to the chosen few. Tonight I am much happier with my lager and Twitter stream. I am sat next to a group of home fans whose only positive comment is that the pitch looks nice. It does indeed, but it is also helping Guiseley to pass the ball. I am expecting more goals, but keep my thoughts to myself. I decide on a walk to burn off some calories and find a place in the new away end behind the goal. I find another dog in a scarf! This Great Dane has been spotted before at Nethermoor, but attending an away friendly confirms that he is the top dog. He has better table manners too, crisps this time, and much bigger than the other canine fan. The floodlights are now on with the sun setting. I count over fifty Guisleley supporters and the banter is great. The toilet facilities are excellent too as they take it in turns to climb the fence to relieve themselves in the pony paddock. The atmosphere may have improved, but the game is unfortunately now a non event. The Thackley keeper in front of us produces a brilliant save which starts some friendly stick. Someone calls him 'chuckles' which I assume is because he does look a bit like a chuckle brother. The shout of "me to you" confirms my suspicions as he flaps at another cross.

Both managers make a lot of team changes, all seven substitutes are used by Guiseley. This results in Thackley getting into the game more and actually score in the 72nd minute. Giles Parry shoots from a loose ball to pull a goal back on a very rare visit into the Guiseley box. In the last few minutes I watch the game from the opposite side as the midges are driving me insane back at the 'paddock end'. I then get the perfect view of Thackley rattling the cross bar which would have created a flattering 2-3 scoreline. The whistle blows and we all head back to our cars. The country lane does get very busy for a few minutes to disturb the non-football dog walking community. The headlights also surprise some young lovers parked up. They look amazed to see fifty or so cars pass them, but at least they now know that Thackley AFC play their football in this part of the countryside. If you are that hungry young man I recommend the ribs, but they do make you thirsty! I leave them with a smile on my face to go home to raid the fridge in the comfort of knowing that I do not own a dog.

Thackley 1 Guiseley 3

Attendance 150
Admission £5
Ground Address Ainsbury Avenue, Thackley, Bradford, West Yorkshire. BD10 0TL
Club website www.pitchero.com/clubs/thackleyfootballclub
Twitter @ThackleyAFC

7

Ferriby across the Humber

North Ferriby United AFC v Grimsby Town

The Rapid Solicitors Stadium

Pre-season friendly. Friday 5th August 2011. Kick off 7.45pm

North Ferriby is another place on my growing list that I didn't even know existed until I took on this extreme ground hopping. The village sits to the West of Hull on the north bank of the river Humber. It is another hot day as I leave Ilkley and I'm feeling happy that it is the eve of the start of the football season. Tomorrow it all starts for real, for the football league clubs anyway, but I have one final pre season game to fit in. The visitors to Yorkshire tonight are Grimsby Town who I still haven't quite got used to being a non league club. They were relegated from the football league only 15 months ago and now play their football in the Conference Premier. I take the busy M62, which becomes the A63 for the last few miles of my journey. Unfortunately, I don't quite go far enough to see the impressive view of the Humber Bridge, but know I am very close to it as I turn off. The bridge was opened in 1981 by H.M The Queen after 8 years of construction. The travelling Mariners will hopefully appreciate the bridge which tonight gives them a short 56 mile round trip compared to the previous 140 mile journey. The vast estuary separates Yorkshire from north Lincolnshire, but the divide must have felt colossal between the 'north bank' and 'south bank' 30 years ago.

I drive into the village which creates a first impression of a well to do area which is, no doubt, popular with Hull commuters. My ground directions are straightforward and I soon see the Duke of Cumberland Hotel, which I am told to pass. It is hard to judge traffic on a Friday, so I am early once again. I don't like being told what to do so decide to see if the Duke is in as he lives in an impressive timber framed building. I soon discover his once quaint inn is now a '2 main meals for £10' pub with free toppings all around. I order a glass of lemonade to save my one beer ration for the clubhouse (if it exists) when I am in the improved company of football fans rather than these culture vultures. I speak too soon and a coach full of football supporters arrive who must be from Grimsby. I can see a lot of orange as the coach pulls into the car park, so assume they must have a new away kit. 'Your coach has pulled up' I hear the landlord shout to his wife followed by the words 'the Blackpool lot'. She then asked him 'if the police have been informed?!' Ah Blackpool must be playing Hull in the Championship. In walks around 50 Blackpool fans with a young Mexican man, complete with drawn on moustache, who appears to speak good English.

Blackpool fans have a good reputation for being well behaved, but I never prejudge a group of football supporters. No Grimsby thugs in thick fishing sweaters invade and most of the seasiders are ordering from the 'sizzling range' menu. This comes with the amazing offer of a free drink, but the pub appears to be safe from destruction as I head back to my car. A short drive to the centre of the village and I am met by the usual line of yellow police cones to tell me that I am near the ground. Athough football has been played in the village from the turn of the century, North Ferriby United were not officially formed until 1934. They first took part in the local East Riding Church League and, in 1938, won the Division One title. The 70th Anniversary Season in 2004/05 proved to be one of the most rewarding in the club's history as the villagers clinched the Unibond League First Division Championship on the final day of the season at Mossley. The following season they entered the Unibond Premier Division and led the table from the off until March. They secured a play-off place by finishing 5th and lost in the final at Farsley Celtic after extra time. Last season, the club last season reached a second successive play-off semi final only to be denied 0-2 at Colwyn Bay.

After a very short walk, I pass an authoritative looking steward to go down a long lane that runs beside some allotments. I soon spot the floodlights and then see not only the ground but the Humber Bridge.

I knew it was there all the time! It's an impressive view and the ground looks well kept but most things do in bright sunshine. I then notice from a sign that I have in fact arrived at another Rapid Solicitors Stadium rather that the Grand Lane ground I was expecting to find. I wonder if Eccleshill United, know or even care, that they are not alone. I can't imagine there would be two Emirates stadiums in the Premiership, but perhaps that is only a matter of time. I pay £9 to get in, which does feel expensive for a friendly, but at least I get change from a ten pound note due to there not being a match day programme tonight.

I have a quick wander and take an instant liking to the ground. The main stand is only 3 seats deep and almost stretches the length of the pitch. The grass is pre season dark green, but does look on the long side. A view of the Humber Bridge could be found from most areas of the ground, so it does dominate in the nicest possible way. I decide, for research purposes only, to see if I can see the bridge from the bar so I enter the club house. I am not disappointed by the view, which includes watching the players warm up from the comfort of my stool. My pint is not as exciting, but at least it is cold. Most people inside are wearing the black and white colours of Grimsby Town, including a group of middle aged men beside me. I couldn't help but listen to their conversation which followed that 'big club arrogance' that I am used to hearing from my own club. In summary, they are not happy with the high entrance fee which is cashing in on their large away support . 'They are taking advantage, they know that we will bring 500 fans with us and can't turn back once we are here'. I can appreciate their argument as turning back would be a brave protest.

I leave the club house just as the players come out and see that printed team sheets are available for a 'donation'. I quickly decide that 20p is a fair price. I don't have the time to establish the going rate, let alone start negotiations to get a bargain, and I take my sheet to study at the back of their main stand. The side ends of the stand are terraced and I am in the mood to stand tonight. The game kicks off with North Ferriby defending my end and the visiting supporters appear to have claimed 75% of the ground. The home side are wearing their usual white shirts, green shorts and stripy socks. Grimsby Town are also in their traditional black and white stripes, black shorts and rather fetching red socks. I have enough height from my spot to also enjoy a view of the allotments and church spire to give the home of 'The Villagers' that village feel. The man on the tannoy is in a cheerful mood and I hope he will make my task of identifying goal scorers easier. I notice that a young father and son wearing the away colours find a ten pound note just a few feet away from me. I decide to leave the possible discussion on the pitfalls of 'finders keepers' due to their high admission injustice. The opening minutes are lively and North Ferriby get off to the perfect start after only 4 minutes when Gary Bradshaw scores directly from a free kick as the visitors defence is caught napping.

Grimsby respond with greater urgency to their play and immediately waste a couple of good opportunities to level the score. North Ferriby have a good chance themselves, but the finish came closer to hitting a large sunflower than the back of the net. After 20 minutes, some good skill from Grimsby's Serge Makofo creates an opening, but he disappointingly shoots straight at the goal keeper from close range. Five minutes later, the home goal scorer Bradshaw is bundled over to win a penalty. Wayne Brooksby calmly makes it 2-0 to the Villagers from the spot, which creates more of a moan than a cheer from the crowd. Grimsby continue to put the pressure on, but the Yorkshire team match the Conference side's creativity with their competiveness. Despite their two goal lead, they continue to play at a high pace and I do wonder how long they can maintain this. Again, Grimsby are denied after 31 minutes with a fine save and a minute later couldn't take advantage from a mad scramble. The 2-0 score is now flattering the home side, but Grimsby are not given much time on the ball. Three minutes before halftime, Grimsby's Andy Thanoj shoots straight at the keeper from close range and then, a minute later, Liam Hearn misses an easy chance by shooting wide. Just as it was starting to look like 'one of those nights', with seconds left until the break, Scott Garner scores during another mad goal scramble to bring the score to 2-1.

I am suffering from that aching 'terrace knee' that gives me a nice feeling of nostalgia. I use half time to sit on the floor to recover. I watch some gardeners start to pack up as the sun is going down. The evening has the feel of September, or dare I say Autumn, so my coat goes on.

The second half kicks off and Grimsby continue where they left off, so the home defence is under pressure immediately. After only ten minutes, Serge Makofo has a great run into the box, weaving in and out, but is eventually chopped down by defender James Williams for the second penalty of the game. This time White comfortably saves from Elding's soft strike.

Grimsby win corner after corner and shot after shot finds the keepers gloves until finally, in the 63rd minute, Serge scores a lovely header from the perfect right wing. The home side have battled but must have known that an equaliser would eventually arrive, which few would argue isn't deserved.

From the restart, Grimsby suddenly look like scoring on every attack and in the 77th minute Grimsby do get the winner. They take a quick free kick from outside the box which finds the corner of the net. It's so quick I didn't see who actually scored, but the enthusiastic man on the tannoy informs us it was Craig Disley. In the last few minutes further chances fall to Grimsby to extend their lead, but the best chance goes to North Ferriby to snatch a draw in the 88th minute. Peat's cross come shot almost surprises everyone, including himself, but falls narrowly wide of the post.

Grimsby Town deserved their win just for how many chances they created, but the home side played a big part in a very good game of football. I notice as I leave the ground that the Humber Bridge is now lit up, much better than the dark lane back to my car, which is the perfect parting image to take away with me. I follow out a man with his young son who are, no doubt, preparing to cross the Humber back to the south. I smile as the child is wearing an orange Grimsby Town shirt. I switch on Talk Sport in my car as I pass the pub, which was still standing, but now has flashing disco lights inside. Blackpool have won at Hull, their first away win this year in fact, and the match report is followed by someone predicting Mexico will win the World Cup in the next 25 years. There will be one very happy lad on a coach behind me and perhaps, by then, he will be able to grow a real moustache. I have had a good evening by the Humber and not even the migraine I am developing on the long drive home will dampen my enthusiasm to get on a coach seven hours later to Southampton. Three grounds in a week will help me for the long months ahead when the weather will not be so kind. I just have time to check the attendance which was a healthy 243. I go to bed feeling sad though that over half of the army of Grimsby fans didn't go through the turnstiles to avoid the admission cost. They missed a good second half performance by their team!

North Ferriby United 2 Grimsby Town 3

Attendance 243
Admission £9
Ground Address North Ferriby, East Yorkshire. HU14 3AB
Club website www.northferribyunited.com
Twitter @NorthFerriby @northferribyutd

8

The birds and the bees

Ossett Albion FC v AFC Fylde

The Warehouse Systems Stadium
Evo-Stik Northern Premier League Division One North
Saturday 20th August 2011. Kick off 3pm

I am not alone on today's trip due to the visit of my sister and her children this weekend. My 14 year old nephew Tim has wisely chosen the Albion ahead of the charity shops of Ilkley. My oldest son George has not been put off yet from this lifestyle so we have a car full. It's another hot day, so memories of numb feet and hot Bovril feel a very long time away. The town of Ossett lies on the outskirts of Wakefield and has two clubs. Today I am visiting Ossett Albion and later this season will need to return to see Ossett Town who both play their football at Step 4 of the non-league pyramid. The origin of Ossett Albion is rare as the club was formed in 1944 during the Second World War. Then a junior club, all the players being students at the local Grammar School, Albion enjoyed great success before moving into open age football. They quickly progressed through the local and district leagues before becoming members of the Yorkshire League with the 60s and 70s being good decades for the club in terms of silverware. In 1982 the Northern Counties East League was formed, but Albion found themselves in Division One as their ground, then Dimple Wells, was deemed sub-standard for the Premier Division. The ground was improved during the 80s and proved a good investment when promotion was achieved in 1987. It took 12 years for them to win the Premier Division title, but promotion was denied due to failing the ground grading criteria. They did go up in 2001 as runners up due to Brigg Town's ground failing this time. They have been relegated and promoted back since this time so now enter their ninth season in the Northern Premier League.

This afternoon's visitors are AFC Fylde who are located between the Lancashire towns of Preston and Blackpool. Unusually, I know how to get to Ossett, but thanks to a road closure on my route for the last six years, I arrive at the ground with only 10 minutes to spare. Yes, I got lost in Leeds! Luckily nobody else in the car is old enough to appreciate how far my way to the M1 is proving to be which I am too embarrassed to commit to paper.

My directions to the ground are good and I easily find this hotbed of sport. I can't help the man asking us where the rugby pitch is, but discover a bowling green and cricket pitch before I spot our destination ahead. I am struggling to concentrate on the Warehouse Systems Stadium until the threat of flying cricket balls passes. I am glad I didn't park any closer, but know that keeping two children safe is more important for the rest of our weekend. I wonder if a batsman has ever hit a lovely shot for a six but then helplessly watched it hit his own car. We survive an over and arrive at the turnstile to one of the strangest signs I have seen at a football match. It reads: 'THIS TURNSTILE CLOSED DUE TO BIRDS NESTING. PLEASE USE THE ONE AT THE OTHER SIDE OF CRICKET SCOREBOARD.' I know that you should never ignore a sign in capital letters and we follow the instructions which involve entering the field of play. I wonder if a nesting bird has ever delayed a kick off? The three of us gain admission and buy a programme for less than £10. I am feeling flush, so can't resist entering the souvenir shop as we weigh up our options of where to watch the match. A lost key to the souvenir cabinet almost stops my unhealthy hobby, but luckily they have a few on standby. Perhaps the nesting bird is a magpie and is responsible for that shiny key disappearing.

The players are preparing for kick off as we head to the main stand. Ossett Albion play in Yellow Shirts, known as 'old gold' according to the programme, with black shorts and socks. Fylde are in white shirts, shorts and socks to give them that Real Madrid look. I notice from the away fans here today that they follow the Spanish theme with a rather nice Barcelona looking away kit. Both strips look fit for the Camp Nou as they benefit from being made by Nike.

We take our seats in the stand at the side of the pitch where the steep slope is at its lowest point. Our stand may have once sat on the far touchline until they got some heavy rain. The black seats resemble the tops of those plastic chairs I grew up sitting on at school. They look like they have been removed and screwed onto the stand and will wobble if the game gets too exciting. The ground is made up of a collection of small stands all painted brown and yellow. It has a very concrete feel thanks mainly to the perimeter walls that surround the pitch. A brown line at one ends suggests that they ran out of paint, so I guess the ground will turn browner upon every visit. The first 15 minutes are pretty uneventful, despite most of the play being at our wing, which is probably due to the slope. In the 16th minute things get more interesting, but unfortunately it's off the pitch thanks to a bumble bee kindly stinging my George in the face. The rules of Chapter 3 had been strictly followed, except that the toy was substituted with his cousin Tom, but it was our sweets that had attracted the attention of the predator.

Once the screaming stops, I go into paranoid parent mode and we take the advice of those around us to head to the Tea Room for vinegar. We then spend the next half an hour calming my little man down and applying vinegar to his cheek with some kitchen roll. The lady, and what appears to be her son, could not be any friendlier and even reward his bravery with a complimentary Finger Of Fudge bar. After all it is 'full of natural goodness' and he was definitely in need of a treat. We eventually return to watch the final couple of minutes of the first half. We choose the terrace behind the goal just in case there is a bee's nest under our previous seat or the bee may want one last sweet before he departs this world. Fylde finish the stronger of the two teams with some good runs into the box, but the whistle blows just as I am settling back into the game. Most of half time revolves around checking the swelling and a few photos, always best to do this whilst the danger of flying balls has halted.

As the game restarts I count around 100 fans in the ground, which sounds accurate as the programme tells me that there was 112 for their midweek home game four days ago. There is an injury to an Albion player and I wonder as he gets some treatment from the physio if she has anything for bee stings in her shiny bag. To take my mind off the swelling, Fylde take the lead in the 58th minute. A good through ball is calmly slotted away by Michael Barnes. Then, two minutes later, the ex Manchester United winger gets his second goal of the match when he latches onto a bad clearance. The Ossett players protest for offside, but it has been one-way traffic since the break. Fylde are showing why they are one of the favourites to win the division. In the 73rd minute the away side take a three goal lead with a headed own goal by Curtis Noble. It looked like he had forgotten which end he was defending. Fylde take their foot off the petal and I switch my attention in looking for revenge from the bees to the birds, that I can now see are swallows, that closed our turnstile. We watch them casually follow a circuit of the stadium, which includes a low flying flight up the pitch. The birds restore George's faith in nature and he hardly notices the game that is going on around them. In the final minutes of the game, Ossett miss two good chances, but 3-2 would have certainly been an injustice. The match finishes and few in the ground can complain about the result, unless you wanted vinegar on your chips.

We make our way out of the ground, but find time to locate the nest. We have at least been in touch with nature today, but I can't say it has been my favourite trip to date. We pass the cricket match which is still on and get to our car without anyone being struck by a flying ball. Now that would sting. One day, I will need to tell my children about the birds and the bees, but can't imagine I will need to worry about them when I return to Ossett in the winter months. Polar bears and penguins are far more likely!

Ossett Albion 0 Fylde 3

Attendance 102
Admission £5 (£2 juveniles)
Ground Address Queen's Terrace, Dimplewells Road, Ossett, West Yorkshire. WF5 8JT
Club website www.pitchero.com/clubs/ossettalbion
Twitter @OssettAlbion

9

Once upon a time in the Midlands

Sheffield FC v Grantham Town FC

The BT Local Business Stadium
Evo-Stik Division One South.
Tuesday 23rd August 2011. Kick off 7.45pm

'The World's First Football Club' is certainly an attention grabbing statement on Sheffield FC website. Club Chairman Richard Tims states 'we have been acknowledged by the FA and FIFA to be the World's First and Sheffield FC are the proud owners of a FIFA Centennial Order of Merit, one of only two clubs in the world to hold this honour, Real Madrid being the other'. There are various interesting links offering browsers an opportunity to become a sponsor of 'The 1857 Club' or buy the 'Sheffield FC Rules' to own a piece of Football heritage for just £9.99. The club was founded in 1857 and is now used as a brand on a variety of products. If all of the above isn't enough, the club also owns a pub! The website advises fans to arrive early to pay a visit to the Coach and Horses for the 'award winning ales'.

So here I am at 6 o'clock relaxing on a very comfy leather sofa in the sort of pub you would happily call your local, not something I can usually say about pubs outside football grounds. I can even buy a copy of their programme, Red And Black Review, at the bar, which is the perfect companion to a pint of Wild Swan. The beer is very good and I may well be enjoying my finest moment so far on my journey around Yorkshire. I am having so much fun I can almost forget that ground number 9 is actually in Derbyshire. Sheffield FC play in the town of Dronfield which is just south of Sheffield. They currently play their football at Step 4 in the Evo-Stik Division One South so I have battled the Ring Road traffic to officially leave the north of England. Tonight's visitors are Grantham Town which is a part of the world close to where I grew up and my parents still live. Grantham was voted the most boring town in England whilst I was growing up and, coincidentally I may add, is famous as the birth place of Margaret Thatcher. I could write about the famous players and managers of Grantham Town, but just because I am in Derbyshire doesn't mean I am now extending the boundaries to deepest Lincolnshire.

There are records of earlier forms of football being played in China that date back almost 2000 years, but it was in Sheffield where a standard set of laws where developed. The club's influence on the modern game cannot be overstated as they pioneered the writing of a commonly accepted set of rules. Sheffield FC played a key role in the formation of the FA, although they may not be so proud of the current FA. They were involved in a host of innovations such as the first crossbar, corner kick, free kick and the floodlit match.

I leave the utopia of the pub for the very short walk to the turnstile. The ground is modern, but not on the same level unfortunately as the club's amazing history, or the pub. In 2007 the club celebrated its 150th anniversary with a 'service to football' attended by Sepp Blatter (no comment) yet we only have two small stands to choose from. With all the money this country has wasted over the years, this club deserves an award winning architectural stadium to match their awarding winning ales next door. Throw in a museum of the history of football and we would have as many visitors as the Camp Nou Experience. It must have been strong that pint...

I enter the ground which is dominated by a large polythene sheet on the opposite touchline which runs the length of the pitch on the bank. This does create a great opportunity for advertising space, but it also makes the ground look a little odd. The teams run out before I get settled and I quickly choose the covered terrace on the opposite side so I can admire the advert. Sheffield are wearing their home kit of red shirts, black shorts and socks to match. Grantham Town look striking in their white shirts with black stripes, red shorts and striped stockings. I count seven Grantham fans as they set up camp behind the far goal with two large impressive flags. One is particularly eye catching with the words 'Forza Grantham Town. The Gingerbreads'. They more than make up for being so outnumbered with cries of ‘come on Grantham, come on Grantham’ as play starts. The away team’s keeper is also very noisy as he shouts instructions to his team members. Dressed in light pink, I would personally keep a much lower profile.

There are chances for both sides throughout the first half which helps to keep those away fans in good voice. The clear evening sky soon turns dark and the temperature drops quickly. This results in most of the half being played under floodlights and reminds me that Autumn is fast approaching. The ground has a traditional cricket style scoreboard which I note will only cope with up to a 9-9 draw tonight.

Sheffield are becoming more effective as the game progresses and get their reward just before half time, just as I was starting to think we wouldn’t see the scoreboard in action. Connor Higginson heads a goal from a near perfect cross to give the home side a 1-0 lead. Grantham have played the better football, but the final ball has let them down. Half time is an opportunity for me to visit the club shop as the Grantham flags change ends with the, now 8, away supporters on the move. The shop is well stocked, but empty of customers as a lot of fans have made their way to The Coach & Horses. They must be more disciplined than me or not driving, the temptation to stay in there must occasionally get the better of supporters.

The second half kicks off in pitch black, so it is hard to count how many people haven’t returned. The Grantham fans now occupy the ‘reserved’ section of seats for visiting supporters behind the end they are now attacking. Like any seated supporter, they instantly become quieter, but then wake up as Grantham almost equalise with only five minutes played. Grantham continue to put the pressure on, but Sheffield cruelly hit them on the break. A good ball is played down the right wing, a couple of neat passes and scorer Higginson turns provider for David Graham to tap in to make it 2-0. Grantham respond with more pressure, but don't actually look like they will score to the frustration of their supporters. One fan leaves his seat to stand on the touchline to protest to the goalkeeper, perhaps about his kit, and, to my amusement, his friend kindly moves the reserved sign next to where he is standing. There is nothing 'boring' about that great comedy moment born in Grantham.

The second goal has clearly killed the game and Sheffield are happy to defend deep and occasionally hit Grantham on the break after soaking up the pressure. The rest of the game is not pretty to watch, but highly effective for Sheffield who ease to victory. It is, I suppose, within the rules of the game to play negative football and, after all, Sheffield did invent them. It is very unfair of me to expect Sheffield to play like Real Madrid, but I know that the beer is not as good in Spain. I am sure when I look back next May at my travels to put together the perfect day it will start in The Coach & Horses. The perfect match day programme would also have the Sheffield FC history in it, but I may be tempted to move the ground a couple of miles north to improve the fantasy.

Sheffield 2 Grantham Town 0

Attendance 290
Admission £6
Ground Address Sheffield Road, Dronfield. S18 2GD
Club website www.sheffieldfc.com
Twitter @Sheffieldfc

10

Egg on my face

Liversedge FC v Thackley AFC

Clayborn Ground
Baris NCEL Premier
Monday 29th August 2011. Kick Off 3pm

I arrive back into Ilkley from our weekend camping later than planned. A long series of events, the bank holiday traffic and life itself almost get in the way of ground number 10. After 3 hours of 'fun' behind the wheel since leaving Whitby, I arrive home just before 2pm. Most sane people would knock a trip to a non league ground on the head, but after dropping my family at home I am back behind the wheel within a few minutes, a suitcase lighter. It is these kind of decisions which will make the difference between completing all 65 grounds or failing miserably. Who would buy a book titled 'Almost Route 66 – the Football Grounds of Yorkshire when I wasn't too tired'? Liversage is just outside Dewsbury so I know the way blindfolded. Doing it blindfolded would be a shame as the views are breathtaking as you approach Queensway. Today I am feeling grumpy, so don't have a problem keeping my eyes on the road. I am beyond tired after three nights on an air bed with a hole in it, three days of shouting at my over excited children and walking around the swamp our campsite had become thanks to the North Yorkshire summer.

I arrive in reasonably good time as most West Yorkshire residents must be in Scarborough, but then spend 15 minutes driving around taking it in turns to ask random strangers where the ground is. Everyone I ask knows that the ground exists, but lacks the ability to give clear directions when it isn't opposite a pub. I am now not even sure where the boundary for Liversedge starts or finishes and I haven't seen a sign to prove the place even exists. I do eventually find someone who has already given directions twice this afternoon and he jokes that it will be a 'bumper gate'. I can see the Italian restaurant that I was told to find, and turn right rather than go inside for the spaghetti Bolognese that I need more than a game of football. Within a couple of minutes I finally see the very welcoming sign that tells me the ground is down a long narrow lane. I make it half way down, twice, but after two long reversing manoeuvres give up and abandon the car on the main road.

Liversedge Football Club, known as Sedge, were founded in 1910 following the demise of the old Liversedge Rugby Club which had been a member of the Northern Union which, in turn, was the forerunner to the Rugby League. They were one of a number of clubs that switched codes around that time. The club eventually rose to the NCEL Premier League where they now play their football. They have enjoyed mixed fortunes, but Sedge are still proud of the fact that they have never been relegated. I do feel that their supporters have missed out on seeing their club go down. Surely you need the lows to appreciate the highs, the pain of relegation will eventually increase the joy of promotion.

In 2005, the famous Clayborn slope was removed as a result of the finance generated from the previous season's FA Cup run to the 4th round. On their new pitch they finished runners up, but were denied promotion due to their changing rooms not meeting Unibond standards. The club were devastated and the following season's merger with local junior club Gomersal & Cleckheaton FC was viewed as a positional move. It was an agreement that suited both clubs with Sedge significantly increasing its membership overnight and Gomersal & Cleckheaton gaining a home after building a substantial club without a ground as such. The future now looks bright for the club with ambitious plans to develop their clubhouse in stages to achieve Unibond status.

Today's visitors are Thackley who I am watching for a third time this season before we even get into September. That's more than the average Manchester United 'fan' in your workplace has seen their team in a lifetime. It will be interesting to see which team I will watch the most come next May. I will surely have a good case to then take my case to the supreme football court to refer to them as 'us', not that I will exercise this right.

It is hard to believe that this football ground exists as I walk down the lane, but finally enter through a gate after handing over my cash to a man. It feels weird not going through a turnstile and hope that I am not topping up someone's Bank Holiday beer fund rather than supporting the club. I arrive beside the clubhouse that looks down on the pitch at its lower level. From my viewing platform, I can see the ground below me and another classic West Yorkshire view, the stone terraces layered on green hills that could be used in a Hovis advert. There are two small stands, one behind the goal and the other on my side of the pitch. They both offer spectators a good view of play as they are set back from the touchline at a higher level than the pitch. It is 2.59pm and the players are lining up to kick off before I have even decided where to stand. I discover that the programmes have sold out, which doesn't help my mood. I am still tense from following tractors, caravans and people who appear to get nervous at speeds over 30 mph on open roads. I haven't eaten since my fried (on a camping stove I may add) egg sandwich at 8 o clock. I am in need of some more comfort food and immediately find the Half Timers snack bar. A chip butty proves to be the best £1.20 spent all weekend and I use the bench on the top of the bank to fully appreciate the moment. It feels like my first meal in a year and helps me, finally, start to wind down.

Liversedge are playing in their usual light blue kit and Thackley remain in their red and white shirts with black shorts today. After Manchester City's fine five goal performance yesterday, I have high hopes for the home side. I decide to stay on my bench, but my thoughts drift away from the play as it dawns upon me that I am still in clothes that I slept in last night. It was very cold in the tent and the only items I didn't sleep in, my jeans, are very dirty. As I examine the tomato sauce stains on my trouser leg I come to the conclusion that I probably smell too. I am glad that I am alone in a place where nobody knows a Michael Mowbray. I struggle to write anything about the first half as nothing really happens, even if I was feeling more co-operative and happy with the world. Thackley do have a chance, of sorts, but not quite good enough for me to get my pad out for.

The half time whistle at least allows me to see if the toilets are better than the campsite facilities. There isn't a mirror to see if I look as bad as I feel but a large pain of glass confirms my worst fears. I know it is me by the clothes I am wearing, but I look a shadow of my former self. A tramp with egg on his face, literally, as my stubble has trapped some yolk from my breakfast in a gale. Perhaps I am developing the look of an author or a freelance journalist where too much working from home withdraws you from the real world.

The game in the second half doesn't improve. Thackley are enjoying more possession and a couple of good chances suggest that they are the most likely winners. Just as I am in danger of finding a cardboard box to sleep in, Liversedge take the lead on 72 minutes against the run of play from a decent through ball. Joe Jagger, who had only come on five minutes earlier, finishes calmly despite looking off balance. In the 80th minute, a good strike by Alex Hallam is the sucker punch number two. I am not sure how the home side have managed to win this game by two goals. It starts to rain as the final whistle blows, but my coat is either in the car or still in Whitby so I head home immediately in search of a shower and a shave. It hasn't been a classic game, Thackley but I have, at least, seen two good goals. I am feeling more relaxed and have even stayed awake without the help of caffeine. I'm not sure it was worth the four hour drive, but I do owe Liversedge Football Club an apology. The club and the other 141 people deserved better than I gave. I hope to be back to my cheerful self again in twenty-four hours when I head to South Yorkshire.

Liversedge 2 Thackley 0

Attendance 142
Admission £5
Ground Address Quaker Lane, Cleckheaton, W Yorkshire. WF15 8DA
Club website www.pitchero.com/clubs/liversedge
Twitter None found

11

Wild Salmon

Rossington Main FC v Eccleshill United FC

Oxford Street

BARIS NCEL Division One

Tuesday 30th August 2011. Kick off 7.45pm

I am in better mood today thanks to a good night's sleep and a bathroom that's within a short carpeted stroll from my comfy mattress. It's chucking it down with rain, but I am actually quite pleased. I may feel differently on a foggy February night in Wakefield, but I am bored with writing how sunny it is at every ground. Tonight I have dropped down to Step 6 in the Non League pyramid. The last time I was at these depths was on the opening day at Eccleshill United who just happen to be tonight's opponents. Rossington is another village south of Doncaster and is not that far from Armthorpe who I bagged on that lovely sunny July evening.

Rossington Main FC was originally thought to have been formed in 1926, but recent delves into the history books shows that a team bearing the name Rossington Colliery played a match in 1919 at the back of the Colliery offices. It moved to the present ground in 1921. The club was formed, like the majority of mining communities, to provide Colliery workers with a game of football and changed its name to Rossington Minors Welfare when the mines were nationalised in 1948. It has competed at many levels since then and its name eventually changed back to Rossington Main. The club has needed to constantly improve the ground to allow it to climb the football pyramid. In the summer of 1998, a merger was finally agreed with the neighbouring club, Rossington FC, who started life as Station FC when it was a mere pub side. The unified club hopes to make better progress as one and has an ambitious committee to drive it forward.

Finding the village of Rossington is straightforward from the A1, but I can feel Mr Grumpy returning as I drive around in circles looking for the ground. A young stray tells me “sorry but I don't like football”. Well young man, I don't like rugby, bowls or swimming, but I know where all of these sporting venues are in Ilkley as I don't walk around with my eyes shut. A second stranger is much more communicative and informs me that they play at the “Welfare Social Club”, which I have passed twice so head back that way. This time I notice on route the large, but now boarded up, Station pub which has roots into Rossington Main.

I arrive at the Legion club, but I am still not convinced that there is a football match here. I ask an old lady who is on her way in who tells me that the pitch is behind the club. I take a walk around the back and I am very confused at the sight of open playing fields. Suddenly, I find myself running as I am being chased by a very large German Shepherd (the canine kind)! Just as his teeth are inches away from my trousers he stops thanks to his responsible owner’s command of “leave him!”.

I am happy to be left and, whilst I am getting my breath back, notice some floodlights in the distance. I come to my own conclusion that I must be able to drive closer and a tweet from follower Tony tells me to take the next right and the ground is at end of street. I turn into Oxford Street, very different from the London shopping paradise, and soon find a portokabin with a small grassed car park... and some very unsavoury characters in hoods watching my car! I am obviously here through choice, but for a split second wish I was watching bowls back in Ilkley.

The dog chase has unsettled me so it’s a relief to see the Eccleshill United team minibus pull into the car park, just as I am pulling myself back together with a wild salmon and cucumber sandwich. I notice Groundsman Nick and Chairman Adrian immediately and head out of my car to say hello. They recognise me and look pleased to see me, which is very comforting on the back of my evening so far. They offer me a pass to enter the ground for free as an Eccleshill United official and I proudly take this role through the turnstile. We have a chat about my adventures to date and Eccleshill's slow start to the season. I wish them luck tonight and I do hope they get more from the evening than a dog bite.

I have exchanged emails with Rossington Main official Pete Murden prior to my visit and was told to say hello. Pete is officially down as the Programme Editor, Committee Member and Website Editor, but I can see immediately that his duties also stretch to PA Announcer. I find him sat in the Press Room. The clue is that the words are written in felt tip on the door, which is situated behind the home dug out. He is in charge of a laptop stood on an old hi-fi that plays tracks into a speaker that, for some reason, is inside a black bin liner. I introduce myself and we chat in between his announcements, so it is difficult to ask too many questions. He has been involved with the club since the merger in 1998 and it is clearly now a huge part of his life. Pete kindly gives me a copy of tonight's programme. This includes a rather good piece on a certain Mr Mowbray, which is why I think it is presented to me in a protective plastic bag. Pete informs me that their average attendance is around 60, but "so many people now come in for free". That is terrible and I swiftly find my place on the covered terrace to hide in shame. Pete announces the arrival of the teams to a heavy metal track and the match kicks off as a very noisy express train passes. I can't actually see the tracks but can tell it is very close behind the trees to my right. I must look surprised as the man next to me proudly tells me that it's the main East Coast line.

Rossington are playing in all blue with white sleeves. Eccleshill have the same combination but in red rather than blue. The Main could not be given a better start when, after 6 minutes, they take the lead. Jamie Green intercepts the ball on the halfway line, runs clear at a great pace to lose the defenders and finishes brilliantly. A fine goal, but my initial feeling is one of disappointment to see Eccleshill go behind after Nick and Andrew had been so positive earlier. Despite me wanting the away side to improve, Rossington dominate the rest of the first half playing good possession football. It is so good, Pete appears with his camera at least three times. It seems I missed Club Photographer from his long job description. The Eccleshill manager's cry of "keep the ball" sums up their problems tonight. The Main are much hungrier for the ball and the quality of their passing is on a different level.

At half time I head to the tea room for a pint and a Vimto chew bar, which is a strange but welcome refreshment. I just cannot resist sweets even with cold lager. I do like it in here as it doubles up as a kind of club museum. The walls are covered in team photos of the various clubs over the years that have formed today's club. There is even a library of old programmes to read whilst you chew, but I am very content with today's issue. I will go as far to say that it is the best I have seen to date, which, I suppose, is why it was voted the best in the division at the annual Programme Awards for 2010/11. I must have an eye for this type of thing and perhaps they will need a famous author next year on their panel of judges. If so, please contact me as I am always available in exchange for a free meal.

The second half starts brightly again for the home side with more possession and they look threatening with every pass. In the 54th minute a perfect corner by Jason Stokes catches the Eccleshill defence static and Lee Holmes makes the score 2-0 with ease. Just after another high speed train passes, the Main score a third goal which is the best move of the game. Liam Charlton takes the ball from the wing, drives inside and pulls back to the edge of the box for Ben Hunter to beat his marker with a fine finish. Eccleshill will struggle to blame that goal on the noise of the trains. Rossington are better tonight in every position.

As the game is starting to come to a close I go in search of Pete to say goodbye. I find him outside his hi-tech castle. I have noticed that the stand on the far touchline is named the Gerry Murden Stand. I assume that Gerry is related to Pete and he confirms that he is his father. I am pleased to discover that Gerry is still on this earth and then actually see the man himself pass us. Gerry has been heavily involved in the club for a long time, from manager, coach and even swimming trainer. He is now the president of the club (and, hopefully, likes having a stand named after him.) Tonight eight people are enjoying the comfort of his stand. It would be nice if the trend of naming stands after people whilst they are still alive continues up the football pyramid. The two of them even named the two ends, the Allotment End and, yes, the Railway End. Sometimes simple is good! Pete tells me that the attendance tonight is 50 but I don't ask if that includes free loaders like me.

Whilst I am chatting to Pete, chance after chance falls to Rossington and I am amazed that the score stays at 3-0. The home defence looks solid to fully deserve their clean sheet tonight, although, in the 85th minute, Eccleshill somehow manage to hit a shot from 3 yards over the crossbar. I am pleased that the railway line is protected with a high fence to stop the striker doing anything silly. I don't hang around as the whistle blows. I am keen to get home to bed to get some more sleep and I didn't want that dog returning either. He may not listen to his owner next time, especially if he smells the salmon.

Rossington Main 3 Eccleshill United 0

Attendance 50
Admission Free (usually £4)
Ground Address Oxford Street, Rossington, Doncaster, South Yorkshire. DN11 0TE
Club website www.pitchero.com/clubs/rossingtonmain
Twitter None found

12

Happy Non-League Day

Guiseley AFC v Vauxhall Motors FC

Nethermoor Park

Blue Square Conference North

Saturday 3rd September 2011. Kick off 3pm

Non-League Day is official as it was even mentioned by Martyn Tyler on Sky Sports during last night's England win in Bulgaria. The top two divisions take a break from the domestic season and "provide an opportunity for football supporters to visit their local Non-League side". I am not sure that I like the concept that non league football should only be an option when the 'big' teams are not playing. However, anything that encourages people to put much needed cash into their local team is a very good thing. After all, 12 months ago I would have needed a nudge myself to give grassroots football a try.

The natural choice for such an occasion, though, is my local team Guiseley AFC who are partly responsible for this tour around Yorkshire. The club are certainly embracing the occasion with an attractive ticket offer. Half price entry can be gained by showing a Football League or Premiership season ticket, match day ticket or programme from this season. I have really missed watching Guiseley this season, they have been the victims of me taking on this project. I am also on the train today as this is one of the few grounds I can leave my car at home for. After a couple of pints in Ilkley, I jump on the 2.21pm Bradford train and 14 minutes later I am taking the short stroll to Nethermoor. This really is the life! I could quite easily fall into this routine, grow a beard and perhaps even bring a dog with me. Perhaps not a dog, but it's a very relaxing match day experience.

Guiseley AFC, known as the Lions, were founded in 1909 and proudly celebrated their Centenary season in 2009/10 with some extensive ground developments that included a new seated stand, lights and installing terracing. Approaching the end of the season, Guiseley were in pole position to achieve promotion to the Blue Square North division after defeating rivals Bradford Park Avenue twice in four days. However, three defeats followed, and the one to rivals Boston meant that they went into the final game against Ashton United needing to win and for Boston's and Avenue's results to go their way. Guiseley ended up beating Ashton comfortably 2-0 while the other two dropped points, ensuring the Lions were Champions and promoted to their highest-ever position in their Centenary year. They are now in unknown territory and last season saw them make their bow in the Blue Square North which became the club's most successful season. Despite losing their opening game, the momentum that followed promotion propelled them to the upper echelons of the league table. Guiseley surprised a lot of people when they achieved a fifth-place finish, putting them in the play-offs and just three games away from back-to-back promotions.

I went to Nethermoor myself to see them overcome Boston United 1-0 in the first leg of the semi-final and they eventually went through to the final on penalties at the Jakemans Stadium. I travelled with both of my children to Shropshire to see the final against AFC Telford United, which is one my finest football memories to date. An incredible statement after thirty years of watching football, but it was quality time on another level. We put the scarf up in the back window of our car, stopped at the services for sausage and chips and even played a game of football in a Telford park. The game itself was another rollercoaster of emotions. Telford started the better and took the lead through a controversial penalty. The scores were level shortly before half-time with James Walshaw keeping cool to fire home the equaliser from the penalty spot. Guiseley came out for the second half refreshed and were on top for large parts of the remainder of the game. The pressure eventually paid off with a header from Darryn Stamp to send the 500 plus away support into raptures. Guiseley were almost there, but injuries and fatigue began to take their toll. Telford eventually broke through to equalise before going on to break Guiseley hearts, scoring a goal with the last kick of the game. The Lions had been eleven minutes from the top tier of non-league football and I am now proud to have been at the New Bucks Stadium that afternoon.

I walk past the Vauxhall Motors team coach on my way to the turnstile and it dawns on me that I have no idea if they have driven 50 or 250 miles today. I assume they have travelled from the North West somewhere, but I am sure that today's programme with give me a geography lesson. I also pass another neighbouring cricket match to arrive at what feels like a busy ground, but it is 2.50pm so that will explain it. I flash my Leeds United season ticket as I enter the turnstile and make a saving that even Ken Bates can't stop. I walk around the pitch to take my usual spot on the touchline opposite the dugouts as the teams appear. Guiseley are in their usual white strip and Vauxhall Motors are in a florescent, highlighter pen sort of yellow, with black shorts. Their goal keeper is wearing luminous orange which is not the sort of kit you would rush out to buy, unless you worked on the railways at night and needed to be seen.

Guiseley look good from the first kick and dominate possession. In the 6th minute they take the lead. Lee Ellington latches on to Gavin Rothery's defence splitting pass to slot the ball past keeper Scott Tynan. On the half hour mark, the Vauxhall goal keeper appears to have made his manager unhappy for some reason. There is a lot of shouting to and from the away bench, which does at least amuse the fans on that side of the ground. On 33 minutes the score becomes 2-0 with a diving header from Danny Forrest. The goal results in some sumo chants as the chubby keeper gets back to his feet for the restart. In his defence, that colour isn't very flattering and he would look much slimmer in black. The game is starting to be very one sided and the lovely surface is helping Guiseley's passing game. Vauxhall Motors look like they could be on the receiving end of a high score. The scouse accents, another clue to where they are based, get louder urging them to organise their defence just as another glow in the dark save denies a third goal. The teams go in at half time at 2-0, but

I didn't want this game to break. I am enjoying the football and feel 'at home' today. I use half time well with a pint in the clubhouse, which was not great but is cheap. Sheffield FC has unfairly raised the bar, literally, in regard to the quality of ale.

The players start the second half slowly, but it comes alive again when Vauxhall's Lee Dames earns a red card for a two footed lunge off the ground. This fine refereeing decision doesn't excuse him for not giving a clear penalty when a Guiseley player is chopped down a couple of minutes later. I am still complaining when the ball is clearly handled on the line to deny the Lions a goal. He almost caught it! The linesman flagged, but then appears to bottle it by putting his flag back down. I lean over the fence to shout in my loudest voice at Paul Curry "you've had an awful game ref, hope you can sleep tonight". Perhaps not the sort of behaviour you expect from an impartial author supporting 65 teams equally. In the 71st minute substitute Simon Baldry gets the 3rd goal with his first touch. It is a simple header from Ciaran Toner's cross that even the officials do not stop to query. I leap off the ground in the 82nd minute as Baldry scores again. This is the best goal of the game and his second of the match thanks to some good play by Alex Davidson to create the chance that deserved my celebration.

Vauxhall's Josh Wilson scores a penalty in the final few minutes after Liam Nethercote is blocked in the box by keeper Steve Drench. The referee gets his revenge on my constructive criticism when he sends him off. Wilson scores with ease from the spot to reduce the margin. The attendance of 522 is announced just as the final whistle blows, which is higher than their usual crowd. A big success particularly if some of them return which, based on this performance is surely an easy sell. Guiseley dominated the game, their passing and one touch football was a pleasure to watch and they must now be serious challengers for a top five finish again. Eleven months after my first visit to Nethermoor, I have bonded with Guiseley to truly make them 'my Non League team'. Perhaps now the fun stops. I have enjoyed the day for lots of reasons, but the main one is simple - Guiseley won.

I will miss the Lions this season, but hope they will have me back when I return, one day, as a supporter.

Guiseley 4 Vauxhall Motors 1

Attendance: 522
Admission price: £5 (usually £10)
Ground Address: Otley Road, Guiseley, Leeds. LS20 8BT.
Club website: www.guiseleyafc.co.uk
Twitter: @guiseleyafc

13

The Wembley of the North

Askern Villa FC v Handsworth FC

The Welfare Ground
BARIS NCEL Division One.
Tuesday 6th September 2011. Kick off 7.45pm

I am going to the Villa tonight rather than watching England play Wales on the box, which most football fans in the country will be doing. Personally, over the last few years I haven't felt any connection with our national team and their overpaid 'stars'. I just can't get excited by England's style of football and suddenly cheering on players I have grown to dislike when playing for their respective clubs. I recall, last season, the cameras at Wembley scanning over a variety of flags from non Premiership clubs (shock horror) and the commentator stating that international football was important to small clubs as their fans are "starved of star players and nice stadiums". I thought that was very condescending and all credibility in his opinion was lost instantly. He just doesn't get it and I am sure he can't have been to The Welfare Ground.

I had a meeting in Newcastle this afternoon, so I am now stiff from the three hour drive, on top of spending yesterday in bed with a flu bug. At least the village of Askern is the right side of Doncaster (the north) unlike Rossington 7 days ago. I arrive into Askern with almost 90 minutes to spare. I decide to pull into the local Co-op to buy some water as I am due some more paracetamol and for an exploration, which I haven't done since Armthorpe. I find loads of takeaways, most of which are shut, a strange mix of shops and a boating lake. The village has that 'seen better days' feel and, despite being starved from my two cereal bar diet yesterday, I decide to head back to my car. I just hope the ground sells food. A Pukka pie would be perfect! The ground is easy to locate this time, set back from the main road on the outskirts of the village. I only just find a space in the car park; the other 16 cars are probably players and officials. I am opposite yet another cricket pitch, but there is no game on tonight. The sky is clear, but it is very windy which may make the football interesting tonight.

I take my chance to look at the Villa website as I know absolutely nothing about this club and find that the first team were formed under the name of Askern Welfare in 1924. In 2008 the club won the Central Midlands League Supreme Division title and were promoted to the Northern Counties East Division. In their first season they changed their name to Askern Villa. The new name suited them as they nearly won promotion again, but finished third after taking only 5 points from their final 6 games. I enter the turnstile and I get an immediate reality check. This is definitely grass roots football! A large open space, with a pitch in the middle, and two tiny stands. There is a small covered terrace between the dugouts and a small seated stand opposite, set back from the pitch. The ground is surrounded by fields which makes the pitch look huge. There is nothing to act as a wind break so it is hitting this area ferociously.

In addition to some changing rooms, there are two portakabins. One houses the ladies toilets and what looks like an area for corporate guests. The other building instantly grabs my attention with a picture of a cup and saucer (although not eggs and bacon) on the door. This gives me hope as the clubhouse I am looking for clearly doesn't exist. Inside I choose a bovril under pressure and to buy me some time to study my food options whilst counting out the loose change from my pocket. My 'options' consists of only crisps or chocolate! I buy some cheese and onion crisps and a Kit Kat but in the panic I ask for them twice as I am convinced that the £1 he asks for cannot possibly be for both items. I remark how cheap this is which prompts a smile as he shows me what is hidden behind his price list sheet. He proudly tells me, and the half dozen other crisp eaters, that the board was originally at Chesterfield's previous Saltergate ground, which they obtained along with some blue seats. He points to the 95p price for a packet of crisps as if it said fifty gold coins. "A little more if I was at Wembley tonight" I reply. He looks back at me blankly as if he is genuinely unaware that England are even playing, or because I have just pissed on his bonfire. There are no chairs so I stand in the corner to sip my bovil and hope that the wind will disguise the sounds of my rumbling stomach. I would kill for a cheese burger and would even pay the tenner it would no doubt cost tonight in our national stadium.

I go to the back of the main stand in hope of getting some shelter, but the wind is hitting us straight on. I have to admit that, for a split second, I do wish that I was on my warm sofa with some post illness sausage and chips from the chip shop. The teams run out to a surreal silence and look as unenthusiastic as I feel. I count only 13 spectators inside with just a minute or so to go. Perhaps there were hundreds of supporters here earlier and the ones that didn't get blown away have found a soup kitchen somewhere. At least Askern look striking in their usual black and white striped shirts, black shorts and striped socks. Handsworth are in red shirts with white sleeves, white shorts and red socks. The teams kick off, which results in the crowd more than doubling as they appear from their confectionery feast.

Within ten minutes of play I discover the main problem with such an open ground. With the few fans there are huddled in one stand, every time the ball goes out of play there is nobody on the touch line to retrieve the ball. The player who takes the throw in has to duck under the perimeter fence and usually chase the ball as it is blowing away in the strong wind. This really does slow down the game. I fear if I stretch my legs later for a wander I will be roped in as a ball boy; that is, if a 39 year old man on the brink of starvation can ever be described as a boy. Within 15 minutes of play it is pitch black which feels a bit odd. How did that suddenly happen I ask myself. I am still waiting for our Indian summer.

Handsworth are starting to have the better of the chances but it isn't a classic game so far. I really wanted to tweet to the nation about news of my 10 goal thriller at the Welfare ground. After 25 minutes the Askern keeper pulls off a save from close range to stop the away side taking the lead. Three minutes later the best chance of the game almost produces a goal for Handsworth, which tells me that the majority of those inside this wind tunnel, last count 31, have travelled from Sheffield tonight. Then their striker Scott Bates weaves in and out of the Villa defence to fire those travelling fans into deliria. Too many paracetomols may have caused me to exaggerate, but Handsworth have taken a 1-0 lead. After their goal they do look the better side now and come close to extending their lead several times. This action on the pitch prompts two fans to gather behind the goal Handsworth are attacking and put up an impressive 'Railway End On Tour', complete with British Rail symbols, flag up. I will make a note to stand in the Railway End whenever I end up in Handsworth. Half time soon arrives and not having a kite there are not many options for me, except to buy another Bovril. This one does taste better as I am now cold through to the bone. The wind is chilling, but as its only early September I remind myself that I will no doubt lie awake in February dreaming about weather like this.

The teams return to the pitch and I move to the window with my hot drink. I can even hear the England game from this sheltered paradise, so stay put for the first ten minutes of play. Eventually, I brave the wind and stand in the open by the corner flag. After only 15 minutes, my fingers can't even type to tweet that the game was better than a home nation's qualifier. I go into the gents for some warm water, but there isn't a towel or a hand dryer to tempt me to stay inside. An elderly man remarks to me as I pass him on the way out that this must be the most windy place in the world. He could well be right. The hood comes up as I leave and it is time to use my head. I notice that I am the only one standing by the touchline. Even the two away fans have now abandoned their flag. I see that the small covered terrace is getting more popular so head that way. As I arrive, complete with watering eyes and runny nose, the wind stops like someone has just flicked a switch! The back of this stand provides the perfect wind break and I can now start to watch a game I had felt I was losing interest in. I am stood immediately between the two dugouts which acts as two speakers in stereo, one for each ear. The Handsworth staff are winning the battle for my attention due to their greater vocal presence, use of swear words and general stroppiness. I am stood next to nine, what look like regular, Askern fans and they create some entertaining banter between the away bench, the players and the linesman at this side of the pitch. There are some great comical moments. My favourite comment is "I hope they catch that barber" to the Handsworth left winger who had a hairstyle that I am not sure the Doncaster villages are quite ready for. Even the linesman got some stick. He had a decent game in my opinion, and the statement "hope you can look at yourself in the mirror tonight lino when you clean your teeth" seemed a little unfair. Handsworth win a free kick on the edge of the box for what looked like assault but our comedian fan shouts "cheat" to start an argument with the away bench. This exchange may have also distracted the players as the free kick was ballooned.

The last five minutes of play see a good Askern penalty shout ignored and a Handsworth sitter missed so badly it even creates a silence on their bench. The away side clearly lack the ability to kill a team off tonight, but at least it gives the majority in the ground some hope that they may steal a draw; a false hope as it turns out. I jump in my car within seconds of the final whistle blowing, mainly for shelter. The temperature dial tells me that it is a tropical 12 degrees. It feels more like -12 in that wind, I am now starting to think like my parents.

I listen to the reports from Wembley on the radio on my way home. Another 1-0 scoreline giving England the win, but it's not a great game. England fans are phoning in to moan with Capello insisting it's all about the result rather than the performance. The Handsworth manager wasn't impressed with his team's performance either, but a 1-0 away win sees them top the table tonight. Perhaps the main difference between international and non-league football is the price of the refreshments; oh and perhaps more food options. Personally I think I made the right choice, I just needed to bring a packed lunch.

Askern Villa 0 Handsworth 1

Attendance 45
Admission £4
Ground Address Manor Way, Askern, Doncaster, Sth Yorkshire. DN6 0AJ
Club website www.pitchero.com/clubs/askernvilla
Twitter None found

14

Hospital Radio

Sheffield United FC v Huddersfield Town

nPOWER League 1

Tuesday 13th September 2011. Kick off 7.45pm

Tonight is a game I have been looking forward to for many weeks and not just because I am making my first trip to a league club. I have been kindly invited to help my friend, Jonathan, broadcast tonight's match on hospital radio. This obviously sounded fun, but it will also give me a unique view of a match day at Bramall Lane from a very different perspective. We arrange to meet up at 6.30pm and soon find the Media Entrance, which sounds much grander than it actually is, at the back of the GAC stand by the main car park. I'm on their list and I'm given a Media Pass which apparently admits me to the Press Lounge and Gantry. I am handed an 'Information for Media/Photographers' sheet which adds to my excitement with the news of free refreshments and some statistics. Wow, I usually have to do my own research (or don't bother, which is the norm). I now have a form guide, details of their last league meeting in 2000, record wins, defeats and even a list of players who have played for both clubs amongst other 'useful' statistics.

Sheffield United were the first sporting team to use the name 'United' and are nicknamed 'The Blades', thanks to Sheffield's worldwide reputation for steel production. The Club play their home games at Bramall Lane, the oldest major stadium in the world still hosting football matches. Sheffield United enjoyed possibly their most successful period between 1897 and 1902, winning the League in 1898 and the FA Cup in 1899 and 1902, with further wins following in 1915 and 1925. They were beaten finalists in the FA Cup in 1901 and 1936, and reached the semi-finals in 1993, 1998 and 2003. In more recent times they reached the League Cup semi final in 2003 and were promoted to the Premier League in 2006, which ended amidst controversy after just one season. Despite reaching the Championship play-off final in 2009, further decline followed, where an over reliance on loan players and the sale of the club's star players saw The Blades relegated to the third tier of English football for the first time in 23 years.

Jonathan, a solicitor by trade, has been a volunteer for the charity Sheffield Sports Commentators for 11 seasons. They report on football, rugby league and ice hockey to the three adult hospitals in Sheffield. Jonathan is part of a small team that covers the Blades for both hospital radio and the blind who attend matches at Bramall Lane. There is also a team covering Sheffield Wednesday and I am told that Jonathan's colleague Terry is at Stevenage tonight to provide us with the highlights of the Owl's match. The home side will always get priority for full match commentary and they edit the programme live between the two grounds. This service is free to patients and is a valuable service. Getting football scores to the sick is definitely my kind of charity, although perhaps sometimes news that your team has been hammered won't help your recovery. The running costs, such as the telephone line and equipment maintenance, is funded by various fund raising events that include a collection at both Sheffield grounds and an annual dog track event. I enter the Press Lounge with Jonathan and restrain myself to casually walk, not sprint, to the free pies and coffee. I am introduced to Tom who is a 6th Form student on work experience. At this rate, there could be more helpers than away fans. At 7 o'clock we are all given a team sheet, which most people seem to scribble on immediately. Jonathan talks me through the facts he knows on each of the players as he also writes on his sheet important details such as that Town player Jamie McCombe is a Wednesday fan.

I am enjoying the excellent facilities the media are given so ask Jonathan which he thinks is the best ground he has commentated at. I recall that he is trying to achieve his own radio version of the 92 Club by commentating at every league ground, which makes my project feels like a walk in the park in comparison. He hasn't commented at Wembley yet but likes the "posh bistro" feel of the press rooms at Chelsea and Arsenal. Andy, a Plymouth Argyle fan now settled in Sheffield, arrives to complete the commentary team. The four of us finish our hot drinks and make our way up the many flights of steps up to the gantry. This is basically a platform in the roof of the stand, situated on the half way line and offers the perfect view of the pitch from this height. I don't do heights but, surprisingly, feel very comfortable up here. It helps that the floor is solid unlike some of the steps I climbed earlier which were transparent. I am, however, relieved that the high winds that we have had over the last few days have now died down.

I am given some headphones to put on and suddenly my friend Jonathan turns into a radio commentator. I am instantly impressed as he confidently chats to Andy, never talking at the same time, as if they are sat in the pub. It is a surreal experience looking down on the players lining up from my roof top position and the noise of the crowd is now in stereo. The Blades wear their traditional red and white striped shirts, black shorts and white socks. Huddersfield Town are also in stripes, their usual blue and white, white shorts and black socks. The visitors from West Yorkshire are currently 5th in the table and only 4 points behind league leaders Sheffield United. I read on Twitter earlier that many town fans will be boycotting this game in response to the £28.50 ticket price for away fans. Yesterday they had sold just 1,049 tickets. By comparison they took over 4,000 fans to Hillsborough last season. We all remain standing and look down at the game as it starts at the fast pace you would hope from a Yorkshire derby with a lot at stake. I could not feel more different watching these players than at my last game in Askern.

We get our first score flash from Stevenage with less than 10 minutes gone. This comes in as a text because Terry's radio isn't working. The news will upset those Wednesday fans keen enough for updates to listen to full match commentary from their fiercest rivals as the Owl's are 1-0 down. This almost inspires Cresswell to put this Sheffield side ahead, but he wastes his chance. The commentary is very geographical which must be due to the blind listeners. It reminds me of listening to the cricket on the radio. It does feel a little weird because I am listening to the game, just how other supporters will be on their radios, except the commentators are stood next to me. I am also surrounded by other commentators which includes the Sky Sports cameras for their updates tonight. We get another text to say that Stevenage have scored a second, which Jonathan announces with a hint of smugness in his voice. A true professional. He even apologises to Andy with news that Plymouth are also losing.

With 15 minutes played, a chip from United's Lee Williamson almost finds the net which results in the gantry shaking. This near miss makes me want to see a home goal just to experience the celebration from up here. A couple of minutes later we get a third goal alert text from Terry which results in a very cheerful response from Jonathan, so perhaps he is human after all. On 20 minutes he gets some of his own medicine as Huddersfield take the lead. Danny Ward hits a shot that the keeper cannot hold and Lee Novak has a simple tap in to put the visitors ahead. Jonathan surprises me with an enthusiastic commentary of the goal. He didn't sit down and fold his arms which I probably would have done in his position.

Jonathan reads out a text from Terry claiming his match is the "worst performance from a professional team I have seen in a long time". He introduces some comedy with his response of "I think he means Stevenage". At our game, Town are starting to take control of possession which prompts the commentary duo to agree that this is the best team that Sheffield United have played so far this season. The Blades then miss another chance which most of the crowd, including the four of us, think is in, but Chris Porter somehow shoots wide from close range. Just as we hear that Wednesday have gone four down, in the 37th minute things also get worse for this Sheffield team as Novak grabs his second after some poor defending. Jonathan is still cheerful, but admits that "United have a big mountain to climb" and Terry adds to the gloom for Sheffield tonight with news that

Wednesday are chanting 'we want our money back'. The town fans then get even greater value for their £28.50 when Oscar Gobern heads in from a corner. The score is now 3-0 which is "game over" according to Andy but Jonathan pulls out the cliché "it's not over until it's over Andy". Believe me it is! Huddersfield have been better than Sheffield United in every single position and look more like the league leaders.

Half time arrives, the headphones are removed and we head back to the press room for soup. I don't finish mine though as missing a few minutes of the second half is not an option when you have listeners getting bored of pop songs. United have made a change, bringing on Ched Evans, who the press were calling for in our soup kitchen, and he almost scores with his first touch from a free kick. Gary is now commentating to allow Jonathan to concentrate on his laptop and chip in with comments like "sadly it is still 4-0 to Stevenage". Evans wastes another chance, Stevenage score a fifth goal and most of our listeners are calling for a doctor. The "poor Terry, I do hope it doesn't rain on the way home as forecast" comment really makes me wish that his radio did work. The impressive Novak is taken off just as Jonathan announces that "journalist Michael" will be choosing our man of the match award tonight. As I am working out who this is, the news that Wednesday have pulled a goal back gives a couple of people next to me some hope. There is very little pitch action now to distract me from deciding who to give the award to. There is lots of pressure from the Blades, but I can't see them scoring if we played all week. I hope that they have enough coffee just in case! Huddersfield are so well organised, strong and very quick on the break that the game has been killed.

The attendance of 17,373 is announced, my biggest so far by some considerable margin, and young Tom is also given a reason to stay awake to read the full time scores. Just as viewers are told that my man of the match is next, I am informed that it has to go to a Sheffield United player to throw my Lee Novak choice out of the window. Under pressure, and to put my own Leeds United signature on the evening, I proudly announce that Richard Cresswell is my choice. I explain that Richard has received a lot of stick from my 'colleagues' tonight when he has faced a brick wall of a defence. I then get a few minutes to plug my book, excellent hospital reading I add. The final whistle confirms that The Blades have dropped to second and Town are now just one place and a point behind. I would be surprised if Huddersfield don't get promoted based on this performance as they look a complete team. Tom then gets his big chance as he reads out the final scores for his work experience. I am unsure what job he is building up to do but, whatever it is, it's a vacancy I am very interested in. He is a little rusty, so looks relieved when Jonathan leaps in with the Champions League results.

We all head back inside for a press conference, which makes a nice change from legging it back to Ilkley. Just before 10pm, Lee Clark walks in to tell us how "delighted" he is and praises their "good work ethic". Seven reporters, plus the four of us, listen to lots of management speak and him discuss their ambitions to finish in the top two to enable him to have a decent family holiday. Those play-off games can get in the way! He looks younger than me, which I later confirm is true as he's only 38. I scribble some notes myself, as old age dawns upon me, but realise I probably don't look out of place in the company I am keeping. Lee leaves the room after five minutes which allows me to grab another coffee to keep me awake on the M1. At 22.12 Danny Wilson enters the room and the Dictaphones all come out. He must have watched a different game to me as The Blades were beaten by "three isolated attempts on goal" and his side "had the better chances". He was happier than Lee Clark which makes me think the coffee downstairs must have been strong. I agree that it is too early to panic, but Huddersfield must have been a reality check for the home side. Six minutes later, Danny leaves with a smile.

The entire evening has been a fantastic experience and I owe a big thank you to everyone. Would I want to do this job for a living? I am not sure, but would love to have a lie in tomorrow, skip a shave and then write up this chapter from Starbucks. Dream on. Instead I get home at 1am, the alarm goes off five hours later and I head to work where the pies are not free.

Sheffield United 0 Huddersfield Town 3

Attendance 17,373
Admission Free with Press Pass (usually from £26 for this category A match)
Ground Address Bramall Lane, Sheffield. S2 4SU
Club website www.sufc.co.uk
Twitter @SUFC_tweets

15

The (big) Boys are Back in Town

Harrogate Town FC v FC Halifax Town

The CNG Stadium

Blue Square Conference North

Saturday 24th September 2011. Kick off 3pm

I am back in Harrogate today and I'm still enthusiastic about the game of football despite a testing 24 hours. I didn't get to bed until just after 5am this morning from my trip to Brighton's new American Express Community Stadium. As the TV advert used to say 'That will do nicely sir' as it is a huge improvement on their previous home, The Withdean. It was certainly an eventful, and long, day! There were the highs of drinking beer on Worthing pier in the warm sun and a blue cheese burger to die for. The low point was our coach breaking down and letting a 2 goal lead slip. Then we had the ecstasy of an injury time equaliser to complete the rollercoaster ride. We made it back home on a different coach and everyone appears to have matched their coats and bags with the right owners - well I am very happy with my new things! I somehow managed to coach twenty seven Under 7's this morning on only 3 hours sleep, but still feel happy to be parked outside the CNG Stadium. Although I am not parked as close to the ground as my last visit in January, due to a large following from today's visitors, FC Halifax, who are very well supported for this level.

Today's history lesson; in the 1907/08 season, a team by the name of 'The Harrogate Town Club' were registered, but didn't get off the ground until 1914 when Harrogate AFC were formed. They secured admission to the Northern League immediately and were due to play their home games at the County Ground behind the County Hotel (now an Indian restaurant). The First World War then got in the way with fixtures being postponed. After the war, a meeting was held at the Imperial Cafe (now Betty's) on Monday 19th May 1919 to consider the formation of the Association Football Club for Harrogate. Eventually Harrogate AFC were formed in 1919 and played their first game on 30th August 1919 against Horsforth at their former Starbeck Lane ground. There was no Town team from 1932 until after the Second World War, but Harrogate Hotspurs were formed in 1935. They became the new Town team and, in 1948, changed their name to Harrogate Town. It is easy to forget poor 'Starbeck' Railway Athletic whilst reading this history, but clearly they are the outsiders being located so far out of town. Town's recent history and success has involved their previous coach and then manager, Neil Aspin. Neil returns today as manager of FC Halifax Town whom he has led them to two successive titles.

I enter the Wetherby Road ground (the name before we knew about the supply of natural gas to businesses) and it couldn't look more different today from my last visit. I am greeted by the sight of hundreds of blue shirts and scarves of the Shaymen fans. There is also a large collection of impressive flags hung all over the ground. There is another 'Forza' banner taking me back to those noisy Grantham fans at Sheffield. I really need to find out the translation. The Harrogate Hornets dancing girls are entertaining us to the 'footballs coming home' tune that we are more used to hearing when we all get carried away with the idea of winning the World Cup.

I select the covered terrace behind the away dugout. It feels like at least two thirds of the crowd are supporting Halifax, which is confirmed by the noise generated as the teams run out. Harrogate Town have their usual white shirts, black shorts and white socks. Halifax are in all blue. They line up to Thin Lizzy's 'The boys are back in town' music which seems to rev them all up for the Yorkshire derby ahead. I have spent the last couple of days exchanging tweets with someone by the name of 'We Beat The Scum 1-0', who is also at today's game. He is here to support Halifax, but is also a huge Leeds United fan (hence his twitter name). It is good to meet him for real and I comment on the huge away following. He responds with, "but they're not really a non league club are they?". I know what he means, but being a bigger club than those around you obviously doesn't guarantee anyone instant success. They may find the slope of this pitch more challenging even with an army of fans, but this strong support could sway today's referee. I have often seen this happen at this level when there is an unusually large crowd.

The game starts at a fast pace and the tackles are flying in from both sides. I can see goals being scored today, but it seems I may have given the game the kiss of death. The first good opportunity falls to Harrogate when Stephen Turnbull's free-kick sends Laurie Wilson clear, but his cross is cut out by keeper Simon Eastwood. The away side respond well to the early chance, but an excellent tackle by Harrogate's Liam Darville halts Danny Lowe's good run. I need to take a visit to the toilets (which usually produces goals) that are situated inside the Cross Bar clubhouse. I enter a very busy bar full of Halifax fans who are getting a bit rowdy and are more interested in drinking than in their team's fortunes on the pitch. We have all been there at some stage, but this is not the norm for a non league game. They look like they are becoming a handful and keeping the barmaid busy with the usual offences such as taking drinks outside and smoking in the toilets. One man old enough to know better gets a good telling off for his bad language.

I escape and return to the game, but decide to take my place by the touchline this time. Being able to watch a game from different viewpoints is another benefit of non league football. Halifax continue to threaten, but it is Harrogate that almost take the lead. Eastwood again blocks striker Lee Elam's effort to keep the score level. I then spot a 'TITS' banner below where a group of noisy Harrogate fans are standing. My eyes are too tired to read the small print underneath, but it does make me smile. The quality of the football and finishing is poor in relation to the last game I saw at this level. That just happened to be Guiseley but, as you know, I always remain impartial.

At half time the club house gets invaded as the dancing girls return to the pitch. The club shop isn't open, just like last January, but I am advised that pin badges are sold in the club house. Great. I am about to enter when I hear the familiar song of "let's go fucking mental" that is popular on my travels with Leeds United. I decide it is wise to double check with the steward outside if badges are on offer today, but he strongly advises me "don't go in there mate". I knew collecting these things would be bad for my health and decided e-bay would be a better option from the comfort of the sofa. As the second half starts, most of the Halifax fans have settled at the club house end where their team are now attacking. I decide, on the back of enough drunken behaviour at Brighton, which probably included me, that the other end was more me today. After all, I am supporting the home side and most of their fans have now also flocked here which includes the local TITS. The visitors begin to dominate and Harrogate have to thank Richard Pell for his battling performance. His team continue to weather every attack, but a Halifax goal now looks very likely. Halifax continue to pile on the pressure and Scott McManus shoots wide with a 30 yard drive. Harrogate's Adam Nowakowski and Richard Pell make brave blocks to keep the score level.

The volume continues to rise from the West Yorkshire fans and the barmy army chant starts outside the club house. Every decision which goes against Halifax gets a roar of disapproval. In the 77th minute there is a huge roar as Jake Picton recklessly tackles Tom Baker in the box. Referee Gary Beswick awards a penalty, which even results in some fans coming outside away from their drinks. This time the roar, a smaller one that includes my tired voice comes from the home fans as new keeper Zac Jones saves with ease from Baker's spot kick. The first 0-0 of my tour now looks a strong possibility. All the action, both on and off the pitch, is now at the far end, including the arrival of a police officer to the Cross Bar. Harrogate create a couple of chances on the break, but find it hard to get through the Halifax defence when it matters most. The attendance is announced, which is almost three times their average this season, as Harrogate throw on all three substitutes in an effort to grab a late winner. However, it is Halifax that finish with a series of corners which almost produce a goal. They have two good chances in the four minutes of injury time, but neither Danny Lowe nor Lee Gregory can produce a goal. It ends with a hard fought draw that I think Harrogate Town will be more pleased with.

I walk back to my car along a very busy looking Wetherby Road. The unusual sight of a line of mini buses and four police vans are waiting for supporters, which is not the usual for match day here. The passing Saturday shoppers know that this Saturday is different. It doesn't feel like a non-league fixture, rather more of a FA Cup tie where the big league club invades for three hours. Perhaps FC Halifax Town are not 'a non-league club' in the usual way, but they will need to put away their chances if they want to climb back to the Football League. A lively atmosphere, but in all honesty I preferred the CNG Stadium on my last visit. I could have a quite pint whilst reading my programme without anyone going 'mental'. I get that from my Championship club and look for something different from non-league football. Perhaps I am getting old.

Harrogate Town 0 FC Halifax Town 0

Attendance 1,107
Admission £10
Ground Address Wetherby Road, Harrogate, N Yorkshire. HG2 7SA
Club website www.harrogatetownafc.com
Twitter @HarrogateTown

16

Mr Scum

AFC Emley v Askern Villa

The Welfare Ground
Baris NCEL League Division One
Tuesday 27th September 2011. Kick off 7.45pm

I leave the M1 at Junction 38, pass the Yorkshire Sculpture Park and find with ease the turning for the village of Emley. A short drive down a narrow country lane and a conversation with a very polite lady, who can communicate with other human beings, and I am outside the Welfare Ground. I have arrived early as I always build in some time to get lost. The tall mast, the Emley Moor Transmitter, stands on the outskirts of the village and can be seen for the entire journey from the motorway to guide other ground hoppers here. The hot weather has returned as we are apparently having a 'mini heat wave'. The temperate is still in the seventies at 6pm. Provided Villa don't bring with them that Askern wind we will have the perfect conditions tonight for a game of football. The village of Emley and the surrounding countryside look great in the evening sun. I have arranged to meet up again with twitter follower 'We Beat The Scum 1-0' who lives locally in Huddersfield. Formally known as Martin, he is a huge Leeds United fan who changed his name by deed poll to stand in last May's election in the Leeds Central constituency. His first name is now We, Surname 1-0 and his middle names are Beat The Scum. This may sound crazy to some, or to most people in fairness, but he received 155 votes. The Lady Mayoress read his name out on TV to bring back memories to Leeds United's famous victory at Old Trafford on January 3rd 2010. He knows Rob, who looks after the twitter account for AFC Emley, as they both work in the same industry. Mr 1-0 does energy surveys and Rob works in his family estate agency business. Mr 1-0 also follows Halifax Town and I had briefly met him last Saturday at the Harrogate game. He is also a bit, or a lot, of a ground hopper and once managed three games in a day visiting Doncaster, Wolverhampton and Swindon. This achievement impressed me when he tweeted about it last month, although my first thought was I wonder if I could manage four games in day!

I receive a Direct Message on twitter as I am sat in the car park from @AFCEmley which reads 'Complimentary entry for you and Mr Scum tonight at the game. Just give your name at the gate'. Poor Martin, it must be common place to get his name wrong. Mr 1-0 to you AFC Emley! The man himself then arrives in his family saloon car and has also heard the news of our fame. He must have read that message whilst driving, an interesting conversation if he had been stopped by the police. Your name Sir?!... We walk through the car park which is the usual mix of hot hatches and white vans that players tend to arrive in. The man on the turnstile is expecting us and as promised we gain entry without exchanging cash. The ground has a good size seated stand on one side and the sort of covered terrace behind the goal that I would love to see crammed full of fans. Opposite the main stand is a fence that separates the football pitch from a cricket pitch. This arrangement is starting to become popular on my visits to the Non Leagues.

We walk to the corner flag and chat whilst the players are warming up. Finding things to discuss is not a problem due to his life story and our mutual love of football. Mr 1-0's full name may not always set a good first impression, but he is a genuinely nice guy. He is clearly also an intelligent man and his middle name Scum doesn't do him justice. Whilst we talk, the ground becomes busier and someone brings over to us our complimentary match day programmes. The warm welcome is extended further when we discover that we have both warranted a mention in the introduction. We then wander over to the main stand where I am introduced to Rob Dixon, complete with his dog, who I discover is also a sponsor of the club, the president and programme editor, which includes writing the match reports. Rob is very friendly and makes me feel welcome instantly. I am told that the average attendance is around the hundred mark, sometimes more with a good away following. I haven't spotted an Askern Villa fan yet so I am not hopeful of reaching these heights.

Emley dates from Anglo-Saxon times and in more recent history was a pit village. Emley Moor colliery closed in 1985 after a year-long miners' strike and is now a business park. In line with Yorkshire tradition, there is a brass band in the village whose members rehearse twice a week in the village band room. As for their football club, the original Emley AFC's history stretches back as far as 1903. The club was somewhat successful in Yorkshire Non League football over the years, winning several championships. It was perhaps most famous for the FA Cup run in the later part of the 1990s which saw it playing against West Ham United. Things started to go wrong for the original club in 2000 after the Northern Premier League Premier Division announced new ground regulation rulings. Emley was unable to improve its ground, and moved to Wakefield to avoid being thrown out of the league. This move and the name change to Wakefield & Emley FC in 2003, alienated the fans from the humble village of Emley who had supported the club throughout the years. The final straw came when the Northern Counties East League discontinued its reserve league. The reserve team had continued to play at the old Welfare Ground in Emley even after the first team moved to Wakefield. As the reserve team was disbanded, several fans and former officials formed the new and current club under the name AFC Emley in 2005, back in their home village. During its first season, the new club finished third in the West Yorkshire League Division One. A year later the club was successful in an application to become a member of the Northern Counties East Football League Division One. It has remained in this division which is at Step 6 of the Non League pyramid. The team play in claret and blue. Askern Villa will tonight play in their usual home strip of black and whites stripes.

Rob is armed with his clipboard and is busy writing the match report which will be used for the club website and the Huddersfield Examiner newspaper. He is clearly the expert, so after gaining his permission to use his report, I decided to sit back and enjoy the match. I choose a seat on the half way line which gives me a great view of play and of Mr 1-0 eating his pie on the touchline. I'm not sure if it's a Pukka Pie or not from up here though!

Match Report by Rob Dixon:
Emley extended their winning run to 6 games despite a below par performance against Askern Villa. Their 3-1 win moves them up to 7th in the table but they will need to improve if they are to get anything out of Eccleshill on Saturday. The game started off in an entertaining manner with Emley looking dominant. David Heagney had a couple of early chances from distance before he put his side in front after 13 minutes. Josh Ingham broke away down the left wing and squared the ball perfectly into the path of Heagney who finished with a clean strike past Liam Copley from 12 yards out. This was the prolific striker's 11th goal of the season and his 10th in consecutive games.
Heagney saw a well hit effort sail over the bar before putting a good move together with full back Antony Leech who eventually saw his header well saved by Copley. Gavin Armitage thought that he had doubled Emley's lead after slotting the ball past Copley after being put through by Mark Stuart but was ruled offside. He also went close with a volleyed effort whilst Chris Wydowczyk had a long range shot saved by Copley. Villa created little in response and it was mostly one way traffic until Stuart received two yellow cards for stamping on an opponent and then dissent to the referee Nigel Haycock. Whilst he will feel aggrieved that the stamp was in reaction to a clumsy foul inflicted upon him he can have little to argue about and will now face a lengthy ban.
Instead of allowing Askern a route back into the game, Emley continued their dominance with Heagney hitting a fine free kick from the edge of the D which curled just wide of the target. Soon after, Heagney linked up well with Ingham who ran free of the Askern back line before returning the ball to the striker who went close from long range. John Cyrus went round an Askern defender before delivering an angled drive which was blocked well by Copley. This would be Copley's final meaningful contribution to the game however as he

too was sent off after elbowing Josh Ingham in the face just on the stroke of half time. Emley started the second half strongly with Armitage hitting an angled drive across the face of goal with replacement keeper Ralph Starkie well beaten.

Then, on the 50 minute mark, Ingham was brought down by a rash challenge in the penalty area. Starkie kept his side in the game, diving to his left to stop Heagney's spot kick. Askern midfielder Andy Towler, who stood out for his side, slipped through the Emley defence before hitting an angled strike past Clarke to draw the scores level on 53 minutes. Emley were back in front a minute later when Sean Hazelden hooked the ball back in a crowded penalty area to see it deflect into the net off the visitor's full back Danny Taylor. Askern worked hard to get themselves back into the game and, if anything, performed better after the loss of their regular keeper. Towler and Lee Pugh both tested Clark from distance before a curling effort from Mark Vicerage 40 yards out almost crept in at the far post with Clark alert enough to palm it over the bar to safety.

The visitors chances were restricted mostly to long range whilst Emley failed to make the best of their possession with the final pass frequently letting them down. They did however wrap the game up on 77 minutes with a well worked move which was started by Marc Townsend down the right flank. The pacy midfielder pulled the ball back for Heagney who laid it off into the path of Armitage who blasted the ball past Starkie into the roof of the net. What began as an entertaining game turned into a scrappy affair following the two red cards with incidents turning the attention to the referee rather than the football. Neither player could complain about the decisions and both would have to hold their hands up and apologise to their teammates after the game.

It has been a good, and eventful, game. At half time, when the score was 1-0, I had a pint with Mr 1-0 in the cosy clubhouse. In addition to admiring the rather fetching carpet featuring the club badge (I wonder if this is in Rob's house?), I did think it would be very fitting if the match ended at this score on the night Mr 1-0 was here. I am starting to think more and more like a writer! Perhaps chapter 65 will be a poem or even a screenplay. The disappointment was that despite warming up on the touchline I didn't get to see Mick Amos play. Mick has recently been in Coronation Street as an extra as a policeman. He is also a policeman in real life, so let's hope he wasn't on duty last week at Elland Road when they played Manchester United. I have to admit I am a big fan of this soap, but if I was in the police force I would want to play a burglar to get some escapism. The highlight for me, in addition to meeting two great people in Rob and Martin, were the enthusiastic score announcements from Old Trafford. At one point Manchester United were losing 2-0 and I saw Mr 1-0 punch the air in delight. As always, they salvaged a draw but it was appropriate that the team from over the Pennines featured in the evening. Mr 1-0 has certainly got my vote and proves again that we really do meet some interesting people at a game of football.

AFC Emley 3 Askern Villa 1

Attendance 103
Admission Free (usually £4)
Ground Off Upper Lane, Emley, Nr Huddersfield. HD8 9RE
Club website www.afcemley.co.uk
Twitter @AFC_Emley

17

One cycling seadog, there's only one cycling seadog...

Pickering Town FC v Scarborough Athletic FC

The Mill Lane Recreation Ground
Baris NCEL Premier Division
Tuesday 4th October 2011. Kick off 7.45pm

Just after setting up my twitter account in June, I received a very enthusiastic tweet from @FrozenMarrow who is better known as Bob. He is apparently part of the 'Cycling Seadogs' and attends some of Scarborough's away games on his bike with some other like-minded individuals. He was interested in my book and I immediately wanted to learn more about his away day experience on the saddle. We arranged to meet at tonight's game as soon as the fixtures were released. Two local sides meeting will hopefully generate a decent crowd so it sounded like a good match to get together. We exchanged tweets and mobile numbers and arranged to meet at the Sun Inn pub in Pickering at around 6.30pm. Bob wasn't sure where the ground was when I asked him, but tells me that he has been to the trout farm and swimming baths in Pickering so he's confident we will find it. I agreed to bring my rod and trunks just in case!

I enter the pub which looks a very good choice. A local's pub in an old stone building with low beamed ceilings and a selection of hand pumped ales. And lots of Scarborough fans! There are no colours on display but I recognise some faces from seeing a lot of them on the road during the last 12 months and I quite like this! Nobody is in cycling gear though and there is not a bike in sight outside unless they are parked at the back. The beer is very good, so I wish I had a chauffeur tonight. I haven't seen the ground yet, but share Bob's confidence in finding the ground as Pickering isn't very big. I hope so as the sky is turning black, a mixture of the sun going down and perhaps rain moving in, creating not so good cycling conditions for their journey home. The mini heat wave has definitely ended. Perhaps it didn't reach this part of North Yorkshire.

The last time I was in Pickering, or a drove through it at speed with the gale force wind behind me, was on route to Liversedge from my camping 'holiday' in August. Just as I am reliving that weekend, four men arrive who could pass as cyclists. Not in cycling gear as such, but all wearing shorts and trainers. They certainly look thirsty and one does look out of breath. I wait for a few minutes and then pounce with the direct question “Are you the cycling seadogs?!” Luckily my detective skills are strong and we all move into the beer garden, just as it is getting dark and cold. I discover that the other three have a bike but don’t support Scarborough Athletic. We have a Leeds United fan, someone attending only his second football match and the third man is “just here for the beer”. “Oh just one cycling seadog then?!” I reply. They have all cycled from York which is around 30 miles away. Bob has been following his Scarborough The Seadogs since he was a child. We discuss my book, their previous trips on two wheels and, like every conversation with a seadog, the subject of playing in Bridlington soon gets discussed. Bob is obviously pleased with the plans for a new ground in Scarborough, but doesn’t feel the new ground matches the ambitions of the club. I am told that the ground will only be suitable to get them to Unibond level. When not cycling, Bob and two others are graphic designers. I am told by the fourth man that he is a “male prostitute” which was always possible I suppose.

To my relief, as I haven’t cycled 30 miles, we all agree that it is getting quite cold outside so go back to the warm bar. I finish my pint, but then it dawns upon me that because I don't have a bike so we need to make our way separately to the ground, wherever that may be. I say goodbye as they order more beer and jump into my car at 7.35pm following their rough directions. I didn't need to worry as the light of the floodlights guide me in. I abandon my car on the neighbouring housing estate and dash to the turnstile with quite a few other late comers.

Pickering Town, known as the Pikes, is an old established club, formed in 1888. The Pikes played in local football, with long and successful spells in both the Scarborough and York Leagues, before stepping up to senior football when they joined the Yorkshire League in 1972. They finished as Third division champions in only their second season, and were Second Division runners-up the following season. The Pikes remained in the Yorkshire League until 1982 when a merger with the Midland Counties League saw the Pikes become founder members of the Northern Counties East League. The club celebrated its centenary in 1988 with a special dinner which was attended by England manager Bobby Robson. They were NCEL Second Division Champions in 1987-88 and have twice been runners-up in Division One, in 1991-92 and 2000-01. Their best ever NCEL season to date was in 1992-93 when they finished runners-up to Spennymoor United in the Premier Division after an exciting campaign that saw them just miss out on the title on goal difference. They first entered the FA Cup in 1993 and the furthest they have been in the competition is the 2nd Qualifying Round on 3 occasions. Recently, the club has recorded its best position in sixteen years when finishing a close third in the NCEL Premier Division. Products of the youth team include former Notts County manager Craig Short who is now the Pike's President. The ground has two 100 seater stands, a large covered terrace and a spacious clubhouse which is soon to undergo new development.

There is a decent crowd inside and the players are just kicking off as I enter. I head to the stand behind the goal that the red shirts of Scarborough are attacking. Pickering Town are playing in their usual blue strip. The away side get off to a lively start and the noise generated by every attack confirms that this ground is mainly following Scarborough Athletic. Just after 8 o'clock I notice the Cycling Seadog (and friends) arrive. Did they get lost or grab a sneaky 3rd pint?! I think I know the answer to this question as they head into the clubhouse rather than watch another Scarborough chance. A couple of minutes later Ryan Blott puts the visitors ahead with a well taken free kick. He hit it sweetly and the ground erupts. This comes after twenty minutes of Scarborough pressure so few inside can complain, even the Pickering Town fans if I find any. I do have some affection for Scarborough Athletic so standing with the Boro fans is great but I don't feel I have connected with Pickering Town Football Club. Therefore, I decide to therefore go for a wander to explore and perhaps I can buy a Pikes' souvenir. I find the club shop, or more of a temporary market stall set up on the top of a pool table and again find myself with a pin badge. Any guesses who I find at the bar? My four new friends are showing me how thirsty a bike ride can be. I then do a circuit of the pitch, or the three sides spectators can access. The pitch has a slope from both sides into the middle which must make it fun in midfield. I stop at the touchline behind the away dugout just as Boro miss another clear chance, which the manager uses as an opportunity to kick the rubbish bin hard. The whistle blows for half time as I am starting to regret that I haven't brought my winter coat tonight. The temperature is dropping despite all the warm air in the dug out. I return to my original position on the terrace hoping that the previous away end will now become the home end and I'll find a Pickering Town fan. The man who sold me my badge doesn't count.

The players return and there is a constant flow of fans passing from the clubhouse to the far end. The 25 or so left must be Pickering fans, although there are no blue shirts or scarves in sight despite the inventive retail outlet inside. I need a Pickering goal to test this theory, but the second half is almost all Scarborough possession and they dominate most of the play from the first kick. Boro finally extend their lead after 67 minutes. A ball from the right finds Bernard who turns and fires past a wrong footed McDonald. The scarfless fans around me, that I had hoped were from Pickering, unfortunately enjoyed that goal a bit too much to be locals. I use this goal as a good time to pay a visit to the toilets which are in the clubhouse. Pickering almost score on my way in from a decent shot and I witness at least five home fans holding their heads; there are six now if we count the shop assistant. My weak bladder also provides me with an opportunity to say hello to the cyclists who are still lubricating their joints for the journey home.

Scarborough are still dominating play as I return and, with a fresh eye I can appreciate the many slopes of the pitch. An M shape may be exaggerating the point but it's certainly not level. Ten minutes from time, Boro get the third goal that their performance deserves. Both substitutes are involved and the move ends with Phillips firing past McDonald. With the ball about to enter the net, Blott makes sure from an inch out. I do hope that goal can be seen from the bar!

The attendance is announced at 564 and at least 500 of them are visitors. They have invaded Mill Lane, but in a nice way. Ok the main stand is full of mature fans all armed with flasks, but the bar is lively too with plenty of drunken people, not all on bikes, but they remain friendly. With five minutes left to play, I say my goodbyes to Bob and his friends and I am told that they did hear the third goal. They are apparently "going steady tonight" and Bob proudly informs me that "we had 12 at Tadcaster and cycled home". I am not sure if there is a legal limit to be over or not in cycling terms. I make my way back to the game just in time to see Bill Law grab a fourth goal for Scarborough in injury time to round off a great night for them. A neat flick by Bernard found Blott who in turn played in Law who easily beat the keeper. A lovely strike to digest as I make the mad dash to my car like the majority of fans. I love how late goals always result in a sprint out of a football ground. The last time Rudy Funk's Scarborough played Pickering Town he saw his side lose by five goals to nil in his first game in charge. This time he watched his new look team exact revenge as they destroyed their hosts. Pickering Town stay at the bottom of the league and, on this performance, face a long season. I face a long drive home, but will pay special attention for cyclists, in particular the hammered variety!

I woke up to find a tweet confirming that the cycling seadog had got home safely at 12.35am. I beat Bob by about an hour, but suspect the alarm hurt him more this morning than mine did!

Pickering Town 0 Scarborough Athletic 4

Attendance 564
Admission price £5
Ground Recreation Club, Malton Road, Pickering. YO18 7DB
Club website www.pickeringtownfc.co.uk
Twitter @PickeringTownFC

18

Risen from the ashes

Brighouse Town AFC v Nostell Miners Welfare

The Dual Seal Stadium
Baris NCEL Premier Division
Saturday 8th October 2011. Kick off 3pm

The Dull Seal Stadium would be a better description today, though slightly unfair, as Brighouse Town Football Club cannot control the weather. It's a horrible grey day and I feel rather grey myself as I sit in the car park at 2.35pm. Also, there is, of course, nothing dull about one of the UK's leading independent processors of High Performance Vision & Insulated Glass Panels for Building Products & Construction. It can't even rain properly today and this constant drizzle is all very depressing. I have to be honest and say that this isn't one of the grounds I have been particularly looking forward to anyway (I've been before!) I feel like collapsing my seat back for a snooze whilst the other scores come through on the radio. If I was a Town fan, not that I have had any success all week in finding one on twitter, I would be outraged by my mood. Any travelling Nostell fans may also want to give me a good shake, perhaps a slap, and tell me how good it is to be alive. Let's engage some positive thinking. The rain may stop - possibly. The sun could even come out - unlikely. The ground may have improved since my last visit, although it doesn't look like it has from the car park. Oh, and we may see a 10-10 thriller, or more likely a 10-0 home win with Brighouse Town sitting top of the Northern Counties Eastern Premier League. By comparison, today's visitors Nostell are 18th.

The weather declines between my car and the turnstile but there have been improvements in the ground. I recall that the club house burnt down a couple of months before my last visit last Autumn. The small temporary portokabin is now a big permanent portokabin, into which I go to apply hot bovril and chocolate to my mood. And a pin badge too! I had been unsuccessful last time on buying such memorabilia with the excuse (a very good one I may add) that the badges were in the club house at the time of the fire. I made this observation to the sales assistant come barman and he proudly tells me that “they have risen from the ashes!” What a lovely response and I hand over the usual £3 with a smile. Another ground hopper arrives. I know of his 'hobby' as he announces it to claim why he “must” have a team sheet. They offer him a handwritten version if he returns later as they need it at the moment to announce the teams. He’s a strange looking man who is dressed for climbing a mountain. I need to beware of my healthy hobby becoming unhealthy. He has found a ground to bag, but think he will struggle to scale a rock face today in West Yorkshire. It’s not really the weather for this pursuit either. I can see the teams come out into the rain to play, but I'm in no rush to move from my dry chair. In a stroke of genius I move my chair a couple of feet to the right and can now see the game through the window. The wire mesh may eventually drive me more insane than my hopper colleague, but can at least report that Brighouse Town are in their usual orange shirts, black shorts and orange socks. Nostell have Yellow shirts and shorts with black socks. Perhaps these bright colours will brighten up a very dreary scene.

The clubhouse clears, which gives me an opportunity to engage in some conversation with the man, who is now the cleaner, who sold me my souvenir. I discover that the fire was in August 2010 on a Sunday night after their first ever FA Cup game. I ask some more questions in an attempt to get some detail about the fire, but he doesn't seem to want to talk about anything other than that they lost the FA Cup tie. He asks me where I am from, almost as if I was viewed as someone asking too many questions. I clam up too and reply Ilkley which he confirms is a nice place. Even in this weather, I add. I decide not to mention my hopping tendencies, let alone my book, as now have image concerns for being part of this ‘profession’. As a soon to be author, I imagine the clubhouse was burnt down by a jealous lover of one of the players or someone who collected Brighouse Town pin badges and wanted to increase the value of his collection by reducing the supply. I give up and even the rain now looks appealing.

Stood at the touchline, under cover at least, I am still struggling for any inspiration and do need some help. I am happy to share my problem with other like-minded budding writers. Let's give this some more thought:

Creative Writing Skills Course

Date: *A grey October day*

Venue: *Standing around in a wet West Yorkshire field*

Cost: *£5 pay on the day*

Course Objective: *To develop the skill of using words creatively to make the dullest afternoon sound exciting to those not lucky enough to be here*

Refreshments: *Tea, Coffee & Bovril*

End of course assessment:

In less than 500 words please make the following first half sound interesting to a non Brighouse Town supporter:

Nostell have two shots, but both are straight at the keeper. Brighouse Town's Anthony Haigh scores in the 23rd minute, but I miss the build up to it. They make it 2-0 whilst I am in the toilets blowing my nose. At half time it rains a bit more and I find out that it was Ben Green who scored the second goal from the penalty spot.

Ok I am alone with this one, but things do actually pick up in the second half. The rain stops, not completely but now it is only spitting. Other than what I can only describe as a horrible little man, who abuses the linesman after every decision, the next 45 minutes can almost be described as enjoyable. He pushes the linesman too far and is told to "shut your gob". He does of course, as someone has bravely challenged him, and the away side start to play some football. A much improved performance by Nostell earns them a draw against this morning's table toppers. A 61st minute goal from Ben Njie followed three minutes later by Graham Marchant, his fifth in four games, gives the Welfare a well earned point.

The final whistle signals the rain to turn heavier and all 66 of us empty the ground very quickly. The other hopper scuttles off with the team sheet across the car park, which eventually turns in a jog to keep his trophy dry. I hope I don't start to run like this man. If so, I will give this all up tomorrow. It has not been a classic, but we need the lows to fully appreciate the highs don't we? Brighouse Town now drop to third in the table with Bridlington Town taking the top spot. I bet Bridlington looks nice in the drizzle. I will need to take the risk of the fashion police finding me when I do make it there. Perhaps I should take a rucksack to keep my programme dry?... No!

Brighouse Town 2 Nostell Miners Welfare 2

Attendance 66
Admission £5
Ground St Giles Road, Hove Edge, Brighouse. HD6 2PL
Club website www.pitchero.com/clubs/brighousetownafc
Twitter @brighousetown or @brighousetownfc

19

101 years of history cannot be bought

Frickley Athletic FC v FC United of Manchester

The Tech5 Stadium
Evo-Stick Premier Division
Tuesday 11th October 2011. Kick off 7.45pm

Frickley Athletic play their football in South Elmsall, pronounced 'em-sull' I am told. The town is most famous for its coal-mining past; it was the site of Frickley Colliery, which was one of the largest in the whole country and a key source of union radicalism. The colliery is named after the nearby village of Frickley in South Yorkshire. During the UK Miners' Strike (1984-1985), there were numerous disturbances in the area. It was one of the last pits to return to work after the strike, as it was picketed by a group of hardliners from Kent who continued to picket Frickley after the NUM had called off the strike. The Frickley miners refused to cross the hardliners' picket. The colliery was closed on 26th November 1993 following closures of nearby pits.

I have read that this area was once one of the most depressed areas of the whole European Union, although fortunes have improved recently. The first impressions of my approach to the ground are not great with all the usual signs of a rundown area. I am greeted by rows of speed bumps, high numbers of hooded teenagers hanging around outside every shop and even an old man going through a bin. You can't rip the heart out of a town by closing its pit without suffering casualties. At the end of Broad Lane visitors are, however, rewarded by what can only be described as a proper football ground like the good old days. I grew up in the East Midlands with fond memories of trips to places like Saltergate, Filbert Street and the Baseball Ground. The facilities were, admittedly, a little dated but they had a soul that a 'replacement' stadium such as Pride Park will never benefit from in my opinion.

Even in the drizzle, the Tech5 Stadium looks great (sorry Brighouse!) The rear of their main stand dominates and wouldn't look out of place in League Two. The ground is overlooked by the huge colliery spoil heap. I love it! Visiting supporters from the south must feel like they have arrived in the industrial north. I leave my car immediately to take some photos before darkness takes all of this away from me. There is a real buzz in the air with over an hour until kick off and a noticeable high police presence which is usually the case when FC United of Manchester visit Yorkshire. I recall problems in Guiseley a couple of years ago when the locals re-enacted the Leeds v Manchester rivalry in a non league setting. The result was the closure of all the surrounding pubs and fighting on the streets. I am told that the away fans singing Eric Cantona songs didn't go down well in Nethermoor either. I doubt whether many, or in fact any, of those involved in the trouble followed their respective clubs the rest of the year.

The history of FC United of Manchester, however short, is very interesting. I purposely use the words from their website to put the clubs argument forward. '"The club set up in protest to Malcolm Glazer's takeover of Manchester United" is a statement often used to describe FC United. But while there is no doubt that FC would not have happened without the American invasion, it was the catalyst, the final straw, but not the sole reason. The material theft of a Manchester institution, forcibly taken from the people of Manchester, was the tip of a pyramid of destruction, with changing kick off times for the benefit of television, soulless all-seater stadia full of 'new' supporters intent to sit back and watch rather than partake in the occasion, heavy handed stewarding and ridiculously priced tickets propping it all up. By May 2005 some supporters had

had enough. The failure to prevent Glazer and repeat the successful repulsion of Rupert Murdoch in 1998 resurrected a 'last resort' idea from that previous campaign and the FC United wheels were put in motion. A group of individuals determined to continue the fight formed a steering committee and FC United of Manchester was delivered. They wanted to maintain the momentum of the protest, to stick together, to sing United songs, to reminisce and bring back the good bits of the good old days. They wanted Our Club, Our Rules and they got just that, a member owned democratic, not-for-profit organisation created by Manchester United fans. A club accessible to all of the Greater Manchester community, dedicated to encouraging participation of youth whether it be playing or supporting and to providing affordable football for all.'

A nice concept, but all I can do is look at this in my own world. If my disillusion with Leeds United grew, becoming even more fed up with the rising ticket prices (in the Championship!) and disliked how Ken Bates is running the club (no comment) then I would have the option to simply swap my season ticket from Elland Road to Nethermoor. This concept is, in reality, not totally out of the question. If Leeds got into the Premier League, prices would rise again and the relationship between supporters and the players (now stars) may widen. In my case, I would probably just watch Leeds less and Guiseley more, but ultimately my local Non League side would benefit. Setting up a new club would be incredibly good fun and a huge fan base will, with time, pretty much guarantee that you rise through the leagues. But what happens when you hit the Conference, or even the Football League, and the novelty wears off? Invading small grounds and the pubs of villages and towns is surely not much different from invading cities in large groups as a Manchester United fan. Perhaps I am missing the point and this isn't just a great big piss up but I doubt this adventure has any longevity to it.

In contrast, Frickley Colliery Football Club was formed in 1910 and initially played in the Sheffield Association, followed by a spell in the Yorkshire League. In 1924, the club joined the old Midland League where it remained a member until 1960 when the League disbanded, upon which they moved to the Cheshire County League. In 1970, the 'Blues' returned to the reformed Midland Counties League and four years later the club changed its name to Frickley Athletic FC. Although Frickley were runners-up in the League in 1971-72, it was after their change of name that their climb up the ladder really began. After winning the Midland League Cup in 1976, they were accepted into the Northern Premier League. The stay in the Northern Premier League was only a short one as in 1979-80 Frickley finished in third position in the League and after their ground, Westfield Lane, was given a 'B' grading they took the place of Redditch United in the Alliance Premier League, now the Nationwide Conference. The 1985/86 season was the club's most successful season ever when they defeated a Football League side for the first time when beating Hartlepool 1-0 away in the 2nd Round proper of the F.A. Cup. History was also made as it was the first time the club had reached the Third Round. However a 1-3 home defeat was to follow against local rivals Rotherham United.

The attendance that day was a record for Westfield Lane at 6,000 although, at the time, the club's average crowd was about 600.

I enter the ground to discover that the inside of the main stand is even more old school, set back from the pitch with a terrace in front. The pitch is surrounded by a wall, which should really catch on in the Non Leagues. Unfortunately, it is now dark so I cannot admire the slag heap, but it is comforting to know that it's there. I already know that this will not be my last visit to this ground. I buy a programme immediately in case they sell out as the ground is getting busy. I overhear a steward tell his colleague that it was his turn to check nobody was climbing in over the wall. £8 entrance is on the high side, but I wouldn't risk it without knowing the punishment. I could watch, but the pull of the Big Fellas Social Club is too strong. Inside is a very cosy (small but warm), AFC Emley style, bar full of FCUM fans. Luckily, there are also some great photos of the ground and past teams to admire. I resist waving these photos at those around me in red and find a table in the corner to wind down with my pint. The solitude slowly diminishes as this small space gets more and more crowded. The noise levels increase and I am soon blocked into my seat with my Yorkshire rose on my coat now looking very lonely as FCUM continue to flock in.

I eventually find a way out of my seat and find the players lining up almost as if they were waiting for me. Frickley are in their usual home strip of blue and white striped shirts with blue shorts and socks. FCUM, unsurprisingly, look like Manchester United with their red shirts, white shorts and back socks. The whistle blows and we get some singing! A couple of hundred away fans are standing in the main stand and deliver an impressive mixture, it hurts me to admit, of new songs and a few old Manchester United numbers for good measure. We get a few cries of “Yorkshire” in response, including from myself but they just keep singing. It wouldn't surprise me if they didn't stop. It takes 8 minutes for Frickley to create their first chance, but an opportunity to quieten the away fans is wasted. Both sides threaten but the final ball is always disappointing.

The longer the games goes on, and the more they sing, the more I am willing Frickley on with every pass. An adopted Yorkshire man I may be, but I have taken an instant dislike to this team, although clearly I am not the “Yorkshire bastard” they referred to in their last tune. Personally, I also prefer the Carpenters version of ‘Top of the World’. Come on Frickley! The hopes of Yorkshire rest with you. The rain starts to fall heavily and the predictable “we all hate Leeds scum” chants start from the main stand. The half time whistle prompts me to find some shelter on the opposite side rather than enter the ‘who can get the most people in a small clubhouse competition’. The stewards are also not playing this game and decide to close the bar on safety grounds or just to dry out those singing voices. The songs do actually stop for fifteen minutes but I still don’t have a mobile signal to communicate this breaking news to the rest of the world on twitter.

The second half starts just as the rain stops, but I decide to stay where I am. This is great position in the covered terrace that runs the length of pitch. The singing and rain start again so I definitely made the right decision. Things also go downhill on the pitch as FCUM go ahead in the 53rd minute with an own goal from Stuart Ludlam that creates a huge cheer, some wooden rattles and a lot of scarf waving. After harassing the Frickley defence with some neat passing play, FCUM worked the ball out wide, Wolfenden's low cross from the right was agonisingly turned into the goal. Three minutes later and the visitors go 2-0 up and more programmes are shredded. More neat passing play, Wolfenden receives the ball inside the area, and after being allowed to turn with the ball, the striker hits a well-placed shot past the desperate hand of Billard. Frickley get a goal back in the 64th minute through Brad Grayson to hopefully start a fight back. A corner from the right caused confusion in the FCUM area, and after a goalmouth scramble, Grayson managed to poke the ball home to reduce the arrears. Within a minute the two goal lead is restored thanks to a lovely finish. United crossed from the right and the Frickley keeper was only able to parry the ball towards Ben Deegan who smashed a powerful first-time volley into the back of the net. The goal results in a song from the home crowd suggesting that everyone in Manchester masturbates and the reply of "come back when your balls have dropped" is sharp, and quite accurate. I lose my sense of humour though on my trip to the gents thanks to three young away fans. They think it is appropriate to come to West Yorkshire to sing songs about the tragic events in Istanbul when two lives were lost. I return to the open terrace with the sounds of "we are the Busby boys" from those delirious tourists. The response of the Munich chant is as predictable as the rain returning now that I am no longer under cover. It was starting to turn a bit nasty inside the ground and unusually for me I leave a couple of minutes early.

As I am driving away I pass four police vans and two policemen on horseback which, I hope, will ensure that the game finishes trouble free. Frickley's average attendance this season has been doubled tonight due to the away following, so the majority here will leave happy. Getting lost in Wakefield on the way home will not dampen my enthusiasm. A couple of mindless idiots can be forgotten, we find these in every ground and town. I have discovered an old fashioned football ground and a town that both have a depth of history that can't be created overnight. I do genuinely hope that FCUM will one day celebrate their centenary year and still have the backing of a noisy fan base. I will struggle to find a set of supporters who generate this amount of atmosphere in Non League football and they put most league sides to shame. My only regret is that I will not be able to return to South Elmsall until next season as this is the best venue of my travels so far. I am disillusioned with the Premier League and for me, the solution is found in places like Frickley Athletic. Why start a club when we have so many on our doorsteps in need of new faces.

Frickley Athletic 1 FC United of Manchester 3

Attendance 497
Admission price £8
Ground Address Westfield Ln, South Elmsall, W Yorkshire. WF9 2EQ
Club website www.frickleyafc.co.uk
Twitter@frickleyafc

20

Amnesia

Doncaster Rovers v Leeds United

The Keepmoat Stadium
nPOWER Championship
Friday 14th October 2011. Kick off 7.45pm

Tonight I am entering the dizzy heights of the Championship for the first time on my Route 66 adventure. This is as high as I will go as Yorkshire does not have a Premiership representative following Hull City's relegation in May 2010. This is not the only debut tonight as on my previous 19 trips, 18 have been in the car and for the other (to Nethermoor last month) I took the train. Let me proudly introduce my readers to the football coach and my local supporters club. I have the day off work, a bag full of beer and I am drinking Premium Organic Pear Cider at 1pm. I think the bus leaves Ilkley bus station at around four o'clock but the pull of the pub is too strong to ignore in the build up to tonight's derby. I have stopped on route at Bar'tat which, in addition to having the words to the Ilkley Moor Bar'tat song written on the walls (then t' ducks 'll come an yet up t'wurums...), serves decent real ale. Despite my appreciation of beer, I decide on a bottle of perry (or the 6% alcohol) to get me in the mood, although the £3.80 price is probably not far short of what the entrance cost to Tadcaster Albion, 24 hours later, will be. I take the short walk to the Station pub and then settle down for a couple of hours of drinking. In between pints we discuss a number of important topics: The subject matters are how much we all love FC United of Manchester, AFC Wimbledon's come back, the insurance market, Leeds United away travel for the next month, MOTs, bobble hats, the new Firestick Peperami, Leeds' team to face Donny, Ken Bates, Beeston as a holiday destination, the catholic church, Wayne Rooney's temper, Jimmy Greeves not playing in 1966, drugs, AIDS, the price of petrol, butchers' shops, 'Movember' moustaches, Dean Saunders, Wales v France in the rugby, church magazines of the 70's, weddings and morris dancing. One of the above is made up - yes that's right we didn't mention tonight's game.

Six pints of beer later, it is 4.30pm and the bus is spotted across the road. The seven of us swap our bar stools for a seat on the coach and my bag is opened. I sit next to my away day partner in crime Patrick, better known as 'The Professor'. Pat lives in Farsley, so I will take on the challenges of summarising this extraordinary character next week when we visit Throstle Nest. We continue to chat and it feels as if the pub is now on wheels but with a great view of the rush hour traffic. The next stop is to collect the Keighley Whites where things usually get more lively, but before we have even passed the Mowbray household the Friday traffic reminds me that it will be a long trip to Doncaster. I will survive though. We pick up a stray in Silsden, pass The Pirates of The Caribbean Rice Bowl takeaway, and the smoothness of the long straight of the Skipton Bypass tempts me to visit the toilet before we pick up some more beer monsters. Have you ever taken a leak whilst going around a roundabout? I should have learned my lesson from Gillingham away a couple of years ago. I attempted then to go for wee whilst being driven on the winding road through Aylesford at speed over many speed bumps. The Little Gem pub was exactly as its name suggested but not quite as good with wee soaked trousers.

We arrive at The Kings Head in Keighley at 5.15pm and 41 well oiled individuals enter the bus to increase the noise levels further. This should be uncomfortable because tonight I am of course a Doncaster Rovers fan. The club was founded in 1879 and has an eventful recent history. They underwent difficult times in the 1980s and 1990s, culminating in relegation to the Conference in 1998. This was the third time Doncaster had been demoted from Football League status, with only Lincoln City leaving the league more times. However, Doncaster's fortunes soon began to turn round, due to owner John Ryan's commitment to invest heavily into the club. The club returned to the fourth tier (known at the time as Division Three) after winning the 2003 Conference Play-Off and they found their best form in 50 years in the 2000s. The club had few financial worries and their new Keepmoat stadium was completed in December 2006. The following 2007/08 season proved to be one of the most exciting in Doncaster's history with only the defeat away at Cheltenham Town on the final day of the season costing them automatic promotion. This disappointment didn't stop the club reaching the League One play-off final at Wembley. On Sunday 25th May 2008 they beat Leeds United 1–0 to move into the Football League Championship after a half century absence from Tier 2 football. A James Hayter headed goal in the 47th minute was enough to secure victory in front of over 75,000 fans that included myself, so the last paragraph was not easy to write, or to read for over 50,000 of those present at Wembley on that day. Doncaster have since established themselves in the Championship building a reputation for playing attractive football. Rovers have however struggled this season and their poor start led to the sacking of manager Sean O'Driscoll and assistant manager Richard O'Kelly. On Friday 23rd September 2011, Dean Saunders left Wrexham to be unveiled as the new boss results have improved.

Keighley is an interesting town with its industrial past and ethnic diversity. The striking image of the old mills next to a modern mosque is probably now taken for granted. Like any football bus there is a heirachy and the front seat is now occupied by the Keithley Whites' organiser. We all know our place and usual suspects have taken the back of the bus like they probably once did on school trips to the zoo. I notice that a couple of people are reading The Square Ball, one in particular reading my article which still feels weird. We crawl through Saltaire and Bradford whilst I take turns between drinking my scrumpy and further trips to the toilet, which is becoming a less appealing place on each visit. A nice puddle is forming on the floor and the concept of flushing has been lost on most fans. The door is also no longer shutting, which does produce the classic "dick in hand, dick in hand" song thanks to some traffic lights turning red. We eventually get on the M606, then the M62 and the M1. By the time we pass Wakefield I am, like the vast majority of the bus, feeling quite merry, boardering on sloshed. It is trips like this when the bus driver earns every penny of his wages and the collection he will receive on the way home. He is now driving fifty very drunk and noisy supporters that, I hope, the Keepmoat stadium is ready to welcome. There will be many other identical coaches heading to Doncaster but all will arrive 'dry' before anyone breaks the law. Thanks must again go to Mrs Thatcher for banning alcohol on football coaches. Can you imagine how drunk we would all be if we were actually allowed to drink? I am not sure this chapter is such a good idea as someone puts the Billy Bremner song on for our own tribute to this legend. We sound great and everyone is in tune! You can't beat a good sing song, but it is thirsty work. Cheers. Let's toast ground number 20...

Doncaster Rovers 0 Leeds United 3

Attendance 12,962
Admission £27 (away end)
Ground Address Stadium Way, Lakeside, Doncaster. DN4 5JW
Club website www.doncasterroversfc.co.uk
Twitter @drfc_official or @DonnyRoversFC

21

Hair of the dog

Tadcaster Albion v Pickering Town

2inspire Park

Baris NECL Premier Division

Saturday 15th October 2011. Kick off 3pm

Before we jump back into Non-League football from the Championship, I feel we should revisit Doncaster Rovers FC as I suspect that the end of chapter 20 is a little vague. I will blame alcohol, which clearly had a part to play, but the Keepmoat stadium was not particularly memorable in all honesty. Clubs such as Frickley Athletic can only dream of league football, but their grounds do have character.

From what I can remember it went something like this: We arrived at a big roundabout off the motorway and had a nice police escort into town. We hid our beer on the assumption that police officers are rubbish at hide and seek, we passed a lot of retail parks (or industrial estates as they all roll into one), we arrived at a stadium, which was lit up like a Christmas tree, and we parked in a very bumpy piece of wasteland (a weak bladder made this a memorable experience). We walked past some 5-a-side pitches with some kids playing in the dark and entered a modern stand. There wasn't anything there to link the club to the town of Doncaster in the present or to their history. Architecturally it is a complete failure. I could have designed the Keepmoat with Lego bricks on my sofa. The game itself was a bit better. Danny Pugh put Leeds United ahead on 20 minutes and then not a lot happened until Leeds got a second on 52 minutes when McCormack scored with a finish that Messi would have been pleased with. There were lots of "Bates Out" chants in the away end and I can't actually remember a single Doncaster song. Going three up with a Tom Lees header on 64 minutes didn't help the home crowd find their voice. We then sang all the way home to the sounds of Neil Diamond. Singing to Sweet Caroline somehow felt appropriate after a second clean sheet for Leeds.

Anyway, back to today and I am now in the car park of the 2inspire Park. My drive through the town of Tadcaster was more memorable that the Keepmoat stadium. The town is famous for brewing beer and the breweries dominate the skyline as I arrive. The smell of beer hits me as I leave my car which is not what I need with a hangover. The ground is practically in the shadow of the John Smiths brewery and I drove past Sam Smiths earlier. There was a time when a hangover didn't last until the afternoon but this one is no rush to leave me today. The Brewers are believed to have been formed in 1892 as John Smith's FC and it wasn't until 1923 that the Tadcaster Albion name was adopted. In the early years, the club played in the local York League, which Albion won in 1948. In the early days, the club played home games on the site of the cricket ground on Station Road, before moving to the Ings ground, near to where the present Samuel Smith Brewery Packaging Block now stands. Changing facilities were in the town, at the rear of the Falcon Public House on Chapel Street, and it was a common Saturday afternoon sight to see nets, corner flags, buckets, oranges, players and officials trekking through the town. Football continued on this ground until 1960, when the club moved 100 yards up river to its present home at the Park. In 1982 they became a founding member of the Northern Counties East League, remaining in Division One until winning the title in 2009-10. Last season, Albion finished fourth in the NCEL Premier Division and won the NCEL President's Cup, beating Farsley AFC 5-1 in the final.

I enter the ground to find a couple of chairs on the touchline, the type of chair popular in offices during the 1970s. They look quite strange, almost as strange as I must look taking a picture of them. I leave this surreal sight to take my bottle of water and programme straight to an interesting looking stand behind the goal that Tadcaster are attacking. The stand is small in width but steep so, importantly, offers me a seat with a very good view of the pitch from the back row. The programme makes me smile as it is advertising tickets for this Wednesday's 'An Evening with Paul Merson' event. This is either very appropriate, or inappropriate, for a player that has publically suffered from an alcohol addiction to visit The Brewers. A couple of other people join me as the players run out. I can feel someone watching me as I open my hangover cure chocolate bar. A Pickering Town scarf wearing Labrador looks pleased to see me and now more interested in my chocolate than the game that is about to start. His owners, a middle aged couple, are also wearing the colours of Pickering town who line up in blue shirts with yellow shorts and socks. The home side are wearing their usual yellow shirts with navy shorts and socks. With every kick, my hangover improves, and my fine view of play makes me instantly interested in the game, when I am not watching the busy ring road in the distance. It is a lively start and Albion create the early chances. Striker Carl Stewart has an effort saved and the keeper makes a double save from Danny Gray's shot and follow up header. The break through for the home side comes after 24 minutes when a corner from Steve Jeff is headed in at the near post by Whitehead. Pickering responded immediately with a shot from Rice that is pushed round the post by the Albion keeper. It was a fantastic save and a good chance to equalise, so deserved more of a response from the army, that now numbers five (including the dog), of Pickering fans.

It has turned out to be a nice day now that the sun has burnt off the morning mist and I am enjoying the warmth on my legs. The dog looks like I feel and soon stretches out on the floor. I am tempted to join him just as Albion make it 2-0 when Stewart runs onto a through ball and fires it under the keeper from 15 yards. The dog's female owner tells us all that this is an "impossible task now" for her side. The players must have heard her as the remainder of the first half was all Albion. The now fragile Pickering defense looks like buckling under every attack. I am enjoying the solitude of a ground surrounded by trees which creates a feeling of quiet isolation. Only the occasional large lorry or flying ball through the leaves brings me back to reality. The half time whistle gives me an opportunity to wake myself up with a walk to the clubhouse. When I was a teenager I would simply have another beer after a night out and within minutes would be cured, so a 'hair of the dog' does actually work. What better place to have a pint than in Tadcaster. Disappointingly, John Smiths is the only bitter option. Would it be too must to ask for some decent ale in a brewery town? I take my pint back to the stand as I assume this is legal in the Non Leagues, but at least I have the defence that 'everyone else is drinking outside'. I am not a fan of John Smiths, but it must be good in the place its brewed surely? Nope. The first sip was always going to be a challenge, but the second, third, fourth... 'hair of the dog' at my age is understandably more difficult, but this beer is awful. With a Samual Smiths brewery a couple of streets away this pint should in fact be illegal, whether drunk inside or out.

The second half starts in a similar fashion to how the first ended except that the dog is now fast asleep. He may have given in on his team but, slowly, Pickering appear to be getting more into this game. Albion are enjoying less possession and doing a lot more defending. The dog's owners are not convinced and the lady declares that "there is a forcefield around our opponents goal like in Star Wars". Within seconds of this statement, a weak clearance by The Brewers falls to Richard Batley who fires home a 25 yard shot into the top corner. It is a marvelous goal which I had the perfect view of as the ball left his boot to fly towards me. That goal was worth the £5 entrance fee alone, but the one spectator who didn't pay, the dog, doesn't even stir. Pickering are now looking most likely to score the next goal now that the force field is down. The away side's cause isn't helped when they get a player sent off for a late tackle from behind on Albion's Terry Taylor. The 10 men of Pickering Town continue to search for an equaliser as Albion try to hit them on the counter attack. The red card looked harsh to me, but I am urging an equaliser by this stage so I'm probably not as neutral as I intended to be. A few goal attempts from Pickering flash wide or are saved by Aaran Reid and silence returns to our stand as the sun is starting to set in the distance. In the end, Albion hang on comfortably to claim all three points despite the brave x-wing fighter pilot's earlier efforts. Our canine friend wakes up moments before the final whistle blows, almost as if he has a sixth sense. I take a leisurely stroll back to my car feeling a better man than when I arrived two hours earlier. It was not an eventful trip but it was exactly what I needed today. A dodgy pint at a Non-League game really is the perfect hangover cure. It is when you enter the last week of your thirties anyway.

Tadcaster Albion 2 Pickering Town 1

Attendance 168
Admission £5
Ground Address Ings Lane, Tadcaster. LS24 9AY
Club website www.tadcasteralbionafc.co.uk
Twitter @TadcasterAlbion

22

On the edge of my garden

Yorkshire Amateur AFC v Louth Town

The Bracken Edge Football Ground
BARIS NCEL Division One
Tuesday 25th October 2011. Kick off 7.45pm

Things have changed in the world of Mowbray since my last ground. I have a new job, which has given me 13 weeks as a full time house-husband and wannabe writer. In short, I am on 3 month's notice, I resign and they enforce the 'gardening leave' clause in my contract as they would rather not have me in the office looking smug. Serving my notice from my garden is not a problem at all. So what else has changed? Well ground 22 will be visited with a bushy beard, perhaps not on David Bellamy's level, but 10 days growth is dominating my face. Despite my 'in the garden' status, I would have been off work this week anyway for George's half term so I had planned to visit Farsley AFC tonight complete with a boozy night out with my friend, The Professor. I turned forty three days ago so it was another excuse to wet the beard and show the world that you are as young as you feel. I had a spare room and a hangover booked, but Farsley had other plans. They drew 2-2 on Saturday with Curzon Ashton in the FA Trophy. The replay took priority against the league and they played this last night rather than give me a night out. They lost the tie 2-0 so I hope they are satisfied. I read last week that Yorkshire Amateur were forced to cancel their league game at Worksop Parramore because they couldn't raise a team. Someone on twitter had suggested that I got to Bracken Edge as soon as possible just in case this was a sign of the club winding up. Therefore, I was happy to discover in the Non League Paper that they are at home today but obviously I hope things aren't as bad as they could be.

Yorkshire Amateur AFC are a long established club who were formed in 1918. In those early days, the club's fixtures largely consisted of playing friendlies at Elland Road following the demise of Leeds City FC on the orders of the Football Association after irregularities were discovered in their accounts. However, in 1920 the club decided that the ground was not suitable for their needs and sold the lease to the newly formed Leeds United AFC for the sum of £250. The aim of the club in those days was to compete as a major force against the professional teams playing in the north of England. This proved not to be viable and the club became one of the founder members of the Yorkshire League. In 1922 the club became the first British team to tour in Latvia and Estonia - now that would have made a good writing trip! The club produced a number of leading amateur international players such as Joe Woodcock who, at left back, was the first Bradford born amateur international. The "Ammers" moved to their present headquarters at Bracken Edge in 1922 after using several other grounds, including sharing with Harrogate Town. This period was by far the most successful for the club and a record crowd of 3,569 saw the 5-2 Amateur Cup Quarter Final replay victory over Wimbledon. This was after a 2-2 draw at Wimbledon before a crowd of 12,000. The "Ammers" had demolished the holders, Wycombe Wanderers, 4-0 in the previous round and the club's sights were now set on a Wembley appearance. Unfortunately, Marine FC had not read the script and triumphed 2-1 in the semi-final replay played at Leicester City's ground. The club became a founder member of the newly formed Northern Counties East League in 1982 and still play their football at this level, Step 6 of the Non-League pyramid.

So here I am, older, hairier and hopefully wiser, parked in a very quiet residential street in a northern suburb of Leeds. I have 50 minutes to spare but this is thanks to my wife guiding me here courtesy of my hands free car kit. Despite this being one of my shortest journeys of the season, I got lost. It’s harder to see in the dark at my age, and in my defence, apart from a meeting once in neighbouring Chapel Allerton, this is not an area of Leeds I know at all. Mrs Mowbray had the luxury of Google maps and a lot of patience, an essential quality for the wife of a serial ground hopper. I walk across a car park, pass through the turnstile and I am relieved to see the pitch to finally confirm that there is actually a football club here to bag. The man on the turnstile asks me if I have come far, so perhaps the beard is not helping me to avoid that ground hopper look that was on show in Brighouse. I'm glad I didn't buy that rucksack with my birthday money. I did, however, buy an anorak! Just as paranoia is setting in I come to the conclusion he must have seen me take a picture of the car park. He was perfectly entitled to call the police as photographing gravel, in the dark, is probably not normal for a grown man. I gain entry and a programme for £5 and then take an immediate sharp left for the tea room. I take my Bovril, rather than the several pints I would have consumed in Farsley, into an empty lounge area in the club house. I am happy to be alone and let the ground fill up whilst I read the programme. I discover that the ground is known as "the edge". Quite appropriate for a man on the edge.

I quickly locate the club statement in the programme that confirms that they 'have been severely hit recently by player unavailability i.e. Injury, suspension and work commitments. This unfortunately caused the postponement of the midweek game at Worksop Parramore which sadly could have far reaching consequences for the club, with the possibility of a large fine and a point's deduction'. They further emphasise that the club is down to the 'bare bones both playing wise and with a skeleton committee who work miracles'. The programme asks for volunteers to come forward to help behind the scenes. Unfortunately, I just can't spare those 'few hours' at this point in my life, but perhaps one day I may find myself involved in a club. It appears that if you want to get involved you will be banging on an open door. I can hear the roar of the crowd, well a few claps anyway, so I decide to leave my chair to soak up some of the atmosphere. The last home game against Grimsby Borough was also on a Tuesday night and drew in a crowd of only 28. Absent fans missed a 5-1 triumph that night. I visit the toilets first and discover that the 'bare bones' includes not having toilet paper. Luckily I have some tissues in my designer bag and decide to leave the packet in the cubical for the next victim. Perhaps not the few hours a week the club is seeking, but small acorns and all that. The 'Ammers' play in white shirts, blue shorts and red socks, giving them that union jack look that Glasgow Rangers would be proud to wear. The visitors from Lincolnshire are wearing blue shirts and socks with black shorts.

The game is immediately a very end to end encounter and I can see the locals, not the 30 or so in attendance, potentially missing another thriller. It's started to rain, so we all huddle under the one stand which joins the back of the club house. It is mild at least and the sound of the rain drops hitting the corrugated iron roof creates an atmosphere of its own. Louth start the game the stronger but the home side are breaking out of defence well. I keep seeing flashes in the distance and assume they are early firework celebrations. There then appears to be a roar of thunder in the distance. The man next to me agrees that a thunder storm is heading our way. This is the first thunder storm on my travels but I didn't expect one in October. The rain starts getting heavier by the minute. However, despite the downpour, Louth manage to concentrate on the game enough to take the lead. Elliott Broughton hits a shot which the keeper parries to the feet of Andy Willoughby who scores from a couple of yards out. A few minutes later we all need to take a few steps back to keep dry as the rain is now torrential and the wind has picked up. Water starts to gather on the pitch and the game slows down as the thunder gets louder. This continues for around 20 minutes and understandably distracts the players. At 8.25pm the rain stops like a switch has been hit and we get a good few minutes play before half time during which the 'Ammers' could easily have got an equaliser. The lightening can still be seen in the distance but the storm has now passed.

Half time gives the players an opportunity to dry themselves and I join the can drinkers around me by buying a Strongbow for only £1.50. Watching the lightening in the distance, the sound of water dripping off the roof and a cold cider is actually one of the nicest Route 66 moments to date. Being a man, I can drink with one hand

and use the other one to look at twitter. A follower tells me that this was in fact an 'electrical storm', a posh term for a thunder storm. I check the definition and we have definitely experienced a 'transient storm of lightning and thunder, usually with rain and gusty winds, produced by cumulonimbus clouds'. I ponder this and go for wander. I discover that the 'one stand' is actually three that run side by side along the touchline. Each stands improves as I pass them, starting with a terrace, then a terrace with a bench at the front and finishing with a seated stand which appears to be the away end tonight. I choose the middle stand just as the players reappear and use the bench to rest my cider on. It was nice not having to drink my pint in 15 minutes. I am stood equally between the two dugouts which reminds me of the entertainment at Askern. Both are very vocal and the linesman has to tell the away bench to calm down. There is so much pacing up and down that the wet grass in front of both dugouts soon turns into big muddy puddles that Peppa Pig would die for. On 59 minutes, the home side equalise thanks to an individual moment of brilliance. Adam Shaw is allowed to run 20 yards unchallenged and then hit a thunderous, no pun intended, shot from 30 yards out which finds the top left hand corner. This goal was so good it left the Louth bench in silence.

Louth respond immediately with a very good chance, but hit the ball straight at the keeper from close range. Both sides then enjoy half chances, but the players look to be tiring. As the grass is drying in the mild air, a mist forms across the surface making it look like we could be on 'the edge' of the world. Perhaps it's just a typical Autumn Yorkshire evening. I have also settled for a draw so make a quick visit to the gents and I am delighted to see that my tissues have disappeared. I have contributed to the running of this football club! I return to the match to news that the Louth manager Paul Walden was sent to the stand for 'comments' made to the referee. Paul will struggle to complain about this decision as he was given enough warnings that the naughty boy step would be used. His team are unaffected and win a free kick on the edge of the area in the dying minutes. However, he probably would have preferred to have been sent into the car park after seeing his side waste their chance to take all 3 points. The whistle blows for the draw which feels fair on a night where credit must go to both sides for producing a decent game in very testing conditions. The club may be down to the bare bones but they do have the basics. If they can get some more players signed, and a few more through the gate like any Non League side needs, they should survive this sticky patch. I will certainly follow their progress from my garden, but if this weather continues I may need to take the paper to my sitting room. I now have the luxury of being able to write this chapter at a more sociable hour so, with that mood decide on grabbing a Chinese takeaway on the way home. I am on holiday after all. The match report on the Louth Town website confirms that they are also happy with a point when they only took 12 players to Leeds due to injuries and suspensions. I will pack my toilet rolls when I head to Lincolnshire!

5/12/2011 Yorkshire Amateur were fined £500 plus home team expenses and deducted 3 points for the unfulfilled fixture at Worksop Parramore

Yorkshire Amateur 1 Louth Town 1

Attendance59
Admission £4
Ground Address Roxholme Road, Leeds. LS8 4DZ
Club website www.yorkshireamateur.co.uk
Twitter None found

23

Gourmet Night

Ossett Town AFC v Farsley AFC

Ingfield

West Riding County Cup Round 1.

Tuesday 1st Movember 2011. Kick off 7.45pm

Movember, the month formally known as November, starts today so the gardening beard came off yesterday. Instead I will be growing a moustache to raise awareness of men's health and to see how ridiculous a tache will look on me. I was too late last year by the time I caught on to why a lot of men appeared to be going for that Kevin Webster in Coronation Street look. Kevin, after all, pulled a young girl with his, although his life has not exactly gone to plan since then. I felt it was a bit unfair to start with two weeks' growth so begin the month with a blank canvas to work on. I searched the internet for some styling ideas, but I'm not sure whether to go for the porn actor (do they act?) or magnum P.I look on my debut. Again, thanks to a high level of twitter activity whilst pruning the roses, I am on the radio again. I did the telephone interview this afternoon with Yorkshire Radio who will play my recording, as if it was live, on their show. Unfortunately, I can't listen to myself as don't have a digital radio in my car and need to concentrate on finding a football ground. The Ingfield stadium, unlike neighbours Ossett Albion, is actually in the centre of Ossett so having an explore is top of my list. I find the ground with ease, park my car and head for the bright lights. The ground is opposite the bus station so I could of gone all green tonight and left the car at home. Perhaps I will do that for another ground and show off my creativity by writing about how exciting going on the bus can be.

I walk past the ground with an hour to spare, but get a little worried when I find it in complete darkness. Their website is not up to date and didn't show tonight's fixture earlier so I am relying totally on Sunday's Non-League Paper. Before I have time to worry further, a car arrives with two men wearing Ossett Town sweatshirts to open up the gates. This moment of panic does make me think about what I will do in such an eventuality. The Yorkshire winter will no doubt make attending games more challenging. The words 'Samuel Smiths' on the window of the Horse and Jockey Inn halt me and, now that it is dark at this hour, the glow of a warm pub is a lovely sight. A perfect place to ponder how I will cope when the frost, snow and ice arrive. I order an organic wheat beer to make up for polluting the atmosphere earlier. The fancy glass may not help me to blend in with a bar heaving with strangers, but I feel much happier when I see a group of Farsley fans inside. I have seen Farsley play away a few times and they usually have a good following on the road. A quiet corner is found and I clear some text messages before my first Route 66 committee meeting begins. My family tell me that my radio interview was good which is nice to hear, although they will probably tell me that I look good as a porn star. The beer, brewed in Tadcaster, is perfect. It is a real shame, or I could go as far to say a travesty, that they don't sell this at the 2inspire Park! So, to my quandary of cancelled matches. The reality is that games will get called off, perhaps abandoned and I need to agree the rules in advance. It's my book so I suppose I can do whatever I want. I do however have a responsibility to my fellow anorak readers and agree the following with Sam Smith:

- Match abandoned after kick off. No need to return as this ground is 'bagged'.
- Match called off after I have passed the turnstile. Chapter written and no need to return
- Match called off upon arrival before I have entered the ground. I start to cry and come back another day.

We may be treated to a mild winter, although this is highly unlikely based on the last few years, but this, in itself, would actually be a problem for me. I need weekend games to be postponed and rearranged in the evening. If you look at the non league fixtures now for after Christmas you will see that the evening games have disappeared. I need evening matches to finish this journey! I do have some comfort from cup games which tend to take priority over the league. Before I have finished my pint, I have agreed that I need all 65 to stay in the various cups and get loads of weekend games called off, many hours before kick-off of course! I have no control over any of the above so I move on before indigestion sets in. Drinking on an empty stomach and stress don't mix.

Tonight's game is a cup game, but the West Riding County Cup doesn't quite have the pull of the other cup competitions, although it does give clubs a realistic chance of some silverware each season. Guiseley were proud winners of this competition last season when they beat Thackley in extra time at Bradford City's Valley Parade. The cup is open to teams from the highest 3 leagues below the Football League. i.e. Conference, Evo-Stik and Northern Counties East Leagues. I daren't attempt to establish the boundaries of this as no doubt a team in Norfolk play in it due to being part of Yorkshire 1,000 years ago until it became separated from the coast and floated down the North Sea. Both of tonight's teams play in the Northern Premier Division One North so there are no giant killing opportunities to write about.

Ossett Town Football Club, known as The Town, were formed in 1936 and have played at Ingfield since the ground was constructed in 1957. In the 1980s, the club were in discussions with the West Riding Football Association for Ingfield to be the new West Riding FA headquarters. The talks fell through and the West Riding eventually developed their own ground in Woodlesford. In 2010, the stadium was renamed Stade France because of a partnership with the local scrap metal merchants Eric France. In 1998, there was a plan to build a sports village on the land next to the M1 off Queens Drive. This would have seen Ossett Town get a new ground and share facilities with Wakefield Trinity RLFC and Wakefield RUFC; the rugby clubs would have had their own stadium next door to Ossett Town's proposed ground. The members of Ossett Town voted against this plan. In 2006, Tesco offered to buy the the site and the plan would entail Ossett Town moving up to Shaw Cross to groundshare with Dewsbury Rams RLFC, but again the members of Ossett Town voted against the plan. It was revealed in February that Ossett Town were again talking to various parties with a view to moving to a new ground within the next two years. These are problems a Non League club has when they sit on land which is worth more as a supermarket. Being in the centre of the town is problematic! Wakefield FC have shared Ingfield with Ossett Town this season which has forced them to cancel their academy and reserve sides due to fixture congestion. It has cost Wakefield FC a rumoured £8,500 to ground share for the season, but at least I will get the chance to sample the Horse and Jockey Inn again.

I enter the ground for £7 which, as a now experienced Non League traveller, is expensive. This is, and the size of the crowd confirms it with a couple of minutes to go, the Johnstone's Paint Trophy of the lower leagues, but without the expensive Wembley final burgers. I find a nice ground with a particularly good stand behind the goal closest to the turnstile. There is a clubhouse, or a function room in these parts, a club shop (closed) and a snack bar which I head for. I am not particularly hungry now, beer can do that, but I still have the mental scares of my Askern famine. I should have asked for the confectionery list. The chips, even at a pound, are a perfect example of the problems we have with food in this country. What chance do we have against such culinary nations as Italy and France when we can't even make a chip edible? They are under cooked and tasteless, which I can live with, but greasy is the understatement of the year. I am not sure why I am continuing to eat them as I am not on the brink of starvation after living two weeks in a cave. I stop after two thirds of them are heading for my stomach. Luckily I have brought some gourmet jelly beans with me for such emergencies. I hope that the strong taste of watermelon or bubblegum will help with the nausea. I even eat the popcorn beans tonight as suddenly they don't taste quite so bad.

The players come out to a couple of claps and, thankfully look more enthusiastic than the spectators. Ossett Town are in all red and Farsley all blue. The bad taste in my mouth is forgotten for a moment in the 6th minute as Danny Toronczak gives Ossett Town the lead. I didn't have a great view of the goal as, inconveniently, a couple of Farsley defenders blocked my view, but not him. Farsley respond with a lot of possession and get a deserved equaliser in the 14th minute when Simon Bambrook runs onto a good through ball to calmly tuck it away in the corner of the net. I am told by the man to my left that if Farsley "play their football" they will beat any team in the land. This comes from a very wise man, a view based on the fact he has brought his own food with him. It only takes two minutes for Farsley to show off this total football, but the striker misses an open net. Just as it is starting to look a one sided match, Ossett also miss a sitter to remind me that they are still in this tie. If the players have eaten the chips I will accept this as a valid excuse for the poor finishing. The rest of the half blends into one mass of players yelling, usually with the F word, at each other with the odd half chance for Farsley in between. Five minutes before the break, Farsley take the lead when Ben Jones cuts in from the left before taking the ball around the goalkeeper to slot it in for 2-1.

Half time comes just as a stomach ache arrives. I started some antibiotics for a chest infection yesterday, or infection of the windpipe to be precise. Too much shouting at football matches my mother told me tonight. They may be the cause of the upset tummy but I am blaming the chips, even if I die in the night. Someone needs to take some responsibility and Gordon Ramsey is in the States at the moment so he can't help. I use the time to pace around hoping that will at least burn some of the 1,000 calories off. I also get the amusement of watching others pass over their hard earned cash for these culinary delights. It gives me some time to analyse why those chips were so bad. I am not ready to move on yet. The conclusion is that they have given a 14 year old girl the job of manning a kitchen on her own, probably without any training. At a similar age I got gainful employment at an exclusive nursing home in their kitchen. I thought I would be washing up, but I soon discovered I had to make them all their tea! I had a mother to cook for me so had barely made myself a sandwich and suddenly I had to make 50! It didn't matter. They were fussy eaters I was told. The staff cleared away the leftovers before their children arrived in their big 4 wheel drive motors and cutting costs increased profits. Non league is all about cutting costs to survive, but I would pay £2, at the very least, for some tasty chips and just think about the cooking oil savings that could be achieved. Farsley make an amazing start to the second half with a third goal inside 15 seconds of the kick-off. The ball is quickly played forward and Jones picks out Mitchell who finishes into the bottom corner to score his first goal for the club. Now, the away side do indeed play their football. Good possession with short passes and Ossett are struggling to get the ball to stay in the cup. Things get worse for them on 55 minutes when Jones gets his second goal of the game to give Farsley a 4-1 lead. Town get a goal back with 18 minutes to play after a through ball splits the Farsley defence and Catton is able to finish past Pecora. It looks offside to me, but it gives them a lifeline. Unfortunately, the players hadn't read the script and any glimmer of hope ends as Farsley stay in control of the game with their possession football. The referee ends the match allowing the majority of supporters here to head back to north Leeds. They will dream of Valley Parade and I will dream of oven chips. If they close the snack bar I may return.

Ossett Town 2 Farsley 4

Attendance 56
Admission £7
Ground Address Prospect Road, Ossett, West Yorkshire. WF5 9HA
Club website www.ossetttown.co.uk
Twitter @OssettTown

24

Men against boys

Kinsley Boys FC v DFS Welbeck Welfare

The Kinsley Playing Fields
Windsor Foodservice Central Midlands. Black Dragon Division Nth
Saturday 5th November 2011. Kick off 2pm

I am over a third of the way into my football tour and this game is my first trip to the depths of Step 7 of the Non-League pyramid. There are 11 clubs at this level, 10 of which play in the Central Midlands Northern Division where Kinsley Boys play their football. The reason for visiting so late is that these fixtures are a nightmare to plan ahead. The websites, if you can locate them, generally don't have fixtures for dates further than the current month. In comparison, it is so much easier to plan ahead for the other higher leagues which is why the lower clubs have been neglected up until today. I purposely left today free as I am conscious that I don't want to leave them all until April. The only plan I could make was to buy the Non League Paper on the Sunday before, study the fixtures and hope for something suitable. Kinsley was the closest and therefore suitable. I didn't want a long drive today with an away day to Leicester City tomorrow with Leeds. I found their website easily, but it wasn't up to date so didn't show today's game on it. It did have an email address though, so a couple of clicks and 24 hours later it was confirmed that the game is on but with a 2pm kick off, not the 3pm listed in the paper. I assume this is because they either don't have, or don't want to use, floodlights, which makes sense but doesn't help give me a relaxing morning. First, I had to coach twenty under 7 children this morning, then get packed away in record time and grab an early lunch before venturing into unchartered territory. Today was also the first day when my moustache was visible to the naked eye, at least in a certain light, so I hope that the people of Kinsley don't judge me on their first impression.

Kinsley Boys has been operating since 1962, then known as Kinsley Village, when its team played in the Fitzwilliam under 18s league (boys). Some of these players are now on the management committee of the present day club. The ground was then known as the 'Cabbage Patch' as it was quite rough land where vegetables were grown and horses grazed. Villagers and miners on their way to the shops and pit used a track through the middle of the pitch. Occasionally a game would have to be halted, once to let an elderly lady return from the shops. The club has progressed from the under 18s side via the Pontefract, Barnsley, Wakefield, Bentley and Doncaster leagues. Throughout the last 49 years the club has won countless honours in the league and cups. They have also run various junior sides of all age groups from 10 to 17. The 1980s and 1990s was the golden period for the club winning trophies. The club then went through a transitional period and it was not until the 2006/07 season when they won the Sheffield Junior Cup and Doncaster Premier League Cup that they got back to winning ways. Kinsley Boys joined the Central Midlands Premier in 2007 and were promoted to the Supreme League the following season. The club then finished 11th over the next two years . Last season saw great improvements to the ground and clubhouse, a new web site and the side finished fourth in the Supreme Division. When I originally put my list together of the 66 clubs of Yorkshire, the Central Midlands League was split into two divisions, the Supreme and the Premier. During the close season the Central Midlands Football League was reorganised to split clubs into a North and South division. This season the club play in the Black Dragon Division North alongside the other Yorkshire clubs.

I arrive into Kinsley and the directions I have are very simple. The ground is opposite the Kinsley Dog Track where I am also to find a large car park. A large free car park I discover upon entry and see the top of six slender floodlights behind. I am greeted by a man at the gate who gives me entry for just £3 which is the lowest admission to date. I wonder if the cost is even lower, or free even, below Step 7, or perhaps, eventually the lower you go, spectators get paid to pass through the gate. I have been warned on twitter all week that this level of football is 'park football with no stands or beer'. My expectations are, therefore, very low so I am actually pleased to discover a small stand, although a corrugated iron shelter would be a better description. It offers fans somewhere dry to stand and by the look of the sky it may grow in popularity soon. The roof almost covers half of the width of the pitch behind one of the goals and a young man is inside drinking a can of lager (the beer I wouldn't find!). The rest of the ground consists of a tarmac path which circles the touchline, two dugouts and a small building which houses the changing rooms. Inside there are also some toilets and a small clubhouse area. I am inside with a minute to spare as the players are already lined up in front of around thirty spectators. The pitch is very uneven and I would go as far to say that the grass on our local park is a better playing surface. I can identify Kinsley immediately by their badge. They are in yellow shirts, blue shorts and strange striped socks that look like they have been washed on the wrong setting. Then it dawns on me that I have no idea who the other team are let alone where they have travelled from this afternoon. They are playing in all white with black sleeves but the Non League Paper is now in the recycle bin. The players of both sides have a less professional footballer look about them which, in truth, is because a lot of them are a bit chubby, or just big boned. In particular the home side who have five 'big' lads.

We are all treated to 15 minutes of seeing who can kick the ball the highest, which I think Kinsley won. More weight behind the ball must help and eventually the ball drops into the penalty area in the 18th minute. Kinsley take advantage of this with a tidy finish from close range to give them a 1-0 lead. The resulting cheer did feel like the noise of a family game in the park even whilst standing in my big stand. The away side rattle the post a couple of minutes later and the game is starting to improve as a spectacle. I can see an elderly man parked on an electric mobility scooter at the corner flag nearest to me and decide it is time that I admit to a stranger than I don't know who the team in white are. He is very friendly but I am surprised, and relieved, to find that he can't remember either. He can tell me that they are bottom of the league and so we should see some goals this afternoon. He shares some other facts which, he tells me, come from the local paper, the same paper who published the kickoff time as 3pm. I am told Kinsley Boys were fined £25 last week for not eating the buffet at their last away game. It all got nasty on the pitch with three players being sent off, so I can appreciate how it could dampen your appetite to share an egg sandwich with someone who has tried to kick lumps out of you all afternoon. He also has a moan about the new league structure where teams without floodlights can now join. We are interrupted by a lady selling raffle tickets and I agree to buy two if she can tell us both (better to show her that I am not the only silly one) who Kinsley are playing this afternoon. "I am not sure" is the response, but she promises to find out for me! So my very silly question isn't quite so silly with at least 10% of the crowd in this same predicament. Within a couple of minutes she returns and excitedly announces "Welbeck Welfare". "Ah, North Nottinghamshire" is my reply to show that my geography knowledge is better than my research skills.

I struggle to get enthusiastic about the game in front of me. It feels like the reason I am watching 22 men belt the ball at each other in a field is because I know one of the players. On 36 minutes it becomes two nil to Kinsley with a headed goal, which I clap as loud as possible in an attempt to make more of an effort. I manage to complete a circuit of the path, retrieving balls on my journey, just as the whistle for half time blows. I use the time to buy a cup of tea which is also a record breaker at only 50p; a double title winner as it is also the worst I have drunk this season. All is forgiven as I get a pleasant surprise when they not only have a pin badge, but have one in stock at the usual £3. I am asked "are you that man writing a book?". I must stand out at this level, probably only because everyone else knows each other. I talk to a few people about Route 66 and everyone is very friendly. I decide that if you lived in Kinsley, knew the goalkeeper and your sister was dating the left back, why wouldn't you come to these playing fields? Just bring a flask!

I take my tea with me back to my stand to be so typically English, i.e. polite. I am now behind the goal that Kinsley are attacking in the hope that a stray shot may spill my tea. The goal is being defended by a larger than life, personality of course, goal keeper who is very vocal. This man becomes the entertainment that was missing in the first half. Within a couple of minutes of play, Welbeck are awarded a penalty which brings out the most of his personality. I also use this distraction to water the weed with some cold black tea. We, ok 'I' as I am the only one on this touchline, are treated to a running commentary from the keeper as his teammate prepares to take the spot kick. I learn that the striker missed the last penalty, which must be the reason he cannot watch. As he hides his eyes in his sleeves, the penalty taker buries his demons as he pulls a goal back for his side with a calm side foot. "That's our lifeline boys, our lifeline!" he shouts after punching the air triumphantly.

This display of passion on the pitch reminds me of coaching the children this morning, evident even in seven year olds. Playing football and belonging to a team is an amazing thing for someone of any age. Today our love of the game of football is more evident on the pitch. I am not suggesting that some of the spectators here are not in love with their team, but this is less visible. The opposite can often be seen in the Premiership, overpaid stars displaying no loyalty or pride to wear their club's shirt, but supporters making huge personal sacrifices to follow their team all over the country week in, week out. It is likely that the majority of players, club officials and spectators of today's teams will belong to their respective communities. This is grass roots football, a reminder to us that the majority of people who play football are found here. In contrast the majority of fans follow teams at the opposite end which, in truth, is a more entertaining football to watch as a spectator.

The Welfare keeper makes another good save a couple minutes later to keep the score at 2-1. "Don't stop believing!" he shouts to his defenders. Just before the hour mark the away side almost equalise and are now the better side. In response to this spell, Kinsley Boys start to create chances again to extend their lead. Our goal keeping leader becomes hero with a string of saves. He is happy to throw himself at every cross and shot. In my son's team we struggle between the sticks; in simple terms nobody wants to be a goalkeeper every week. A seven year old wants to score goals. Letting goals in is less fun and usually produces tears rather than practiced goal celebrations. The frustrating thing for a coach of a junior team is that a keeper is the most important position on the pitch. I should have hired a bus and brought them to Kinsley with me to see this fearless display.

Welbeck clear another shot off the line to generate the cry of "another fucking lifeline" to remind me that this may not have been suitable for young children. The keeper then saves again and, although this lifeline is still technically in place, it does now look like a matter of time before Kinsley will score a third. Thirty seconds later, a Kinsley Boy (or man) rounds the keeper calmly and we watch our hero lie on the floor helpless to the ball slowly rolling over the line. We are treated to some silence in the goalmouth which is broken with his observation to his teammates of "more fucking mistakes". A home supporter shouts "where's your lifeline gone now son?". A very cruel but humorous line which he offered on a plate to anyone is ear shot.

At 3-1, Welbeck will need a second goal for any kind of lifeline to return. In contrast, Kinsley are now stronger on the ball and quicker in every position. Within five minutes of their third, the score becomes 6-1! Lots of "fucking mistakes" now and even the Welbeck keeper is looking poor. I start to feel sorry for him when Kinsley get a seventh goal and his question of "we've given up today have we?" was fitting after an eighth goal followed. As the score changed to 9-1 he did at least announce to his right back that that goal was his fault. Perhaps dropping the ball didn't help, but the Welbeck midfield appears to have gone back to Nottinghamshire. The greatest goal keeper in the world couldn't keep a clean sheet today. His best comment was saved to the end when he updates his team "two minutes left lads. Let's get through this without conceding". A more realistic target, but it was almost ten when Kinsley struck the post from close range. The referee kindly blows his whistle, almost like a vet putting down a sick puppy dog. He sat in the mud whilst the goal posts were being taken down behind him. I was surprised to see the goals being dissembled, which is another first. Any lower down the leagues and I may need to use my jumper as a goal post. With no programme available, I haven't got any idea who scored today.

I find the man who sold me the badge and, after discussing this with his friend, it was agreed that Craig Rouse and Scott Collins both scored four, giving them second half hat tricks. It was Callum Stapleton who scored the final goal to complete Welbeck's misery. This feels like the time to ask my burning question, "how much would turning on the floodlights today cost the club if you kicked off at 3pm?"£30 is his immediate reply. That small saving summarises how every penny counts at this level, although I would have donated this amount for a more leisurely lunch. I have enjoyed my afternoon, thanks mainly to the seven goals that I saw bulge the net right under my nose. I think I can also confirm that Kinsley Boys have today showed me that they are definitely men whilst Welbeck will leave feeling like the boys. I hope they get served in the bar tonight, a stiff drink can only help! I pass a football ground on Wakefield Road on my way back which grabs my attention thanks to two enormous St George's flags which can be seen from the road. I later discover that this was the home of Hemsworth Miners Welfare. I do hope that these flags are out when I visit the Fitzwilliam Stadium next year!

Kinsley Boys 9 DFS Welbeck Welfare 1

Attendance 42
Admission £3
Ground Address Kinsley Playing Fields, Wakefield Road, Kinsley. WF9 5EH
Club website www.kinsleyboysfc.co.uk
Twitter None found

25

Something Changed

Parkgate FC v Scarborough Athletic

Roundwood

NCEL Premier Division

Tuesday 8th November 2011. Kick off 7.45pm

I had to pass Leeds this afternoon to get on the M1, so used my gardening leave free time to stop off. I had the practical task of collecting my new glasses, but on route from my car I found myself standing next to the coffin of the late Sir Jimmy Savile in the Queens Hotel. Also on display is the last cigar that he smoked and the two 'This Is Your Life' books. Paying my respects to the legendary Sir James Wilson Vincent Savile was something I could not resist. He sadly passed away on 29th October, just two days short of his 85th birthday. This man is part of some of my best childhood memories. Saturday nights felt like Saturday nights because of Jim'll Fix It and then Top of the Pops was part of the next stage of growing up into a teenager. Sir Jimmy was due to switch on the Christmas lights in Ilkley later in the month and I was lucky enough to shake his hand on his previous visit. As an adult, I can now also appreciate what an amazing man he was beyond the tracksuits, chunky jewellery and big cigar. He raised over £40m for charity in his lifetime and the world of showbiz is now one character lighter.

He claimed to be the first disc jockey and who would argue. I hope that inside his coffin he is dressed in his favourite tracksuit. Sir Jimmy was born in Leeds and died in his home in Roundhay. His funeral is tomorrow in Leeds Cathedral and he will then be buried this Thursday in Scarborough, his coffin inclined at 45 degrees to fulfil his wish to "see the sea".

A couple of months ago I was proudly told on twitter that Parkgate FC are the highest team in the football pyramid to play in Rotherham. Roundwood is situated in the suburb of Rawmarsh to the north of Rotherham, but is certainly not in Sheffield which is where League Two side Rotherham United play their football. Parkgate FC should make the most of this fact as the Millers are hoping to leave the Don Valley stadium next season and return to a new ground in Rotherham. Tonight's visitors Scarborough Athletic may not be backed by their usual army of supporters due to a suggested boycott. This has stemmed from Boro's game with Parkgate last month. Their FA Vase defeat at Roundwood ended in controversial fashion. The match report on the Boro website stated, "After twenty three minutes the whole game was turned on its head, Blott was fouled, as he got up he tried to take a quick free kick to Law, Clayton tried to block his path so Blott gently nudged him in the chest, Clayton went down clutching his face as though he'd been felled by Apollo Creed, Parkgate's players surrounded the referee in protest, to the utter amazement to everyone in the ground he showed Blott a straight red card, Skipper Tony Hackworth also received a booking for trying to be a peacemaker. This was the catalyst to the officials completely losing all control of the half as the home side were falling over at every opportunity looking to get other players booked." Scarborough were reduced to nine players in the second half and a player was shown a yellow card for removing his shirt after the final whistle because he hadn't left the field of play. Since this match the club has been hit by three separate charges from the FA and manager Rudy Funk has publicly supported a boycott.

I find the Crown pub easily upon arrival at Rawmarsh but have to ask a passing young family for further directions. Yorkshire Amateurs have knocked my confidence and even my wife can't help me tonight in this part of South Yorkshire. I am relieved to hear that I just need to continue on this road and take a right past the Chinese takeaway, although passing such establishments is not a skill I have. It's shut, there are no spare ribs to resist and I drive down a dark lane to find a large car park. There is a sign confirming that I have arrived at the

Roundwood Sports Complex and also that this is where Rotherham United's training ground is situated. A traditional signpost, the type more at home on a coastal walk, provides me with some options. I choose the 'Spectators' path, as authors or ground hoppers don't get a mention. The rain is starting to get heavier so I take an immediate sharp left to the Pavilion bar. The 'Members Only' sign slows me down until I see a group of Scarborough fans go in. I climb the steep stairs to find a modern bar at the top full of supporters, the majority wearing Scarborough Athletic colours. So much for a boycott, although I am pleased that a few red cards hasn't stopped them supporting their team tonight.

Parkgate Football Club, known as the Steelmen, was established in 1969 as B.S.C Parkgate by the Steelworks Wire Department. They went on to to win the National Wire Drawers Cup four times and joined the Yorkshire League in 1973 which is now known as the Northern Counties East Football League where they compete today. Parkgate FC installed floodlights at their ground at Roundwood Sports Complex in 1992 and Dave Bassett, then the manager of Sheffield United, brought a team for the switch on. The team was hugely successful last season. They finished second in the league and just missed out on promotion to Farsley AFC.

A pint of Stones later and the bar is starting to empty, so I make my way to the ground to see some football. We all go through the one turnstile and enter the ground behind the goal. I can't think of a better word than strange to describe my first impressions of the ground. A nice strange as it is obviously far superior to my last visit to a park in Kinsley. To my left there is a hedge the length of the pitch which feels more like a bowling green. I believe this sports complex can also offer this for visitors. There is a decent stand behind the nearest goal, five seats deep which is above average in Non League football. Most fans seem to be gathering on the bank running the length of the pitch which includes a small covered area with a corrugated iron roof ideal for this wet weather.

I watch the team run out as I am reading the introduction in the match day programme. Who says men can't do two things at the same time. The editor uses his page to confront the 'moments and issues' from last month's match. Dave states 'everyone has the right to be passionate on the terraces and voice their opinion' but warns 'that the majority of spectators, some of them children, do not want to become involved in over zealous behaviour. Although vitriolic language and aggressive behaviour shouldn't be involved in football at any level, I do believe this is even more important in the lower leagues'.

It certainly sounds like the players at the previous fixture were not the only ones to lose control. There will always be two sides to every argument, with the truth being a third version, so it is impossible for me to comment. I do however agree with his sentiments that 'most people come to watch and are involved in non league football because they love football, not for the glory and we should try and promote behaviour that welcomes people to our grounds and promotes non league football in a positive manner'. A very long sentence but he hits the nail on the head in a non aggressive manner. This is the reason I take my 3 year old son to Non League games when he is not ready for the bright lights, and colourful language, of a league ground. Dave calls for supporters to keep their passion 'in perspective and show respect for the players, officials and our fellow supporters'. This page is worth the £1.20 alone as this appears to be what all the supporters are discussing.

A passing Scarborough fan asks me if I am Jarvis Cocker so my new glasses have made an instant impression. I reply "yes" and he walks away looking a little confused. Jarvis doesn't have a moustache silly. Boro are in their white away strip as Parkgate play in all red. The steelmen take the lead after only 45 seconds as Nathan Forbes-Swindells lashes home from 15 yards after Scarborough poorly clear an attempt on goal. This has caught me by surprise as I am still reading the programme. I withdraw the comment about men able to do two things at once.The away side immediately pin Parkgate back with wave after wave of attacks. Off the pitch going a goal behind increases the banter between the Scarborough fans, which is friendly although with the theme being what happened at the previous game. Every decision by the referee that goes against their side is made into a joke. As the rain continues to pour down, our stand gets increasingly cramped, it is four deep by the time Boro equalise in the 7th minute with a deflected header from Patrick Miller after a corner is swung in from the left. One Seadog fan celebrates the goal by jumping on the front of the stand to give an aggressive two fingers to the home bench. It certainly has an edge!

A couple of minutes later, the referee doesn't give the away side a corner which results in a lot of abuse being aimed at him. On closer inspection it is just three individuals that are hounding him and ‘performing’ to the other supporters. On 27 minutes, only a good save denies Scarborough from taking the lead. The Seadogs look far superior tonight so I do wonder how they lost to this side, although playing with 9 men probably didn't help!

Unfortunately, the abuse continues towards the referee and after half an hour it is getting a bit boring. We all know someone who has a tendency to continually repeat the same joke which was once funny; why think of new material when you can just use the same line over and over, and over, again? I now recognise the worst offender from watching Scarborough play last season at Dinnington Town. A woman at that match was telling him that he was a disgrace and wished he wouldn't follow her club. I didn't see the start of that argument, but I am now starting to appreciate her views. A lot of fans in our huddle are still laughing at his constant shouting, but the majority of these are hopefully laughing at him and not with him. Is this passion? It depends on your definition, but he is certainly not showing any respect for the players and officials. I decide against performing a citizen’s arrest whilst waving my match day programme in the air.

The visitors continue to bombard the Parkgate goal as Curtis Bernard draws a fine save from Jamie Bailey after pouncing on a mistake in the home side's rearguard. Scarborough are constantly pressurising Parkgate, but a well organised defence with some composed goalkeeping from Bailey survives the onslaught. On 42 minutes, Scarborough have the best chance to take the lead, but a header from Ryan Blott is excellently cleared off the line by Gareth Clayton. The whistle blows and somehow the scores stay even at half time.
I decide to use the break to move to the stand behind the goal that Parkgate will be attacking before one individual dampens my soft spot for Scarborough Athletic. I could tell him of course that he wasn't positively promoting Non League football but being so typically English, I vote with my feet.

As the second half starts I can still hear him! Reassuringly, to prove I am not just a grumpy old man, most people in this stand feel the same and remark how they wish that man would shut up. He has a very deep voice which is very grating. On the pitch, the game continues to be an entertaining contest with end to end play throughout. Scarborough come close again on 50 minutes as a goal mouth scramble sees an effort courageously saved by Bailey and blocked by substitute Joe Jerrison. The frantic pace increases as Parkgate's Ashley Worsfold keeps the pressure on the Scarborough backline which forces a mix up between Martin and Hackworth. Worsfold nips in between the two players, flicks the ball over the full-back's head and his vollied strike is cleared off the line by the covering Boro defender, Kemp.

It suddenly occurs to me that the foghorn fan has gone very quiet, in fact silent. He may have braved the rain and now be behind the far goal, but I would expect to still hear him. However hard I concentrate, I cannot locate where he is. He could have choked on a hot dog or, more likely, someone has shut him up. We may read on page 2 (the front page is held for Sir Jimmy's burial) of the Scarborough Evening News that a sweet old man hasn't returned from South Yorkshire where he travelled to watch his beloved team play. Oh, the panic is over as I hear the deep cry of "referee you complete c***". What a relief to us all. Then we are all treated to a firework display in the distance, taking some attention away from this fool. The final period of a cracking game is filled with some tireless work from both outfits, but some stern defending restricts the forwards to half chances and long range efforts. For the record, referee Nigel Smith had a very good game tonight. He blows the final whistle to end a decent game which will be appreciated by the vast majority of the 252 people inside Roundwood. I have enjoyed the game and the cup of tea was worth the extra 20p too. On a day where the famous people, including myself as a pop star, mix with the 'common people', not even the thick fog on my drive home will take the smile from my face.

Parkgate 1 Scarborough Athletic 1

Attendance 252
Admission £5
Ground Address The Roundwood Sports Complex, Green Lane, Rotherham. S62 6LA
Club website www.parkgatefc.co.uk
Twitter @parkgatefc

26

Hide and seek

Northallerton Town FC v Morpeth Town

The RGPS Stadium

Skills Training Ltd Northern League Division 2

Saturday 12th November 2011. Kick off 3pm

I feel like I have just been hit by a steamroller. The world has stopped for a moment. Five minutes have passed without seeing him. Time begins again, but is now in slow motion. Everyone is looking at me. He has vanished. I have looked everywhere. Where has Lucas gone? I've been watching him all day. He always comes back. "George where is Lucas?!" "Where is he?!!" I keep asking the same question. Stop. I need to use my head. Quickly. I run one way, then the next. I just want to see that little blond head bopping up and down in the distance. Nothing. He is not on the touchline anymore. Ok. The clubhouse. Nothing. Toilets? No. Back outside. Nothing. What's behind the ground? I run to the other end where I last saw him. A park. An empty park. Too empty. I don't like how this feels. I run back to the clubhouse. What's behind it? I find the car park. Not a sole in sight, but I can hear the traffic of a busy road. No he wouldn't go this far would he! I start to shout. "Lucas, Lucas!" I am running again, still shouting. How have I lost my 3 year old son? I have got the attention of other people. They have started to look for him. "He has blond hair and is wearing a Barcelona shirt with his name on the back. Lucas". I stand still. I want to phone my wife. What can she do 50 miles away. I am not sure what to do. I feel sick. My mouth is bone dry. "We've found him". "What, where?" Someone tells me that he is in the cupboard in the clubhouse. I run inside. What cupboard? I find it, not sure if seconds or minutes have passed, open the door and inside I find two small boys looking up at me. I grab Lucas and shout. I'm not sure what I shout, but I am suddenly aware that everyone inside is listening as the room is in silence. I pick him up and hold him. George is crying his eyes out. I go back outside just as Northallerton score a goal. I am now hit with relief, unbelievable relief. I squeeze Lucas very tightly and tell George that everything is ok now. "Is it 2-2 now then?" I ask.

I am confused and am now confusing others who start a debate on what the score is. In my defence, my world was falling apart. It was 3-2 to Northallerton before I lost my son. We all agree that it must now be 4-2, which soon becomes 4-3 with 10 minutes left. The whistle blows to give Northallerton the win, but I have to admit that I have now lost interest in this game. I have just been staring at the last twenty five minutes of this match. That's a shame, but probably understandable. It was a good game up until my personal crisis. Northallerton took the lead on 2 minutes when Carl Chillingsworth was brought down on the edge of the box. The shout from the terrace "he's been doing that all match ref" was a brilliant one line that I may recycle one day myself. Peter Bulmer curled the ball round the wall into the top corner to make it 1-0.Chillingsworth almost made it two as he rounded the keeper but saw his shot cleared off the line. The visitors equalised on 25 minutes when a cross was headed home by Dormand. Town regained the lead on 35 minutes when Colin Anderson broke and squared for Chillingsworth on the edge of the area. Just as he was about to shoot, a defender stretched to clear the ball and diverted it past his own keeper into the bottom corner. Town almost added to their lead straight from the kick off, Gavin Parkin's well struck shot was saved by the visiting keeper. It was 3-1 on 55 minutes when Stuart Dunn crossed for Bulmer who beat a defender before firing across the keeper into the bottom corner. Morpeth made it 3-2 when a cross was pulled back to Johnstone to score from 6 yards. Then my world fell apart but I am told that there was almost an equaliser as a header struck the angle of post and bar before being cleared to safety. Northallerton had regained their two goal lead on 65 minutes when Bulmer showed great composure rounding the keeper before slotting home to complete his hat-trick. Morpeth pulled a goal back thanks to Dormand on 79 minutes whilst I was staring into space.

Off the pitch it had all started so well. I found a Northallerton Town fan yesterday on twitter! James Tosh tweeted 'be sure to try the chips' which instantly grabbed my attention after my potato poisoning in Ossett 10 days earlier. I enquired about these chips and he told me that they have 'the best chips and clubhouse in the Northern League'. A brave statement, but a safe one to make when, to date, I have only dined in the grounds of Ashington, Bedlington Terriers and Whitley Bay. I used to search for Pukka pies which only ended in disappointment and hunger. Chips must be easier to hunt down and know they can only improve from those consumed at Ingfield.

A couple of hours after our exchange of tweets, I receive a message from James to say that he has arranged free entry to the ground for me and will introduce me to the 'characters that make up Northallerton Town FC'. Perfect! Provided they don't run out of chips of course; oh and I am bringing two monsters with me (my children George and Lucas). I phoned James from the car park and he let me through the turnstile like he was inviting me into his front room, which bought back memories of how I was made to feel at Eccleshill United. James is on the committee of Northallerton Town who play in the Northern League Division Two, which is at Step 6 of the non league pyramid. They are the only Yorkshire team in this league with the vast majority being based in the North East. Today's visitors, Morpeth Town, have travelled from Northumberland.

The exact date of the formation of Northallerton Town Football Club is uncertain, but The Elliott Bowl, a trophy donated by local MP Sir George Elliott and contested for the first time in 1895, carries the club's name as its first winner. Known previously as Northallerton and then Northallerton Alliance, Northallerton Town played for many years on the Bluestone Ground behind County Hall until they were forced to leave in 1974. The North Yorkshire County Council placed a compulsory purchase order on the ground in order to extend County Hall which never took place. It still remains a football ground! The existing ground looks good with a covered terrace and seated stand on either side of the clubhouse. The concrete steps of the terrace behind one of the goals look old fashioned and, therefore, I love it!

James introduced me to various supporters around the ground, most of whom were also on the committee of the club. I also met 'Patto' who is part of their loyal away following of between 20 to 30 every week. I was told that they like to sing and indeed they do. Every goal, from either side, was greeted with a full rendition of a selection of chants. Patto formed a huddle of around ten fans who didn't stop all match. It was good to chat to the club's chairman Les Hood and, particularly, seeing him join Patto's gang on the terrace for large parts of the game. The equivalent of Ken Bates standing in the kop, although he wouldn't be shown the warmth like these supporters do towards Les. I can't see Ken mowing the grass though, which 'our Les' does too. He has served as Chairman, Vice-chairman and Treasurer, being part of the management committee for 30 years.

The main difference with non league and league football is that the club officials are true supporters. Their motivation is based on their commitment and dedication to their team alone. Northallerton Town FC is a good example of this labour of love. This is a very good club that I have been warmly received by and I am only richer for discovering it. I believe that every Premiership supporter should be made to visit this club before they are allowed to renew their season ticket. This is real football and the perfect match day experience, provided you don't lose your children. Northallerton Town produced Spurs and England defender Michael Dawson, but even more impressive than that is they know how to cook chips. The statement of 'best chips in the Northern League' was inaccurate; the best chips I have ever tasted at a sporting venue! Hand cut and cooked in a deep fat fryer, importantly by a more mature lady who actually had a pride in what she was making. I praised her for her fine work and she looked pleased to hear what she already knew. I could have told the girl in Ossett that her chips were rubbish but she would have probably

just laughed and put it on facebook. The clubhouse has been recently refurbished and was one the best I have visited so far.
Everyone today has been friendly and I have seen most of a decent match. Once I have had a lie down, drunk a bottle of cooking sherry and confessed to my wife that Christmas was almost cancelled, I will look back on my trip to Northallerton with fondness. We start to listen to the England v Spain match on the radio as we make our way back to Ilkley, but I felt the need to switch it off to talk about what happened this afternoon. I ask Lucas why he had hid in the cupboard to which he replies "I was playing hide and seek daddy". I wish I had known we were playing. In his defence, I think he won, which would be a first as Lucas is usually terrible at this game. He always chooses the same places and usually the sound of giggling gives him away. George asks me if anyone has ever not found "their little boy?". "Yes George". "But when do you go home dad?". "Never George. I would stay there until we found him". Perhaps the only excuse for not completing this book. George tells Lucas that, despite them always arguing, he does love him. A good moment to tell them that I love them both too. Three men in a car getting emotional, in Yorkshire. It was time to turn the radio back on. We had seen real football today and were now listening to England. Back to reality with a bump.

Northallerton Town 4 Morpeth Town 3

Attendance 95
Admission Free entry (usually £4)
Ground Address Ainderby Road, Northallerton, N Yorkshire. DL7 8HA
Club website www.northallertontownfc.net
Twitter @NorthallertonFC

27

Following Scarborough Athletic hurts

Scarborough Athletic FC v Staveley Miners Welfare

Queensgate

BARIS NCEL Premier Division

Tuesday 15th November 2011. Kick off 7.45pm

Have you ever decided to do something without really thinking it through? Then you make a commitment to do it to a lot of people (I recommend using social media) Then, when you have all of the information to hand, you realise it's suddenly not such a great idea and it is too late to change your mind. Well, that's what I did for this game. Scarborough Athletic currently play their football in Bridlington and, upon learning that it is only 20 miles away, I had an idea. I would walk to tonight's match at the Queensgate Stadium from Scarborough to emphasise their plight. I am reasonably fit so a walk of this length is not the real problem. I also have the time to do it as the garden is looking good, well good for a back yard with nothing growing on it. The real problem slaps me across the face when I buy the map and discover that the route is not as straightforward as I assumed it was when composing my tweet last month. The coastal path appears to end at Filey when I had assumed it ran the length of the country, all nicely signed and easy to follow, i.e. keep the sea on your left and walk in a straight line. I also didn't appreciate that even if I could walk in flip flops on the beech the entire route, it wouldn't be the shortest way of getting from A to B and a lot further than the anticipated 20 miles. Oh, and I forgot that since turning back the clocks it gets dark at about 4 o clock!

I used twitter to get some reassurance, but lots of Seadogs tell me that I am mad. There isn't a footpath from Filey to the Queensway

Stadium and one twitter follower suggested that the 121 bus service from Filey is my best option. I lose count of how many messages I get telling me "the A165 is not a safe road to walk along". It's "dangerous" I am told, particularly in the dark. Despite warnings that I should not do this, I have no choice but to do this. I will be there by 4pm, no? Someone on twitter calculated that it will take me 10.3 hours to walk it, without a stop, and I should pack some spare batteries for my torch. I can't really leave Scarborough until the sun rises at 7.37am. Sunset is at 4.04pm so I'll just have to walk quickly. Another big, and quite important, issue was how to get home to Ilkley afterwards. After much thinking, involving paper and pen, a plan comes together. I will drive to Filey on Monday, stay the night at my friend's holiday flat, get up early, drive to Scarborough and abandon my car, walk as soon as the sun appears, watch a game of football, get the shuttle bus back to Scarborough, drive home and then collapse in my own bed in the small hours. So the plan is set and I embark on my journey. I had a good afternoon in Filey! A run on the beach, a pub crawl, Singapore noodles and an early (ish) night. I had enough beer to not realise that I have forgotten my towel. My face must of been a picture at 6am when I got out of the shower and realised. Yesterday's pants did the job though.

So here I am climbing the steep path out of Scarborough at 8am. I spend half an hour finding a car park that would still be open when I returned later after the match. The first eight or so miles are breathtaking with the path following the sea all the way to Filey. The stretch of coast by Cayton Bay is the highlight despite the constant warning signs that I mustn't dangle off the end of the cliffs, not that I was planning on doing this. I pass through a couple of empty caravan parks which feel quite eerie. I pass more signs, these telling me that breaking into the caravans is a waste of my time as they have been emptied by their owners. I don't meet a single person until the outskirts of Filey when I hit the dog walking circuit. I arrive into Filey at 11am happy with my progress so far. I have earned a break and even a bad coffee tastes good on the seafront. The sun is shining now and before I know it 20 minutes have passed so I need to crack on, once I've throw another pound away trying to win a cuddly sheep. I am sure I can buy one in Bridlington for less than a fiver, but I wanted the glory. I follow the promenade until it ends and find the footpath onto the cliff at the first attempt. I walk alongside Filey golf course and eventually find another sign reminding me that there is no access to Primrose Valley, where the coastal path just wants to continue through, and this path 'leads to the A165'. I can't wait! I then find another warning sign which certainly gets my attention. This is actually spelt Varning so must be more important. It warns, or varns, 'MEMBERS OF THE PUBLIC ARE WARNED OF THE DANGER FROM FLYING GOLF BALLS'. Gosh nobody on twitter had warned me of this. The words 'CROSS WITHOUT DELAY' are still in my head as I am crossing the final fairway when my rucksack is struck by a golf ball! I am still working out the odds of that happening when a lady at retirement age appears. I am preparing my 'don't worry about it' type speech when she demands, "hurry up! You are getting in the way". Unbelievable. I have kept to the footpath, well followed the poles, yet I am somehow in the wrong. I just keep walking, perhaps due to the shock of it all, but within a couple of minutes I regret not defending my position. I could have phoned the local rambling society and we could have rioted in the bunkers.

I find the A165, impossible to miss, and turn left onto the pavement. The speed of a passing lorry is enough to confirm that this road will not be very safe when the pavement disappears. I arrive at the first roundabout and can see that the road beyond gets much faster with just a grass verge for me to walk on. I take the side road to the village of Reighton that runs parallel to the A165. The road sign earlier read 8 miles to Bridlington, but I know this route, with the relative safety of the country roads, is further. The mile into the village feels like ten as I am developing a blister on the base of each foot. All the preparation was focused on the logistics of today and I forgot to bring the essentials including some plasters. A plaster now would make all of the difference. My spirits are low as I feel worse with each step.
My walk has turned into a hobble as I arrive into the village at 12.45pm. The bus shelter looks a good place to sit down for a

sandwich. Whilst I am chewing, my eyes drift to the bus timetable on the wall. It is for the 121 service and I see that there is a bus at 1.07pm which would get me into Bridlington bus station at 1.30. I sit back down, put my map into my rucksack and start to prepare to get on the bus. What am I doing?! The blisters are bad but I can't give up. I also think about how I would fill 6 hours and then remember that I have left my book in the boot of my car. This is enough for me to jump to my feet, lace up my boots tightly and, without thinking about it, I start to walk again. The bus does stop in the next village so decide to see how I feel then as I am still not convinced I can complete the next 10 miles or so.

Just as I am leaving Reighton, I see a footpath to my left signposted to my next stop Speeton. I consult my map just as the bus passes me. It doesn't look like this route will shorten the distance, but walking across fields will be much more interesting. I cross a crop field, almost expecting to be chased by an aggressive farmer with a shot gun. The flying golf ball has put me on edge! The sign at the next gate reads 'Bull in field'. That is the last thing I need! It is not the words that worry me but the picture of a bull in a warning triangle. His picture looks quite aggressive with his ring through his nose and don't think I have the feet to outrun him today. I hobble as quickly as I can and soon see that the bull is, thankfully, at the other side of the field. I stay calm, despite him watching my every step, but I'm relieved to climb the fence at the other side. I get back onto the road and, without really thinking about it, push on. I could pick up the coastal path here but don't have enough daylight hours for this to be an option. The long lonely road from Speeton Gate to the next village of Buckton is the hardest stretch so far. I am surrounded by miles of open countryside and, despite it still being early afternoon, it is starting to get dark. This is a constant reminder that I can't really afford the stop that my feet are asking for. The traffic is also getting busier and the long straight road is encouraging them to drive faster. I am forced to mount the bumpy verge, sometimes ditch, as nobody seems to want to slow down for a lonely ground hopper. I hop past the sign that welcomes me to the East Riding of Yorkshire as my right blister is now very painful. I don't really have any choice but to keep going. I pass through Buckton which tells me that I am still 3 miles from Bridlington.

The passing cars now have their lights on as I arrive at the suburbs of Bridlington at 3.30pm. The local school has just finished and I feel finished too when a group of school girls tell me that my Movember moustache makes me look like Adolph Hitler. It is not the morale boost I am looking for! During the next half an hour I draw attention to myself from other children as my limp has now slowed me down to a snail's pace. I am struggling to cross roads as can't achieve the required speed to do this simple task in the early rush hour traffic. I hope that my 'great outdoors' look, last seen at Brighouse Town, will make it obvious that I am struggling because I have been on a long walk. I arrive at the busy Queensgate road at 4.15pm and continue towards the town centre in search of a chemist.

I feel one of my blisters pop whilst in the middle of a very busy road. Ouch! I hop to the other side of the road as a large lorry focuses my mind. I find a bench and collapse on it, only my third stop since 8am which up to now has totalled thirty minutes. I am getting cold so rise again and I continue despite every single step now hurting. I eventually see a Boots sign in the distance which must be similar to how a lake looks to someone stranded in the desert. The young shop assistance kindly states the obvious that I "should of packed these" as I buy some compeed plasters and ibuprofen tablets. I even generate a giggle as I drag my right foot back onto the high street in search of a Starbucks. I would have more chance of finding a cruise ship in the harbour, but I do locate an indoor shopping centre. I use the toilets as a base to attempt to patch my feet up in one of the cubicles. This is not an easy task! Firstly because my feet are a complete mess, so bad I would lose all of my followers if I put a picture of them on twitter. Secondly, I can't even bend my knees! I collapse in the nearest cafe and swallow my tablets with a cup of tea. I did it!

After half an hour, I take the hint of them hoovering under my table as a sign that I need to become mobile again. Ah, Ah, Ah... my muscles have all stiffened up, so I leave the shopping centre with a silly walk that John Cleese would be proud of. The whole of Bridlington town centre appears to shut at 5.30pm and the streets quickly become very dark. There are no cosmopolitan coffee bars to welcome me, just dodgy looking pubs where walkers with a tache may draw attention to themselves. It is a good mile back up the hill to the ground but there aren't any other options really open to me other than to start walking again. I get some sausage and chips to break up the journey, but my inability to walk smoothly results in me dropping my sausage on the pavement. I finally arrive at the ground at 6.15pm. I am very early but this is not a problem when I see the inviting glow of an open clubhouse. Entering the Bridlington Town Supporters Club to watch Scarborough would feel a bit weird under different circumstances. I assume the 'Boro supporters must now be used to this experience. Scarborough FC were one of the oldest football clubs in England, formed in 1879, before they were wound up in 2007. In the 2006/07 season Scarborough competed in the Conference North. They started the season with a 10-point deduction, for a breach of league rules, and finished in 20th place which would have resulted in their relegation to the Northern Premier League. Their last ever game, on 28 April 2007, was a 1–0 win at Hucknall Town.

A new club was established by the Seadog Trust under the banner Scarborough Athletic on 25 June 2007 and one year later a new club, Scarborough Town, also came into existence. The Scarborough Athletic FC Society is the formal term for the democratic entity which began and now runs the club. The Society is registered with the Financial Services Authority as an Industrial and Provident Society. They began life in 2006 as the Seadog Trust when supporters formed the group to try to gain fan representation on the board of Scarborough Football Club. A steering committee was formed and, in April 2007 the Seadog Trust's first board was elected. The Society membership quickly rose to over 500 and has stayed around this level since. Membership can be taken out in four levels, from £15 a year for Bronze or £25 per month for Gold membership. Members can stand for election each year, vote in official ballots and receive a badge. I have joined the Society as I am fascinated to follow the fortunes of the club and want to be of part of their future. I have not joined just for the pin badge, I promise!

Tonight's opponents are Staveley Miners Welfare who are directly below Scarborough in the table, a 4th against 5th clash for two teams with promotion inspirations. A home win will open a five point gap over the visitors from Derbyshire, which could be significant come next April. Scarborough's manager, Rudy Funk, used to manage at Staveley in the 2000s before moving on to a number of other jobs around the Midlands. Rudy arrives whilst I am reading 'The Funk Files' in tonight's match day programme, which feels a little surreal. He walks through the clubhouse, greeting everyone he knows and I even get a smile from the great man. He looks a lot better than me with a moustache, but perhaps his 12 months a year tache is part of his growing cult status with supporters. Some of the best club merchandise that I have seen is based on Rudy. These include a Funky Notebook, the Funkmeister mouse mat and a very nice 'funk' t-shirt based on a similar high street retailer's logo. The programme features a piece on Movember under the title 'Rudy's got a tache, have you?!'. I am obviously just not cool enough to carry the look off, certainly not in these clothes anyway. The travelling souvenir shop arrives and is set up on the top of the pool table, Pickering Town style. Everyone seems to know each other and clearly the fans have made their rival's club feel like their home. I was, of course, at Parkgate a week ago for their league match with Scarborough and the chairman's notes in tonight's programme is used to discuss the 'carry on' in the previous FA Vase tie. Scarborough Athletic have been reported for 'failure to ensure supporters conducted themselves in an orderly fashion' and the North Riding FA will meet soon to consider a suitable sanction. How can a club control the actions of a minority of supporters? It takes me a while, long enough to draw attention to myself, to get out of my seat but I decide to have a look at the ground. Plus keeping active may be better than turning to rigor mortis.

The game kicks off, but does feel dwarfed by the rest of the day in all honesty. The Scarborough players look like they have walked here too as they make the worst possible start by going a goal behind after only three minutes. Some neat interplay from Staveley and Boro's inability to clear their lines gives Chris Coy the chance to cut inside Denny Ingram before firing past Kevin Martin. Boro try to respond, but struggle to find any rhythm due to the away side's high work rate and play being stopped on a regular basis by niggling fouls. Boro create a couple of half chances and start to pick up some momentum, although this creates chances for Staveley on the break.

One home fan is distracting me, and most of the people around me, for his constant shouting of abuse at anyone not wearing red on the pitch. I wonder if he has read the programme notes. I lose count of how many people around me make disapproving sounds, but of course nobody says anything to him. This individual is at least 60 and really should know better. He is probably someone's sweet granddad until he stands at a touchline. His constant swearing and the warmth of the snack bar influence me to move away. My coat has been designed for keeping warm whilst walking and not for standing still at a cold touchline. Boro do manage to find an equaliser right on half time, Bernard beats the offside trap, turns and crosses for the unmarked Naylor to lash home from six yards out. I find enough energy to let out a small cheer.

At half time I just collapse with a diet coke in the clubhouse. I just stare out of the window until the players arrive and don't quite manage to finish my drink. Boro start the second half on the attack when Bernard sees his shot cleared off the line and the follow up by Luke Fletcher is well wide of the target. The game quickly becomes a bit scrappy as both sides fail to make any in roads to taking the lead. A flow of substitutions doesn't have any impact. The visitors still look dangerous on the break and Andrew Fox fires over the bar from a good position. Boro have a few chances but you never feel that they will score tonight. They are now pushing so many players forward and this is their downfall when Staveley break away in injury time to take all three points. Boro lose possession and Staveley make a speedy counter attack, the ball eventually finding its way to Joe Thornton who lets fly from twenty five yards. The ball cannons in off the underside of the crossbar giving Martin no chance and me an excuse to find the bus.

I eventually get on the bus but because it is "private hire" the driver refuses to take any money off me. My response of "I walked here" to his question in regard to a ticket may have confused him. I settle down upstairs too easily and the sound of fans discussing the game is my final memory of Queensgate. "No replacement for Blott... We have no pace up front... They had 3 chances and scored 2 of them" and someone wakes me up outside of Scarborough railway station. I limp to my car and the drive home doesn't get any easier.

The Scarborough Athletic moto is, No Battle No Victory. At 1am I climb into bed after a drive through thick fog and the constant pain from every time the accelerator pressed against my blister. This helps me to understand the true meaning of this. Playing games 25 miles from their home town is all part of the battle. Getting back to Scarborough will feel like a victory before a ball is kicked. I feel a long way away from my personal victory of completing Route 66. I didn't knowing watching a football game could be so painful.

Scarborough Athletic 1 Staveley Miners Welfare 2

Attendance 393
Admission £7
Ground Address Queensgate, Bridlington, East Yorkshire. YO16 5LN
Club website www.scarboroughathletic.com
Twitter @safc or @SeadogUpdate

28

Erik The Viking

Goole AFC v Belper Town

The Victoria Pleasure Grounds
Evo Stik League Division One South.
Tuesday 22nd November 2011. Kick off 7.45pm

A view of the Glass Works dominates the landscape of Goole as visitors leave the M62. Goole is a town with a port located 45 miles inland on the confluence of the rivers Don and Ouse in the East Riding of Yorkshire. The port is capable of handling nearly 3 million tonnes of cargo a year, so is one of the most important ports on the east coast of England. I did some research today on Goole AFC which made for interesting reading. Goole have had a semi professional football team since the 1900s competing in various leagues throughout their history and achieving varying degrees of success. In the 1995/96 season, because of ever-increasing debts and falling attendances, the Goole Town committee had no option but to close down the club. For the last few die hard supporters it must have been a very sad time in their history.

In the autumn of 1996 a Leeds Businessman, Mike Norman, who was at work in the Goole area, happened to stumble across the Victoria Pleasure Grounds and, hearing that the town had no football team, visited the local council regarding the possibility of starting a brand new club. It had been his dream to run a semi professional club and he set to work immediately, recruiting local people to help him with his vision. In the summer of 1997, Goole AFC. advertised for a club manager with John Reed being the most outstanding candidate. He had taken Bridlington Town to Wembley and had enjoyed five non league Championships with many clubs. The first game of the new season was a sign of things to come when local man Paul Gibbon hit Blackwell Miners Welfare with five goals. The final score saw Goole hit their highest score to date winning by eight goals to nil. The first year was more successful than anyone dare imagine. That season ended with Goole crowned as Champions of the Central Midlands Premier Division winning 27 games, drawing 4 and just one defeat. Goole also managed to top 100 goals in a season, finishing with 102 league goals in all. The new club's second season also provided more success, achieving promotion to the Northern Counties East League. Their third season was traumatic when, in January, it was announced to a sombre crowd that founder and Chairman Mike Norman had passed away. Mike, who had had the ambition and motivation to start a club so soon after the last one folded, had received the backing of the council and more importantly the general public. John Reed went public and stated that he would win the Championship for Mike and his family he did it in style by finishing eleven points clear. After a few years of making progress both on and off the pitch, Goole achieved the dream of Unibond Football when they gained promotion in the 2004/05 season.

Visiting a club who play at a ground with the word 'pleasure' in it are known as The Vikings, and whose badge features a Viking long boat, sounds like a fun trip. I stop at Morrisons upon arrival into Goole for some food with the scars of Askern Villa not quite heeled. I am surprised to park next to an old building in the car park which I can only guess was once a windmill. Perhaps this supermarket does a range of fresh flour but, instead, I raid the 'almost out of date' range, which is very popular tonight. I think I am close to enjoying the pleasure of ground number 28 but, to save time I ask a girl for directions. Her reply of, "I didn't know we had a football ground" said it all. I had been told earlier on twitter that the crowd tonight would be around the 70 mark. Rattleknackers (yes, it was difficult to take him seriously) told me that it would be around 130 on a Saturday, though it used to get over 200. I change my question to ask where Carter Street is. "Oh yes. It's near the new Sainsburys further towards town". Great. I am still hungry and maybe the store will have a lighthouse in their car park to admire. I settle for my bargain beef sandwich and drive down Carter Street where I immediately see a large water tower in the distance. I can also see the ground thanks to a floodlit football pitch. I have seen enough of Goole already to remind me how diverse Yorkshire is. This town feels very different to my previous 27 visits.

I follow another car through the gates into the ground assuming that this was the way to go to park my car. I do indeed find a small car park but I should not have made assumptions as, I do feel an ass getting out of my car. It is clear that I am not in a car park for supporters. The biggest clue is that I have entered the stadium without passing the turnstile which, I suppose, makes this car park excellent value for money. A middle aged man, who looks official, asks me who I am I.
"A fan. Sorry should I have parked there?".
"Not really but it's too late now. Are you from Belper?".
"Ilkley. I am writing a book about the football grounds of Yorkshire". That was a good response. I got his attention and he instantly becomes friendlier. He asks me if I have read the Tyke Travels. My blank look results in being asked to follow him.

We end up in an Aladdin's cave, a cross between a souvenir shop and club museum. He holds up a copy of the Tyke Travels by a Steven Penny which gives me a flash back from Northallerton Town when I was in fact asked if I was the "new Steve Penny". I avoided answering on that occasion as I wasn't sure who Mr Penny was. He offers me his copy and I am so bowled over by this act of generosity, I accept. I then get a sixty second history of the club delivered with amazing enthusiasm. I wish I was armed with my pad and pen, but I haven't mastered short hand yet. The highlight is that the Vikings did land in Goole he tells me, then "just four cottages", on their way to York. I also learn that the tall building is a water tower, in fact the largest one in Europe. I buy a programme and leave the gates just as they are shut behind me. I need to find a pub just to digest the last few minutes of my life. I am told that there are a couple of clubs on this street and I promise to return later through the turnstile. A bit early for a Night Club, but as long as I can get a beer.

I find The Victoria Club half way down Carter Street and ask the man on the door smoking if I need to be a member to go in. The look on his face suggests that I have just asked the most ridiculous question of all time. I thought clubs had members, otherwise aren't they just pubs? I follow the man in, who then goes behind the bar to serve me. I am asked again who I am and then enter a surreal, particularly as the bar is empty, conversation where, because I am not from Goole or Belper I end up talking about my book again. To say that the bar man, who I assume is the owner, is a character would be a huge understatement. I warm to him even if he suggests my book will be "crap" but I've always got on with people that others don't find so easy.

I take my pint and find a seat where I can make some notes about what is already turning into an eventful evening. To my surprise, I am politely asked by the barman to move as "this is my seat". I look around a very large empty room. At least I have plenty of options. The walls are covered with photos of football teams, the majority being of Victoria Rangers and Mansfield Town. I resist telling him that his team are crap. A young man interrupts the silence when he comes in to settle his bill from the weekend. I wonder if I can arrange credit on the back of my free entry to the ground earlier. A quick study of the programme tells me that Goole have lost their last five home games but they hope that this bad run will end tonight. After being told I will "never write a book without paper", I make notes on my phone, finish my lager and venture back to the ground. Now that the gates are firmly shut, I notice the sign that clearly states 'strictly no entry'. Whoops. This time, I enter the ground after an exchange of money.

Tonight I have witnessed some moments of comedy, based on my sense of humour anyway, which you just couldn't write. Or I couldn't write it. I could return to Goole one day to film a comedy series to rival anything Peter Kay produced in Lancashire. My Victoria Nights would surely put this Yorkshire town on the map.

Episode 1 - The Match. Scene 6:

Man on turnstile: You don't look like you come from Goole. Are you from Belper?

Me: No. Ilkley.

Man on turnstile: Oh.

Me: West Yorkshire.

Man on turnstile: Are you one of those ground hoppers?

Me: Yes, I suppose I am.

Man on turnstile: We had someone from Reading once visit Goole. Can you believe that?

Me: I can yes.

Man on turnstile: Did you find a pub?

Me: I found The Victoria Club. Interesting place.

Man on turnstile: Isn't he.

Me: He is certainly a character. I could probably write an entire book just on him.

Man on turnstile: I'm sure you could. Enjoy your evening.

After my nice chat with the man on the turnstile, I find Mr Goole AFC again who I discover is called Eric Lawton. Eric tells me, enthusiastically of course, how great the word Goole is, which is apparently why Google have been so successful. I had never thought about how they simply added a 'g' to Goole. Eric once contacted Google wanting them to sponsor the team, but he wasn't successful. I suppose they could have named their search engine Gleeds. I thank Eric again for my book and go in search of a hot Bovril. I use my time in the queue to enter Eric Lawton into Google on my phone, which tells me that he was the chairman in 2001. Much better than a pad and pen! Although I am not sure it is working properly as I can't, at first glance, find any connection between the town and a Viking landing. The ground feels very spacious due to the pitch being surrounded by an athletics track. There is a main stand on one side, covering both a terrace and some seats, and opposite there is a small stand similar to a bus shelter. The teams run out and, as I recognise the Viking badge, I note that Goole play all in red. Belper are wearing yellow shirts with black shorts and socks.

After 10 minutes Belper take the lead to the cheer of one, just one, very excited gentleman. It was a well taken finish by Greg Wright and I am sure if I had travelled all the way from Derbyshire I would also wave my hands in the air. On 16 minutes, an attempted chip looked like it would be 2-0 for a moment. Another decent shot by Belper a minute later suggested that Goole's barren home form is set to continue. Whilst I am admiring the steam coming off my Bovril, the referee stops play after a foul. I didn't see the incident, but the Belper player looks like he may have been shot. I am starting to worry that we may have a bad injury and the shout from the stand "get up you big fairy" feels a little harsh, until he jumps straight up. After half an hour Goole finally get their first real chance, but shoot wide of the goal. That opportunity seems to give the home side some belief and a couple of minutes later they get another chance. However, the Belper keeper judges the through ball perfectly and comes out to take the ball off the forward on the edge of his box. Just as things are looking bright for Goole, one of their defenders makes an awful mistake on the edge of his box. Belper's Jonathan Froggatt pounces, loses control initially, but eventually dribbles the ball into the area before shooting into the roof of the net. 32 minutes have gone and Belper are two goals up. A few minutes later it's almost three. A brilliant pass cuts a now fragile defence in two, but the striker blasts it over the bar. On 39 minutes I hear the sound of the Belper Town players celebrating their third as I am returning my plastic cup to the tea room. I am told that Ashley Longstaff scored, which is "game over for Goole". I thought they may need the cup back before half time, but I let my readers down.

I use half time to do a couple of circuits of the track, or, I suppose, I can call them laps. I get a lot of different views of the water tower and then discover there are actually two towers. A narrower, but slightly taller, much older tower stands behind the first. I use Google again, which tells me that these twin towers are dubbed the 'salt and pepper pots'. Why didn't I enjoy History to school? Listen to this:
An Act of Parliament in 1881 allowed Goole and the surrounding villages to have a piped water supply. To achieve this, the brick water

tower was built and opened in July 1883. The new ferro-concrete tower was completed in 1926. Every year, on the anniversary of the tower's opening, flags were flown from the top of the tower. When this coincided with Queen Victoria's jubilee in 1887, it was decided to have a firework display from the top of the tower as well. This ended in tragedy when one of the organisers was blown from the top by an explosion and fell down the inside of the tower to his death.

A week ago I was warned after every step of my walk to Bridlington of the dangers that I faced. Yet I can't see a single sign telling me not to climb on the water tower to attach a Catherine wheel. A train passes to alert me how close we are to the railway line. It is another image of the industrial north, even if tonight's passengers are just going to Doncaster to star in Booze Britain. Their families will be so proud when they are still watching the re-runs on Bravo in 5 years time of them emptying their home cooked meals on the pavements of Priory Walk.

The shout of "let's play for some pride" greets the players as they run out for the second half. I am outside the bus shelter stand so decide to stay put, but I keep mobile as the temperature is dropping. I need to start bringing a hat and gloves with me. Play starts with another Belper attack which makes we wonder if we will see a second half goal feast like that last seen at Kinsley. I notice that the wall around the track stops the majority of stray balls reaching the crowd. It would be much more fun if play could continue after the rebound similar to some of these indoor tournaments.

There is a man behind me watching the game over a fence on tip toes; and not just watching, but getting quite vocal. First the referee, then the home players and eventually a cry of "how long are we going to persist with this manager?!" Surely it should cost £7 to share this opinion? He must have been there for the first 45 minutes as Goole are actually playing better now. Unfortunately 'playing for pride' has killed the game! This man, at least I assume it's a man based on the top of his head, is starting to annoy me. Not because of his strong views, or the fact that he hasn't come through the turnstile, but because the sound is coming from behind me. I take a few steps to my left onto the terrace just as he starts to bother a man inside the stand.

Scene 46. (All 3 characters are shouting)
Man behind fence: Come on Goole. This is shite
Man in red hat: Get behind your fence. You haven't paid for that opinion so shut up!
Man behind fence: Bollocks
Man in red hat: Linesman, you are dreadful. A bloody disgrace!
Lady at touchline: Shut your mouth tosser. The defender was playing him on side
Man behind fence: She has paid for her opinion! You're a tosser. It's official!

Brilliant! I just wish the drama on the pitch was at this level. The game is now awful, so I start to play with my phone and think about how I will get my car out of the ground. I take a slow walk around the ground for the final quarter of an hour. Nothing really happens on the pitch and soon the referee puts us all out of our misery by blowing the whistle. Someone on twitter suggests seeing my photo of the water tower on the basis that this was all Goole had to offer. Now that I have been to the Victoria Pleasure Grounds, and the club, I would strongly disagree. Although, admittedly, the Vikings did move onto York...perhaps. There is a friendly football club, whose team probably just need some confidence and, of course, a very secure car park. Once they open the gates I will be on my way. I wonder if the man from Reading ever got back to Berkshire. He may have stopped at The Victoria Club on his way home and has never been seen since.

Goole AFC 0 Belper Town 3

Attendance 115 (plus the man behind the fence)
Admission £7

Ground Address: Marcus Street, Goole, East Yorkshire. DN14 6SL
Club website www.pitchero.com/clubs/gooleafc
Twitter:@GooleAFC

29

Speed

Glasshoughton Welfare AFC v Bottesford Town

The Glasshoughton Centre
BARIS NCEL Division One
Saturday 3rd December 2011. Kick off 3pm

Leeds United play Millwall today and because of the usual fun and games outside the ground, the police have brought forward the kick off to 12.30pm. Some of this is justified as there has been a lot of trouble at previous encounters, but now that the away allocation, or demand to travel north, has dramatically reduced, it all feels a bit over the top. Today, there are just 200 Millwall supporters attending, yet it feels like there are enough police officers on duty at Elland Road to hold the hand of each away fan. The early kick off was too much of a temptation not to bag a Route 66 trip on the same day. I will be doing this with George as he is my partner in crime for Leeds games. Wakefield FC are at home, but I have chosen Glasshoughton Welfare who play their football on the edge of Castleford. The AA Route Planner tells me that the ground is 15.1 miles away from Elland Road and will take me 18 minutes to drive there. My worry is that it can take 18 minutes just to get out of the Elland Road car park. The tragic death of former Leeds United midfield legend Gary Speed last Sunday has generated a larger crowd than normal as the club will be paying their respects before the match. Gary Speed started his career at Leeds, winning a League title after making his debut as a 19-year-old in 1989. Between then and 1996 he made 248 appearances during his time at the club. Gary finished his playing career in Yorkshire last year after playing 37 games for Sheffield United, where he also managed before moving to the Welsh job. He played 85 times for his country and remains the most capped outfield player for Wales. He was well respected by everyone in football for his abilities and manner on and off the pitch. An amazing man who touched a lot of lives. This can be seen by the messages on the shrine that has grown over the last 6 days at the foot of the Billy Bremner statue. We spend a few minutes in silence to read some of the messages, which I can see has got George's attention.

Inside the ground the atmosphere is very different today. Nobody is discussing the actual game and the only moans are from people who tried to buy a programme after they were sold out. A four-minute video of Speed's greatest goals, he scored 57 in 291 games for Leeds, is shown on the giant scoreboard before the players arrive. Above the applause we can hear Oasis' Stop Crying Your Heart Out. This song, along with some amazing images of his time at Leeds, helps to prove that northern men do cry. It is also a lot for a 7 year old boy who looks overwhelmed as the players enter the pitch. Both teams line up around the centre circle for a minute's applause, only interrupted by singing the name of Gary Speed. We get a very composed announcer who reminds us why most of us are all getting very emotional without getting emotional himself. Former player Gordon Strachan, along with managers Simon Grayson and Welshman Kenny Jackett, lay wreaths on either side of the halfway line, and everyone applauds thunderously at the words: 'A player who will never be forgotten, Leeds United No 11 Gary Speed.' More tears in the crowd! At this point I look down and see that George is sobbing uncontrollably. "I feel sick daddy. Poor Gary Speed". I hug him and my nose gets very runny. I must have caught a cold. I tell him that it's ok to cry, more than ok and I am very proud of him, yet hide my own tears.

The game starts and we hear how many tunes the words Gary Speed can be sung to. This happens at almost every moment of the game from somewhere in the ground. Gary wore the number 11 shirt, so in the 11th minute fans started to chant his name. The travelling Millwall fans joined in, capturing the spirit of the day and, at the conclusion of one 11-minute bout of singing Speed's name between the 11th and 22nd minutes, everyone in the ground stood to give a rousing finale. Unlike previous home games, the fans today are united. The first half in comparison was flat and an anticlimax. This is totally understandable and I have barely noticed how cold the weather is this afternoon. There was a feeling at half time that there only was going to be one winner today and a five minute spell wins the game for Leeds. Just after the hour mark, Robert Snodgrass fires a free kick into the top corner and then scores a second with a diving header two minutes later. The chant of two nil to Gary Speed was the start of more singing of their hero's name and, once again, the players on the pitch get lost in the noise.

My attention turns to how to break the land speed record to Glasshoughton in front of the entire West Yorkshire police force. Leaving five minutes early is the only solution and we both jog back to the car park, only held up by the steward who has to get radio clearance to let a man and a school boy out of our stand to riot. We get into our car and get out of the car park just before the ground empties and, luckily, within moments of the road outside the Billy statue being closed. To my relief, a kind policeman lifts his cone to let me through. You could be excused for thinking that the American president is due at the club shop by the policing outside the stadium. We race, all within the speed limit of course, down the M621, onto the M1 and dodge the Christmas shoppers to get onto the M62. We arrive into Glasshoughton at 2.55pm and, luckily, find the ground easily. We park on a side street with ease and get into the ground just as the players come out of the changing rooms. This day would be impossible in reverse!

Glasshoughton Welfare AFC was formed in 1964 as works outfit Anson Sports and initially used a variety of park pitches to compete in the Castleford Sunday League. A change to Saturday football and entry to the West Yorkshire League saw the policy of only playing company employees scrapped. However, the lack of a regular home ground prevented them progressing. In 1974, an approach was made by the Glasshoughton Colliery to adopt the name of the Colliery Welfare's disbanded club and play on its Leeds Road ground. This enabled the move into senior football through entry to the West

Yorkshire League, progression to the Yorkshire League and to their current position in the Northern Counties East Football League. The retirement of almost all the Committee in 2007 threatened the Club's existence, but funding and public awareness raised by the involvement of former Liverpool goalkeeping legend Bruce Grobbelaar ensured the Club were able to survive. They finished bottom of the league in 2007/08 and were relegated to Division One where they have remained since. Today's visitors have travelled from North Lincolnshire near Scunthorpe. I grew up near a village by the same name and once had a girl friend who lived there. My parents still rave about the giant car boot sale there every Sunday morning so was disappointed to learn it wasn't the same place. Bottesford Town have already visited Leeds Road this season in the FA Vase, but lost 6-0 on that September evening. They have in fact lost their last six games. Glasshoughton are also not in great form, going out of three cup competitions in the last two weeks, although currently they sit fifth in the table.

The players are followed onto the pitch by a crowd of supporters all leaving the warmth of the bar, part of the modern Glasshoughton Centre. This community centre offers fitness classes, runs parent and toddler groups and you could even hold a conference here if you chose to do so. It's not far from the motorway so Ken Bates is not the only one to have such football club owned facilities! There are two stands, similar in size and construction. The stand behind the goal is terraced and the other is seated on the half way line. Most fans gather in front of the clubhouse, almost as if they are having second thoughts on braving the wintry conditions. The home side are in their usual blue and white hooped shirts, blue shorts and blue socks. Bottesford are wearing red and black striped shirts with black shorts and socks. The wind blows me to stand behind the goal in, surprisingly, our own stand, particularly as Glasshoughton are attacking this goal. George is very excited about our private enclosure and uses the space well to run around.

The home side attack from the first kick so we get a great view of play from the offset. In the 8th minute they take the lead after an awful mix up by Bottesford's defence. It shouldn't have even been a half chance but eventually the ball is picked up and struck in to the net by Carl Fothergill. "Why is the goalkeeper lying on the floor daddy?". "Because he made a mess of that George". I am not sure if he has even met his defenders before and nobody spoke to each other. I may be still in Championship football mode so possibly being unfair. Four minutes later it is 2-0 to the home side. This time the defence could not be blamed. It came from the perfect corner which Alex Booth powerfully heads into the net. I may give the game the kiss of death, but I remark to George it will be five or six today. In the 38th minute Glasshoughton get a third with a simple tap in from Liam Radford after a good cross. The keeper just swore this time, which was noted by my son. I defend his language by pointing out that his defence let him down again. This goal is enough to draw two other boys into our stand to where all the excitement is. Our new friends are too late as the referee blows his whistle to start the stampede to get into the warm bar.

I have had my pint today, so buy a Bovril at just 60p, my last one 3 hours earlier at Elland Road was £1.50. This is, in fact, still cheaper than some Non League grounds. We buy more badges and George goes to the toilet "to check my hair". My advice is to keep his woolly hat on . He is growing up quick. I do get some 'me time' thanks to FIFA 12 on my ipod. A boy of similar age comes back from his toilet stop in a rush and knocks a cup of tea to almost ceiling height. The thirsty man takes it well and just ruffles his hair. George would have seen that as a punishment. I get time to catch up on some scores which confirms that we didn't miss a goal Elland Road as a result of our high speed dash.

We swap ends for the second half; George's idea to "see all of the goals", but there is no stand to shelter us from the cold wind. My son then talks solidly for the next 45 minutes, which probably keeps him warm. Bottesford do win a penalty which they miss, in front of the warm terrace, I am told. I was playing with my ipod. "Most of the game is at that end now Daddy" confirms that the away side are much improved. A couple of minutes later I am reminded how cruel football can be when Liam Radford grabs his second with a lovely shot that flies into the top corner in front of us. "Shall we stay here now dad?" "Yes, as long as it doesn't rain George". It doesn't and at 4-0 we have found a new game to play. The rules are simple, you stand behind the net, you know the ball can't hit you but the loser is who ever flinches at the next goal. It doesn't take long for us both to flinch. In the 72nd minute, Jack Nodder shoots in the roof of the net from close range. "Is it really five now daddy?". The Town keeper shakes his head. George looks up at me for a response. "It is, yes, and we have seen all five". We then see a firework display from a neighbouring garden and the away side miss two easy chances that would have flattered them. Bottesford have been well beaten today and they look relieved as full time arrives.

We walk leisurely to the car having rushed around too much today and drive home at a much slower speed. George has finally stopped talking and I suspect that two matches, one of which was emotional to say the least, has tired him out. We get to Ilkley and just as I am thinking George is asleep I hear "Can we see 3 games on another Saturday?" That's crazy, I think. Although the man that changed his name by deed poll did this. Oh yes, he is crazy. "Perhaps one day". Gary Speed gets another mention and, given today, this seems only fair. He was far too young to go and still had too much to give to football. He touched a lot of people, even those who didn't know who he was a week ago. I do hope that George remembers today when he's grown up. He will also remember his trip to Glasshoughton if he keeps his pin badge. George then hits me with, "It's a good job that Gary didn't wear a shirt like Ross McCormick". "What do you mean?" I ask. "44 minutes is a long time to sing his song". A good point, although I sense the Leeds fans would have done just that if that was required. "Nobody shouted at the Leeds players today. It was nice. We have seen 7 goals today daddy!" We certainly have and

I feel like I scored all of them myself. An early night, I think, for both of us!

Glasshoughton Welfare 5 Bottesford Town 0

Attendance 54
Admission price £4 (£2 Juveniles)
Ground Address Leeds Road, Castleford, West Yorkshire. WF10 4PF
Club website www.pitchero.com/clubs/glasshoughtonwelfare
Twitter None found

Gary Andrew Speed, MBE

8 September 1969 – 27 November 2011

30

Christmas Shopping

Pontefract Collieries FC v Hallam

The White Rose Stadium
BARIS NCEL Division One
Tuesday 6th December 2011. Kick off 7.45pm

Three hours! That's how long it has taken me tonight to get to the town of Pontefract. The cause of this irritation was a broken down lorry in the rush hour traffic and, no doubt, a few late night Christmas shoppers starting to panic. This is why I leave the house so early and, therefore, why I usually end up arriving before the stewards open up. Listening to Talksport was supposed to relax me, but I ended up shouting at the radio in the absence of whoever was to blame for not maintaining a certain HGV. The question put to listeners was, are Liverpool in crisis? They lost last night at Fulham to keep them at 7th in the Premier League. I had high hopes for one caller who quite rightly said "no" until he added "you want to try being an Arsenal fan. We know what a crisis is!". Poor Gunners. With their amazing stadium, playing total football in the Champions League... these people, who may well unfortunately be the majority, who claim to 'support' a football team don't really understand football at all. I will not get on my non league high horse as I am, of course, a fairly new convert, but let's look at my trip this Saturday to Valley Parade as an example. Bradford City and Plymouth Argyle are two well supported clubs with a great history, who are both in danger of dropping out of the league. These two groups of supporters are entitled to phone in to discuss a possible crisis. Rant over. If you are reading this book, I am preaching to the converted.

Tonight's game is only a couple of miles away from Glasshoughton where I was only three days ago. I leave the same junction of the M62, but this time on the other side of the motorway. It has turned into a filthy night and, believe me, I have had long enough to study it. We had some snow yesterday, but now it's turned to rain; that really cold icy type of rain. Perhaps I can go as far as calling it sleet. The 2 degrees Celsius on my temperature gauge does not take into consideration the chilling wind that awaits me outside. However, I'm prepared with my long johns under my jeans and an extra pair of socks. A pair of gloves would be useful, but I am moving in the right direction.

Pontefract is a historical market town in West Yorkshire and known for its medieval castle, which is featured on the football club's badge. The town suffered throughout the English Civil War. The castle was noted by Oliver Cromwell as, "one of the strongest inland garrisons in the kingdom." However, three sieges by the Parliamentarians left the town impoverished and depopulated. After the Third Siege in March 1649, Pontefract inhabitants, fearing a fourth, petitioned Parliament for the castle to be demolished. In their view, the castle was a magnet for trouble. On 5 April 1649, demolition began. Although efforts were extensive, the crumbling sandstone ruins of the castle remain today and may be visited. The town is called Ponte by its locals and I have heard some refer to it as Ponte Carlo. This theme is continued in the name of bars in the xscape complex, between Pontefract and Castleford, referred to locally as 'Cas Vegas'. Pontefract's deep, sandy soil makes it one of the few British places in which liquorice can be successfully grown. The town has a liquorice-sweet industry; and the famous Pontefract Cakes are also produced here, though the liquorice plant itself is no longer grown there. The town's two liquorice factories are owned by Haribo and Monkhill Confectionery (part of the Cadbury's Group). A Liquorice Festival is held annually and poet laureate Sir John Betjeman wrote a poem entitled "The Licorice Fields at Pontefract". I notice that there is a sign as I enter the town that says that I have arrived at the home of Haribo. This is fitting as, thanks to arriving late, this is what I may have for my tea tonight. I skipped lunch earlier as I went to the cinema this morning. I hadn't planned coming out at twenty five to three when I understood the film started at 10.30am. The three hour masterpiece, with interval, was worth the hunger pains. I went alone, and garden leavers qualify to join the senior citizen screening. I did at least get free tea and biscuits!

Pontefract Collieries play at the White Rose Stadium, sponsored by White Rose Tools, and play near to the old Prince of Wales Colliery. Pontefract is known to have had a football club as far back as the 1890s when a side, presumably composed mainly of soldiers, competed in the West Yorkshire League as Pontefract Garrison. Much of the history of the game in the town is still in need of further research, but it is known that a Pontefract Borough club reached the dizzy heights of the Yorkshire League in the late 1920s. They failed to finish the 1929-30 season though. However, by 1935, a club called Tanshelf Gems managed to acquire a ground on Ackworth Road, moved there, and became Pontefract United. United ruled the roost in local football before the war, but when hostilities ended in Europe, they were rekindled in the town with the appearance of a Pontefract Collieries side, who by the late 1950s had gained slight bragging rights over their town rivals, both playing in the West Yorkshire League. In 1960 the old Collieries club became extinct, only for the name to return a couple of years later when United merged with a local youth side and adopted the name for them. The new club quickly gained in stature and found considerable success in the West Yorkshire League, before joining the Yorkshire League in 1979. Progress on the field continued, culminating in a Yorkshire League Division Three Championship win in 1982. This was the last season of the old Yorkshire and Midland Leagues, which then combined to form the Northern Counties East League. The Colls were founder members of the new league and have remained there to this day. The team are sitting third in the table tonight following their 5-0 win on Saturday at Appleby Frodingham. In 12th are tonight's visitors Hallam who I have not yet visited - the oldest football ground in the world I have learnt.

The ground is very easy to find, a left turn down Beechnut Lane just before the Tanshelf Railway station. A long lane and few pot holes

later, I arrive in a waterlogged car park. I have somehow ended up with the luxury of ten whole minutes spare to grab some food. I enter the turnstile and head straight to the snack bar. The offer of a steak sarnie is a pleasant surprise and a very easy decision to make! In fact, I am spoilt for choice with pork pies, sausage butties, burgers and hot dogs on the menu, which all look very good. Inside the ground there is a good sized seated stand running two thirds the length of the pitch and a covered area to stand behind one goal. It isn't terraced, but nicely painted blue like the rest of the stadium. The Colls play in all blue and Hallam, known as the Countrymen according to my programme, are in all yellow. As the teams enter the pitch the sound of their boots on the grass tells me how heavy this pitch is.
The match kicks off as a train passes. The railway line is a lot higher than the level of the pitch so passengers will be treated to a birds eye view of the game included in the price of their train ticket. As always, I buy a raffle ticket with tonight's prize being a tin of Quality Street. The tin I bought for Christmas has suffered the damage of garden leave so this prize would be very welcome. The steak sandwich has at least ensured that I am no longer in a desperate need to win some confectionary tonight. Two trains later Hallam have a couple of good chances to open the scoring, but both are wasted. After 18 minutes Pontefract take the lead thanks to a fantastic strike from Ryan Poskitt from the edge of the penalty box. The ball does take a slight deflection so there is a shout of "it was an own goal" when the scorers name is read out on the Tannoy.

The lead lasts less than a minute as Aaron Moxam gets the final touch to bring the scores level again. Like most of the crowd I miss the build up play as it happened so quick from the restart. Before the home side can recover, Hallam hit Pontefract in the 25th minute with another goal to take the lead. Liam Morris heads the ball into the net almost at ground level. Pontefract look stunned but eventually start to play some football again, which results in two very good chances to equalise. The final ball is disappointing and Hallam then create some better chances themselves from a string of corners. The away team are growing in confidence as the game progresses and are putting a lot of pressure on the Colls defence. The man next to me keeps shouting "wake up Ponte!" which they certainly need to do before the game is beyond them.

The referee blows his whistle to start the charge for hot drinks. It has been a good half of football considering the state of the pitch, so good I hadn't noticed how cold it has become. I decide to head to the warmth of the clubhouse and manage to secure a table next to the heater and under a picture featuring the 'Legends of Elland Road' which, of course, has Gary Speed on. They also have a couple of motivational sport pictures that seem to be quite popular at non league grounds. These pictures tell visitors to 'walk the talk' and 'pull together'. It feels very cosy inside, even with an ice cold lager, almost as if I am in someone's front room. Everyone appears to know each other and £2 for a can of Carlsberg is also welcoming, although I do have to ask for a glass so must now stand out.

I return outside to see that the rain has now completely stopped. The clear sky does, however, make the temperature drop further, so my new hat makes its ground hopping debut. I am distracted from the start of the second half when I hear someone shout out the winning raffle number. I eventually find my screwed up ticket and see the winning number is staring back at me! I am not sure if I have ever won a raffle before so quietly go back into the clubhouse to ask for the numbers again, just in case I have misheard through the thickness of my woolly hat. I am indeed the winner, so I am handed the tin which I take back to the touchline. I was in two minds to open them and share them around. That would have been a very generous act, but I am too much of a fan to let anymore near the strawberry and orange creams. I stand in silence and watch the game as before, just now with a tin of chocolates under my arm. I lose count on how many times I hear people ask who has won the raffle and nod on each occasion to the numerous congratulations. On one occasion I am even referred to as "that 'lad"! My new hat has certainly taken years off me; about thirty since I was last a 'lad'. It is nice that people appear genuinely pleased for me although a do get a few 'can't believe an outsider has won our prize' looks. Unfortunately, the quality of football on the pitch is not as eventful and despite all of their continued pressure I don't feel that Pontefract will get back into this game. The Hallam keeper is not helping them with a couple of fine saves from close range. The pitch is only getting worse which the man next to me blames on "too many games", just like the Liverpool supporters earlier for their loss of form.

Most of the last quarter of an hour of play consists of pressure from the home side. Hallam stay solid and respond by hitting their opponents on the break to suggest that the Colls are running out of time. During this period Hallam do get a good shout for a penalty after, in my opinion, a clear handball which would have killed the game completely. Another Pontefract attack should have given them the draw they probably deserve, but instead Hallam get a third goal in the 85th minute when Liam Morris gets on the score sheet again. If that was cruel, Craig Getliff grabs a fourth goal in the dying seconds to twist the knife on the cold Pontefract fans. A 4-1 defeat has certainly flattered Hallam, but it just hasn't been the Colls night in the penalty box. On a night when a lot of Christmas shoppers have flocked to retail parks such as the White Rose Shopping Centre in Leeds, a handful of brave souls have chosen the White Rose Stadium. At least they will go home at least with some colour in their cheeks and more money in their wallets. My raffle win could well be used as a Christmas present so I definitely made the right choice. I have got the bug now and there are enough games left until the 25th to win the rest of the family a gift too. With a crowd of only 39 people, even in this weather, and with the number of shopping hours until Christmas diminishing, I can't help feeling that there must be more people in Pontefract that would enjoy a visit to Skinner Lane. Just bring a torch and some wellington boots as chocolates are not the only thing I am taking home with me. I now have a very wet foot thanks to the fish pond that someone built beside my car during the game!

Pontefract Collieries 1 Hallam 4

Attendance 39
Admission £4
Ground Address: Skinner Lane, Pontefract, W Yorkshire. WF8 4QE
Club website www.pontecolls.co.uk
Twitter: None found

31

Barmy

Bradford City AFC v Plymouth Argyle

Coral Windows Stadium
nPOWER League Two
Saturday 10th December 2011. Kick off 3pm

Don't feed the pigeons! Everyone knows this. If I had my children with me today I wouldn't let them do it. However, a few bits of grated cheese later and my sandwich is being attacked. It ends up in pieces on the floor. The pigeons retreat and I'm now hungry. Nobody wins. Except an old lady who chooses, and enjoys, to tell me that I "shouldn't encourage them". She is, of course, right. This assault, at the Ilkley train station, was totally my fault. I can always buy another one I tell her to salvage some pride. I am now on the 12.21 to Bradford Foster Square drinking a can of lager, just because today I can! The car is redundant for the ground once known as Valley Parade. I am also on my own as it was decided that today would be the game that Lucas had to miss as his punishment for his heart attack inducing play at Northallerton Town. Therefore, I thought that it would be the perfect opportunity to leave the non leagues as I am all alone. As soon as I saw who Bradford City were playing this afternoon it was a very easy decision to make.

Bradford City are currently sitting third from the bottom of League Two with the two below them staring relegation from the Football League in the face. The team at the bottom, only three points below Bradford, are today's visitors Plymouth Argyle. Bradford City Association Football Club, known as The Bantams, was founded in 1903 and immediately elected into Division Two of the Football League despite not having played a previous game. Promotion to the top tier followed in 1908 and the club won the FA Cup in 1911, still its only major honour a hundred years later. After relegation in 1922 from Division One, the club spent 77 years outside the top flight until promotion to the Premier League in 1999. City stayed up, with a then record low of 36 points, in their first season in the Premier League. Relegation followed the following season and since then a series of financial crisis have pushed the club to the brink of closure. The financial pressures have resulted in two more relegations to its current position in League Two. They are the lowest-ranked of all former Premier League clubs. I know a couple of Bradford fans and their claim to fame is that they have seen their team play in all four divisions, which is unusual. The lowest point in their history was when Valley Parade was the site of a fire on 11 May 1985 which took the lives of 56 supporters. Plymouth have certainly had their own problems and many supporters will be happy to still have a club to support. After Hull City earned promotion to the Premier League, the city of Plymouth is now the largest in England never to have hosted top-flight football.

I fancy another beer and it is bitterly cold so I don't want to get to the ground too early, even though I probably should do as I don't have a ticket yet. I follow some Bradford fans off the train for the short walk into the City Vaults in the centre. A decent pub, full of supporters from both teams and they sell one of my favourite beers Saltaire Blond that is brewed just up the road. Everyone around me, and my blond bombshell, are discussing the game. Clearly, despite some people arguing on twitter this week that it is too early in the season to have a 'must win' game, this is a huge match. In my humble opinion, as a neutral supporter of 65 teams this year, the truth is somewhere in the middle. It is not a must win for the bantams as, indeed, there are a lot of games left, but it is not a game that Bradford would want to lose. Plymouth would then be on the same number of points as them which would be a physiological blow. This is certainly a game Plymouth cannot afford to lose either, the resulting six point gap would be a huge gulf for a team that has only won three games in the league all season. I am really looking forward to kick off myself, but I better have another pint first as nobody else seems in a rush.

Another beer and I am now feeling more socialable. It must be the time of year. I find some Plymouth fans to chat to and their view is that this is a 'must not lose game'. A draw feels as predictable as me squeezing in another beer. Mrs Mowbray works in Bradford and tells me to pay a visit to the Sparrow on the way to the ground which I will, apparently, like. I decide to do as I am told, sup up and follow her directions after speaking to a couple more Argyle fans. I still haven't found one who has travelled from Devon. The latest guy is from Cumbria, but tells me that you would need to leave Plymouth by 7am at the very latest to be in West Yorkshire for the kick off.

The city of Bradford rose to prominence during the 19th century as an international centre of textile manufacture, particularly wool. It was a boomtown of the Industrial Revolution and amongst the earliest industrialised settlements, rapidly becoming the "wool capital of the world". The area's access to a supply of coal, iron ore and soft water facilitated the growth of Bradford's manufacturing base, which, as textile manufacture grew, led to an explosion in population and was a stimulus to civic investment. As a result, Bradford has some fine Victorian architecture including the grand Italianate City Hall. The city is a very different place today as the rise and fall of Bradford is a stark reminder of the rapidly changing fortunes of Northern cities. In its heyday, Bradford was generally regarded as a more important city than Leeds just nine miles away and proudly boasted of having more Rolls-Royces and Telex machines per capita than the City of London. The centre is now dominated by discount shops and has a very run down feel. Bradford as a city has huge potential, but I am sure that the two teams today get fed up of being told that they are a 'sleeping giant'. The teams play on grass unfortunately and not paper. Multicultural Bradford should celebrate these cultures. For example, just think of the range of amazing foods the city can offer visitors. The cobbled streets and old stone buildings from their industrial past can only further enhance its unique identity. Don't try to be another Leeds, celebrate how you are different! The signs claiming Bradford to be the 'first city of film' is a good start. I can confirm that the National Media Centre, with free biscuits to mature gentlemen like myself, is a fantastic facility.

I find the Sparrow which confirms what I already knew, that my wife knows me very well. What an amazing bar! English real ales + strong continental beers + well behaved football supporters = a winning formula for me. In fact, most inside are quite cool. I am flattered that I passed the bouncer on the door, which I put down to my new pom pom hat. I choose a dark German beer which, at 6.5%, gets my respect even at £2.75 for a half a pint. This trip is turning out to be a bit boozy, but it is Christmas and all of that. Garden leavers don't have a Christmas party, so I can justify trying a Pere Noel on their Winter Guest list. I have time to grab some homemade cake for £1 and make my way to the ground with the kick off now fast approaching. It strikes me as I arrive at the ground how few Asian faces there are at Valley Parade area. Why is this? A question that I couldn't possibly answer in my book, but one the club must continually ask themselves. The potential for the club would be huge if they can change this. It's 2.45pm, which is late for me, but still early enough in my opinion. The 'TICKETS ONLY' signs above every turnstile concern me. The huge queue for the ticket office is not what I was looking for either. So you queue here, buy your ticket, then cross the road and then give the ticket to the man on the turnstile. How does this help anyone?! I question this policy, very politely, to a steward who tells me that I "should've got out of bed earlier" I got up early enough to take fifteen under 7 boys to an away game thank you very much. Clearly this steward needed a little longer in his bed. I keep walking until the first 'cash' turnstile is found after almost completing a circuit of the ground. However, this is for the visiting supporters which I suppose I can be categorised as. This is not the Carlsberg Stand, or the kop as it's known as, that I had planned, but it could be fun. Bradford City are actually not that far from the non leagues, but this reluctance to make it easier for paying customers to part with their cash is a million miles away. In Bradford City's defence, although not an excuse, this is a Football League problem and not isolated to watching the Bantams.

I pay twenty pounds in cash to enter the ground and I am given a ticket. There we go, that was relativity simply wasn't it? I join my new friends from the West Country who are all making their way to their seats. I select my position near to the front as nobody is following the seat numbers on their tickets. There is a good following here to support Plymouth and we have been given the far end of the East Stand. The ground is big and, despite there being at least 10,000 inside, the view of empty seats is striking. The atmosphere is good though with Bradford supporters singing from both ends. The Plymouth response of "you're just a grim northern shit hole" makes me smile. Bradford are wearing their usual claret and amber striped kit and Plymouth have an all white away strip on. There is a rather amusing man on the touchline in a Bradford kit complete with a Santa hat and beard. I take a photo of him which unfortunately results in a steward running towards me which takes me my surprise. "What have I done?". "Put that bloody camera away or you will be kicked out". He was quite aggressive, so my defensive response of, "I can't see that I am doing any harm" may not be the best thing to say to defuse the situation. However, I can't see that this justified him watching my every move for the entire first half. I could of entered the Bradford prison based on the behaviour of steward number 017! I can safely say that the first half on the pitch is much less eventful and very scrappy, which is understandable for a game that neither side can afford to lose. Open attractive football was just not going to happen today and the players certainly look nervy under the pressure.

The best chance of the game so far occurs in the 44th minute when Plymouth clear the ball off the line to stop the Bantams taking the lead. I use this distraction as an ideal time, with four minutes of injury time announced, to beat the rush and get a Bovril. On the way out I am told by my own personal steward to "watch it". Watch the game? I had. Behave? I had done that too and had even opted out of the ten minute "green and white barmy army" chant. His behaviour is a big disappointment as now, as a result I actually want to see

Plymouth score just on the off chance he actually supports Bradford City. I see this type of stewarding all of the time on the road with Leeds, but this doesn't mean that his behaviour is acceptable. I do wonder if this is a problem caused by individuals where power goes to their head or if they are simply following instructions from the club, or police, on how to supervise an away crowd. The second half improves because the steward with the attitude has disappeared. His replacement is a friendly middle aged man who manages in just five minutes to get some banter going with the away fans, even a jig to the barmy army chant that runs throughout the second half. What crisis in Plymouth? The support for their team is simply amazing which gets rewarded in the 59th minute with a goal. Craig Sutherland puts Argyle ahead when he turns in Simon Walton's shot to claim his first goal for Plymouth. The away end goes bananas as ten outfield players in white run towards me! Bradford respond strongly and create a lot of chances that makes Argyle much more cautious on the ball. It looks like Plymouth will attempt to defend this 1-0 score line, which makes the fans around me nervous. The home side do eventually force a deserved equaliser with just four minutes remaining. Kyel Reid crosses the ball for James Hanson to hammer his first-time shot in from eighteen yards out. The ground erupts as I sit in silence. More finger nails are bitten around me as Bradford then push for a winner with some good half chances falling to them. Plymouth have to see out the injury time with ten men after Onismor Bhasera picks up his second yellow card of the afternoon after a reckless challenge. The home side run out of time and the final whistle gives everyone a chance to breathe again. The draw will probably be a relief to everyone in the ground, but Bradford City could well have won this at the death.

The attendance of 10,143 is announced, in a ground that holds 25,136, so why make it so difficult for fans to attend? And when they are in the ground, whether they have travelled 15 or 325 miles, please don't be so off hand and aggressive with them. The draw keeps Bradford out of the relegation zone, but if they do drop to the non league they will need to change. Forget stabilising the finances, keeping your best players or investing to bounce straight back. Non league grounds are much more welcoming! I do hope that Bradford City keep their league status though and I won't let one bear with a sore head take the edge off a very enjoyable day. I will never feed a pigeon again though, so my apologies to all the non greedy pigeons. That one has unfortunately let you all down. I can see myself humming that Barmy Army tune throughout the night though. A draw keeps everyone happy as predicted, but probably more so for Plymouth who have moved off the foot of the table. There is still plenty to play for with Bradford City only having a three point comfort blanket. Is there really a crisis at clubs such as Liverpool and Arsenal? Now that is barmy!

Bradford City 1 Plymouth Argyle 1

Attendance 10,143
Admission £20
Ground Address Valley Parade, Bradford. BD8 7DY
Club website www.bradfordcityfc.co.uk
Twitter officialbantams or @BradfordCityFC

32

You little liar

Selby Town FC v Barton Town Old Boys

The Rigid Stadium
BARIS NCEL Premier Division
Tuesday 13th December 2011. Kick off 7.45pm.

The North Yorkshire town of Selby is situated 12 miles south of York and its origins date from the establishment of a Viking settlement on the banks of the River Ouse. Archaeologists have actually found Viking remains so this is more than just a good story. However, for the record, I do believe Vikings stopped at Goole, why wouldn't they? The town's position on the Ouse eventually gave it wealth from a large shipbuilding industry, but in recent times it has given it some serious problems with floods that made the national news. If you are someone that is more likely to choose the Entertainment category than History when playing Trivia Pursuit this Christmas, you may be more interested to know that Tommy Cannon lives in the Selby area! Tommy was one half of the comedy (personally I use this term loosely) duo Cannon and Ball who were huge in the 1980s. As Tommy would say, "I'm all excited" as I have never been to Selby. Perhaps not. I may be a "little liar" in this icy wind and the dark. I head straight into the warm clubhouse!

It is, indeed, warm inside and feels very cosy in comparison to the arctic conditions outside. It has been stormy and wet all day, but the sky has now cleared resulting in the temperature dropping. Other supporters start to enter and there isn't one person that doesn't remark on how cold it is tonight. We are a nation obsessed with the weather after all. There is a tea room as you enter, complete with blackboard with the words 'chip butty' waving at me. This will be my reward at half time and, instead I opt for an ice cold lager from the bar at the opposite side of the room. In between there are some tables and chairs which, unusually, all seem to match. The room is seasonally decorated, which is another first on my travels. Christmas is now upon us. There is a range of interesting team photos that have been blown up onto large canvases. There is one of David Beckham during his Manchester United days when they must have visited Richard Street for a friendly. "1999. Lost 5-1" an elderly man kindly tells me. There is also an old scene from 1953 against Bradford Park Avenue in the first round of the FA Cup when there were "7,000 packed into the ground". "I would be surprised if they get 70 tonight" I reply.

Selby Town Football Club was formed in 1919, adopting the nickname The Robins, becoming the first senior club in the town since the First World War. In 1920, they became founder members of The Yorkshire League and are the only club to have played in this league for all 62 seasons. Selby Town's golden era was in the 1930s when it won the league three times, The West Riding Trophy three times and The League Cup. More recently, success was achieved in 1996 when they won the NCEL Division One title and finished runners up in the Premier division 9 years later. The club are currently bottom of the league with only 9 points from 2 league wins and 3 draws to date. Tonight's visitors from North Lincolnshire are in the safety of tenth with 28 points. There is one of those Form Guide tables in the programme based on the last six games that I usually ignore. This one, however, catches my eye as it shows the Robins at the bottom, no surprises there, and Barton Town are top. A 6-6 draw is unlikely then. I make it a priority to enter the raffle as planned to fund some Christmas presents with the £20 prize on offer.

I take a few brave steps outside and the wind hits me before I have even shut the clubhouse door. It is bitter cold and the gusts have got stronger during the last hour. I will try, to avoid sounding like my parents, to only mention the weather again if it does something different; or if, of course, it has some significance on the game of football I am about to watch. Otherwise, this chapter will be very dull.

Tonight, my new fingerless gloves are making their debut. I feel like I could work on a market stall as an extra in East Enders, if only I could perfect that miserable look. They were actually a very thoughtful present from Mrs Mowbray to help me with updating my Facebook and Twitter followers on these cold winter nights. The ground is tidy, even with the crisp packets flying around, and with a spacious covered terrace at each end. The Barmy Army banner brings back memories of my two hours as a Plymouth fan on Saturday. We are probably all a bit barmy tonight.

Selby Town are all in red with a hint of white down each side and Barton are in sky blue and white striped shirts, black shorts and blue socks. The crowd divide into two huddles, one in each stand to enjoy some shelter. I join the biggest gathering behind the goal that Selby are defending. This is not the norm, but it does offer greater protection from that thing I can't mention, or perhaps they are expecting to see a lot of goals conceded this evening. After ten minutes of play where not a lot happens on the pitch, there is a crisis developing in the stands. The four balls in circulation have quickly become two; the latest casualty has gone into one of the neighbouring gardens. They can't reach it and the man who lives there is apparently on the other terrace. After a quick discussion between some official looking supporters, with the weather mentioned at least twice, they decide that he can throw it over the fence in the morning. The other one is "lost" which is blamed on the conditions.

After 21 minutes, the statistically proven form side Barton take the lead with a cross that floats into the net from Ashley Dexter. The keeper gets a touch but it only helps the ball to go in a bit quicker. In the keepers defence, he did look like he had been fouled and up to this point it has been difficult to separate the two teams. The game soon returns to its former scrappy self with very little to justify not having fingers on my gloves. The home side almost score an equaliser just before the break, so I am told anyway. The man who told me all about the pictures informs me that Barton hit the post with a shot.

I was making a start on my chip butty and Bovril when this key moment took place. They are both delicious but only because they are red hot. Burning the inside of my throat has never felt this good. I didn't win the raffle so my family will just have to go without this Christmas. This has not been a good game so far and I don't have much hope it will improve as I head back outside. My negativity might just have rubbed off onto the players, or perhaps they also had a chip butty, as the rest of the game is awful. The only highlight on the pitch, and I am being very generous, is when Barton put the ball in the back of the net midway through the second half. It is ruled out for offside and nobody complains. The disallowed goal does at least allow me to count six away fans in the crowd who will no doubt enjoy the windswept Humber Bridge on their departure from Yorkshire. Barton-upon-Humber is at the foot of the bridge, on the opposite end to where North Ferriby United play.

There is more entertainment on offer from the supporters than the players tonight, which I am discovering is quite common at this level of football. My favourite moment is when there is a huge roar from a group of home fans when the ball hits the roof of a house. "Do you want to bloody send us bankrupt Barton!?" was a lovely line to the defenders clearance. The game just peters out without much quality from either side and it feels as if everyone just wants to get out of the cold, including the referee who has let play run without much interference. As I leave the ground, a fan tells me, as one supporter does to another, how unlucky Selby have been tonight. "One goal. That's all there was between us and that only went in because it blew into the net". Personally I thought the cross was a good one so I am tempted to respond "you little liar, Tommy". This may have been lost on him, particularly as another fan refers to him as Tony. I make my way back to the car but this time I manage to avoid all of the big puddles thanks to the floodlights illuminating the car park. It is also nice to see all of the festive lights in the houses as I leave Selby. I am starting to feel Christmassy, but I am not sure if I will get another ground in before the 25th. We are spending this weekend with my parents and I haven't found a game yet for next week. We are, however, all going to see a football match on my 'day off'. I have recently inspired my father to watch his local non league side Grantham Town. It will be quite an occasion with myself, my father, nephew Tom last seen at Ossett Albion, George and Lucas all watching the Gingerbread men. It is quite fitting that they are playing my birth town team Loughborough Dynamos. It will be a new ground for me but it's not in Yorkshire I'm afraid. Now I wonder how many football grounds there are in Lincolnshire...

Selby Town 0 Barton Town 1

Attendance 70
Admission price £4.50
Ground Address Richard Street, Selby, North Yorkshire. YO8 0BS
Club website www.pitchero.com/clubs/selbytown
Twitter None found

33

It's a Wonderful Ground

York City FC v Kidderminster Harriers

Bootham Crescent
Blue Square Premier
Monday 19th December 2011. Kick off 7.45pm

I have found a game, so we're half way there in the words of Bon Jovi. I am also living on a prayer, namely that we get some weekend games postponed soon! When I was planning December's itinerary last month I couldn't find a single Yorkshire game, let alone a ground still on my reducing list, for my usual Tuesday night slot. But thanks to Premier Sports, I (and their subscribers forking out £8.99 per month) can see tonight's match at York City against Kidderminster Harriers. I am always happy to come to the city of York which is one of my favourite places to visit, and that is even without a football match.

York dates to the beginning of the first millennium AD. 1,000 years ago this was a major city in the Viking world, once they had managed to tear themselves away from Goole of course. This is one of the reasons, along with attractions such as an iconic minster and some fantastic architecture, that over 7 million visitors a year flock here. York City would surely have the best case to use a longboat on their club badge, rather than the existing coat of arms with five lions. Their badge has changed over the years. It once featured York Minster, but there has never been any reference to these warriors. York City Football Club was founded in 1922 and joined the Football League 7 years later. They have spent most of their history in the lower divisions but briefly rose as high as the second tier of English football, spending two seasons in the Second Division in the 1970s. York have enjoyed more success in cup competitions than in the league, with highlights including an FA Cup semi-final appearance in 1955. In the

1995/96 League Cup, York beat Manchester United 3–0 at Old Trafford; Manchester United went on to win the Premier League and FA Cup double that season. Also, in the history of FA Cup, they beat Arsenal, as well as holding Liverpool to a draw on two occasions to earn their giant killing reputation.

After being relegated from the football league at the end of the 2003/04 season, York City have experienced mixed fortunes in the conference. The highlights so far being a play-off place in the 2007 season when they lost to the eventual winners Morecambe. Both of tonight's teams have enjoyed life in the Football League in my adult life and are now established in the top level of non league football. York are currently better placed at 4th in the table on the back of a 12 match unbeaten run. Fans are hopeful of a return this season and a win tonight will move them to third place. The programme tells me that 13 years ago today York beat Manchester City 2-1 in front of 7,527 fans at Bootham Crescent in the Second Division. The club still reside at this ground but how things have changed, for both clubs! It has recently been renamed as the Kit Kat Crescent after the club offered Nestle naming rights to the ground. This caused a lot of amusement to many but no doubt embarrassment to the York fans, who own 25% of the club through the Supporters Trust. The club is now progressing with plans to move to a new stadium by 2015. Last month, the plans for The New Community Stadium were submitted and the club are encouraging fans to send letters of support to the council. This would be a new home for both York City and the York Knights Rugby League Club. It would be part funded through a retail development including a new Marks and Spencer nearby. The club's view is quite strong. "Without the retail development going ahead the stadium will not be delivered and York City will struggle to survive. Some do not want to see this retail development go ahead and this jeopardises the future of sport in the city of York". A report is being put together offering four options, one of which is to redevelop Bootham Crescent, but chairman Jason McGill has come out heavily in support of building a new stadium. Lots of celebrities have put their name to this campaign, talking of creating better facilities for the community, holding concerts and boosting tourism.

All of these plans sound great with exciting times ahead until you see the artists' impressions of this "stadia and new open public space for York". The picture of the ground could actually be a photo from a variety of clubs, such as Chesterfield or Shrewsbury to name a couple of examples of lower league teams that have moved home. The man on the drawing dressed in a suit by the fountain does look happy to be using the open space to make a phone call and on paper moving to a new stadium makes complete sense. The beautiful historic city of York is filled with interesting individual shops, so it is a shame that they feel the need for a big out of town retail park to rival one of their main strengths. By joining forces, the people of York will no doubt get both. I visited Coventry City's new Ricoh Arena last season and enjoyed the advantages of buying a sandwich in the biggest Tesco I have ever seen during my walk to the ground armed with my favourite Starbucks coffee. It all felt wrong though. The Leeds fans drinking supermarket beer in the subways or those trying to recreate an English pub in the car park didn't look comfortable either. These new stadia usually have very little atmosphere without their vocal home end, the terraces have gone and the ground now lacks character. It can all go wrong if you build your ground too big, which is easy to do without a crystal ball to predict the future. Just look at Darlington FC's Northern Echo Arena. A 25,000 capacity, but two days ago it pulled in a crowd of only 1,784. It will be interesting to see what the York City fans, the opinions that matter most, think. I am sure it will happen and will be another nail in the coffin in the growing number of lost old football grounds.

I often think that this level of football is a nice happy medium between the extremes of the Premiership glitz and the collapsible goal posted parks at each end of the football pyramid. Upon arrival at Bootham Crescent this thinking is quite evident. I could well be in the Football League after my twenty minute search for a car parking space, buying a match day programme priced at £3 and ticket prices pushing towards the £20 mark. My walk around the ground feels a long way from last week's game at Selby Town. I am reassured to discover I can at least pay on the turnstile tonight which buys me enough time for a quick pint of real ale in the very non league feeling Pitchside Bar. £2.70 for a very good pint of Christmas Spice is definitely a world away from the Championship bars selling overpriced smooth beer. I choose the cheapest option, the David Longhurst Stand, where the majority of the late comers are all heading. I enter the ground behind the goal into an old fashioned covered terrace which is just what I would have asked Santa for tonight. It takes me back to my teens when these home ends were the norm in the Football League. The East Midlands alone provided me with some fond memories of Forest's Trent End, the Osmaston End at Derby's old Baseball Ground and a, then, scary Spion Kop at Leicester City's previous Filbert Street home. It feels like a decent crowd is gathering with the terrace getting busier. A young man arrives with a drum and the teams enter the pitch, almost as if they were waiting for his arrival. York City are wearing their usual kit of red shirts, blue shorts and white socks. Kidderminster Harriers are in their change strip that is a sort of dirty yellow. I used to live in Worcestershire so I know the town of Kidderminster quite well. It was always known to me as 'Kiddy' so have no intention of breaking this habit tonight particularly when I can see a large Forza Kiddy flag. Google finally comes out after asking myself the same question for the third time this season. It turns out Forza is an Italian phrase meaning force and strength. It looks good on a flag too! The away fans are stood on the opposite open terrace. Around fifty have travelled north with at least ten of them looking very festive in their Santa suits.

Kidderminster make a lively start and York look nervy in response. The last thing that York needed was to concede an early goal, but this happens after only four minutes with a well taken header from Jack Byrne. A goal that I get the perfect view of as it hits the back of the net. Mickey Demetriou's free kick picked out the unmarked midfielder who made no mistake as he found the top corner. "Come on City" is the immediate response from our stand. I notice during the post goal discussions that a lot of people around me seem to know each other. I imagine, and hope with nostalgia, that they will all keep returning to their own special place on the terrace.

The Minstermen are really struggling to make their mark in the game and are not coping well with the cut up pitch. It could have got even worse had Kiddy's Callum Gittings not fired his shot wide of the target after a smart turn in the box. Against the run of play York's Matty Blair levels the scores against his former side with his team's first attempt on goal. Ashley Chambers displays a quick turn of pace to get away from Demetriou before picking out the striker with a low cross for an easy finish. Our terrace is still celebrating when York find themselves a goal down again as Gittings puts Harriers back in front. The striker manages to wrestle his way past Jon Challinor and into the box before poking the ball in off the post to silence the York faithful. I just about manage to see the ball roll towards the net from Callum Gittings, but a very tall man blocks the build up play. I am sure I will survive. The groans from the supporters around me are louder than the celebrations from the away end.

The York mascot, a lion, gets my attention and I watch him, or perhaps her, for the rest of the half. They are clearly just a supporter in a cuddly suit. At one particular flash point, I am not sure how the referee keeps a straight face as the lion uses his paws to mime the Kidderminster players dive to the official. After 33 minutes, City's task soon gets that bit harder as Harriers' Jamille Matt catches Jamal Fyfield dallying on the ball on halfway before racing away. He beats a couple of players before his powerful near post finish gives the visitors a two goal cushion.

York respond with several chances to score, but the moaners on the terrace tell me that the York passing is usually of a better quality. Off the pitch, this is great fun. Standing with others in a confined space does make you feel part of the crowd, rather than just a spectator of a game of football. At half time my utopia is shattered when I pay

£2 for a Bovril. This is 20p more than at Elland Road! The arrival of the "Minster Men", which sounds more like 'Mr Men' on the aging speakers, is announced over the festive song 'All I want for Christmas...' Someone shouts in response "3 points" which really would be quite a comeback tonight. York are kicking towards us in the second half so we can all suck the ball into the net. Well we can at least try.

Unfortunately, despite enormous amounts of pressure on the visitors' goal, York cannot make the early breakthrough they need, but with thirty minutes left City are handed a golden chance to get back in the game. Chambers breaks into the box and Kidderminster's Luke Jones decides to handle the ball. "Handball" is the universal opinion at this end and the referee points to the penalty spot. The locals point out that their regular penalty taker, Walker, is sat in the stands. On hearing this fact I am not surprised when I, and nearly 3,000 people, watch Chambers' spot kick saved. Keeper Tony Breedan guesses the right way and saves the shot to his right. In response to York's disappointment, the volume from our end increases, but I sense that it's just not going to be York's night. A minute later City almost make me eat my words when the ball almost finds a route through a sea of Kidderminster legs. The resulting corner is headed into the net by David McGurk with the help of a Kiddy defender. At 3-2 the game changes. There is now a belief in the crowd and chance after chance falls to York to get an equaliser. Kidderminster look panicked and waste a lot of time that at least allows our terrace to count out loud the seconds the keeper is taking for each goal kick. The Minstermen are now in the ascendency, but Kiddy almost deliver a sucker punch as they break on the counter attack. Several Harrier chances get blazed over the bar and they hold on for the victory. I sense York have simply had a bad day in the office but I am impressed with the standard of football tonight. To me this didn't look inferior to the League Two game in Bradford I saw recently.

Someone on twitter suggests to me that the only thing keeping Bootham Crescent up is sentimentality. It does need some work, the toilets are more frightening than an evening game at The Den, but surely this is worth the effort. Do we knock down every old building because it is cheaper to replace it with something new? I leave the ground and let Mrs Mowbray know that I am on my way home, perfectly happy to stand next to a bus shelter rather than a pretty fountain to make my call. A new ground would leave me with even less money in my pocket and I very much doubt that even a York win in their new home would create as good an atmosphere as I have experienced tonight. People can just turn up at Bootham Crescent and may not do that when the David Longhurst Stand doesn't exist, particularly when it will cost them more money to watch their team. I heard on the radio this afternoon that the Scottish Premier League are discussing the possibility of bringing back terraces. They use Germany as an example of how fans can stand in safety and, importantly, their grounds have a great atmosphere. It is not just about getting bums on seats. Supporters are much more likely to return if they have enjoyed the overall experience regardless of the performance on the pitch. I will definitely return to Bootham Crescent and that has nothing to do with the spirited performance I have watched. I will even pay an inflated price for my favourite beef flavoured beverage to do so. It really is a wonderful ground!

York City 2 Kidderminster Harriers 3

Attendance 2,830
Admission £15
Ground Address Bootham Crescent, York. YO30 7AQ
Club website www.yorkcityfootballclub.co.uk
Twitter @yorkcityfc

RIGHT
You are my Guiseley

BELOW
Sitting comfortably at Armthorpe Welfare

LEFT
The big boys visit Harrogate Town

ABOVE
Frickley Athletic art

LEFT
A quiet pint at Tadcaster Albion

BELOW
Hard times at Yorkshire Amateur

RIGHT The pain of visiting Scarborough Atheltic

RIP Gary Speed

My pre crisis meal at Northallerton Town

RIGHT Away at Bradford City

Huddersfield Town under the spotlight

LEFT A sea view at Whitby Town

RIGHT Back to college for Westella & Willerby

ABOVE Bentley Colliers all seater stand

LEFT Refreshments at Yorkshire Main

LEFT Bar side at Kirbymoorside

Handbags at Farsley

RIGHT Kermit visits Phoenix

LEFT This way to Easington United

BELOW Sheffield Wednesday's impressive Hillsborough

A wet Kiveton Park

RIGHT Ossett again for Wakefield FC

Leeds United LUST

Rotherham United pitch invasion

34

Prizes mean points

Huddersfield Town FC v Carlisle United

The Galpharm Stadium -
nPOWER League One
Friday 30th December 2011. Kick off 7.45pm

In one of my recent daily panics about not completing all of the grounds, I was delighted to discover that an unvisited Yorkshire club are playing tonight. These odd match days, this time on a Friday evening, will all help me to squeeze in those extra trips. It is not ideal to be here tonight though as I am going to Barnsley tomorrow morning and have a busy Monday planned. I have had my Christmas break so I need to get back in the saddle and I never do things in half measures! I have, of course, already watched Huddersfield Town this season and on that occasion, at Bramall Lane, they were very impressive. Since that win, the team went on to break Nottingham Forest's long standing 42 match unbeaten league record with a 2-1 win over Notts County on 19th November. A week later they finally lost a game, 2-0 to the current league leaders Charlton. However, this run doesn't include the 3-0 defeat last May in the play-off final to Peterborough United at Old Trafford. It feels strange, and a bit unfair too, that a club can register such a magnificent achievement yet not win promotion as a result. A Forest fan may argue that the record doesn't stand when they did lose a match during this period. Huddersfield are currently sitting fourth in the League One table, but a win tonight will see them jump into second place and take an automatic promotion spot. I have heard a lot about their in-form, and now much sought after, striker Jordan Rhodes. I am looking forward to watching the Scottish International, who scored, on Boxing Day, his 20th of the season for his club. This is a phenomenal feat before we are even into the New Year and may justify being compared with Alan Shearer in terms of his finishing; luckily; not his personality. This form must almost be worrying Terrier fans with the January transfer window opening on Sunday. West Ham have recently had a £3m bid turned down but everyone has a price. He is only 21 and goal scorers are always in high demand, although previous Ipswich Town manager, Roy Keane, was happy to let Rhodes leave.

Manager Lee Clark is another highly rated prospect who has reportedly snubbed many job offers to join bigger clubs, the latest is reported to have been Leicester City. Lee took charge of Huddersfield Town in December 2008 and has since built up a reputation of playing attractive football from a mix of youth and experience. Tonight's visitors Carlisle are currently eighth in the table, but a win would move them to sixth and a play-off place. I have been to the Galpharm stadium, sponsored by a local healthcare company, a couple of times but always in Leeds' colours. It is a nice change to be walking to the ground tonight feeling much safer and relaxed. The first time I came here it was a night match when they hadn't played Leeds for a number of years. It was certainly fun getting back to my car that night! The following year I took the train, as I have done tonight, and the heavy policing certainly made that the best option. A return ticket from Ilkley is only £5.60 and I couldn't face the drive in this wet weather. I promise that the opportunity to have a few of pints is not my motivation! I did admittedly have a couple in the Head of Steam upon arrival, but purely for research purposes only. Huddersfield is a large market town and well known for its important role in the Industrial Revolution, the birthplace of rugby league and for being the birthplace of the late British Prime Minister Harold Wilson. Train passengers are greeted by a statue of Wilson as they leave the station. The rain is far too heavy tonight for any sightseeing so I take the most direct route to the stadium.

I arrive with half an hour to spare at the Galpharm which I still think of by its original name the Alfred McAlpine Stadium, after the construction company involved in its creation as part of a ten year sponsorship deal. In 1994, the new stadium replaced their previous

Leeds Road ground which had been their home since when they were formed in 1908. Rugby league side Huddersfield Giants also share the stadium. In football terms, in 1926 Huddersfield Town became the first English team to win three successive league titles, the reason for the three stars above the club badge. This feat has been equalled by only three clubs, Arsenal, Liverpool and Manchester United, but no team has bettered. They won the FA Cup in 1922 and have been runners-up on four other occasions. The club hit the headlines locally in 2008 when they offered season tickets for just £100 as part of their centenary celebrations. They sold 16,123 during this offer which was more than twice the number sold the previous season. Attendances this season tend to be around the 13,000 level which is high for this league. It looks like I can pay on the turnstile, but I have enough time to find the ticket office. I am greeted by a very friendly man. He politely organises his line and within just a couple of minutes I have a ticket in my hand. I had intended sitting in the south section of the Britannia Rescue Stand which is situated next to the away end and is the singing section. It is full tonight, so it is a good job that I hadn't brought my trumpet with me. I do recall reading that in the early days of the new stadium there was a band occupying the top of one of the stands. They disbanded following a dispute with the club over the concessions they received in return for their services. I use the universal language of pointing to the stand above me and ask for "somewhere in the middle". I apologise to the passing Carlisle fans for not joining them, unlike on my last trip to the Football League, and enter the Direct Golf UK Stand.

The four stands are all arch shaped, half of which have two tiers. Based on my visits here, it does feel like the Huddersfield fans are happy in their purpose built stadium. There is usually a good atmosphere and tonight does have that big match feel. This proves that new stadiums can have character, helped, in my opinion, if the stands are not all identical. Beautiful bowl shaped stadiums such as the Emirates are the exception to this rule! The Galpharm is also an interesting design and personally I like it. I am also happy with my seat that is positioned in the lower tier and close to the half way line giving me a very good view of play. This section is almost full and the noise levels rise just as the teams run out of the tunnel through an arch of flags. The home side are in their traditional blue and white striped shirts, white shorts and black socks. Carlisle United are wearing their away kit of yellow shirts, black shorts and white socks.

Both sides start the match slowly, but after only eight minutes Carlisle take the lead whilst I am still taking photos of the ground. On the back of my experience at Bradford, I time each snap when the steward has his back turned to me. A cross from the left wing is pulled back to Liam Noble who times his finish perfectly from eight yards. Carlisle's five hundred plus followers and a large inflatable banana jump for joy. They are having so much fun a steward takes the banana away. Perhaps there is a ban on fruit so the steward's hands are tied? Technically it is still Christmas so I'll will give him the benefit of the doubt. Two minutes later Huddersfield get a very good chance to equalise but the ball is ballooned into the away fans. The home team has responded well to going behind and create a couple of further chances. However, this pressure does allow Carlisle to break on the counter attack so any game plan that Lee Clark had has now gone out of the window.

The next goal is vital to the outcome of this match and the away side are looking much stronger on the ball and better organised. The Huddersfield fans are getting frustrated and it looks like its making their players nervous. Just as Carlisle are beginning to look the better side, Jordan Rhodes shows us why Huddersfield are so adamant that their prize asset is not for sale with a clinical finish. After some good build up play, finally the ball that Rhodes has wanted all night is played to his feet in the box. He is unmarked but shows great skill to wait for the keeper to commit himself before rolling the ball into the net. The equaliser lifts the home side immediately and within a minute Rhodes gets another opportunity, but doesn't quite control the ball in time. He is so good at losing his marker and gets into some dangerous positions like all good strikers do.

Half time arrives and I spend most of it waiting for my usual Bovril, which is about all I can justify at these prices. I see the end of the cross bar challenge that provides an opportunity for a section of Huddersfield fans to single out one plump man from Cumbria. They get much joy from telling him that he comes from a small town in Scotland that hopefully takes their minds off their expensive refreshments. I am not sure how I ended up buying a chocolate bar for a pound when I have a house full, including the Pontefract Collieries prize winning sweets.

Within four minutes of the restart, Huddersfield hit the post from close range and then have a flurry of chances to take the lead. Most of the pressure is now from the home side, but Carlisle look quite capable to soak this up. The Cumbrians then almost take the lead themselves in the 70th minute, but Keeper Ian Bennett comes to the rescue with a brave block from Francois Zoko's attempted chip. The man to man marking from both sides gets tighter so the game is starting to look like a draw now. The fans around me look devastated that their team may not win tonight, but I think they are underestimating Carlisle's own ability. Winning games at home against fellow promotion rivals is not easy as they will always raise their game for these clashes. It's easy for me to take a step back and call for patience when, in similar circumstances, I would be calling to the gods that we need to win these games and then return home in tears wishing that we had a cat.

With less than a minute or so to play the stage is set for Rhodes to make the headlines again. Jordan receives a pass that allows him to scamper away from former Leeds United defender Lubomir Michalik. With the crowd rising to their feet, he does the unthinkable and rolls the ball beyond the post with the Carlisle keeper beaten. He is human after all! A dramatic winner would have been welcome by most inside the ground, but in all honesty a point is the fair result. Winning football matches is, of course, not about who deserves the points, which is the exact reason why prolific strikers are worth so much money. Natural goal scorers do at least create chances to miss by being in the right place at the right time. The home crowd still look in shock as the final whistle ends a very enthralling match. I leave the ground with a small group of teenagers wanting desperately to congratulate the departing away fans on their hard fought point. I manage to avoid being rounded up like sheep by the stewards and slip away before anyone finds the apple in my bag. I jump on a train to Leeds, incidentally with about fifty Carlisle fans so those little terriers looking for a scrap should have come with me.

It was a decent game played on a nasty night and provided my coat dries by the morning it has been a successful trip. I am not sure if Mrs Clark can book that early summer holiday quite yet though as Lee's side remain in contention for the play-offs. The timing of their break may depend on whether Huddersfield keep their prize asset. A week is a long time as Harold Wilson said about politics. Jordan Rhodes is clearly quite a talent and the more chances you give him the more goals he will score, which I am confident he could do at a higher level. On another night, even with a below par midfield behind him, he would have taken the match ball home with him. Thankfully, whether their prize asset stays or goes, these supporters will keep returning rain or shine and regardless of whatever they call their home.

Huddersfield Town 1 Carlisle United 1

Attendance 13,962
Admission price:£22
Ground Address Stadium Way, Huddersfield. HD1 6PX
Club website www.htafc.com
Twitter @htafcdotcom

35

Brassed off

Barnsley FC v Leeds United

Oakwell

nPOWER Championship

Saturday 31st December 2011. Kick off 1pm

The train didn't quite get back to Ilkley last night thanks to a power failure. I did eventually find six other stranded strangers at Menston to share a taxi with. I finally climbed into bed just after 1am and within 8 hours I am leaving the house again for South Yorkshire! Today's match does at least kick off at lunchtime to ensure that football doesn't eat into the evening. Hopefully, I will be home before seven to see in the New Year with my loved ones.

The history of former industrial town Barnsley is centred on coal mining and glassmaking. These industries have obviously declined in the 20th century, but their local culture remains rooted in this heritage. The town is also famous for Barnsley born former international umpire 'Dickie' Bird and for brass bands that were originally created as social clubs for the mining communities. To me, however, I think about Hovis bread when I visit Barnsley. Not that Hovis make their bread in South Yorkshire, but the 'Boy on Bike' advert of the 1970s looked and felt, in my opinion, very Barnsley. I have recently discovered that it was actually directed by Ridley Scott who, 6 years later, went on to make the blockbuster film Alien. The ad, complete with catchy brass band tune and slogan 'Go On Lad', was voted Britain's favourite advertisement of all time. My first visit to Oakwell was in the early nineties with a friend who supported Leicester City. Leicester won that evening and their fans, then standing at the former away end on open terracing, hummed the Hovis tune throughout the match. The resulting sound was so impressive that even the home fans smiled.

Barnsley Football Club, nicknamed the Tykes, was founded in 1887 under the name Barnsley St. Peter's. The club have played at their current ground Oakwell since 1888. They joined the Football League in 1898 and have spent more seasons in the second tier of English football than any other club in history. In 1910 they reached the FA Cup final, where they lost to Newcastle. However, they reached the Cup Final again two years later and beat West Brom in a replay to win the trophy for the first and only time in their history. Over the past decade, Barnsley have experienced a number of highs and lows as a football club. In 1997, Barnsley reached the top tier of English football for the first time in their history but were relegated the following season despite their efforts. They are one of a small number of clubs to have completed only one season in the top flight. I pass row after row of terraced houses layered on the hills as I arrive at the ground. I can almost feel myself humming! It feels like there will be a good crowd today helped by a third of the people wearing Leeds United colours. It is a lovely clear and sunny day to end the year on a high giving both teams the perfect conditions for a game of football. I have time to stretch my legs and visit the club shop. A competively priced badge at £2.50 makes me suspicious and I decide that it will no doubt fall apart before next year. There is high police presence as always for this fixture, but everyone today seems more in the mood for eating fatty food and drinking more alcohol than engaging in any street battles. Barnsley on the pitch have a very good record against Leeds in recent times. The Tykes won at Elland Road only last month and battered Leeds 5-2 at Oakwell last season.

The turnstiles are very busy with late comers as I enter the ground with less than ten minutes until kick off. Oakwell has been developed in recent times, their West Stand being the only original part of the old stadium left standing. It was, however, made 'all-seater' in 1995 and the seats in the upper tier are the originals from the early 1900s. The corrugated iron roof that houses the main television gantry is also a blast from the past. The stand also incorporates a traditional tunnel in the centre but, while this is used for access to some of the facilities, the main players' tunnel now feeds out from the north-west corner. The changing rooms were relocated to the North Stand which is where their very large, holding 6,000, away end is situated. Opposite is the East Stand , a two tier development completed in 1993 to replace the large covered Brewery Stand terrace. Upon completion of this stand, Barnsley became the first football club in Yorkshire to incorporate 'executive boxes' into their stadium. I like Oakwell a lot because, even redeveloped, it remains very much a football ground with each stand having an identity. It may have been cheaper to move to a new site and build four identical red seated stands but that would have meant leaving all of that history behind.

Leeds start the match well and striker Andy Keogh's attempt goes close. The rest of the opening 15 minutes are largely lifeless. The game is soon ignited after Leeds' Ramon Nunez sends a shot wide from 25 yards before Barnsley's Jacob Butterfield limps off following an earlier challenge from Darren O'Dea. Butterfield is one of their star players but, within moments, the man who replaced him, Ricardo Vaz Te, slots under the Leeds keeper after Patrick Kisnorbo fails to clear the ball. Barnsley are ahead and three sides of the ground erupt. It could have become two immediately if Matty Done had shown a better far-post touch when Vaz Te played him in. Nunez again goes close and the game is now wide open. Barnsley have a reasonable penalty appeal turned down when Aidy White appears to handle in the box and have a couple of other good chances before the break. I am certainly looking forward to the second half as I can see a lot more goals being scored this afternoon. Barnsley use half time to introduce the "newest OBE, Dickie Bird". He is paraded on the pitch before the ink on the New Year honours list is even dry. He takes this attention to his head, after the away fans chant "Yorkshire Yorkshire" at him, by showing us his dribbling skills on the ball. The Leeds fans should take care with their chants of "sign him up". Their owner may well do this tomorrow. After all he should be cheap to buy, perhaps even a free transfer at the age of 78.

The "Super Reds" are welcomed back onto the pitch to the sounds of Queen and within only five minutes add a second goal. A corner finds the unmarked Vaz Te at the back post and, even though he was eventually closed down by Danny Pugh, he had already picked his spot beyond Lonergan. The away end stands in silence as the cuddly bulldog mascot Toby Tyke punches the air in front of them. The nearby Barnsley fans taunt them too and the familiar song "If you hate Leeds United have a go" is greeted by two kids playing an imaginary violin to them. The comedy mime may have been lost on them and their sense of humour is tested again on the hour as Craig Davies whips in a delightful third goal. His strike gives Lonergan no chance from the corner of the box as the ball flies into the top corner. It was a very good goal, but the Leeds defence is now nonexistent and fail to clear the ball at every half chance. At 3-0 many Leeds fans leave the ground and I can see the constant flow of them climbing the hill back to the coach park. The day belongs to Vaz Te as he wraps up a well-deserved treble with 18 minutes left. He turns past Leeds defender O'Dea one way and then the other before casually finishing under Lonergan. The flow of supporters up the hill now becomes a rush within seconds of the fourth goal. They do miss Becchio nod in an injury-time consolation for Leeds from a Nunez free-kick, but those still present decide to "go fucking mental". The whistle blows and this sarcastic chant is drowned out by over 11,000 very happy Tyke fans.

So Barnsley have once again beaten their Yorkshire rivals, a first league double over Leeds United in 22 years, turning up the pressure on United manager Simon Grayson in the process. The atmosphere inside Oakwell has been good and the Barnsley fans will begin their New Year celebrations in high spirits. Me? I am impartial as always but in all honesty I am leaving Oakwell gutted. I watched today's match in the away end, my team played awful and I now enter New Years Eve feeling fed up. We lost this game because of silly defensive mistakes; there was no heart, no passion and no flare from any of our players. From the 40th minute the Bates Out chants started which is always the sign that the fans have given up hope of getting anything out of the match. It was only 1-0 at that point! Leeds fans are unhappy with the lack of investment off the pitch but are in danger of self destructing with their unrest towards the players on the pitch. These supporters are so despondent that they are not getting behind the players at a time when they most need it. "Can we play you every week" is the departing chant from the Barnsley faithful as I get on my coach. No thank you. Happy bloody New Year!

Barnsley 4 Leeds United 1

Attendance 17,489
Admission £30
Ground Address Oakwell Stadium, Barnsley, S Yorkshire. S71 1ET
Club website www.barnsleyfc.co.uk
Twitter:@BarnsleyFCNews

36

High Noon

Nostell Miners Welfare FC v Tadcaster Albion

The Welfare Ground
BARIS NCEL Premier League.
Monday 2nd January 2012. Kick off 12pm.

Almost a month ago to the day I proved that it is possible, with a well timed exit and a turbo engine, to bag another ground on the same day as watching Leeds United at home. On that occasion the nonexistent match day traffic in Glasshoughton generated by only 54 spectators made arriving moments before kick off simple. So why am I today going to attempt the same feat but in reverse? Leeds are playing Burnley at 3pm, but a 12pm kick off at Nostell has tempted me. Well it's a little more than a temptation as I am now sitting in my car outside the Crofton Community Centre. I had found a couple of other fixtures that kicked off at 1pm but that would have made getting to Elland Road impossible without the use of a helicopter. This high noon showdown near Wakefield was too good an opportunity to miss, once it had passed a 9.30am pitch inspection anyway. I was very impressed that the result of this inspection was put on their website within five minutes. George is with me again as raiding Non League grounds now come free with his Leeds season ticket. I have been to Nostell MW before, so I know how to get here without getting too lost around Wakefield. I will need a perfect run back to the M1 as, despite Saturday's miserable performance at Barnsley, the traffic will be busy today. After a couple of days of cabin fever with our loved ones, the nation will flock to the streets in panic looking for a shop that's open or, hopefully, a football ground.

Coal mining in Nostell began in the 9th Century and continued until 1987. Nostell Colliery was known locally as 'the family pit' due to the welfare schemes introduced by the Winn family far in advance of similar schemes prior to nationalisation. In 1880, terraced houses were built close to the colliery and the settlement was nicknamed 'Cribbins Lump' after the builder by the inhabitants. The settlement was later renamed 'New Crofton' by Lord St Oswald but the nickname remained until the houses were demolished in the 1980s. Prior to the current club, a team under the name of Nostell Colliery Football Club played in the village during the 1890s and early 1900s. The team won the Wakefield and District League during this period. The current club, Nostell Miners Welfare Football Club, was founded in 1928 after they purchased of a plot of land for £400 where they remain at today. In recent times, the club has worked its way up to the West Yorkshire League Premier Division to enter the most successful period in their history. Alan Colquhoun took over as manager in the late 1990s, helping the club gradually improve in the league, becoming champions in 2004-05. They finished well during the following season and, as champions Leeds Metropolitan Carnegie were not eligable for promotion, Nostell, along with AFC Emley, were promoted to the Northern Counties East Football League Division One. This, Step 3 of the Non League pyramid, is the highest the club has ever been in their history. In 2009, Nostell won the Northern Counties East Football League Presidents Cup when they beat Scarborough Athletic 3-2 on aggregate.

George spots a big wheel near the entrance as we leave our car which he just has to run towards. I tell him that it was once used to mine coal, not really knowing the technical term for what was now a climbing frame to a seven year old boy. Once we have looked at the mining equipment on show in the reception area we go inside the community centre. We have 15 minutes to spare so, after discussing how tough it would have been to work underground, we head to the bar. A couple of diet cokes, to start the year with good intentions, and some gaming time for my son provides me with some peace and quiet. George has talked non stop from Ilkley with most of the conversation consisting of asking questions about football. The poor lad didn't stand a chance with me as his dad, so perhaps this is now my punishment for my toddler brain washing. He is also happy because he is not alone in his Leeds United shirt in the bar where the others are still discussing what happened in Barnsley 48 hours ago. I avoid giving my opinion as crying in front of strangers is not one of my New Year resolutions. We leave the warmth, and Manchester City verses Liverpool on the PSP, to go in search of the game. We follow the signs to the pitch via the maze of corridors, leave the back of the building and eventually locate the turnstile. George gets his pin badge, but is disappointed that they don't sell footballs. The club have missed an income generating opportunity. He still has some Christmas money burning a hole in his wallet and would have been happy to take the dirty used ball on the floor that he enquired about. There are no programmes either as they have all sold out because “there are more here than we thought would turn up“. The shops must be shut in New Crofton!

The game has already kicked off as we and quite a few others make our way into the ground. Nostell are in their familiar yellow shirts with black shorts and socks. Tadcaster are wearing all red. I recall from looking at the tables last night, without a programme to remind me of the exact numbers, that Tadcaster are currently second in the table. They can’t quite go top if they win, even with an earlier kick off than league leaders Retford United’s game. The pitch may have passed an early inspection, but could be described in racing terms as soft, heavy in places. Albion adjust immediately to the surface and open the scoring after only 7 minutes. Jamie Hopcutt weaves in from the right and curles a 20 yard left foot shot into the top corner. That was a good goal! The strike also helps me to discover that some of the unexpected visitors today are supporting the away side. At least fifteen cheer which is probably more than ten percent of the crowd. The ground is easy to describe. There are two covered rows of white seats running down a third of one side of the pitch. This stand is sat on top of a bank, giving a good view, with the rest of the pitch being circled by a concrete path.

The goal results in a lot more possession for the away side, but their keeper still feels the need to start an argument with the linesman, who actually argues back for couple of minutes. George's comment of "the linesman has a much better view than the goal keeper" is a very good point from a seven year old. On 25 minutes, a brave block from the Nostell keeper keeps the score at 1-0. Three minutes later Tadcaster miss an easier chance. A home win is looking very unlikely. George is a bit restless, perhaps after 48 hours indoors, so we go for a wander. I see the pitch is even heavier further down the wing as that area is in the shade of the community centre. It is also colder at this end so we soon return back to our spot in the sun. I didn't feel in the mood for our usual supermarket sandwiches this morning so just before half time we dash to the snack bar, hoping that we are not going to be forced to eat even more chocolate. The food options are not extensive but at least hot. Two chip buttys and a Bovril are ordered for just £3.10. I ask the lady if we can eat our food in the club house, a silly question judging by her friendly "yes of course love" reply. It is always polite to ask I tell my son.

We take our food to a table perfectly positioned under the large TV screen showing a live match from Scotland. We sit in silence both enjoying the moment, only broken when Hearts miss a penalty. It took me 24 hours to prepare our Chistmas lunch, but I am sure that this chip butty tastes as good as my goose did. It is time to get back to the second half although I am very tempted to buy another chip butty and join the play a little later. George wouldn't have noticed as he is playing his new FIFA 12 game and Sergio Aguero is having another decent match. I somehow find the motivation to put our coats back on and return to our previous position. I check that the score is still 1-0 as we arrive back and George decides that continuing to be Manchester City on his PSP is much better than the match. He misses a good shout for a Nostell penalty. It looked like handball to me but, as George would have said if he had seen it, the referee had a better view than me. Nostell would need to field a couple of Argentinean internationals to compete with FIFA 12 today I feel. A nice thought, although this would only result in the food prices increasing.

Tadcaster are by far the better side, but the one sided game is not great to watch for the majority here today. The away side strike the bar, the keepers chest and almost the post but somehow Nostell manage to stay in the game. After 65 minutes Jamie Hopcut grabs his second goal of the day to put the home side out of their misery. We all knew that a Tadcaster goal was coming, but this one is an absolute peach and probably worth the £5 entrance fee alone. We also get the perfect view from the height of the bank where I am standing. The number 7 accelerates to beat his man like he is just changing up a gear, skips into the box, waits for the keeper to commit and then calmly slots the ball into the net. His composure and confidence reminded me of Jordan Rhodes' finish on Friday night. In relative terms of course, Hopcut stands out at this level of football just as Jordan does in League One. Five minutes later, Hopcut gets the hatrick that his performance deserves. The Nostell defender gives the ball away too easily, but Hopcutt fires in a 20 yard shot from the edge of the area to cap a very good afternoon for him and his team.

Nostell respond with a couple of good efforts that require top class saves from Arroan Reid to deny a goal. Near the end, Albion conceded a penalty after Rob Pell handles (almost catches) the ball. The penalty is struck to Reid's left side but he manages to push it away to preserve a clean sheet. With a couple of minutes left, and my thoughts now on match number two of the day, we slip away for a quick exit out of the car park. With the pressure now on, I successfully navigate myself around Wakefield and the traffic is not as bad as I had feared. Elland Road does look busier than normal, but there isn't much else on the roads this afternoon. We are parked and walking to the ground by 2.40pm and get to see Leeds United finally win a football match. A 2-1 victory against Burnley is quite an achievement when they were losing until the 88th minute. So I have managed to see four games in four days that have produced 13 goals and, importantly, added three Yorkshire grounds to my total. Provided I don't return home tonight to find my clothes are in a suitcase it has been a successful smash and grab operation. This high activity will of course create a lot of writing but I still have two weeks left of my garden leave. I will at least be far too busy to panic, not for a few days anyway. And the really good news is the weather forecast suggests that some wintry weather is finally coming our way. Happy days!

Nostell Miners Welfare 0 Tadcaster Albion 3

Attendance: 120
Admission price: £5 (children free with paying adult)
Ground Address: Crofton Community Centre, Middle Lane, New Crofton, Wakefield.WF4 1LB
Club website: www.pitchero.com/clubs/nostellminerswelfare
Twitter: None found

37

Oh, yes it is!

Whitby Town FC v Chasetown

The Turnbull Ground

Evo-Stik Northern Premier League

Saturday 7th January 2012. Kick off 3pm.

Every January Mrs Mowbray goes to the pantomime at the Theatre Royal in Newcastle with her mother, niece Hannah, George and Lucas. This is due to her family living in Northumberland and because, for some reason, they all find this type of slapstick buffoonery, complete with cross-dressing humour and audience participation, entertaining. Today it is the turn of the classic tale of Sleeping Beauty to be ruined with mild sexual innuendo and squirting water. You may guess that I am not blessed with the talent to be able to appreciate this. I had chosen, although I am not sure I was ever invited, to stay home alone and of course find my 37th ground. In my own way, a game of football provides me with more drama than any theatre. Although booing is often frowned upon in football, whereas it is actively encouraged at the panto! I checked the fixtures last month and getting Whitby Town under my belt, the furthest ground with a 180 mile round trip, made sense once I saw they were playing at home today. However, Hannah's baby sister, Lola, was born four days ago, so going further north after the match to see her was a must. Money is tight at the moment, so taking two cars would make this ground very expensive in petrol. The solution, after much debate, was agreed. I drove us all up to the north east last night, I got to see Lola and I have driven to Whitby this morning. I will return after the game and we can all go back together to Ilkley tomorrow.

I leave the house at 9am sharp before the children start to bounce off the ceilings from their pre panto excitement. I go back through the Tyne tunnel onto the A19, past Middlesbrough (again!) and then

I take the scenic drive to the North Yorkshire Moors. Around 10 miles before Whitby, I cross the border between Cleveland and Yorkshire, reminding me of the twitter debates I have sparked in regard to where the county starts. I passed the Guisborough bypass many miles back before I got welcomed to North Yorkshire, but will discuss this topic at length later in the book. Unusually, my approach into Whitby today is from the north on the A171. Thanks to my wife's built in Sat Nav, I take a short cut through Lythe ending up on a breathtaking coastal road. The view of the West Cliff beach is simply stunning on the approach, in-between concentrating on the hairpin bends. I arrive near the ground just before 11am, intentionally early, to have a good exploration of Whitby and to be fed and watered as a tourist. I did come to Whitby as recently as August when we were camping nearby; hence the bag man that arrived at Liversedge for ground number ten. I was beyond tired that day. Today I can have a much more relaxed wander. The weather is perfect, cold but a clear sky and sunny. I take a leisurely walk into town along the sea front. Whitby's skyline is dominated by the ruins of St. Hilda's Abbey high on the East Cliff. Spreading below is a maze of alleyways and narrow streets running down to the quayside. I wander down, cross the river and explore the old town shops. I brave the 199 steps up to the parish church of St. Mary to get a glorious view out to sea, and down on the town, from the churchyard. This view, apparently, gave Bram Stoker the inspiration to write his famous book Dracula. It has inspired me to want to eat!

The pace of life slows down for the next few hours as I wander aimlessly, with the main event being my lunch in Hadley's Fish Restaurant. The food is so good I soon forgot the disappointment that the famous Magpie Cafe is closed this week. A few more shops and I'm thirsty. I stumble across The Golden Lion which tells visitors that 'ye be supping in the official meeting place of the Whitby International Pirates Society'. The bombardier is good and 'ye be warned' that they only meet on Fridays after 8pm. Three middle aged couples from Sheffield arrive though to entertain us in the absence of Blackbeard. Yorkshire humour that would have shadowed Queen

Rita's or Muddles's performance this afternoon. There was a long build up which I can't attempt to repeat, one of the ladies says "you know how tut treat a woman". Her husband says "Aye, leave her at home next time" at which the entire pub roars with laughter. They may have been rehearsing all night but it had me spilling my beer. The joke will be lost on readers, but the timing and delivery made our pub a theatre for fifteen lucky punters. I wander back up the hill towards the ground now with a very full stomach. The ground is a stone's throw, with the wind behind you, from the West Cliff beech. Despite a great effort whilst circling the ground, I cannot take a photo (without being in that helicopter again) to show how close the Turnbull Ground is to the sea. Whitby Town FC, known as the Seasiders, play at the heights of Step 3 of the Non League pyramid, effectively just 3 seasons from the Football League, although this is a lot easier to write in a sentence than actually achieve. However, they are currently 21st in the league, just one place and two points off the bottom.

Whitby joined the Northern League for the first time in 1893, but went back to the Cleveland Amateur League only two seasons later. They returned in 1899 and won the Second Division the same season. The cost of travelling forced the Club to leave the Northern League and, for a time, Whitby reverted to playing friendlies, which only served to put the club into near obscurity. After World War One, the town of Whitby had two clubs, both playing in the Scarborough and District League, Whitby Whitehall Swifts and Whitby Town. Ever conscious of Whitby's more illustrious past, the two clubs decided to amalgamate as Whitby United in 1926. The new club was admitted into the Northern League and the club's name was changed to Whitby Town in 1949. Over the years, Whitby have had several illustrious managers. Ex Leeds United star Eddie Gray managed and played for Whitby Town in Northern League matches. Other ex-internationals to grace the Turnbull turf include Peter Lorimer (Leeds and Scotland) and Sunderland's FA Cup winning skipper Bobby Kerr. In 1997-98 the Club won the UniBond League First Division Championship by a margin of 7 points at their first attempt as well as beating York City

3-0 in the final of the North Riding Senior Cup to become holders for a fifth time. The club play at The Turnbull ground and I am not disappointed with what I find inside. There is a large, almost Football League standard, main seated stand that dominates my attention. Opposite this is a covered terrace that is part seated. The rest of the ground has two steps of terracing and has a well maintained feel. There are six floodlights, four on the far side and two chunky towers, one either side of the main stand.

Armed with my competitively priced £1 Bovril, I climb the steep steps of their big blue stand to the back row. As I had long hoped, I am rewarded with what I have been searching for all of these years - a sea view from a football stand! As Basil Fawlty says to Mrs Richardson in Communication Problems, 'You can see the sea. It's over there, between the land and the sky'. Today's visitors from Staffordshire are currently in a more comfortable 13th in the table. Chasetown made the headlines in December 2007 in the FA Cup when they defeated league side Port Vale. They became the lowest ranked side to ever make the Third Round with a 88th minute goal against the League One side. The scorer of that dramatic winner, Danny Smith, is on the bench today and will be live on ITV tomorrow from Wembley to make the Fourth Round draw. A few of their supporters have made the trip this afternoon and some of them have made a day of it as well. I recognise some of them from my sightseeing earlier. Three large flags are put up to my left to show that, despite the sunshine, it is very windy. By the time the teams come out, the three flags have become eight. They are all a decent size too and very well decorated. It is a miniature version of a scene from an England away game. One flag even has an England badge on it, so it may be spotted in Oslo in May. The Scholars, after the club were originally formed as Chase Terrace Old Scholars Youth Club, are supported today by flags from The Junction and Uxbridge Arms pubs and even someone from Cardiff. I have seen a few away supporters, but the wall of flags gives the impression that there are hundreds of them inside the ground.

Whitby Town play in an all blue kit with a red and white stripe down one side. Chasetown are in their red away strip. During the first ten minutes the ball spends most of time high in the air which helps me to realise I can also see the Abbey from my seat. The ball eventually settles down but the football is poor. We get to see a few chances from both sides, but it doesn't look like anyone will show enough quality to put the ball in the net. After twenty minutes there is a good long range shot by Whitby, but it is hit straight at the keepers chest. Three minutes later, Chasetown do exactly the same. A good cross is finally played into the box from the left wing just before the half hour mark, but the Chasetown keeper manages to punch the ball clear and eventually catch it. Jamie Clarke has the best chance to score in the 37th minute, but makes a mess of a good cross into the box. It generates a laugh from the crowd rather than the goal cheer they'd hoped for. With five minutes remaining until the break, Tom Portas picks the perfect time to score his first goal for the Seasiders. The nineteen year old links up well with Clarke before advancing into the box and calmly firing past keeper Ryan Price. James Brown's "I feel good" chorus is blasted around the ground which makes me jump, but I feel better for seeing Whitby take the lead. The home side win a corner immediately after the goal and Clarke attempts a bicycle kick. He doesn't score, but it is a far better effort from a much harder chance and shows he hasn't been put off from his previous comedy moment.

The whistle blows and I use half time to visit the club shop and go for a wander to get warm. The top of the stand may offer a great view but we are all getting battered by the cold wind up here. I buy my usual souvenir badge but it just doesn't feel enough today. I decide on a mug that could be useful on my desk to keep my pens in, particularly as my current employers won't let me have my old one back. This is a sign that the Turnbull Stadium has made quite an impression on me! I will need to promise Mrs Mowbray that this is NOT the start of a collection of mugs! The other shoppers in the well stocked store are joking about the Chasetown flags. "I swear there are only seven of them here but eight big flags. One lad brought two with him!" Perhaps they were made for their big FA Cup tie four years ago.

For the second half I move to behind the goal that Whitby are now attacking. The Chasetown fans, I actually count seventeen of them, have now joined their big flags at the opposite end that had looked lonely earlier. I arrive just in time to see Andy Appleby give his team a great start in the 48th minute. I have a good view as he runs onto a cross from Jeff Smith and slots the ball past the keeper with his second touch. "Sea, sea, Seasiders" is the noisy response from the home fans, which almost drowns out the Proclaimers on the tannoy. A very appropriate chant for someone who has just paid £4.50 to have these words on the side of a mug. Whitby are now playing a lot better and are also backed by an increasingly vocal support. The away side do have opportunities to break but don't really look like scoring when they do. I now wish that I had had another Bovril as the club must have put something in the half time drinks. The crowd have come out of their shells and I am treated to a variety of songs. The team respond well with some other good chances to increase the score. First Clarke's free-kick after a foul on Smith is hit straight at Price's gloves from 25 yards. Shortly afterwards, substitute Matty Tymon scuffs wide after some good support work by Appleby. An elderly man to my left starts a song aimed at the young lads to my right who happily join in. This is very entertaining and the reaction of those around me suggest that this is a weekly ritual. Despite more pressure, the Seasiders just can't produce the final ball to get that third goal. The flags have now all disappeared just as Chasetown's Ashley Lyth misses a simple chance to score in the dying seconds. Perhaps the fact that their fans have lost belief affected the player's confidence. The home fans have to suffer four minutes added time, but finally the whistle blows to generate a chant of "we are staying up" from the noisy terrace. The PA man excitedly shouts "Finally we win at home".

This is the club's first home win in the league of the season at the thirteenth attempt! I am delighted that my presence was all the club needed and take a slow walk back to my car. The Turnbull Ground, and the town of Whitby, make the perfect place to watch a game of football. I have had a 276 mile round trip to get here, but the scampi and chips were the best I have eaten outside of South Shields. The sea air and coastal walk has blown away the post Christmas blues and I have seen a very entertaining second half played in a good atmosphere. I am sorry Frickley Athletic and York City, but this is definitely now my favourite ground so far on this journey around Yorkshire. It will take some beating but let's see if anyone else manages to flog me a mug! And, importantly, I had a cuddle last night with my own sleeping beauty, Lola, to make this time, and money, very well spent. Oh, no it isn't I hear you shout. Oh, yes it is!

Whitby Town 2 Chasetown 0

Attendance 238
Admission £8
Ground Address Upgang Lane, Whitby, North Yorkshire. YO21 3HZ
Club website www.whitby-town.com
Twitter @whitbytownfc or @TurnbullTweeter

38

A rebel with a cause

Bradford Park Avenue AFC v Loughborough Dynamo

The Horsfall Stadium

The Doodson Sport Cup Fourth Road

Monday 9th January 2012. Kick off 7.45pm.

Tonight I will complete the list of the Yorkshire clubs at Step 3 of the Non League pyramid after my previous visits to Whitby Town, Frickley Athletic, North Ferriby United and Stocksbridge Park Steels. Bradford Park Avenue are currently 6th in the Evo-Stik Premier Division, just one place away from a playoff place. On many occasions, I have heard Bradford City fans joke that they may soon be playing in the same league as Park Avenue. Promotion this season would see them just two leagues behind; only one if the Bantams don't keep their league status. Bradford (Park Avenue) Association Football Club were previously known as Bradford FC and have an incredible history. The football club was founded in 1907 and joined the Second Division of the Football League the following year. They made a steady decline through the leagues after the Great War and were eventually voted out of the Football League in 1970. The club entered financial problems as a non league side and were forced to sell their ground in 1973. They ground shared with Bradford City, but went into liquidation in 1974 with debts of £57,652. They were immediately reformed as a Sunday League club playing in the former team's colours.

The stands and buildings of the old Park Avenue ground were demolished in 1980, but the pitch and terraces remained. The derelict stadium was made fit for amateur football in the mid 1980s and the Sunday League club actually played at their spiritual home for a full season in 1987/88. An indoor cricket school was built on part of the pitch the following season and I recently read that the site is still a cricket ground today. Only a perimeter wall of the football ground remains and some of the bricked up terrace entrances can still be seen on Park Avenue with admission signs still in place. The club reformed as Bradford Park Avenue, their name from the former old stadium at Horton Park Avenue. The new entity was established in 1988 and played at the Horsfall athletics stadium where they have remained to date. They started in the West Riding County Football League and reached the heights, as founder members, of the Conference North in 2004. Former chairman, Bob Blackburn, unveiled plans in 2008 for a new 20,000 seat stadium at Phoenix Park in Thornbury and, also that year, claimed that the club would reach the Football League within four years, neither of which has happened.

Tonight, Avenue play the Evo-Stik First Division South outfit Loughborough Dynamo in the cup. I watched Loughborough play for the first time less than three weeks ago at my father's new love Grantham Town. That day they lost 1-0 to the league leaders. I was actually born in Loughborough, but have only returned to the Leicestershire town on a handful of occasions since we moved when I was just a toddler. After that match, my parents reminded me that I was born at home and not in a hospital. When we looked on a map we discovered that I was, in fact, born only a couple of streets away from their Nanpantan Sports Ground. I plan to visit the ground soon and was delighted to see that they are playing in Bradford this evening. The away side are now 7th in their league, just two places off a playoff position, after Saturday's home draw with Leek Town. They beat Stamford in the previous round to earn tonight's giant killing opportunity against their Premier League opposition. Bradford beat Stocksbridge Park Steels in the previous round on penalties. The Doodson Sport Cup is the sponsored and rebranded name for the League Challenge Cup. This cup gives the Evo-Stik clubs, Premier, North and South, a chance to win some silverware in addition to the FA Cup, FA Trophy and county cup competitions.

The stadium is to the west of Bradford, so I go the long way around, via Keighley and Queensbury, to avoid the rush hour traffic. It was a good plan and I am in the clubhouse by 7pm with a beer and the programme. Inside, I find around 30 Dynamo fans, all older than me, proudly wearing the yellow and black club colours. I assume they all came on the coach that I parked behind. The programme tells me that my club, well I am entitled to use this phrase if I want, were formed in 1955 by a group of boys from the Loughborough Grammar School. They had rebelled against the school's rugby only policy and secretly formed a football team. I dislike rugby more than pantomime so I like to think that I'd have joined the rebellion. At the time, Moscow Dynamo visited England to play Wolverhampton Wanderers. They took the name Dynamo and adopted the colours from Wolves. I proudly leave the clubhouse with the other Dynamo fans, hopefully to find an oval shaped ball to burst. The traditional colours of the former Bradford Park Avenue were red, amber and black, but I see that this has changed as the teams are now on the pitch warming up. Avenue now wear green and white striped shirts with green shorts and socks. Loughborough are in gold shirts and socks with black shorts. They do look like Wolves!

The Horsfall is an athletics stadium with just one stand, although it does run the entire length of the pitch with modern green plastic seats. There is a small terraced area on each side of the stand, but it is behind the goal line. I ignore the 'No Standing' sign. The clear sky has made it too cold to sit down, but I'm not that rebellious as I'm not alone. There is a building on the opposite side, where the players came from earlier, which looks more like a house. A couple of spectators have chosen to stand at the front by the advertising hoardings, but even there they are a long way from the play. The crowd feels very sparse tonight and will be lower than their average of 453 this season. I will be surprised if the attendance reaches 100. This cup has obviously not got the Bradford people excited. In contrast, a third of the crowd have travelled from Leicestershire. The game kicks off and the Loughborough fans appear to have blended in as there isn't an 'away end' as such to join. This is not helped by the stadium having just one stand of course. The seats are more full at the other end though because that is where Avenue are attacking. I stay at my end, now all alone, waiting to see my first Loughborough goal. It only takes twelve minutes to see Dynamo miss a good chance to score, but the ball goes wide from close range. Avenue respond with a similar miss two minutes later to suggest that we may see some goals tonight to warm us up. There are a few other half chances but the first half is not a spectacle for anyone. Loughborough Dynamo are doing enough to frustrate the home side. The away side become more resolute as the games goes on, dampening out any of Bradford's attacks, and come the closest to scoring. A defensive mistake by Jordan Deacey sees his attempted pass to James Knowles intercepted, but top scorer Jamie Clarke's right footed effort skims wide of the far post from just six yards. Clarke gets another good chance soon after, but his swerving shot from 25 yards is superbly tipped over by Avenue keeper Clark Lydon on his home debut.

Half time arrives just as I am getting restless. I really do not like watching football in an athletics stadium and this one is the worst I have been to so far. I didn't complain once at Goole or Grantham Town this season. I feel like I am miles away from the pitch, which even from my view has cut up with every tackle. And they have even run out of Bovril! The game itself has been ok with chances for both sides and probably just needs some goals. Loughborough should probably have gone in leading so they will be happy with their performance as the minnows. I just don't feel like I am part of the game from wherever I stand. This is so unlike Non League football where you can usually hear every sound in the game.

The game restarts as I begin my circuit of the ground with the intention of settling at the other goal where Dynamo are now attacking. I look up just as the game swings dramatically in favour of the home side. With only two minutes gone, Michael Duckworth strikes a stunning left footed shot from 30 yards that flies into the top corner. The Avenue now began to dominate proceedings with Rob O'Brien nearly doubling the score within minutes. The captain then gets on the scoresheet with another fine strike. He receives the ball 25 yards away from goal and hits a bullet into Loughborough's top corner. The keeper had no chance again with that goal and suddenly Dynamo are two goals down with only eleven minutes of the second half gone. Loughborough will now struggle to stay in this competition. I don't have much faith in them I'm afraid, so decide to stay behind this goal, all on my own.

The game and atmosphere gets flatter with just five noisy teenagers voicing any opinions. Everyone else is sitting in silence. Avenue still look the better side, but the manager makes a substitution in an attempt to liven things up again. He swaps John Deacey for James Knowles who gets his first goal of the season within minutes of his entrance. This time the goal is just a simple header from 8 yards, but it is enough to secure a quarter final place for his side. There is time for one final goal when, in the 84th minute, the impressive Duckworth gets his second and Avenue's fourth. This caps a miserable night for Loughborough. He hits a free kick from 20 yards that squirms under the arms of the Dynamo goalkeeper. The score line flatters Bradford, but they have managed to score three incredibly good individual goals. I am probably Loughborough's newest supporter, but I think the club will prefer it if I stay away in future. It was like watching two different Avenue sides tonight, so perhaps the players also needed a hot drink at half time to get them going. I leave this ground without a mug tonight and, unfortunately, I was not even tempted. It was always going to be a come down after Saturday's trip to the Turnbull Ground, but my vote is to leave athletic tracks for athletics. I would love to be a rebel tonight on this subject, but I suspect most football supporters will share this opinion. Let them play rugby in them!

Bradford Park Avenue 4 Loughborough Dynamo 0

Attendance 91
Admission £9
Ground Address Cemetery Road, Bradford. BD6 2NG
Club website www.bpafc.com
Twitter @Bradford_P_A

39

Fool

Harworth Colliery FC v Phoenix FC.

The Recreation Ground
Windsor Foodservice Central Midlands Football League
Black Dragon Division North
Tuesday 10th January 2012. Kick off 7.45pm.

Tonight I start a period of time at the basement of Step 7 with the next three trips, and perhaps more depending on the fixtures, being in the Black Dragon Division North. To date, I have only visited Kinsley Boys where a second half goal feast saved the day. I was, of course, at a running track only yesterday, but I feel the need to cram in an extra game during my last week of gardening leave. I actually did some gardening this morning which was cut short when I lost my wedding ring. After a mad panic, and losing an hour of my life, I somehow found it at the bottom of the gardening recycling bag. That will teach me to leave the sofa! Last summer when I put together my list of the then 66 clubs I looked at the websites of every club I hadn't heard of to double check that they were in Yorkshire. If you look at the Location section Harworth Colliery FC, on website www.pitchero.com/clubs/harworthcollieryinstitute ,it lists their address as 'Scrooby Road, Bircotes, Doncaster, S. Yorks DN11 8JT'. Tick and onto the next ground. But no, that would just be too simple. On Sunday night, after updating my Facebook page with my week's plans, I received the comment 'Harworth now in Yorkshire Michael?' with a link to another site. This 'Friend' certainly grabbed my attention and I quickly found myself staring at the following paragraph on Christopher Rooney's excellent website:

'The village of Harworth is situated further north than Sheffield, Liverpool & Stockport. It has a Doncaster postal code & Doncaster telephone number. However, do not let the Royal Mail & British

Telecom's South Yorkshire categorisation fool you. Harworth Colliery Institute are very much a Nottinghamshire football club.'

You bastard was my first thought but, yes, I am indeed a fool. Oh well, one less ground will certainly help me. Yes, but actually no. I had to come to see for myself. And here I am in the car park of Nottinghamshire's most northerly football club, but a couple of miles outside of God's own county. I am still studying my road atlas to see that I am further north than Dinnington Town (on my list and definitely in Yorkshire) and only a few miles from Rossington, but a comfortable distance from a certain vicious dog though.

The club was founded in 1931 and forged close links with the neighbouring Colliery that was established only twelve years earlier. Over the years, the colliery has been at the centre of the political battles of the miners' strikes. The club has played most of its football in local Yorkshire leagues and their glory days were in the 1980s. They reached the 3rd Round of the FA Vase and also won the Central Midlands Supreme Division title in 1988. In 2006 the colliery closed, but the illuminated huge concrete shafthead towers that remain guided me into Haworth from junction 34 of the A1. The ground is straight forward to find in my South Yorkshire Street Atlas! I get bored of sitting in my car. I have no idea where the pitch is, so head towards the bright lights of what appears to be some kind of clubhouse. I enter a very busy room, one half youth club that has a bar and a lot of people staring at me. I order a pint of Stones in my deepest voice before I am stoned to death for the Yorkshire Rose badge on my coat. I now know why the previous visitor came straight out and back into his car. The other people soon get back to whatever they were doing before I opened the door, which it seems was shouting swear words at each other. At least I still have an East Midlands accent and will watch darts on the TV if needs must. Someone on twitter tells me to smile and call everyone youth. I think I need the F word too in any sentence spoken in this room.

I finish my pint quickly, but in a casual manner, and go back outside in the hope that some floodlights have now been switched on. The full moon is now making me nervous as I'm not sure they are used to strangers around here. That was yesteryear you may say? No its still here in these parts. I drop my money into a Quality Street tin as I go through the gap in the wall. I had read that the ground needs some tender love and care. The one stand, a solid home-made steel box with corrugated iron roof, would indeed benefit from a lick of paint. The stand offers standing room only but protection from the elements. There is also the remains of a brick building on the opposite side but it looks too far away from the pitch to be a stand. In the absence of a running track, the usual perimeter fence, or even a wall, the boundary tonight is a length of painted rope. To my left it looks like there is a BMX track behind the goal, which is a first on my travels. Harworth Colliery, with the Institute word now dropped from their title, have orange shirts and socks with black shorts. Phoenix are wearing a Notts County style black and white striped kit. The away side have travelled from Rotherham and they will get the privilege of my company in the coming weeks. The match starts, but I decide that tonight is not going to be a game I will want to describe to my own family, let alone the nation. I think honesty is important and feel I have gone beyond my duty just being here. I am not even in Yorkshire, my battery is almost flat, I left my notepad in the car and without a programme I haven't got a bloody clue who anyone is running around in front of me.

At half time I am surprised to find both a programme and a pin badge can be bought from the clubhouse. Three sheets of A4 for a pound is steep, but the badge is impressive at the usual price. I notice that Black Dragon made this particular badge. I knew I had seen this logo before, which is appropriate in a league that they sponsor. The programme lists a different website address which may make it clearer that they are not a Yorkshire club. However, it just redirects me to the pitchero site when they had Institute in their title and a different club badge. No doubt it will trap another fool in the future. I do chat to a few locals and everyone, in fact, is very friendly. I stand behind the goal in the second half, which lasts for twenty minutes before I return to my tin shed. I got fed up of fetching the ball for every goal kick and corner! Every time it happened all twenty two players looked straight at me. I watch the game and the details are simple. It isn't pretty. Neither team ever really looked like scoring. I survive and manage to watch almost 88 minutes of a poor game of football. Yes I am a fool. Although, I expect there is a better word, even a medical term, to describe me. Let's find the A1 and head north. I even resisted singing a song that was playing in my head all night. Now that I am in the privacy of my own car: "My garden shed, my garden shed, is bigger than this....."

Harworth Colliery 0 Phoenix 0

Attendance 68
Admission £3
Ground Address Scrooby Road, Bircotes, Doncaster. DN11 8JT
Club website www.harworthcolliery.co.uk
Twitter None found

40

Twix inspection

Bentley Colliery AFC v Westella & Willerby

Bentley Miners Welfare Ground
Windsor Foodservice Central Midlands League
Black Dragon Division North.
Saturday 14th January 2012. Kick off 2pm.

I may have stayed in the Step 7 Non League basement but I am definitely in Yorkshire this afternoon. I packed away the Under 7's kit this morning in record time despite not being able to feel my fingers. I bolt my lunch without getting indigestion and jump in the car at 12.30 as planned after some extreme de-icing of the car. I take my wife's car as it is fitted with a DVD player for my passenger Lucas. I can also see the benefits of her Sat Nav following my day, last Saturday, in Whitby. I head to the market town of Thorne, which, I believe, is the usual mix of brass bands, surrounding moors and a coal mining history that you would expect to find in South Yorkshire. Thorne is a "tough town with a friendly club "according to one of my twitter followers. The ground is outside of the town centre in Moorends, so I don't think I will get to see very much to confirm if this fact is true or not. I read up on the area and football club last night so I am very well prepared today. I have learned that the town has been called, by more than one person I assume, Little Holland. This is because of the flat countryside, big skies, canals and windmills. If the football team play like the great Dutch sides I will be happy. I start my new job on Monday, so it will be harder to find time to do my research and I may not appreciate the mad rush that the 2pm kick offs generate. I am both excited and nervous in the same emotion. I have enjoyed my three months at home, but I am now very ready to go back into the rat race. On Thursday we got confirmation from a scan that I have achieved something incredible from my garden; Mrs Mowbray is eleven weeks pregnant. Oh and he or she will even be born outside of the football season!

Today's visitors to Thorne are Kinsley Boys who gave me my debut at this level of football. To make up for the half time cup of tea, the team scored nine goals on that November afternoon to cushion my reality bump. It will be tight, but the computer in the car tells me that we will arrive at Thorne Colliery FC with ten or so minutes to spare. We are not far into the journey when we get a telephone call from Mrs Mowbray to say that the game is off due to failing a pitch inspection earlier. I had feared a frozen pitch after playing this morning on grass that felt more like concrete. Therefore, I had introduced my wife to the Central Midlands website and asked her to check the other games closer to the kick off time. All that research and preparation! Bentley Colliery's game is still on so I pull over and the DN8 postcode of Moorends is changed to DN5 0PN. I have no idea where Bentley is in relation to Thorne and put my complete trust in Tom Tom. I drive to the edge of Doncaster and a long series of right and left turns take me to the bumpy car park of Bentley Colliery Cricket Club. I can see the back of a small football stand in the distance and head towards it. The small screen doesn't quite get me through the turnstile, but I manage to get to the ground with less than ten minutes of the match played. Without the invention of Satellite Navigation ground number 40 would not be happening today as it would not have been easy to find this ground unprepared. The ground doesn't have any floodlights to guide me in.

No computer system in the land could have located the turnstile anyway as they don't appear to have any. Instead we are greeted by a man sitting at a table at the corner of the pitch. He does at least have a menu styled board with the prices of admission and a handful of souvenirs. He looks quite pleased to take £10 off me when he was probably preparing to take his tin away. That price included two pin badges and a programme so I am happy with my part of the bargain too. The ground is basic, as you would expect, but the size and structure of the main stand exceeds my expectations. The solid brick build covered terrace gives this venue a much more football ground feel than my previous two trips in this league, Kinsley and Harworth. On closer inspection the ground looks very neglected in places. We head to the steep steps set back from the pitch and just catch a goal being scored. A player in the black and white striped kit strikes the ball from close range is as good a description as I am able to provide. I don't see anyone cheer from the small number of supporters and can just about match the badge on the other team's shirts with my recent purchase. After a quick glance at my programme, I can confirm that Westella & Willerby have taken the lead. Bentley are playing in a dark blue kit with a lighter stripe down each side. After 22 minutes a well timed sliding tackle stops the away side increasing their lead. The brave lunge stops the striker on the edge of the penalty area when he looked confident to score.

The inside wall of our stand is painted white which allows the locals to express themselves with a lot of graffiti. Lucas likes the large centre piece, a rather well endowed "monster". We are sharing our stand with one other person, sat on a plastic garden chair on the top step, who comments to my son that "it's a good job you can't read". Indeed I think, as I read it for myself. I see graffiti all the time, but this is particularly attention getting! The ground is in an area that looks, using the non offensive phrase from twitter, tough. The parts of the village that I saw are a mass of speed bumped streets in a large council estate that feels unloved. These teenagers, a huge assumption I know, are not wanting to love each other. What they want to do to poor old Demi is much more physical and I wouldn't repeat on these pages. I now notice that a couple of the other spectators are also watching from matching chairs on the touchline forming a kind of mobile stadium.

I drag myself away from my literary adventure and back to the match. After 30 minutes, Westella get another good chance from a cross into the box. The Bentley defender scrambles the ball clear just as the forward is preparing his tap in. Westella look the better side and the league table in the programme confirms that they are currently

4th in the table. Bentley are 11th in a division of only 17 teams. The rest of the half is nearly all pressure from Westella. I am getting cold in the stand which is shading us from the bright sun, the very reason this game has survived the freeze. I hope that this is the reason our neighbour decides to up sticks and move his chair to the touchline.

The half time whistle blows allowing Lucas and I to also get some sun, but only after we have visited the tea bar. There isn't a clubhouse, so I suddenly appreciate the facilities that Harworth actually have. We do at least learn that it was Jonny Slater that scored the goal. The club make the offer in their programme that we can join them for a 'drink and a bite after the game in our clubhouse just over the road in "The Jet" at the cricket club'. The pitch may have survived the subzero temperatures but the chocolate bar we buy is frozen solid. It is, in fact, so hard that Lucas cannot bite into it until the last stretch of our lap of the pitch. Believe me, he tries at regular intervals! We discover that the tarmac path ends at the first corner flag so the frozen muddy bank slows us down. The players arrive back on our final stretch and an immediate attack by Westella & Willerby forces me to be a ball boy again. Lucas is not happy with my new role either and screams "I want to get the ball daddy". "Sorry we don't have time as they are waiting to take a corner" gets a smile from the players. The Bentley fans are soon calling for me to be replaced as the quick corner results in a goal for the away side. After a couple of attempts the ball is crossed to the head of Phil Winn who is standing on the goal line. Westella & Willerby take a two goal lead and their players' voices are the only cheers to be heard as there doesn't appear to be a single away fan here today.

We sneak back onto the stand which now has four people standing at the back. Within 5 minutes of Lucas running around in front of them we are on our own again. He was in a lively mood so I needed to watch him now more than the game. I am very happy to do this. The game has now died and I nearly died on his last game when I lost him. I haven't counted a crowd for a while, more difficult at recent trips to places like Huddersfield and Barnsley. After two attempts I arrive at the same number 23, I count just the adults including myself. After 65 minutes Bentley have a good long range shot which the keeper can only push away for a corner. They waste the corner and a minute later Westella should have scored a third goal. The shot is inches wide of the post to everyone's surprise, including the home keeper who was preparing to get the ball out of his net. The sound of church bells at a nearby wedding and the distant view of some cooling towers are now getting more attention than the players. The away side get another good chance, but their number 10 is pushed to the ground as he is about to head the ball in the net. His cry for a penalty is rewarded by a good telling off by the referee which looks harsh. The last ten minutes are uneventful so I manage to read the programme from cover to cover to learn that Bentley Colliery FC were re-established as recently as 1976, in The Doncaster Sunday Alliance League. They won just about everything in the Sunday League so turned to Saturday Football, firstly in the previous Bentley League and then to the Doncaster Senior League. Again, they were so successful they obtained promotion to the Central Midlands League in 2000.

Today I have visited, despite Jack Frost's best efforts to sabotage my plans, my 50th Non League ground. This is not a bad number when you consider that I only ventured outside of the Football League 15 months ago. The Avenue just needs someone to love it again! One of my twitter followers, Tony, tells me that it was once "great", complete with floodlights and proper changing rooms when the old Bentley Victoria, which folded in the late 80's, played there. I am sure that they had enough cupboard space then to store their chocolate bars and keep their cold fridges for the milk. The Thorne-Moorends Town Council website uses the slogan "There's No Place Like Thorne" but in my little world there isn't any place quite like The Avenue. Without Route 66, I would probably have gone to Selhurst Park today to see Leeds. Wherever you go in this division, it is an awful long way from the Championship in every way! At least the early kick off will allow me to listen to second half scores on the radio, or Pepper Pig is the reality today. The cold weather is the thorn, or should I say

Thorne, in the side for other Non League fans, but to me I will take this hassle every week. I am in desperate need for more Tuesday night fixtures to stand any chance of completing all of the grounds. In addition to Thorne Colliery, there were also postponements at unvisited Hall Road Rangers, Dinnington Town, Hallam and Farsley. Just don't play them all on the same evening and I will be a happy man!

Bentley Colliery 0 Westella & Willerby 2

Attendance 25
Admission price £3
Ground Address 105 The Avenue, Bentley, Doncaster. DN5 0PN
Club website www.pitchero.com/clubs/bentleycollieryfootballclub
Twitter None found

41

Every cloud

Hutton Cranswick United FC

Rotsea Lane Sports and Recreation Centre
Sunday 15th January 2012. 10.25pm

I am on my sofa reading the Bentley Colliery match day programme to wind down. I start my new job tomorrow so I am attempting an early night. Pete Tooth's 'Secretary's View' page grabs my attention with, "Due to Hutton & Cranswick's departure from the CML we have had no home game since November". I know that name. They are on my list! Where have they gone? As always, Twitter is asked this pressing question before I go to the internet. Follower Tony, once again, provides me with the answer within minutes; they "packed up last month". I am not sure how I missed this news as a regular browser of everything Non League. If Tony ever writes a book of his own I recommend that you buy it! The penny drops with this author as I remember wondering on Tuesday night why the Northern Division only had 17 clubs in it. It is unusual to see an odd number of teams in a league.

I am directed to an excellent article by Richard Lusmore who is the kind soul who recently told me on Facebook that Harworth Colliery are not in Yorkshire. Richard is on the committee of Easington United AFC, still to be visited, and is another individual who exposes my relatively low knowledge of the local Non League scene. I am sure it must take years to get to this level of an anorak. The piece was written on the 1st December after the announcement came though that Hutton Cranswick United FC resigned from the Central Midlands League with immediate effect. The club had done so well to battle from the Driffield & District Football League to Step 7 football in the CML in just two decades. The reasons cited for the club's demise are mainly financial. Richard writes, "Lack of support in the local area has proved a major factor. Despite a recent showpiece occasion against Hull City in the ERCFA Senior Cup, which managed to pull in a crowd of just under 200 to Rotsea, the wolves weren't kept far from the door for long. When the two league games either side of that tie brought in 14 each (with 7 and 6 away fans, from Glapwell and Parkhouse respectively) and the cost of the match officials is over a hundred quid, it doesn't take a genius to work out the difficulties".

Richard goes on to say that, "My league season will not be the same without the trip to Rotsea, where the post-match hospitality was quite rightly lauded as the best in the league and where, whatever the result, the likes of Denis and Chairman Jim would always be on hand for a pint and a chat afterwards. When I express my disappointment at the loss of this club, I speak for many at Low Farm past and present (it was no surprise that both the current and previous First Team bosses were among the first to get in touch to express their sadness at the news). Not for them or me the 'told you so' smugness that may well emanate from certain quarters of the East Riding at what may be seen as another club that got too big for its boots. Always 'better to have tried and (ultimately) failed than never to have tried at all'. And as Denis is keen to point out, it was bloody good while it lasted".

It is sad when a football club departs but, personally, I am surprised that more don't close their doors more often. The silver lining is that my list of unvisited Yorkshire clubs has reduced from 25 to 24 all from the comfort of my sofa. Although, I now wish that I could have experienced that hospitality before they disappeared. I better get to bed before I disappear from the wage roll!

42

I quit

Bridlington Town AFC v St Andrews

The Neil Hudgell Law Stadium
East Riding Senior Cup Quarter Final
Tuesday 17th January 2012. Kick off 7.45pm

It is my second day in my new job and after 3 months of pottering around at a leisurely pace, to say it's a shock to the system would be a huge understatement. I am exhausted already just from the change in routine. In all honesty, I just want to hibernate after dark until I have adjusted to life back in the fast lane. The cold, dark mornings do not help, but today I swapped the warmth of the train, and more time under the bed covers, for scraping ice off my windscreen at 6.30am. This was to enable me to leave work in my car to stand in the cold at a football ground. I obviously love standing in a freezing field, but tonight it is going to take quite a match to make me really want to be there. I have enjoyed every single match so far, only the damp Brighouse car park managed to fizzle out my fire. I feel that I have therefore earned this mood! Tonight I am going to watch Westella & Willerby play in the Phoenix Trophies Floodlit Cup North. Now you can see why I have made the effort!

Just as I am starting to tidy up my desk, and get more interested in visiting a sports village in a college, I have one final check of the Central Midlands Football League website. It now shows the match as 'postponed due to frost'. I am not sure whether to leap for joy or weep. After a couple of minutes of thought, I decide that this news is a bad thing based on the huge effort I have made earlier to get to this point. After a ten minute spell of searching the bookmarked websites, I come to the conclusion that the only game to survive the frost is Bridlington Town. Why did it have to be one of the furthest away? And a ground I had already hobbled around! I don't trust the website so phone the club. It is only 5.20pm, but to my surprise a female voice answers with a cheerful greeting of "hello brid town“. I suppose the word Bridlington does have a staggering 11 letters. My direct question gets the response, "The nets are up but we have only just arrived". I explain that I am about to leave Leeds which not only gets her attention, as if I am a traveller from a foreign land, but she seeks guidance from her colleague. "I think you should call back in half an hour". I do just that, but a little nearer from a multi-storey car park in Leeds, and in plain clothes. I receive a more confident, but not totally risk free, response of, "We think it's on". A 160 mile round trip is a long way to travel for a "think" but, hey, there is at least hope, and I am beyond hope.

The drive soon feels like the longest 75 miles of my life. It takes twenty minutes to just get out of Leeds thanks to my fellow working community joining the rush. I can't help thinking of them all heading to the warmth of their sitting rooms. I follow the signs from the M62 to Brid (its catching) but, I must have come off the motorway far too early. The A164 from Howden is nothing short of awful. It is not a great road to drive when you are in a rush but the freezing fog is now questioning my sanity on every blind bend. The temperature is dropping fast, but my internet assistant, Mrs Mowbray, who is checking their site from home doesn't call me, so I just keep driving. I arrive into Bridlington, but then go round and round in circles in search of the ground. I may have been here in November but I was approaching from the opposite side of town and, of course, on foot! At least I see the harbour this time, twice, but eventually I recognise the chip shop where I dropped my sausage last time so things become clearer. I finally arrive with the temperature at minus two. To my relief, the flood lights are on and I can hear the sounds of the players shouting at each other to boot the ball a bit higher. I enter the turnstile and I am quite relieved that it is only 7.55pm, so I haven't missed that much of the 'action'; just ten minutes feels like a positive result in my mind. 'Can I go home now?' is my first thought. Bridlington Town are in their all red kit with white sleeves. The away side are wearing blue and white hooped shirts, blue shorts and socks.

The club were formed in 1918 as Bridlington Central United. They joined the Yorkshire League in 1959 under the changed name of Bridlington Town. In the mid to late 1960s, Town built up a rivalry with fellow Bridlington side, Bridlington Trinity. During the 1966/67 season in the Yorkshire League, Town won the championship while Trinity finished second. The following year it would be Trinity who took the title and Town finished in third. This rivalry continued until the early 1970s when Trinity became part of the Midland League. Town marched on to the Northern Premier League Division One. The 1992/93 season was the most successful in the club's history, they finished as champions of the NPL Division One and they finally took the FA Vase at Wembley, beating Tiverton Town 1–0. Alan Radford scored the only goal of the game. The bright spell did not last. Due to legalities, the team were forced to play their home games at Doncaster Rovers' Belle Vue ground. The club went into turmoil. They finished 21st in the NPL Premier Division and were deducted three points. Instead of going into NPL Division One, they folded. A local pub team, The Greyhound, approached the lease-holders of Bridlington Town's former stadium, Queensgate, looking for it to become their base. A deal was struck under the condition that the team would change their name to Bridlington Town AFC, essentially bringing the old club back to the town. They agreed and a new club crest was designed and a new motto "*Pergere et Eniti*", meaning "*Onwards and Upwards*". The club returned on 10 September 1994, and were put into the league where they had originally played during their formative years; the Driffield and District League.

In the first half we have a goal from Craig Hogg (19 minutes), some sausage and chips (26), and two more goals from Josh Greening (30 and 44) to give the home side a 3-0 lead and me a full belly. At half time, exhausted by writing the above detailed match report so far, I head to the clubhouse to buy my usual souvenir pin badge. The words "the shop's closed tonight" slap me across the face. Closed? What! The fact that there isn't a programme is absolutely fine. It is a small crowd after all and there was some doubt to whether there would a game at all in this weather. The lack of souvenirs, however, is unforgivable. My mood is worsening and the fact that I can't feel my fingers isn't helping, even though this is totally my own fault for leaving my gloves in the boot of my car. There is no diet coke at the bar, but the battered, and greasy, sausage went in the bin so I have calories to play with. All of these other things I can live with, but, please, someone sell me a bloody badge! I storm out, back to the match, feeling short changed that won't change even if the game now becomes a twenty all thriller.

The second half only gets worse for the minnows, St Andrews. I don't know anything about this team except that they are below the Step 7 of Route 66. They get punished by Billy Logan (58 minutes), Danny Brunton (65 and 73) and Robert Hawkes (70) to make them, no doubt, feel as low as I do. The 7-0 score line is a little embarrassing. St Andrews' Ross Ellerby does at least try to make things more respectable in the 76th minute by pulling a goal back. The whistle blows to remind me that I need to get home. Off we go again! I decide to head out of Brid towards Scarborough and pick up the road to Leeds at Filey. It's going to be a long journey home, but it is my last ground after all of Route 42. If you don't like my match report then please complain to someone who cares. I quit. In fact, I bloody quit.

I pick up a message on my Facebook page just after midnight. Thanks to the involvement of the very familiar Richard Lusmore I have a Friend Request and Direct Message from 'Brid Town Leon':

Hi Michael,

Please send me your address and i will sort you out with a badge. Really sorry that club shop was shut. Joe who normally looks after it lives in Ripley. It is Derbyshire I think and probably chose not to travel due to the cold weather. I will hopefully get you a badge on Saturday. If not it will be at our next home game.

Cheers
Dom

I click the Like button, whilst pulling a face, and head upstairs with my tail firmly between my legs. Let's see how I feel in the morning...

Bridlington Town 7 St Andrews 1

Attendance 73
Admission £5
Ground Address Queensgate, Bridlington, YO16 7LN
Club website www.bridtownafc.webs.com
Twitter @BRIDTOWNAFC

43

Ready

FC Halifax Town v Gainsborough Trinity

The Shay

Blue Square North

Tuesday 24th January 2012. Kick off 7.45pm

I had last weekend off from Route 66 duty which gave me some time to reconsider my position after my resignation. A stay in a 5 star hotel and a trip to Ibrox was exactly what I needed. We had planned a weekend in Barcelona for my 40th, but, thanks to the Spanish changing the fixtures, I chose Rangers verses Aberdeen instead. To some this would be a disappointment but it was actually the perfect weekend. Sometimes it is the simplest of things that make a weekend when the usual demands of our children have been removed. The best cooked breakfast I have ever eaten (even at the £17 per person price tag) served at a civilised 10.30am is just how to start a day. The large freestanding bath full of hot soapy water that was waiting for me after the 1-1 draw felt like heaven. Ibrox is an incredible stadium that only gets better with 46,000 lively Rangers fans inside. I sat in the middle tier of the Archibald Leitch designed Bill Struth Main Stand. It was built in 1928 and quite rightly granted a listed building status in 1987. It has more character in every single one of the red bricks on the facade than the majority of today's grounds. I would have loved to have sat on one of the original seats, then made of cast iron and oak. The noisy 'Ultras' to my left were more entertaining than the match and, surely, can only put on that level of performance with a lot of rehearsing. The Broomloan Stand Theatre!

Tonight I am going to try again to watch Westella & Willerby play Kinsley Boys in Round 1 of the Phoenix Trophies Floodlit Cup North. This match may feel a little small in comparison to my last ground! I am more positive today than I was seven days ago, helped by the milder weather at the dizzy heights of 6 C. I needed to come to work in my car anyway today for a meeting out of town. A much improved build up, that is until 5.25pm when I check the Central Midlands Division website that gives me the surprising news that tonight's cup tie is postponed again. This time it is a waterlogged pitch. It has rained a lot today, but not enough for me to even consider this happening. I had, however, found a plan B match last night at FC Halifax Town, to be prepared for this very scenario. I had planned many months ago to visit the Shay on 14th February when Guiseley will be the visitors, all very romantic as I know, in their case, that absence does make the heart grow fonder. I cannot, unfortunately, see that any of the other unvisited teams are playing at home. We may well have six feet of snow on Valentine's day so I decide that a ground in the hand is definitely worth two in the diary at this stage of the season. I join the rush hour traffic for the much shorter drive from Leeds, which is welcome now that the fog has appeared.

An hour or so later I arrive into Halifax and I am now really looking forward to my first visit to The Shay. The name 'Shay' is derived from the old English word 'shaw', which means a small wood, thicket or grove. The two words are used interchangeably in ancient references to the property upon which the Shay Stadium was eventually constructed. The team are therefore known as the Shaymen with the ground being home to the club since 1921. It is also now the home to Rugby League side Halifax and once to the Halifax Dukes Speedway team. Please note that it was the Shea Stadium in New York where the Beatles played in 1965! This information proves that my smart phone is much smarter than me. I have caught a view of the tops of the floodlights on numerous occasions as it stands beside my favourite route to the west bound M62 from Ilkley. I am well overdue a look inside this famous old ground.

The West Yorkshire town of Halifax was the centre of England's woollen manufacture from the 15th century onwards and, in more recent times, known for the Halifax Building Society. Nothing stands still and the Building Society, founded in 1853, was first taken over but eventually became part of Lloyds TSB in 2009. The once largest residential mortgage provider in the UK needed 'A Little Extra Help' themselves to stay afloat and the local workforce breathed a sigh of relief after their survival. I arrive at the stadium and then quickly head off towards the town centre in search of a cash machine, which really should not be a problem in this town! I have the money, almost £15, for a Step 7 cup tie and probably enough for every chocolate bar that the Bishop Burton Sports Village ground sell, but the £12.50 admission sign here panicked me. I return within fifteen minutes with some readies and enter the ground through the back of the modern East stand. This seated stand was only opened in March 2010 after the previous Family Stand was demolished in 2000. Relegation and financial problems slowed, and even stopped, the completion of this stand. I am immediately drawn to the pitch for my first look inside. There are two deep covered terraces at each end, so it looks more like a League One ground. One of them appears to be home to the majority of Halifax fans with the opposite end closed, unless you are a large flag needing a lie down. I recognise some of the collection of flags from my September trip to the CNG Stadium. On the other side there is the older seated Skircoat stand, which is also closed tonight. I instantly warm to the Shay, even with half of it out of bounds, and would love to return for a big match. They drew a crowd of 4,601 in November for the 4-0 FA Cup defeat to League One leaders Charlton Athletic. This tie had tempted me but we had family staying with us that weekend.

Halifax Town AFC went into administration during the 2007/08 season after finishing 20th in the Conference National. They were demoted by three divisions to the Northern Premier League Division One North when the club failed to get a Company Voluntary Arrangement passed. The club owed over £800,000 to Her Majesty's Revenue and Customs making them more than £2 million in the red. At a meeting of the Football Association, discussing the makeup of the football pyramid for the 2008/09 season, Halifax Town were not placed in either the Football Conference, the Conference North or the Northern Premier League Premier Division. Their appeal against the decision to remove them from the Football Conference was unsuccessful and the club was wound up. The Supporters' Trust prepared a back-up plan to form a new club should it be required, but the club was reformed by the same directors of the previous legal entity under the name FC Halifax Town. They were accepted to play in the Northern Premier League Division One North in the 2008/09 season. After a season of consolidation, they won back to back promotions to climb the pyramid to the Conference North. The former club once spent more than 80 years in the Football League and could be back within less than 18 months from now. Promotion again this year would clearly be a huge achievement for Neil Aspin's side.

The teams run out into what feels like an empty ground with the Shay having a capacity of 14,061; this is huge for Step 2 of the Non League. Halifax Town are all in blue and the visitors from Lincolnshire are in yellow. The Shaymen make a very lively start knowing that a win will move them to second in the table. I decide to put away the match day programme, which is from New Years Day when the game was postponed but with a new cover on, as I can see a lot of goals being scored if the visitors' defence stays this open. After just 9 minutes the Shaymen put away their first good chance of the game to take the lead. The number 10, Lee Gregory, accepts the pass and then comfortably curls the ball into the bottom corner, which the keeper had no chance of saving from close range. The home side now have most of the play and almost grab a second after 25 minutes. The shot is wide, but it is enough to prompt some singing on our terrace that inspires more pressure from Halifax. With five minutes or so left of this half I suddenly realise that I have not had anything to drink all day except for a lot of coffee and a beer at lunchtime. This must be the reason that I am so thirsty. I decide to beat the half time rush in search of water, which is bound to produce another goal. The walk from the back of the terrace to the half way line does almost do that for Gainsborough, but the ball is hit straight at the keeper. Halifax then hit them on the break away, but the striker's legs run out of steam and he falls to the ground in the box. I'm sure he looks around to complain that I am still watching play!

I return just £1.50 lighter and to the sight of a group of players in yellow celebrating. I really do have this knack! The whistle blows whilst the 20 or so away fans are still cheering Andrew Boyce's strike. I sneak back to my previous place on the terrace hoping that nobody links my disappearance to a very unjustified equaliser. Half time is given to a junior 5 a side match and their skills certainly impress me. Their ability to pass the ball at their age is great to see, now with my Under 7's Coach hat on. I think, and also hope, that these boys are much older than my side.

The players arrive and I will now stay on this step until that final whistle blows tonight. Halifax are attacking this end and they can concentrate on their next goal now that I am not going to collapse of dehydration, although I have to admit thinking that it would help Guiseley if they do lose! Halifax now look less adventurous and I can also tell that the equaliser has given Trinity a boost. Chances fall to both sides and on the hour mark Halifax deserve a solo goal from Danny Holland, but his final shot doesn't match his skillful run. Someone on Facebook, whose brother in law is here tonight supporting the away side, asks me how they are doing. I write "second best in every position but growing in confidence... Oh yes, Trinity now 2-1 up". There is a good break down the wing, a cross and then a tap in from Connor to give the visitors the lead that looked impossible for the first 45 minutes. At least I can offer my Facebook friends live match commentary!

Halifax react well after going behind and have several good chances to score. They play some good football on each occasion to get them in a good position but only to shoot wide of the post. Tinity have dropped back to absorb the building pressure from the home side. Halifax substitute, Cameron Darkwah, picks the ball up 25 yards from goal, he turns skilfully, but his drilled effort goes just wide of left post. The on-loan man from Stockport is starting to cause problems down the right hand side. His low cross finds Dean, but the striker can't apply the required finish. Just when it doesn't look like it will be the Shaymen's night, Garner must have read my thoughts and puts the ball in the net for 2-2. A low cross finds Dean, his shot is blocked and Garner hits it hard to generate a huge cheer of relief. Needham almost grabs a third straight from the restart and it is now all Halifax. Gainsborough are panicking every time they lose the ball but, despite constant pressure, they survive to earn a good point. Halifax stay unbeaten but the crowd look disappointed as they depart the ground. They really should be very happy with the progress made both on and off the pitch, but expectations have risen in this part of West Yorkshire.

It wasn't the trip that I had planned, but The Shay has restored my enthusiasm for Route 66. It is a fantastic old fashioned football ground. They just need to grow back into it to feel the benefit of all that space. The Football League will one day be richer with FC Halifax Town there. Last Tuesday's tantrum at the seaside was just a blip and I probably just needed a hot bath and a cooked breakfast to draw a line. Ibrox is probably the best ground I have visited to date but, in its own right, I have found a little gem here that is only 23 miles from my doorstep. Although, in thick fog, it does feel like I am crossing the Scottish borders as I return home. The Rangers motto is 'Ready' and with the Bridlington wobble now well and truly behind me, I am now ready to finish this hopping marathon.

FC Halifax Town 2 Gainsborough Trinity 2

Attendance 1,300
Admission £12.50
Ground Address The Shay Stadium, Halifax, W Yorkshire. HX1 2YT
Club website www.halifaxafc.co.uk
Twitter @FCHalifaxTown

44

Ball boy

Thorne Colliery FC v DFS Welbeck Welfare

The Welfare Ground
Windsor Foodservice Central Midlands League
Black Dragon Division North
Saturday 28th January 2012. Kick off 2pm

I am hoping that Thorne Colliery isn't going to turn into the new Westella & Willerby. I am going back to the Step 7 basement today for my second attempt to tick Thorne Colliery FC off my list. After the usual rush that these earlier kick offs bring to my Saturday mornings, following football training, we are on the road for 12.30pm. George is with me but, quite wisely, Lucas used his party invitation as an excuse to avoid the cold. We listen to the radio commentary of the Liverpool verses Manchester United FA Cup clash to amuse us on the hour and twenty minute drive. We also have sandwiches to eat on the way to save time and avoid any disappointment over poor refreshments. As we drive down the M18, the sky does actually look huge as promised on my visit to the 'little Holland' I have read about. The surrounding countryside is flat and it is a clear day so there is a lot of sky to observe. I leave the motorway at junction 6, turn left on the edge of the town centre and a mile later we are in the village of Moorends. I drive through a 'tough' estate and we arrive at the Welfare Ground with five minutes to spare. There is another one of those big wheels at the entrance, which I now know is the 'headgear' of the shaft tower of the former pit. Thorne colliery was worked until 1956 at which time it was closed for major shaft repairs. It stayed shut, but was kept on a care and maintenance basis with the intention of reopening should the market for coal improve in the future. I read last night how the locals were shocked in 2002 when the decision was made to close the mine. Many thought it would eventually be the last working coal mine in England due to the massive reserves of coal still left underground. The pumps were turned off in 2004 and the following years they started to fill the shafts.

Records show that Thorne Colliery FC was formed in 1929 where they originally played football in the Yorkshire League. The club attracted a crowd of 750 for one match in the early days on what was described as the best playing surface in the County. The current side finished 7th last season and are now one place higher to suggest that they are making good progress. The back of the large main stand, marked TCFC, dominates our approach from the car and confirms that we are at the right ground. I also recognise the stand from some pictures I found prior to my previously planned visit. It looks like it needs a lick of paint, but it is certainly big for this level of football! Someone on Twitter told me that the ground has been home to the club since 1929 and he believes that the stand dates back to the 1930s. I have also been told that some of the 'Colliery Boys' supporters are quite lively. Perhaps they get excited by their big stand! One old photo from the car park included the shaft towers beyond the pitch which have sadly gone. We follow the back of stand around until we find a middle aged couple at an open gate. The players are also arriving at the same entrance from an outbuilding behind us. There is a programme to buy but I get a response of "I knew I should have brought some with me" to my pin badge enquiry. To my surprise, she then offers to sell me hers from her coat! I don't have the heart to tell her that George wanted one too, but feel I have done well for my £2.50. I assume that it has been discounted by 50p for wear and tear.

Thorne Colliery line up in their blue kit with the visitors, Welbeck, wearing black and white striped shirts, black shorts and socks. The huge concrete construction naturally draws us inside without the need for a discussion. It runs two thirds of the length of the pitch with the rest of the touchline benefiting from a rope to lean on. There are wooden benches on the edges of most of the steps but we decide to stand at the back, unlike the other six people inside. The rest of the crowd, ten or so people, have all chosen the warmth of the sun on the touchline. Disappointingly, there are no noisy fans here today with just the sound of the players and one very noisy visiting keeper. Yes, I am fairly certain that it is the same player who entertained me at Kinsley, but just need to hear the phrase "lifeline" to be absolutely certain. He let nine goals in on that day, yet, despite that, in my opinion he played quite well.

The game enjoys the usual end to end start where the players haven't quite settled into an organised formation. Both teams are handed a similar chance in the first ten minutes. A good through ball, or a bad defence, but the keepers both read each chance perfectly and get to the ball first on the edge of the box. It doesn't take long for George to find a friend, a boy of a similar age, but the main draw is he has a football. Without the need to communicate any rules, they start to play a game of throwing the ball to each other. That sounds harmless; accept George is standing on the top step of the stand with his partner being at the bottom. This game soon becomes irritating to the others in the stand, which includes me. In the 24th minute Thorne score a goal. I miss the final touch thanks to the other ball in play almost hitting me in the face. George doesn't learn his lesson and within a couple of minutes his misjudged throw results in a second ball being on the pitch. I am relieved to see the linesman retrieve the ball, but then hear a cheer to my left. Welbeck have equalised. I have missed the goal again and it is game over for George.

Two other boys start to play a similar game and the ball again goes onto the pitch, "three times" according to George who now has serious ball envy. I witness the third crime myself which forces a Welbeck defender to kick it away. It doesn't appear to be a problem for anyone taking on the parental role for these juvenile delinquents. The Thorne number 11 continues his good game and scores with his second attempt on goal after 36 minutes. A good cross comes into the box, he hits it straight at the keeper who can only palm it back to his feet for 2-1. In the 40th minute Thorne score again with a header, but the linesman's flag goes up. I don't think it has been allowed, but then I get distracted with some excitement between the away bench and someone in the crowd. Liverpool have apparently scored an 88th minute winner which spreads to the players. Two of the Thorne players even let out a cheer at this news whilst continuing the other game that they are involved in. The whistle blows to end the first half and allow the Thorne keeper to check the result from Anfield. That produces another cheer because he apparently had £5 at 17/2 for a 2-1 home win.

At half time we head towards a portokabin expecting to find a toilet, so have mixed feelings when we discover it is a canteen. My usual Bovril is an Oxo cube in water, but at least it is hot and only 50p. There isn't a clubhouse, but George is happy to eat a burger with crossed legs and tell everyone around us that he wants to go to Ibrox one day. He is proudly wearing his new Rangers top, an obvious present from our abandonment of him last weekend.

As the second half starts, we finish our wander and settle behind the goal where Thorne are now attacking. I can see now that it is definitely the same keeper who entertained me in Kinsley. We arrive just as the ball needs retrieving. The players all look at me, but this time I have a ball boy, the perfect Non League accessory! George loves it before anyone calls Childline. "Shall we stay here daddy?" "Why not George!". The Welbeck keeper, who is called Tom Chambers, also looks happy with our setting up of camp. On the second occasion George passes Tom the ball, I ask him my burning question if he was in goal at Kinsley. "I was. We were unlucky that day". I smile and enjoy the moment. This really is just perfect. George can finally play with a ball whilst I enjoy the warmth of the South Yorkshire sun in peace. The score remains 2-1, or perhaps 3-1 if the previous goal was allowed, thanks to our hero's efforts in goal to maintain that lifeline. Eventually, his defence make an awful mess and the home side get the goal they have been threatening for a while. His response was very accurate, "That's come from our own goal kick boys" after the Thorne player runs through unchallenged and fires in from close range.

It is all one way traffic now, but with most of the shots on target so helper George is not as busy as the home domination warrants. Corner after corner, save after save and I am kept busy giving George instructions to keep play flowing. He sometimes wants to give the ball to Tom rather than the player waiting to take the corner and we have a responsibility to the Yorkshire side to keep the game moving. With around 5 minutes left, the lead is extended with a lovely shot from outside the area into the top corner . A couple of minutes later, the Thorne striker runs through again and this time chips the keeper for another goal. ”You can have that one” he says with a smile. That was a fine strike in any league. Despite the scoreline, the Welbeck keeper has played well this afternoon. Tom may need to change teams though as his side are firmly rooted to the bottom of the league without a single point. What would their minus 79 goal difference be without a decent player between the sticks?!

The final whistle generates a groan from the small boy standing next to me who just doesn't want to leave his duties. "There are no more balls to chase now George. Let's go home”. His work is done this afternoon. ”Nine times I got the ball”. It felt like more than that but ”good work” is my response. ”But I wanted to get to ten daddy". There really is no pleasing some people. I now know why they don't charge admission for children. If only there was a pit to send them down to earn their keep.

The following day, after many hours of searching the worldwide web, I find one line of text that confirms that the goal scorers for Thorne were Callum McCormack, Scott Rhodes (4) and Neil Sheppard with Welbeck's goal coming from Mark Stirland. Yes, that is 6 goals for Thorne and not 5! I can't find the time of the goals, let alone a match report, so I can't even attempt to lie to my readers. Quit? I should be sacked. You'll have to excuse me as Manchester United getting knocked out the FA Cup got us all a bit flustered in Yorkshire.

Thorne Colliery 6 DFS Welbeck Welfare 1

Attendance 48
Admission £3 (children free)
Ground Address Grange Road, Moorends, Thorne. DN8 4NA
Club website www.clubwebsite.co.uk/thornecollieryfc
Twitter None found

45

Bingo!

Westella & Willerby AFC v Yorkshire Main

Bishop Burton College
Windsor Foodservice Central Midlands League
Black Dragon Division North
Saturday 4th February 2012. Kick off 2pm

On Tuesday I had planned a third attempt to watch Westella & Willerby against Kinsley Boys in that now well known Phoenix Trophies Floodlit Cup that just doesn't want to happen. However, when I checked the website at lunchtime the tie had been switched to Kinsley 'due to the pitch at Bishop Burton being declared unfit'. I do hope that the hoards of away fans got the news in time. Instead, I chose a lot of cider and a trip to Elland Road to see the 7 minute defensive collapse that lost manager Simon Grayson his job. If the only Yorkshire ground I don't manage to visit this season is the Genix Healthcare Stadium please beat me to death with a copy of the rough draft of my unfinished book. A 4-1 defeat to Birmingham City was not a great result for Leeds but sacking a manager just hours after the transfer window has shut says a lot about the ambitions of the club in my humble opinion.

Back to today's match. It is minus 2 degrees outside with heavy snow forecast for the afternoon. I definitely need more than a plan B and, despite having ten options, I don't really expect to see a ball kicked today. I arranged the games last night in order of priority with my original plan of Kirkbymoorside now sitting in tenth. The steep climb up, or slide down, Sutton Bank is really not a place to be in snow. I hate driving in snow anyway, so I put the nearest grounds at the top of my list for the shorter drive. I am now sitting on the sofa to check my bookmarked League websites. I will cross them off as they get postponed to play a kind of Route 66 version of bingo. It is 11.30am and within minutes, after checking four sites, nine games have fallen to frozen pitches. I will not be blessing Garforth Town, AFC Farsley, Hemsworth MW, Albion Sports, Worsborough Bridge, Maltby Main, Hallam, Handsworth or Kirkbymoorside with my presence today.

There is just one match still on and once again the words Westella and Willerby are staring back at me. If their pitch was unfit on Tuesday it will surely be on its knees today. I check their own website that I know from the previous disappointments is usually up to date, but it still shows it on. There isn't a telephone number listed to call so I spend my time refreshing the news section and checking the fixtures on the Centre Midlands site. At 12.15 I grab some lunch, refresh Mrs Mowbray's memory of the sites to enable her to keep checking and jump in the car. Of all the games to survive, or appear to present a glimmer of hope, it is the furthest away and with the earlier 2pm kick off! It has started to snow as I leave Ilkley, so I decide it is worth having a full tank of fuel just in case. The friendly young man in the petrol station asks if I am going far as the weather looks "grim". He tells me, whilst pointing at his screen on the counter, "11cm of snow in Ilkley between the hours of 3pm and 6pm" and it really makes me think long and hard; well long and hard enough to phone Mrs Mowbray who calmly and confidently tells me that "the main roads will be fine". Indeed they are and by the time I pass York the snow has completely stopped. The temperature gauge is still below zero which makes me very nervous. I don't understand how the pitch can be anything but as hard as concrete. I phone Mrs Mowbray again to check she hasn't forgotten all about me, but both the club and league websites still say that the game is on. I concentrate my efforts on how hard I am going to hit the person who tells me the game is off but didn't update the website. I clearly have a problem.

As expected, I don't quite manage to make kick off and arrive at 2.10pm, which could have been later if the entrance to the College wasn't so well sign posted. I take a left turn before I get to see the village of Bishop Burton that is on the edge of the market town of

Beverley. The club were formed in 1920 and were long time members of the East Riding County League. The 1960s were a successful period for them. After a lean period in the 70s and early 80s, there was an influx of new young players into the club, primarily from Wolfreton Secondary School. Some of these youngest are still involved in the club today, such as the current Chairman, Secretary and Director of Football. In 2003, Westella & Willerby became the third FA Community Club in East Riding along with North Ferriby United and Hessle Rangers. This season, the club will field a record 24 teams at a wide range of age groups and including a women's team.

I pull into the car park and drive up to an area that, at first glimpse, looks like tennis courts but then I see there is actually a football match taking place. This is the sort of scene you will see at any 5 a side centre with 3G pitches. I recognise the kit of Westella & Willerby so I presume the reserves must also be playing. I wonder where the game is? The penny then drops. No surely this is not it?! I leave my car, with my mouth still wide open, in search of a gap in the fence to take a closer look at the play. I find the entrance on the far corner which has a Bentley Colliery style table and chair turnstile. There is also a small notice board that confirms that the action on the plastic (a modern version accepted) in front of me is the Black Dragon Division North fixture I have rushed across Yorkshire to see. Before I can even think about exchanging any cash I have to ask a burning question to the man blowing warm air into his hands. "I can see how this game has survived the weather because of the artificial pitch. But what happened on the previous three games that were called off?!". This is a very good question, but I wasn't expecting the very simple response of, "We only get this pitch on Saturdays". This is the reason I have struggled to see this venue under the floodlights but it now appears to be the only Non League fixture being played today.

They don't have any pin badges in stock and after my eyes check his coat for souvenirs to bid for, I also check that the score is still goalless. I do at least buy a programme for a pound to take inside what I am now wondering would stand up to the definition of a 'ground'. There are some dugouts and that is basically it! There isn't even a perimeter fence to separate the crowd, a handful of people admittedly, from the touchline. I had always thought that this was a basic requirement to play at this level. We are, at least, close to the action, emphasised when a Westella player runs down the wing and a couple of spectators feel the need to take a few steps back. I have seen Westella play already on my travels, so I recognise them instantly in their usual strip of black and white stripes. Yorkshire Main are playing in red with a black stripe on the shoulder of the shirts. The visitors are currently fourth in the table, just one place below Westella, and have travelled from Edlington. This is a town near Doncaster that I will hopefully be familiar with before May.

The game is competitive enough, but no team has been able to create a single chance as such. Some goals may take my mind off the bitter cold wind that I cannot shelter from, or whether I will get back to Ilkley in the snow that the wise oil man warned me about. In the 32nd minute the home side do get the first good chance but Jonathan Slater heads the ball against the crossbar. If I was to add any more detail to the first half I would be being creative for the sake of it; not that I could actually write anything down if it did happen due to my numb fingers.

At half time I wander the corridors of the modern college building to find the toilets that appear to be used by the gym. It all feels a bit strange as I read the notice board on how it's never too late to learn a new skill. I arrive back to see the end of the team talk, on the pitch, and they soon restart the game in attempt to keep warm. I am told, as I examine my watch, that they have chosen a shorter break today because "snow is on the way". Yes, a fact that is now finally sinking in. Westella start the half in a positive manner and the players look like they have got a 70 mile drive home afterwards too. In the 54th minute the home side miss a good chance in a game that will surely finish 1-0 at the very best. Craig Havercroft's fine shot is tipped over the bar which, unfortunately, is as exciting as this one gets.

I have to admit that this ground is just too Non League for even me (if that sentence makes any sense). It is not the 3G pitch that makes me feel this way. I actually think these are a great idea for Non League football played in the winter. It is rather that standing on the same flat surface as the pitch with a dozen other people in the grounds of a college is just not how I would choose to spend my free time. I am so cold and, with no shelter from the chilling wind on offer, I decide to watch the last fifteen minutes of the game from inside my car. This is certainly a first for me, but I feel better that I am not the only person who has this idea. I actually get a good view of play after driving my car close to the fence. It feels like a drive in cinema but without the drama, although Westella look like they have had a couple of chances to win during the final ten minutes of the match. I have at least paid my money to earn my opinion that these teams wouldn't score if they played all weekend. The whistle blows to move Westella to second place as I turn the key for my quick escape.

The snow is starting to settle on the ground as I leave, but I fear that there is a very different scene in Ilkley based on some of the texts from my wife. The final one tells me to leave the car at the front as I will only get stuck if I attempt to park it at the back of the house. If someone on the outskirts of York would have offered me the freezing fog of Bridlington, I would have snapped their hand off as the roads are progressively getting worse with every mile. I soon discover that these roads are nothing compared to the fun and games that is waiting for me for the last 20 miles of the journey. The tyres are now sliding with a blanket of snow covering every surface. I'm not sure when the roads around Otley were last treated, if at all, but the packed snow is only made more interesting with the freezing slush underneath . As I pass the Ilkley petrol station, I curse under my breath for ignoring the wise man's advice. However, within minutes of the comfort of my sofa I start to smile. Only now can I appreciate that I have been very lucky to visit ground number 45 today and I can finally put a large tick next to Westella & Willerby. More importantly, there are nine evening fixtures to come at grounds that I still need to visit. There is some hope at last. Today may be that pivotal moment in my season. I have turned that corner and really do believe I can do this now!

Westella & Willerby 0 Yorkshire Main 0

Attendance Not recorded
Admission £3
Ground Address York Road, Bishop Burton, Beverley. HU17 8QG
Club website www.westella-willerby.co.uk
Twitter None found

46

A passion

Garforth Town AFC v Ossett Albion

Genix Healthcare Stadium

Evo-Stik Northern Premier League First Division North.
Tuesday 14th February 2012. Kick off 7.45pm

I clearly love football and I'm sure that my recent fling with the non leagues has enough longevity to go beyond the lust I am feeling for the grass roots game. Therefore, standing on a touchline is the natural place for me to be on Valentines Day. Mrs Mowbray luckily agrees that this day is just commercially driven nonsense, at least enough to not be having a candlelit supper with the milkman tonight. I do go as far as buying a card but always use the space to write something to emphasise that our love is 365 days a year and not when the retailers need to fund the gap between Christmas and Easter. Clearly my wife loves me, or, I suppose, she hates the sight of me, to not show any resistance to my passion of visiting every ground in Yorkshire in a single season. Passion is the word that I have chosen to use and is very appropriate today. The gap between ground number 45 and 46 was prolonged due to the cold spell but it became very mild yesterday. Almost the entire Non League fixtures were wiped out last week and over the weekend to create many midweek fixtures to look forward to. Tonight I am in Garforth as it is quite simply my only option. I am, of course, happy to be here, particularly with a short journey across West Yorkshire on offer.

Garforth Town, known as The Miners, were established in 1964 as a local pub side called The Miners Arms and played in nearby Swillington until 1976. They soon acquired their own ground in Garforth, a former rubbish dump, and changed their name to Garforth Miners to enable them to gain entry into the Yorkshire Football League as pub sides were not permitted. In 1985 they changed their name again to Garforth Town and moved to their current ground in 1998. In 2003, life got more interesting for Garforth Town with the arrival of Simon Clifford. Simon bought the club, cleared their debts and eventually managed the team. He expressed a strong ambition to climb the pyramid and use his strong connections to Brazilian football. He went on to achieve 2 promotions in just 3 seasons to get them to their current status. Simon grabbed the attention of the media nationally and internationally with the signing of Brazil player Socrates on a month's loan deal as player coach. He played for 12 minutes as a substitute against Tadcaster in front of 1,385 fans during the 2004/5 season. The following season, another former Brazilian international, Careca, arrived after coming out of retirement. On 26 September 2010 it was announced that former England star Paul Gascoigne had become manager, but he apparently changed his mind at the last minute. All of this for a team playing at Step 4 of the Non League Pyramid!

I have already been to the Genix Healthcare Stadium when I saw Chester win promotion here last April in a dramatic game. Despite the away side being spurred on by the majority of the 2,428 crowd that day, they lost but still went up on goal difference. The ground looks very different tonight upon arrival, but I enjoy getting a car parking space with great ease. It is probably the most accessible ground in Yorkshire, just a mile from junction 47 of the M1. A left turn, through a modern housing estate and you will see the very recognisable shape of their main stand. Its height and distinctive roof can be seen from the motorway in daylight. I buy a programme and head straight into the clubhouse, mainly because there is one on offer tonight. Also, I couldn't get in here on my last visit due to some very thirsty Chester fans. The first thing that I notice are the various framed Brazilian shirts on the walls but, thankfully, no red roses or chocolate hearts. Just the words Ronaldo, Romario and Pele are enough to excite me even before I see the photos of Rio behind the bar. Understandably, the programme is the edition from 4th February when the game was originally due to be played, when I was having much more fun in the Beverley snow of course. The news of Rangers

FC entering administration today is dominating the news on the big screen. I promise this decline had nothing to do with my recent visit to Ibrox. It is very sad and a reminder that it is not just non league clubs that sail close to the wind. Living within your means is vital for a football club of any size.

I enter the turnstile and manage to complete a quick lap of the touchline before the players enter the pitch. The large main stand looks good from every angle, not just from the motorway! There is also a small bus shelter styled area behind one of the goals that 6 away fans with their 2 large flags make into their home. The rest of the ground is surrounded by a solid perimeter fence and a concrete path. It looks very windy up in the big stand so I find a nice spot on the touchline exactly on the half way line as the game kicks off. Garforth Town play in Brazilian style yellow shirts, blue shorts and white socks. The visitors, Ossett Albion, the ground where visitors risk a bee sting rather than a greasy chip, are in white shirts with black shorts and socks. The crowd feels small as the sound of the players shouting echoes around the ground.

Garforth make the better start and their flowing football is usually only broken by a rash challenge from the away side. The Miners deservedly win a free kick on the edge of the box after 9 minutes. The resulting strike hits the cross bar despite it looking like a goal from the moment of leaving Paul Walker's boot. There are a lot of hard challenges from Albion that produces some good banter off the pitch and some good football played in between. After 24 minutes Ossett score against the run of play when Simon Poole's cross is met by the head of Adam Hayton forcing Ben Higginson to parry it away into the path of the Richard Tracey with all the time in the world to slot it home. The next 20 minutes see some lovely possession football for Garforth, but apart from a couple of free kicks they don't actually look like scoring. Although they do hit the bar and then the post in the 40th minute with a header that looked very much the equaliser they deserve. The Garforth players all scream for a goal as they appear to think the ball may have crossed the line. I am not sure so keep out of the squabble. In one of the final kicks of the half, Ossett almost score themselves from a shot that is deflected just wide of the post.

I return to a very snug bar at half time to shelter from the cold wind. I enjoy the moment thanks to some latest scores, a diet Pepsi and a lad selling a range of pin badges from the corner. The time flies in my club house heaven, but that's life really. The football I have seen has also been enjoyable. Garforth are clearly the better football side, but I can see this physical Albion side getting another killer goal on the break. Just like how England would approach a game in Brazil if we are going to continue with the South American theme.

I brave the gale as I climb the steep steps of the main stand. You would struggle to find a better view from the back row at this level but, as feared, it is bitter cold up here. I get rewarded with second half radio commentary, focused on the Leeds United game at Coventry, via the man in front of me. As well as the game, I have a good view of the motorway and what I think may be the Emley mast in the distance. My grasp of the local geography has improved over the last six months. The game follows the trend of the first half, with Garforth having all of the play. The final ball is always disappointing and Albion continue to hit them on the break. In the 58th minute it is no surprise when Ossett take a two goal lead despite it looking like one of their players had handled the ball in the build up. The play continues and Matthew Patterson applies the finishing touch with a neat chip from outside the box. The height of my position in the stand gives me the perfect view of the very confident finish. The huge cheer from the passionate few was justified and inspires some singing from both sides. Garforth again respond immediately but, again, don't make the most of their chances to pull a goal back. The Miners get even more frustrated in the 75th minute as a claim for a blatant foul on David Brown by goalkeeper Jody Barford, which is a clear penalty, is turned down. A header from the resulting corner has power but it is directed straight at the keeper.

Just as I write down the words 'I can't see them scoring tonight' the tables turn with just over ten minutes to go. Garforth finally get a goal thanks to Price's cross to Paul Walker who forces Jody Barford to make a good save. Luckily Matthew Mathers is there to apply the same type of finish as Tracey had done earlier. The tempo is raised and the home players now have a renewed confidence on the ball. They get a second a moment later with some good play on the right by Paul Walker who plays in Mathers. His cross is eventually tucked in by Ben Thornton to get the equaliser which looked impossible at the hour mark. I am still updating twitter when I look down from the gods to see the Ossett players celebrating after being awarded a penalty. The fans around me look gutted, but they are not complaining about the decision. Adam Hayton calmly steps up to score the winner from the spot in injury time. This feels cruel, but Ossett had controlled the game for the majority of play. It has not been the Miners night, but I hear two fans blaming their fortunes on the windy conditions. I am tempted to tell them all about my night at Selby Town, but decide instead to leave with the others to return to our loved ones. We have all seen a very competitive game and, appropriately, the romance of a last minute winner. Not bad for the price of a bunch of roses!

Garforth Town 2 Ossett Albion 3

Attendance 79
Admission £7
Ground Address Cedar Ridge, Garforth, Leeds. LS25 2PF
Club website www.garforthtown.com
Twitter @GarforthTownAFC

47

I get my kicks from Route 66

Yorkshire Main FC v Thoresby Colliery Welfare

Edlington Lane

Foodservice Central Midlands Football League North Division.

Saturday 25th February 2012. Kick off 2pm

I am standing in a cemetery on the edge of the South Yorkshire village of Edlington with George and his uncle Archie. "I've found it!" I shout enthusiastically. Although it was always going to be me who did as George doesn't really know what he is looking for. Archie is just going through the motions whilst texting Auntie Tina and wondering what he's doing here. I read the words out aloud in an attempt to generate some more enthusiasm, "Born James Town, Accra 28th October 1865. Died Edlington 13th December 1930". This is the grave of Arthur Wharton who is widely considered to be the first black professional association football player in the world. The words on his grave continue with the statement "The goalkeeper with the prodigious punch who would crouch in the corner of his goal until the last moment then spring into action to make fantastic saves". He was given a headstone in 1997 after a campaign by anti-racism group Football Unites, Racism Divides. It is an unusual way to start a game, but without twitter follower Tony's help (once again) giving me the instructions of "half way down on the left" we would surely have struggled. It may well have taken us, or me, several hours to check every headstone, and knowing my OCD tendencies I probably would have done just that.

It's now 1.45pm, so we need to get moving on the short walk back to the ground where we parked the car earlier. I could easily use this start to ground number 47 to discuss the vast subject of racism in football and find a link with the game ahead of us. It would be very topical at the moment after the recent events and, in my opinion, disgraceful behaviour witnessed at Anfield. Thankfully, we have moved on since Arthur's playing days, and probably with every decade that passes, except for what I consider to be isolated cases where certain people really should know better. I appreciate, however, that we shouldn't rest until racism is totally kicked out of football as it has no place in a modern society, let alone a sport that is governed by highly paid professional people. My view on this subject with my Route 66 hat on is quite simple. Yorkshire is an ethnically diverse county and I would love to see this reflected more at games, both on the pitch and in the stands. Today I will watch 22 players and 3 officials take part in a game of football and their skin colour, religion or culture has no relevance to me at all.

We turn left after the fire station, pass the cricket pitch and follow the view of the tops of six floodlights to where Yorkshire Main play their football. The club started life in the 1920s as a village Colliery side under the name Edlington Rangers. In the late 1950s a committee split led to a new name and the formation of Edlington Welfare FC, which later became Yorkshire Main FC. In 1983, the team joined the newly formed Northern Counties East league, but the following year disaster struck with the start of the miners strike. In December 1985 the Yorkshire Main Colliery closed, but the club continued despite losing many committee members and players. In 1991, the new requirements on the league included floodlights so many clubs, including Yorkshire Main, were forced to leave. Not having floodlights was still a problem at a lower level, but they eventually got these fitted in 2010 after 3 years of applying for grants. Fittingley, they then won the Phoenix Trophy Floodlit Cup in their first season with lights! Last season they also won the Doncaster & District Challenge Cup, the Central Midlands League Challenge Cup and Premier Division Championship to achieve their most successful season in the clubs history. Following the reorganisation of the Central Midlands Football League last summer, they now play in the Step 7 North Division where they currently sit in 4th position in the table. This afternoon's visitors from Nottingham are two places behind them, but have seven games in hand on the leaders Clipstone Welfare.

We arrive at the tea bar that stands before the 'turnstile' and I am immediately impressed by paying just £1.35 for two Bovrils and a Fruit Shoot. The inside walls are covered in interesting looking football themed pictures and old team photos. I need to return at half time when we have more time. We put our money in the tin, pick up our free programme and even the pin badges are priced at the rock bottom price of just £2 each. This is definitely the cheapest ground to date and I will struggle to spend more than £10 today. We make our way to the pitch as the teams run out of the changing rooms, which are also housed in the same outbuilding. Yorkshire Main are in red with a black stripe on the shoulders of the shirts. Thoresby are all in blue with hint of white on the shirts to match their white socks. Inside the ground, or perhaps a more accurate description would be through the gate, it all looks a bit odd. It doesn't take me long to solve the mystery as I realise that there isn't a perimeter fence of any sort. A sign tells visitors to either stay behind the wire fence around the clubhouse or go to one of the two shelters that are situated either side of the half way line. The majority of people flock to the bigger of the two stands on the far touchline. There are numerous crumbling concrete posts surrounding the pitch to suggest that there may have once been a fence. The stand is small but solid. The walls are made from breeze blocks and support a corrugated iron roof to cover some shallow terraced steps. This is only the second ground to date without a fence. However, it still feels very much like a football ground, perhaps because of the stands and a grass pitch, although Archie is less enthusiastic and describes the surface as, "A field with lines on it". No, fields don't usually have floodlights is my response.

A group of young children distract me by their continuous shouts of "Steff...Steff...Steff" who, Archie says, is one of the home players after finding a Stephan in his programme. This is confirmed when, during a throw in, a player turns around to tell one of the kids to "shut the fuck up". You can just imagine David Beckham shouting like this at Brooklyn before taking that last minute free kick against Greece at Old Trafford. It is becoming a day of firsts when I also notice that the linesman has got the largest beer belly I have ever seen on an official to date. It is also the first time anyone has openly smoked cannabis at a football ground. The smell is unmistakable from the nearby group of teenagers. I'm sure this will cause much less damage than the problems alcohol can bring to our football grounds. At least if they get the munchies the snacks here are cheap! On 22 minutes we see the first chance of the game when Yorkshire Main win a free kick on edge of the box. Unfortunately, the shot hits the wall and, a couple of rebounds later, the number 7 balloons the ball over the bar from close range. After 26 minutes the second spliff is lit and the first bag of sweets is eaten at our end of the stand. To the trained eye, as it's not that obvious, it seems the Yorkshire side are having more of the ball than the opposition, but the sky is still seeing more of it than both sides. On 34 minutes, Thoresby get their first chance, although I am being kind with my choice of language after the striker attempts a volley that ends up in the middle of the wicket of the neighbouring cricket pitch.

The award for best drama in the first half belongs to the Yorkshire Main's manager who gets over excited by a decision from the referee that he must have seen differently. His language gets extremely colourful and he soon self destructs. It is similar to watching those police reality programmes when the drunk man just needs to shut up and walk away, but he doesn't and he's being pinned to the floor by six officers. The ref sends him off, confirmed by our chilled out neighbour's shout, "They've sent Dave off". He simply takes two steps back to the fence from the touchline and continues to swear at the ref from his new position. I buy a raffle ticket with today's grand prize consisting of 4 cans of lager. In my opinion this is still a good investment of my quid, unless the 4.0% proof will result in me starting a fight with the locals. On 45 minutes there is a strong run by Yorkshire Main's number 9 from the half way line and he hits a good shot from the edge of the area at the keeper. The ball is dropped, but none of his team mates are close enough to take advantage of the fumble.

The whistle is blown for half time and we head straight back to the tea bar. George enjoys our direct route across the pitch. This time, a packet of crisps and a Mars Bar set me back a staggering 90p. They are consumed whist studying the photos, but I am soon drawn to a large map on the wall. It is covered in pins in for each club in the North Division. I don't know where to look first and decide instantly that I really want one of these for Yorkshire on my wall! I then notice where Easington is and I now understand the "Hull Riviera" comment on twitter last week. I had assumed it was a suburb of Hull rather than a village practically in the sea. Going to this ground in daylight is now a must and I may take my trunks. The sound of the players' studs walking on the path outside stops me from counting the number of clubs in Nottinghamshire.

Within a minute of the restart the home side shoot over the bar from close range giving me hope for some goals today. George finds a stray ball to play with on the sidelines so we come out of our stand to ensure he remains in our sight. The match ball does come to Uncle Archie who actually shows some skill to trap the ball and pass back. "Careful. You'll be on in a minute" I warn him. Now that would definitely be a first. There is a lot of pressure from Yorkshire Main who now look more likely to win it. They look good until they reach the edge of the box where they seem to get blinded by the sight of the goal. Thoresby occasionally break out of defence but that always ends in disappointment too. With just over 5 minutes left of the game, there is a great move by Yorkshire Main, but it is halted by the flag of our pot bellied linesman. He looks onside to me, but it doesn't deserve the abuse from a group of lads. When the play is at the other end he turns around to politely explain his decision to them and a man on crutches who has hopped over to him. It was a well constructed argument for his decision which shuts them all up and prompts them to light up another spliff for the road.

Thoresby get a corner in injury time as we are starting to prepare for home. To my surprise the ball lands on the head of their number 9 and it flies into the back of the net. The cheers from the away bench drown out the final whistle and Yorkshire Main have suddenly lost the game nobody in the ground would have predicted. Obtaining the number of fans who have witnessed this goal will be a challenge, so I ask the man, who looks official, as we cross the pitch what the attendance is. "We don't record it". I prompt for a number and make some progress with "about 20". I continue my questioning, but this time to one of the coaches from Nottinghamshire who tells me that Gary Panting scored that dramatic winning goal. I am learning! I, like those young men, will also leave this ground on a high. This is not just down to seeing a lively ending to an otherwise ordinary game of football. I am lucky to be able to actually get a kick from watching a dull game of football without anything stronger than an Oxo cube.

Yorkshire Main 0 Thoresby Colliery Welfare 1

Attendance "About 20"
Admission £3 (Juveniles free)
Ground Address Edlington Lane, Edlington, Doncaster. DN12 1DA
Club website www.clubwebsite.co.uk/yorkshiremainfc
Twitter None found

48

A room with a view

Kirkbymoorside FC v Silksworth Rangers

The Recreation Ground
Wearside Football League
Saturday 3rd March 2012. Kick off 2.30pm

Today I have gone all strategic. Over several evenings last week, I put together an (almost) earth moving spreadsheet. It came very close to cracking the Route 66 code in linking the remaining times I can attend a match with the fixtures of the 18 clubs left. I am now just one match away, which isn't a bad effort when you consider it looked like I would be 13 short before the cold spell. I was planning to visit Phoenix FC today, then follow the other 16 dates, somehow finding a way of getting to Kirkbymoorside before they go on their summer holidays. I was on the way to the recycling bin this morning with the Non League Paper and saw that the Moorsiders are at home today. I quickly came to the conclusion that I needed to go there today. It is quite a trek from Ilkley and therefore ideal for an afternoon where I am on my own thanks to two children's birthday parties. Mrs Mowbray may need a spreadsheet herself though to plan how to collect George and Lucas from different locations in Yorkshire at the same time. Secondly, I am not sure if Phoenix have floodlights for the option of a future evening game, but I know for sure that Kirkbymoorside don't have them thanks to Twitter. And finally Rotherham, where Phoenix play, is a lot more accessible than this North Yorkshire town. A structured argument to why this ground needed to be under my belt.

It was indeed a 'trek' and I arrived after a two hour drive caused by the Saturday shoppers of Thirsk and a few tractors who want to sabotage my book. The views from my climb up Sutton Bank were spectacular though on such a clear day. Kirkbymoorside FC were founded as early as 1890 and competed in local leagues, including the Scarborough League, for over a century. In 2006, they made the decision to try their luck at a higher level. After two seasons in the Teesside League, finishing as runners-up in Div2 and then runners-up in Division 1, they were accepted into the Wearside League at Step 7 in the Non League pyramid for the 2008/09 season. They finished a respectable 10th place in their first season and improved this finish by one place 12 months later. Last season they finished sixth and got to the final of the historic Monkwearmouth Charity Cup, losing out by a single goal late in extra time to Ryhope CW. The market town promotes itself as the 'gateway to the moors' and, on first appearance, it looks like a very nice place to live. We are only 24 miles from Scarborough and I must have passed this ground without noticing it loads of times as it sits just beside the A170. In my defence, it is just a pitch on the roadside. I park just after the sign at the entrance of the Kirkbymoorside Sports Field that also hosts cricket, bowls, tennis and a pigeon club. I cautiously approach the pitch as I know what pigeons do best and see the sign warning me that there are 'DEAD SLOW CHILDREN PLAYING' ahead. The group to my right look quite fast to me, but I discover that it is much more than a pitch on closer inspection. Despite the surface clearly needing the lines remarking, there are 4 corner flags and 2 dug outs! I first visit the hatch in the small wooden shed and, for a total of £7, I gain admission (the cheapest at £2.50 to date in Route 66), a match day programme and my usual badge. I could have spent a lot more too, with a scarf, car sticker and tie on offer. I can't see £2.50 being beaten if the other clubs in the Foodservice Central Midlands Division maintain the £3 I have come to expect.

Half of the ground is roped off, but the remaining two sides enjoy the luxury of a metal fence. I follow the other fans to where there is a raised bank of grass running along the pitch. That is it really; and not a great deal to photograph I tell my social media friends. There is a building behind the goal housing the changing rooms and, what I hope, is some kind of bar. There is a whiteboard on the outside wall with the teams written on it, but, again, the local doctor has contributed by writing them on. Or perhaps it is just me who can't understand joined up writing? The Moorsiders are the only Yorkshire side (well I hope and pray that they are) that play in the Wearside League. The other teams in this division are all based in the North East. Today's visitors have travelled from Sunderland, no doubt hoping for a better result today after losing 8-1 to Kirkbymoorside earlier in the season. They are currently second from bottom and just one place, but ten points, behind Kirkbymoorside. The Moorsiders are in red with a hint of white on their shorts. Silksworth are wearing blue shirts with white sleeves, black shorts and blue socks, and have strong mackam accents. I can count just 16 fans including myself, 4 of which are wearing wellies. This is the equivalent of 11,230 and a half (one boot on) supporters wearing their wellington boots at the game playing today at Anfield.

In the 16th minute the Silksworth number nine swings his leg aimlessly at a cross into the box. He is unmarked, but can only clip the ball as if he is also wearing inappropriate footwear. Our grass area is at least a real sun trap on what is now a lovely mild afternoon. I get my sandwiches out and it feels more like a country picnic looking out to the open countryside. Why is it that whenever I bring food there is always hot food on sale? Today I get to drool over the burger that the man next to me is currently destroying. It does look at bargain at just £1.50 as advertised in the programme.

After half an hour, Kirkbymoorside try a long range shot which strikes the large tree behind the goal. A minute later Silksworth have more luck and take the lead. The ball is headed against the inside of the far post but rebounds kindly to the feet of the number 10 for a simple tap in. Only 30 seconds later Rangers score again after the keeper drops a shot, but our much slimmer linesman puts his flag up. "Fucking embarrassing" is the defender's analysis, but I think he was offside. With ten minutes left to half time 11 people leave the clubhouse and gather behind the goal. This almost doubles the attendance and their casual shoes also spoil my wellington boot statistic. The away side win a couple of corners and now start to look the better side with more of the ball. However, with seconds left of the first half, Kirkbymoorside equalise. I get a good view of a well timed run onto a long ball, he rounds the keeper who has charged out and slots it in calmly to make it 1-1. After discovering the goal scorer was "Rob McDermid", I use half time as an opportunity to see why some had chosen the clubhouse ahead of the first half.

I go inside and I am sold instantly. This is indeed a nice space. My can of Strongbow and I are very happy. There are a lot of kids, all well behaved, and everyone is very friendly. Lucas would have liked it here with there being a couple of girls his age. I am, however, enjoying this complete relaxation time as, even when he is behaving himself, you can't completely switch off. There is a pool table, a large flat screen TV showing the latest scores, a jukebox and the usual team photos that I think are a must. Time certainly flies, which is not helped with the teams coming out five minutes early. Most of the Kirkbymoorside players stop to peer in to see the scores. The large window also gives me a very good view of the game so I don't feel any need to rush back out, despite my drink being portable. There is no mesh on the window like at Brighouse and it does look like it is clouding over outside. The officials are not out yet so nothing can happen without them. Cheers!

Within a few minutes of the restart Silksworth almost take the lead, but the shot is directed straight at the keeper from close range. I see all this from my barstool and I am not alone. There are a lot of people with the same idea and they all shake their heads to the Moorsiders' defending. The goals are flying in around the country and, I have to admit, I do get addicted to the high drama created by goals being scored in games I really should have no interest in. I can imagine how strong the pull of this room would be in bad weather, particularly with no cover on offer in the ground. I can see why you would pay your £2.50 to drink some cheap cans whilst watching your local team play from a far. This is much better than following the scores from your sofa. Of course, I am driving so I sip my cider slowly. You can bring your children to the game after they have spent the morning

playing for the junior side. If I had this set up at Ilkley Town... I would probably still travel the country to collect more grounds. In the 59th minute it becomes 2-1 to the home side. I see the ball hit the back of the net and the middle aged man in front of me punches the air, with his other hand safely on his pint. The sky outside is now black, but the rain hasn't arrived taking away that excuse for still being inside. I hear how Arsenal won earlier with a last minute winner at Liverpool and now they are going around the grounds I seem to have lost the use of my legs. Apparently, it's not a classic at the Britannia Stadium so the travelling Norwich fans are asking the Stoke people where their famous atmosphere has gone. This reminds me exactly why we stand outside for games, it's the atmosphere!
In the 65th minute Rangers make it 2-2 to the sound of people tutting whilst the other Rangers are winning at Ibrox.

This goal is enough for me to finally leave my seat and see the last twenty minutes in the fresh air. So far I have seen 4 goals, even if 2 were from afar. That works out at less than 63p per goal. Should I add the £1.80 for my cider to this equation? I seem to have jinxed this game by coming outside as the goals have now dried up. Both teams look like they have settled for a point in this bottom of the table clash. With around ten minutes remaining, Kirkbymoorside win a free kick on the edge of the box. There is a long build up and a quick glance to my left confirms that the tension extends to the clubhouse with at least 8 faces close to the window. The ball is struck well but, again, straight at the keeper who palms the ball away for safety. A few minutes later at the other end there is enough time to squeeze one last drop of drama for our money with a winning goal. A scramble in the box, a simple side foot and the goal price comes down to 50p. The Yorkshire side has been a little unlucky to lose this game but have provided great value for money in my opinion. I run to my car as it is starting to rain and before anyone asks me how much I have spent on petrol to get here. A bargain! Although I would pay more for names on their shirts.

The Wearside League website (eventually) tells me that Kirkbymoorside's goal scorers were Robert McDermid and Jack Chadwick. Gary Tyzack got the first two for the away side with Paul Muir getting the winning goal.

Kirkbymoorside 2 Silksworth Rangers 3

Attendance 43
Admission £2.50
Ground address Kirkby Mills, Kirkbymoorside, N Yorkshire. YO62 6DY
Club website www.webteams.co.uk/kirkbymoorsidefc
Twitter None found

49

A is for Apple

Hull City AFC v Leeds United

The KC Stadium

nPOWER Championship

Tuesday 6th March 2012. Kick off 7.45pm

Most books don't have as many as 66 chapters. After 48 chapters I am starting to think like a writer so I'm conscious that my book could get a bit repetitive – I arrive after a rush and getting lost in Wakefield, it's cold so I have a Bovril, I describe the ground, then there is a game of football and I go home wondering what normal people do with their Tuesday evenings. Therefore, I will attempt to give my readers a break and allow me to use my mind more than my pen. This is the A-Z of my evening...

A is for Apples. Crushed and fermented they produce a refreshing beverage that is absent from the vast majority of chapters. Tonight I have left the car at home and intend to be reacquainted.

B is for Boothferry Park. This was the tigers home until ten years ago and once held over 55,000 spectators. I have heard some refer to it as a "dump", but I may have found it beautiful if I had ever been lucky enough to visit it.

C is for Coach. This is definitely the most relaxing way to travel. Door to door transport without the hassle of driving and finding somewhere to park.

D is for Dull. It rhymes with Hull, but the recent games between these sides have been anything but, usually with lots of goals. That's the kiss of death then, so I now expect a goalless draw.

E is for Expectations. These are high for both sets of supporters who believe they must be in the Premier League. Hull enjoyed a recent taste of it and now they want more. Leeds are a huge club and "belong" there. It could all end in tears.

F is for Flat. The landscape on the approach to Hull doesn't exactly excite me, although it is nice to have some daylight to see the world we are passing, even if that world is the town of Scunthorpe.

G is for Grafton. The street in Hull where the band, The Beautiful South, were formed from the wreckage of the Housemartins. Their 1989 album Choke includes the track called 'The Rising of Grafton Street'. G is also for Google where I found this out thanks to having too much time on my hands with my phone replacing my steering wheel!

H is for Hull City AFC. The club was founded in 1904 but didn't reach the top tier of English football until 2008. Dean Windass scored an amazing goal to beat Bristol City 1-0 at Wembley in the Play Off final to promote his hometown club to the Premiership. Phil Brown became their most successful manager of all time and then defied the odds to keep them up in their first season.

I is for I am already struggling with this new wave of creativity. I need another drink!

J is for Jack Scrumpy. I am a great admirer of your work.

K is for KC. The stadium was opened in December 2002 and is now one of my favourite modern grounds. It is worth every penny of the £43.5m it cost. It is architecturally pleasing on the eye, mainly due to the imaginative roof design. Most importantly, it generates a fantastic atmosphere when full. Tonight it can't be far away from its 25,586 capacity.

L is for Leeds United. Tonight's visitors and now under the stewardship of Neil Warnock who is looking for his first win in his 3rd game. This is yet another 'must win' game for the large travelling army of Leeds fans.

M is for Match. A lively game played at a fast pace, but I don't really feel that anyone is ever going to score. Hull finish the first half strong, but Leeds have the better of the second period. Both sides lack quality in the final ball.

N is for Noise. The levels are high and one of the best atmospheres so far on Route 66. The stadium appears to trap the noise and spectators feel very close to the action on the pitch.

O is for One point each. Not enough for either side is the overwhelming opinion on the coach.

P is for the Premiership. The Premier League would be a much better place with some representation from Yorkshire, but I can't see either of these teams getting to the promised land this season. The top six are getting further ahead.

Q is for Queen. HRH apparently came to East Yorkshire in 1989 and she met former Hull manager Phil Brown. He described the experience as, "Better than winning promotion at Wembley". I wonder if her majesty felt the same?

R is for Roundabouts. The enemy of coach toilets! Perhaps they could turn this challenge into an Olympic sport. It is not a skill that this hopper possesses.

S is for Snograss. Robert had a disappointing game tonight. The word on the street, or the back seat, is that there is too much reliance on one player for Leeds.

T is for Tigers. "Tigers, Tigers rar rar rar" is probably one of the worst songs to ever be sung at a football ground. That is my thought of the night whilst others snooze around me. This number is now sung by the away fans in an ironic manner, complete with paw action.

U is for Unfair criticism on Neil Warnock from the man behind me. 3 games!!!

R is for Reading the match day programme to avoid an argument. This is a task that is much easier when you are not driving.

V is for Vikings. They may well have also stopped at Hull? Perhaps they are still there...

W is for Wetherspoons. The scene of the crime in Ilkley where ground 49 started at 2pm. I insist that my creative writing of this chapter is purely coincidental to my liquid lunch.

X is for Xpensive. I'm not great at spelling, but today has cost a lot of cash in comparison to the average trip and particularly to my last game. Add the price of the coach, which is actually cheaper than the petrol, to the ticket and I have spent over £50 before I even buy a programme.

Y is for Yorkshire. Where else in the world would you experience an atmosphere like this in the second tier of football? A disappointing result for both sets of supporters but playing this fixture next season is really not the end of the world.

Z is for Zzzzzzzz.... I am so tired. It must be all that fruit. Good night.

Hull City 0 Leeds United 0

Attendance 22,676
Admission £24

Ground address Walton Street, Kingston upon Hull, E Yorkshire. HU3 6HU
Club website www.hullcityafc.net
Twitter @hullcityteam

50

Wakefield A to Z

Hemsworth Miners Welfare FC v Penistone Church

The Fitzwilliam Stadium
Sheffield Senior Cup Quarter Final
Wednesday 7th March 2012. Kick off 7.45pm

Perhaps this A-Z will work better as I am sober...

A is for A roads. I have left the top flight motorways to return to Non League football. The A629 from Pontefract sounds simple enough but I end up on the A639. I turn around, just so I can then give the A645 a try. After wasting more of my life and petrol around Pontefract, I find the road I wanted by pure chance. Sign posts must be for soft southerners. I only chose this route to avoid getting lost in Wakefield again!

B is for Bovril. My beverage tonight and I could now murder one after negotiating the country roads to Fitzwilliam where Hemsworth Miners Welfare play their football.

C is for Cup tie. Tonight's game is in that well known Sheffield Senior Cup. I know I got lost earlier but, still, I didn't think that we were near Sheffield. I obviously still have much to learn. It is the Quarter Final and described as a "massive game" by the Hemsworth manager in the match day programme.

D is for Double burger. At £2.50 this wins the battle to be in my stomach and I settle down in the club house to tuck in.

E is for Emmerdale. There may be some 'tough' looking people around me, but all eyes are fixed on Emmerdale on the big screen. The quick read of the programme tells me that Penistone Church FC recently celebrated their Centenary by playing an Emmerdale All Stars XI where over 1,000 people turned up to watch the match! They will need to change channels to the Champions League soon to ensure the players receive a warm welcome onto the pitch.

F is for Frost. The freezing temperatures have returned and an overnight frost is forecast. Despite finding a window view of both teams lining up whilst also able to see the Barcelona v Bayer Leverkusen game on the big screen, I brave the cold wind. Hemsworth are wearing their usual royal blue kit with Penistone in black and white.

G is for Ground. It is basically two small seated stands opposite a modern clubhouse, although one stand appears to be just for the home and away dugouts. It is basic, but I am a man with basic needs.

H is for Hemsworth Miners Welfare FC. The club were founded in 1981 out of Hemsworth Colliery FC. They currently play at Step 6 of the BARIS NCEL Division One.

I is for Ipod. The one next to me tells us all that Barca have just taken the lead. Boring; another world class finish from Messi no doubt. Let me just have a peep through the window...

J is for Joint. The weed smells good in this part of Yorkshire too.

K is for Kitchen staff. Dawn, Jane and Alison are all listed on the honours page of the programme. A nice detail, but possibly not one for league clubs to introduce in the interest of saving trees.

L is for Linesman. The official on the far touchline may look good in his tight shirt but he certainly likes to wave his flag at every opportunity. This is winding up the Penistone fans, who must make up over half of the crowd.

M is for Mitch Savage. The number 9 gives Penistone the lead when he fires a shot into the top corner to generate a huge cheer from the travelling fans.

N is for Novelty condoms. These are discussed at length at half time and I couldn't help myself but listen. The conclusion is that savoury flavours are “just so wrong". No Bovril ones then?

O is for Oxo. Another 50p is spent on a cube. As a beef stock connoisseur, I definitely prefer Bovril.

P is for Pin-up. Turn to page 37 of the match day programme and you get a photo of a young girl in her underwear titled ‘One for the boys’. Priceless!

Q is for Quick glance at the TV on the way back outside. I am rewarded with a goal from "the best footballer on the planet". Messi completes his hat-trick in the 49th minute with a beautiful chip that actually backs up ITV's statement.

R is for Riley. Alvin steps up in the 65th minute to take a penalty with a confidence that Messi himself would have been proud of. 2-0 to the giant killers.

S is for Semi finals. These surely now await Penistone with just Worksop, Sheffield and Frickley Athletic standing in their way of a final at Hillsborough on 8th May.

T is for Tray of meat. I didn’t win tonight’s raffle, but, in all honesty, I am not that disappointed.

U is for Unknown OG. This is how the BARIS NCEL website describes Hemsworth’s lifeline in the 85th minute. In their defence, I can’t shed any light on this one! The whistle blows and Penistone Church have won the tie 2-1. Their fans and players celebrate with a passion that I used to associate with the FA Cup.

V is for Value for money. A great evening for less than a tenner! Obviously, the standard of football was lower than last night, but in its own way it has been just as good. There is room in my life for both top flight and Non League football where each one is as enjoyable in comparison to the other.

W is for Wine gums. An elderly lady following Penistone offers them to strangers "to celebrate". I wonder whether she will hand out gourmet jelly beans if they win the cup. I may go to Hillsborough just in case.

X is for Xtra time. I did fear this in all honesty. I really need my bed, so I hope that I can finally master Wakefield tonight as I have decided to tackle it head on in an attempt to speed up the journey home.

Y is for Yorkshire (again). This game had a real 'Yorkshireness' quality that other counties just can't compete with. The people, on and off the pitch, make Route 66 different from any other game of football in the world. A unique humour and, of course, accents to match!

Z is for Zappy. A real word worth 21 points in Scrabble and the best you will get from me. Believe me, doing this after a couple of pints of gravy rather than scrumpy is much harder!

Enough A-Z fun I promise. Normal service will be resumed on Saturday.

Hemsworth MW 1 Penistone Church 2

Attendance 110
Admission £4
Ground address Wakefield Road, Fitzwilliam, Pontefract, West Yorkshire. WF9 5AJ
Club website www.hemsworthmwfc.sm4.biz
Twitter @hmwfc

51

You muppet!

Phoenix FC v Kinsley Boys

Phoenix Sports & Social Club

Windsor Food Service Central Midlands Football League Black Dragon Division North.

Saturday 10th March 2012. Kick off 3.00pm

We have a 3pm kick off! There isn't the usual Step 7 rush after football training to get there for a 2pm start. Phoenix don't have floodlights. This is the important fact of the week and is why I decided to travel to Rotherham today. The Spring is now fast approaching, we are noticeably getting more daylight hours and today it is a staggering 15 Celsius. I've had a busy week at work (the day job) and my 'hobby' has also been hectic. Today is my third game in five days so a relaxing afternoon is what my doctor would demand if I ever gave him the opportunity to assess me. Buy the book like everyone else! I have Lucas with me today who is now 4 years old and, luckily, hasn't grown out of wanting to come to the football with his father, or unusually he doesn't have a birthday party invitation as his joker card. I follow the Silsden AFC rules so decide that we will take Lucas' birthday money to Meadowhall on route as it is only a couple of miles from where Phoenix FC play their football.

I think this is good idea and arrive in plenty of time at 2.10pm. I announce that we are going "straight to the toy shop Lucas as we don't have much time". We are in total agreement - two men who know how to shop. It is a military operation to hit the toy shop and flee to the car with a bag full of goodies within budget. "I just need to find a car parking space". It takes ten minutes and then a reversing manoeuvre that deserved a least a cheer from the watching South Yorkshire public (two men smoking). We enter the shopping centre and I have an immediate question, "what are all of these people doing here?" We stay focused and head to our one shop. I can see an obstacle ahead, but I am helpless as Lucas sees a giant picture of the Muppets in the shop window in front of us. He went to the cinema recently to see their new film, and also got given a box set for his birthday, but I still feel the need to ask the closed question, "Do you want to go in the Disney shop?". Within seconds Lucas is holding a large Kermit the frog soft toy in the air. I then spend over ten minutes in a long queue with our £18.

We dash to the toy shop, but Lucas is very disappointed on arrival with the poor selection on offer. I am also disappointed, and a little bemused, that around a thousand people have decided to cram into this small space on such a lovely day. We escape, but I then get dragged back into the expensive world of Walt Disney. We find a large set of racing cars this time and join a now longer queue to throw another £20 at the shop assistant. Upon arrival at the till she asks "you do know that the wheels don't go around on these cars". I am a little confused by this fact so I consult my boy as clearly I didn't know this. We both agree that toy cars that you can't push along the floor are as much use as me coaching rugby. "I think we will find some real cars elsewhere then" is my response. I can't imagine that I am the first victim, but I feel like I am the muppet for thinking that I could pop into Meadowhall as if I am grabbing a loaf of bread from the corner shop. A few tears later, not mine this time, and we are back in the badly stocked toy shop looking for cars that work. I am then relieved to hear the words, "Let's just get Kermit daddy". We are out of there as if Miss Piggy herself was chasing us. We get some more tears as I drag Lucas at speed past the soft play area and we get back to the car at 14.52. The map studying last night pays off as we fly to the ground going through every light on amber. It's not big or clever readers. We get the boost of a large sign directing us to the ground and hear the whistle blow for the start of the game as we are climbing out of the car.

It is believed that Phoenix FC's origins date back to the early years of last century. The complex of Phoenix Sports & Social Club started with a football pitch and a wooden hut for the local steel works. Football was played in the 1920s as shown by the match reports in the works newspaper. The club began as the football section of Steel Peech & Tozer, later to be part of British Steel and now known as Corus. Phoenix have been winners of the Rotherham County Cup, previously played at Rotherham United's old home, Millmoor, on three occasions. When forming the Central Midlands League, administration problems resulted in the side having to adopt the title of Phoenix Sports & Social Club FC. In 2010 they were allowed to revert back to Phoenix FC. The team are currently 12th in the table with today's visitors in 4th place. Kinsley Boys were, of course, the team who introduced me to this level of football. They are wearing maroon shirts and socks with light blue shorts as we arrive.

After only one week, Kirbymoorside's admission record is shattered by 50p when the man at the table says the words "two pounds please". My look of surprise does prompt, "The league tell us to charge three quid". Well what do they know. I am cash rich so I buy my raffle ticket and badge immediately. A bottle of wine, even if it is white and I have a pregnant wife, will always come in handy. Phoenix are wearing an interesting looking kit that is blue and claret striped shirts, blue socks and shorts. Lucas reads my mind with the comment, "Look daddy, Barcelona are playing". I just couldn't write lines like that! He makes a lot of people smile including the Kinsley bench who probably fancy their chances today, even without the tactical genius of Mourinho.

I can appreciate from the side of the pitch that we are at a height as we have a good view of the surrounding area. There is a large forest in front of us and a good view down to the centre of Rotherham to our left. I see what looks like a ground, or one being built, so ask the man next to me if that is Rotherham United's new stadium. I half expect him to laugh but the response of, "Oh, yes it is. I have never noticed that" confirms I have an eye for spotting these things. I am also surprised to discover that the club have a small stand. Lucas is very happy with his green frog so, despite the unexpected rush to get here, I can now finally relax. Once I get these sweets out I will be able to concentrate on the game and, luckily, I haven't missed too much so far.

We move to the stand. This is constructed from corrugated iron over a flat concrete surface, but with a few raised bits which another little boy soon trips over at high speed. There are a lot of tears and Lucas soon joins him with some crying as I put Kermit back into my bag. The frog now has a large dirty mark down his back! Phoenix were defending a free kick so I didn't notice the other game of running Kermit along the filthy walls of the stand. Silly me for watching this game, particularly as, after 25 minutes, I am struggling to write anything positive about the play in front of me. This is a 0-0 game for sure! The shouting on the pitch gets louder and we almost get a goal, of sorts. Kinsley try a long range shot which just goes over the bar on 30 minutes. Lucas missed it as he has now made friends, to replace Kermit, with the little boy who had tried to fly earlier. I must again stand out to the locals as I get asked the usual two questions of "where are you from?" and "are you one of those ground hoppers?" when they learn I have travelled from Ilkley. I now just reply "yes" to the second question, but this man wants more information. "Did you come on the train?". My dull reply just makes him more interested and follows up the question of "what car have you got?!". I am just about to give him details of the make, model, colour and details of which pocket the car keys are in when I remember that I am talking to a complete stranger. "A Volkswagen" is much safer. "I have a Vauxhall Vectra. 3.2 litre. And it's an estate! I only bought it to go fishing, but it is fast. Wednesday are winning 3-0" comes the reply. Our conversation, however riveting, is broken when a Kinsley player puts the ball into Nottingham rather than the back of the net.

At half time we go to the tea bar, which is in a long wooden building. It has everything you would expect to find at a Step 7 football club, cheap snacks and gravy, but we also have pop music. Lucas and I sit on one of the benches and tap our feet with the others. It is a lovely moment and I no longer feel like the stranger in this town. I am even starting to appreciate the Oxo cube and may just buy some for home. Ok, perhaps not, but it just shows that you can wean yourself onto most things. I can see that the players have left the social club and are crossing the cricket pitch for the second half. On the way back to the touchline I get chatting to two of the committee members. My first question is, of course, if they record the attendance. They don't, but I get a "10 not on a free pass". I also learn that the club is planning to get some new changing rooms, but this will only become a reality if they can raise £25,000. On gate receipts of £20 this is not going to be easy! I ask about floodlights as there appears to be some confusion at this level if clubs will need them or not. The league is apparently voting on this soon, but as it stands now they do need them. That's another £45,000 to dream about. The club is still attached to the steel works by "name only", but this fact makes getting a grant for these improvements much harder. Few people could argue with their parting comment of "it will kill this league if they insist on floodlights". More alarming to me was their view that their attendances have fallen due to the economic climate when admission is just £2. If this is true, I really don't know I'm born.

On 55 minutes, a floating cross from the right wing lands perfectly onto the head of a Kinsley Boys player to give the away side the lead. It is a lovely goal! My eyes follow the celebrating player in an attempt to see his number but I get distracted by Lucas who has found a piece of string to wrap around his neck. Therefore, and understandably, I now have no idea who the goal scorer was, but the string has at least been confiscated. I may ask someone in a minute, but first I watch Kinsley come very close to making it 2-0 with a header from a corner that goes just wide of the post. The Kinsley bench are happy with the news that Sunderland are beating Liverpool. Kinsley then get caught offside in this game and Chelsea are in the lead against Stoke elsewhere. It is like being back in Kirkbymoorside but with more fresh air. Phoenix almost equalise with an inviting cross, but unfortunately there is nobody, from either side, in the box. We then get a spell of chances for Kinsley but they keep crossing the ball without looking, something I have been telling my Under 7s about this morning. I recognise someone from Kinsley who I chatted to all of those months ago. He will know who scored the goal and I am told "Mark Lefferty... The manager". I wasn't aware that they had a player manager. I look around to see the ball in the net and it is 1-1. I was looking at the man at the time so missed what happened. Another fan shouts "Dave Gleason" to me before I can even ask the name of the scorer. There is almost a dramatic winner for Kinsley but the shot can't find a way through the sea of defenders legs.

Lucas and I return to the car and I am happy just in the knowledge that he has had a nice afternoon. I needed this as Lucas hasn't been as keen to join me recently. I think the cold weather has not helped his enthusiasm. This has been a very child friendly ground once I had cleared the broken glass so it's a real shame that there weren't more children here today. It is free to bring them and the weather has been lovely. Surely this is a better option than dragging them around a shopping centre? Although looking at my son, shopping is a much cleaner activity!

Phoenix 1 Kinsley Boys 1

Attendance 10
Admission £2 (children free)
Ground address Pavillion Lane, Brinsworth, Rotherham, S Yorkshire. S60 5PA
Club website www.pitchero.com/clubs/phoenixfc
Twitter None found

52

Ladies day

Farsley AFC Ladies v Pontefract S&S Ladies

Throstle Nest
West Riding County Women's League First Division
Sunday 11th March 2012. Kick off 2pm

This is a very special ground today with Mrs Mowbray making her long awaited debut! It is the turn of the ladies, both on and off the pitch as the notepad has also been passed on. I'm going to relax in the sun, eat loads of sweets and I may even have a cider or two with my wife driving. Over to you dear!

This morning started as most others do in the Mowbray household, with my husband searching out yet another football match that he could go to with Lucas whilst I ate breakfast dreaming of the few hours peace I would get thanks to his obsession. Things were soon to change, however, once he discovered that the only match that was available, at a yet to be counted ground, was the Farsley ladies fixture. For some reason Mr Mowbray thought it would be a good idea for me to come along and be a guest writer for this chapter. For some strange reason I agreed to this. You never know, I may even begin to understand where this ground hopping madness comes from. So, here we are, a chapter from the usually left at home and long suffering wife of a ground hopper. I hope I don't disappoint! I will warn you in advance that football isn't really my thing. Please don't expect a detailed match report or talk of the technicalities. In fact, I have only ever been to two football matches in my life, so I'm definitely no expert. My two previous experiences, both many years ago, were Leeds United v Chelsea in the FA cup at Elland Road and Roma v Lazio at the Stadio Olimpico in Rome. I'm sure today's home tie for Farsley ladies will live up to the tension of those battles!

We set off for the match with plenty of time to spare. However, as is fairly usual for me and thanks to a few road works, we are a tiny bit late. There are stands on two sides of the pitch, one being seated and the other a covered terrace at the far goal end. We choose a nice sunny part on the edge of the fairly impressive stand. I think we are on a terrace but decide to sit on the steps rather than stand. From what I've heard of non league grounds, Throstle Nest is pretty impressive and I noticed a lot of training facilities too as we parked up. As we are settling into our space with Lucas happily running up and down the terraces, I am surprised to discover just how much of the action you can hear when you're this close to the pitch. The blue team, Farsley, blast the ball towards the goal but, unfortunately, it hits the crossbar. It strikes me how loud the noise is as the ball strikes the bar. The other thing that's really loud today is the Farsley team coach, or at least I think that's who it is. Whoever he is, he is certainly making himself heard! Just as the Farsley girls are told off for gossiping instead of playing, the red team (Ponty) move in for their number four to score the first goal of the match. You will notice that names are not my strong point, but, helpfully, Lucas teaches me that I can tell they are different players because they all have numbers on their back.

Farsley fight back from their one goal deficit, with most of the action coming from their number 21 who shows plenty of effort but fails time after time to get the desired result. There are corners, free kicks and plenty of confusion as a ball, from what turns out to be another match going on behind the ground, finds its way onto the girls' pitch. Now I could make a joke about ladies and too many balls to play with, but that wouldn't be very appropriate for a mother would it? With the confusion corrected by the referee, play continues. I forget that these are apparently ladies playing for a moment thanks to some more than colourful language from the Ponty number 11. I have to admit though that I'd probably be swearing too; even if it was just at the pain that is no doubt caused every time the ladies chest the ball. Ouch! Farsley's number 21 continues to try her hardest for a goal, yet still it is not going her way today. Luckily there isn't any action that requires the linesman to make any tough decisions. He is a bit busy being handed a Next carrier bag to "pass to Sarah", one of the Farsley players I think, at half time. I'm not sure that the linesman at my previous matches would have been so accommodating to this request!

Despite the sunshine, it is now starting to get a bit chilly. I decide to relieve my coat from its job of keeping my bum warm on the cold concrete step. I'm very jealous of the only other spectator in our area who has clearly come more prepared than me, with both a coat and sunglasses. Play starts to get a bit rough in the run up to half time, with Farsley pushing forward. They end up giving away a free kick, which Ponty cannot turn into a goal this time. Just before half time, a penalty decision goes Farsley's way and finally the number 21 gets her goal from the spot to reward her continued effort!

Half time arrives with a 1-1 score line. It could easily have been a great deal more goals for Farsley had their goal scorer's luminous boots been more on form. I take the opportunity to have a little wander with Lucas as he wants to show me the ground. I manage to see my first pair of butterflies this year. Perhaps it really is nearly Spring! I doubt Mr Mowbray would have even noticed this fact on his travels. My husband makes his way to the bar to "pay a visit".

As the second half starts, Lucas and I are watching from the perimeter fence which is nice and high for him to sit up on. The nice moment doesn't last long though when Lucas loudly announces "Mummy, that lady with the number 7 has a fat belly". As I know how much detail we can hear from the pitch to the stands, I decide to make a very hasty retreat back to my previous step. I can see from my new position that we seem to have a new linesman; and it seems that he is part of the Ponty team! The previous linesman turns up next to us in the stand and I realise from his supportive shouts that he is part of the Farsley team. I assumed that all match officials would need to be impartial? Perhaps not then at this level of football. One of the Farsley players, who may be a new addition as I hadn't noticed a number 5 before, grabs my attention. However, this is not because of her ball skills. I notice her first because she looks about 12 years old. Annoyingly, she is playing the whole time with her hands tucked up inside of her long sleeved top like a moody teenager. She has a stroppy look to match her posture. This is one of my big bug bears and it takes all of my strength for the rest of this half to not shout at her. Farsley have definitely come out fighting in the second half, but what strikes me most is that their number 9 needs a better sports bra! Despite this, Miss bouncy boobs, the moody teenager and the ever present number 21 work really well together. They attack the goal with purpose but, unfortunately, without the desired finish.

Just as play is getting interesting, we get another stray ball onto the pitch which is cleared away by a spectator who is carrying his baby. I think I must have got distracted by the baby as I almost miss the second goal from Farsley. I'm not sure exactly how the build up came about, but it ended with an easy kick from the teenager with no hands. Not long after, the hard working Farsley number 21 manages to stand on the ball and fall over injuring herself in what sounds like a very traumatic experience. There are tears and everything! As they are tending to her (aka telling her to stop crying like a baby and get on with it), I see an aeroplane taking off from the hill in the distance that again distracts me. I had been wondering the whole match what that noise was as I didn't think we were close enough to the airport for it to be aeroplanes. I was wrong and a nice bit of plane spotting with Lucas follows. It seems that number 21 was really hurt and she is taken off. She deserves to leave the pitch to a standing ovation for her hard work. I give her a clap anyway.

Mr Mowbray decides it is time for another cider which makes me want one. However, guess who's driving...and pregnant! He times his journey quite nicely though as he manages to give his services as ball boy on his route back to our step. It seems that I have also missed a goal from Ponty while he was away. Lucas and I were distracted by our sweets and the planes. The linesman kindly turns around to tell me that it was scored by their number 9, Debbie. Is this the norm?

This brings the score to 2-2. Another injury occurs, this time it's Miss bouncy boobs who manages a pretty impressive roll across the pitch. It appears that the linesman is also the first aid man. He's being kept busy today! As the second half is coming to an end, Ponty get a corner. This is taken really well and converted into a third goal for them. The scorer is again their number 9. I'm fairly sure that I hear the corner taker being referred to as "Foxy"? I can't imagine any girl would actually want to be called this so I pretty much disregard this instantly!

The game comes to an end for a 2-3 win for Ponty. I can't help but feel this would have been a different story if number 21, complete with fashionable boots, hadn't had to be taken off. No one else in the Farsley team seemed to have her spirit going forward. We leave the ground happy with our afternoon's viewing though and, although it was no Serie A match, it was certainly an entertaining introduction to non league football for this long standing football widow! I am not sure I will be writing a book about my three matches, but they will all be memorable for different reasons.

Farsley AFC Ladies 2 Pontefract S&S Ladies 3

Attendance Not recorded
Admission Free
Ground address Newlands, Farsley. LS28 5BE
Club website www.farsleyafc.co.uk
Twitter @FarsleyLadies

53

The bright lights of Dunswell

Hall Road Rangers FC v Winterton Rangers

Dene Park

BARIS Northern Counties East League Premier Division

Tuesday 13th March 2012. Kick Off 7.45pm

My name is Lucas Mowbray aged 4... sorry to disappoint you but passing the journalist reins to members of my family was a one off. An enjoyable day was had by all on Sunday afternoon. I did feel a bit redundant without writing every few minutes, but relaxing in the sun with a pint was good. Unfortunately, my main observation on my introduction to women's football was in regard to the linesmen. They really do need to be someone who is neutral and who can actually be bothered to keep up with the play. We had two linesmen in casual clothes and the worst offender was wearing a Pontefract tracksuit top. There was one decision that forced me to find my voice and take up with him. A beautiful ball was played through the middle and, with just the keeper to beat, could have put Farsley ahead. It was judged offside by the person who probably didn't want her to score. I admittedly had the advantage of being higher than the level of the pitch but he was on the half way line! "That was on side!" got the response of "No it wasn't". I managed to bite my lip as didn't want to start a blazing argument at my wife's first game with me. But how could he possibly make that judgement when he was so far from the line of play. I had spent the previous 70 minutes mystified why he wasn't even attempting to follow the line. Laziness! The women should surely receive the same treatment as the male footballers. The standard of football was good and surely deserved a lot better from the 'officials'.

I am still in shock from Mrs Mowbray's 20 week scan this morning when we discovered that life will only get more fun with a third little boy. Gulp. Most importantly he is healthy and doing the things in the womb that he should be doing. I have therefore had a big smile on my face all day. Despite my good mood, my lead into tonight's game is far from ideal. The days of picking matches to fit around my work diary are long gone. With just 14 matches remaining, I need to strictly adhere to the spreadsheet. I left Chester Le Street this afternoon in the rush hour traffic and began questioning my sanity when stuck in a jam near Sunderland to get onto the A19. I'm not saying I had a Bridlington moment, but crawling around the York ring road, needing a toilet stop and petrol, was a challenge to my positive thinking. Route 66 is of course my choice, but occasionally life can get in the way. However much I love a game of football, I wouldn't have chosen, under any normal circumstances, to drive 120 miles tonight. Collapsing on the sofa in front of the Merseyside derby may have been the closest I got to a live match. I pass the entrance to the Bishop Burton College, without the snow this time, and even a sign to the KC stadium where I was only 7 days ago.

Hall Road Rangers play their football in Dunswell, which is on the outskirts of Beverley and on the northern side of Hull. This is my first visit to the area as I have always entered Hull from the west on the M62. The club was formed in 1959 by a local man named Ted Richardson and was originally set-up as a youth club for teenagers and as a Sunday league side. They moved to a senior division in 1968 from the Yorkshire Football League Division Two. In 1970, they were moved to the newly formed Division Three and won the title twice in eight years either side of a relegation in 1976. Rangers were founding members of the Northern Counties East League in 1982. In the 2007/08 season, Hall Road finished as runners up in the Northern Counties East League Division One. They won promotion to the Premier Division where they play today at Step 5 of the Non League pyramid.

I finally arrive at Dene Park, very hungry and drained, after the long drive here with just one short stop for petrol. Parking is my next challenge with other cars arriving as I am trying to turn around as the main area is now full. I get changed into my jeans and hoody in the front seat in between the passing car headlights. This is a task that I have mastered over the recent months and achieve this successfully so avoid exposing my semi naked body to the people of East Yorkshire. The large 'Welcome to Dene Park' sign on the clubhouse roof may have been constructed with weary travellers like me in mind, although a large lit up hot dog, like those American diners in the movies, is what I really want. I go through the turnstile and I'm pleasantly surprised by the ground. There is a substantial stand behind the goal end that I have entered from with four steep rows of wooden benches. There are also three other small shelters scattered around the ground to provide additional cover from the elements. It is dry and mild tonight so I don't think I will take advantage of these areas. I have also been sitting down for the last 3 hours so I want to be on my feet. Tonight's visitors have made the short trip from Lincolnshire thanks to the Humber Bridge. They are well placed at fourth in the league, just six points off the top. In comparison, Hall Road have struggled at the other end of the table and now lie in 17th place. The home side play in all blue and Winterton are in red to create our own version of Liverpool v Everton perhaps with a bit less pace to the game. The crowd also looks a bit lighter with no more than 50 here!

I find a snack bar, but it is, of course, closed! I am almost in tears as the teams arrive, but my attention is suddenly grabbed by another fan carrying a tray of chips. I ask for directions immediately and head back out of the ground to the clubhouse. I can now see from inside that this is a big space. There is bar, a huge screen showing that other match, a dart board and some snooker tables. There doesn't appear to be a menu, so the lady runs through my options like my mum used to when I got home from school. I decline an egg and settle for sausage and chips for just £2. On a scale between the heights of Northallerton Town and that dark night at Ossett Town they are somewhere in the middle. I go back into the ground and they must have delayed kick off just for me as I catch them starting at 7.51pm.

I find a large lonely space in the open by the corner flag. I have developed a headache which I hope the food will halt in its tracks.

Winterton open the scoring after just 5 minutes before I have even polished off the second sausage. After some poor defending of a corner, the number 9, Jake Stannard, back heals the ball into the net. It deserved a clap, but I am not risking another dropped sausage moment for his show boating. Twenty minutes later it should really be 2-0 but the same player scuffs his shot with just the keeper to beat. His colourful language confirms his disappointment as well. My head ache is getting worse and it is making it difficult to concentrate on the game. Therefore, I miss the incident, whilst squinting, that gives Hall Road a penalty in the 33rd minute. Steve Gawthorpe coolly places the ball in the goal to equalise. The home keeper is very noisy and is actually starting to bug me with his constant yelping at every outfield pass. Although, in his defence, the bright floodlights are doing more harm to this bear with a sore head.

I use the half time break to go back to my car for some paracetamols as the pain has now moved to my eye socket. I sit in the car for ten minutes with my eyes shut, which seems to help a bit. I can hear the players return so decide to persevere, not that I can just pop around the corner to a bed in a darkened room.

I return to a different part of the ground and hope this change in viewpoint will also improve my match day experience. At least the fog horn keeper is at the other end of the pitch to me now. He is kept busy from the start by pressure from the away side. Winterton are looking the more likely team to win this game and they test the keeper three times in the opening ten minutes. These bright lights really do need dimming, but I'm not sure they would do that even if I was a world famous author. The match is so one sided that the timid looking man nearest to me feels the need to shout "come on Rangers". I could have explained the need to be more specific with his support to both Rangers teams, or even asked him to keep the noise down, but my poorly head doesn't need to be punched. After all the early pressure from the away side, Hall Road almost score in the 60th minute. The visiting keeper reads the striker's run and shot perfectly to keep the scores level. A couple of minutes later, Winterton's James O'Neill dribbles the ball into the box and deservedly fires his team into the lead.

The goal kick start's the game, but I am struggling so much that I decide to upgrade my headache to a migraine. I also need to stop writing down every half chance the away side has. Winterton score a third goal, that I couldn't describe if my life depended on it, to put the game to bed, which is exactly where I want to be. This is a second goal for Stannard according to the loud man on the tannoy system. After a lot of pacing around and with around 15 minutes left to play, the only option is to head home. This crime against football happens every week at the Emirates Stadium so, as a one off, I am sure I will be able to look at myself in the mirror in the morning. Perhaps five games in a week has finally caught up with me. It is more likely, defending my devotion to football, that I have not drunk enough water, or it could just be the stresses of life. Something I need to get very used to when my three sons take over the family home!

Footnote: It always happens when you leave a game early doesn't it?! Danny Ricketts scored a goal for Hall Road to bring the score back to 2-3 at the time I must have been starting my engine. James O'Neill scored again in the 84th minute to restore Winterton's two goal lead. The lights of Dunswell would have been a distant sight in my rear view mirror as the final whistle blew. At that time I was more focused than I had been all day on getting back to my bed!

Hall Road Rangers 2 Winterton Rangers 4

Attendance 30
Admission £5
Ground Address Beverley Road, Dunswell, E Yorkshire. HU6 0AA
Club website www.pitchero.com/clubs/hallroadrangers
Twitter @HRRFC

54

Home and away

Dinnington Town FC v Louth Town

Phoenix Park

BARIS Northern Counties East League Division One

Tuesday 20th March 2012. Kick off 7.45pm

When I wrote the introduction to this book last summer and planned this hopping marathon in my mind, I had every intention of continuing to watch Leeds United home and away as normal. My confidence was based on the fact that I could comfortably commit to 9 months of Tuesday evenings, in addition to the handful of free Saturdays due to International breaks and when TV dictates the fixtures. It became quite apparent, however, around the turn of the year that this would not only be a challenge but it was actually impossible. Even with some input from my old friend Excel, it was out of my control. If we had had a Siberian winter it would have been just about achievable, but not with the mild temperatures we have 'enjoyed' to date. I have, therefore, been forced to pick and choose my away games since this reality check. To my surprise I haven't really missed the long away days, which I'm not sure is a good or bad thing. I think it became too much of a habit that I just didn't know how to break. The danger in stopping such things is whether I will now ever want to start these days again. I can now fully appreciate what a huge commitment this was. Watching Non League football locally, instead of travelling to grounds around the country, has given me more money and more time with my family (both away from and at the games) and I do really enjoy the more relaxed environment. Goal text alerts have allowed me to feel involved with how Leeds are getting on. Occasionally, some texts, when resulting from goals scored rather than conceded, have much improved my Route 66 'away' day. I could shame myself with the tale of when I threw my phone into a flower bed in temper, but let's concentrate on the positive experiences.

I have some decisions to make next season, which may be very easy in the short term with a new baby arriving in July. I can safely commit to continuing my home season ticket, which leaves me in the minority of football fans with this level of commitment. I intend to continue this particular habit well into my retirement and beyond. Tonight, Leeds are playing Nottingham Forest at Elland Road, but, as a landmark moment, I am currently sat in my car in the South Yorkshire town of Dinnington. Saturday's home draw against West Ham was fantastic in terms of atmosphere and showing the impact Neil Warnock has already had on the pitch, so I would love to return to my seat tonight. Apart from Wakefield FC (thanks again for moving tomorrow's home match forward 24 hours!), I have planned a strict schedule to ensure that I visit the remaining 12 clubs over the next 6 weeks. At least the equation is now simple. Dinnington Town will be missing from my book if I go to the match at Elland Road. In conclusion, completing Route 66 is more important to me than watching Leeds. I now feel cleansed, like an alcoholic telling his group that he does in fact have a drink problem. I have no intention of moping around Phoenix Park, particularly on such a beautiful evening, and will make the most of what ground 53 can offer me. It will probably be a boring goalless draw back in West Yorkshire.

Dinnington is another on my growing list of 'tough' towns with a mining past. The colliery was closed in 1992 with the loss of 1,000 jobs that must have devastated the local economy. A business park on the old colliery site has gone some way to helping generate a recovery. 7.29pm on Tuesday 17th August 2007 was a significant moment in Dinnington Town FC's history. Not only was it the start of the club's centenary year but it was also their first encounter in the FA Cup. What's more, they were playing their closest rivals, Maltby Main, and the game was chosen by the FA to kick the competition off; hence the unusual kick off time. They won the game and went on a great cup run, beating Rossendale United, Penrith

Town and Cheadle Town until losing to, then high flying, Bradford Park Avenue. They celebrated reaching 100 years of existence by winning Division One to get promoted to the Premier League with five games spare. They were relegated back to Step 6 in 2011, where they remain today. Dinnington Town currently sit 13th in the table, just one place and one point above tonight's visitors. I have already watched the Lincolnshire side, Louth Town, this season.

Dinnington Town have one of the most interesting playgrounds I have seen on my travels. The apparatus resembles various pieces of gym equipment, yet it stands on open wasteland. It is situated immediately outside the ground, so it may well be used by the players. Tonight, however, it is the setting for some chav culture. Five teenage boys pass me carrying a large drum so I decide it is time for me to leave my car to soak up the atmosphere. The ground is basic, but given that I am now happy just to find a perimeter fence, I am almost giddy when I discover two stands. They are both small but offer some covered seats. The one behind the far goal is home to the drummers who have recruited three other young men to join them. They have also erected a large St George's flag with the letters D T F C between the four squares. There are at least ten minutes until kick off, but the singing has already started. Elland Road would probably benefit from this kind of backing, the one with the drum can borrow my season ticket if he gets his skates on. I find a wooden bench in the other stand at the side despite the potential fun I could have with the noisy locals. I quickly go for a wander to the tea bar for my usual Bovril. I pay 60p and I am offered some ground black pepper? I may not be a beef stock connoisseur after all.

The players enter the pitch and the noise levels rise. The home team are wearing a very striking yellow and black kit. Louth Town's all blue number does at least have a white stripe on one side. The drum beat gets louder as the game starts. Dinnington are kicking towards the singing and go on an early charge towards them, which gets the teenagers quite excited. It is amazing what a difference just nine boys can make to create an atmosphere that I'm not used to at this level.

Most of the home players appear to have their own songs and whoever Ivan is, sat in the home dugout, “we all love you". Every time their heroes cross the half way line they all shout something and sometimes they even cheer every pass. After 13 minutes the Dinnington number 10 makes good contact with the ball with his head from a corner and forces the Louth keeper, in light pink, to pull off a great save. The stand behind him almost explodes with all the excitement. The resulting goal kick creates another opportunity for the locals to try to put him off, which may actually be working based on that effort. On 19 minutes, I just manage to catch the ball fly into the opposite net for Louth Town to take the lead. Jamie Coulson was outside the area going nowhere, but manages to hit the ball sweetly for 1-0. “We're going to win two one" is the song from our undetermined youth.

I look down at my phone to discover that I have two texts, it is 1-1 at Elland Road. Four more home fans join the party late whilst Louth are starting to have more of the ball since Jamie’s thunderbolt. They almost grab a second goal five minutes later, but the Dinnington keeper manages to hold the shot when it looked like he was about to drop it at the feet of the approaching striker. On 35 minutes there is a blatant handball in the penalty box in front of the youth club. Despite the vocal appeal, the penalty isn’t given. This generates the very familiar response of, "We only get shit refs" that I usual hear from the Elland Road kop. Dinnington’s number 11 agrees with his supporters and almost gets booked for his arguing. The linesman’s cry of, "Shut your mouth gobbie" surprises me, but appears to calm him down. There is time for a further penalty claim before half time for Dinnington. This again falls on death ears and our official just laughs this time. A middle aged man leans over the fence and offers him his glasses. I'm not as sure about that one, but the earlier handball I could have seen without my specs. I get a goal alert to confirm that the other away side in my evening have just taken the lead at Leeds.

I use the half time period to follow the players into the leisure centre in search of some toilets. I half expect to find a bar inside, but without one I can't justify calling this building a club house. There is a strong smell of whatever that stuff is that athletes spray on their muscles. I manage to find the hottest hand drier in Yorkshire and return to the touchline with less skin on my hands but no beer. I enjoy a few minutes of silence as the drum also takes a break.

The second half starts and the drum is fired up again. This time it is the turn of Louth's attacking number 17 to receive their attention. If he could finish, he would have killed this game after just five minutes of the restart. The drums would be the excuse I would use for why the ball ends up in Nottinghamshire. It must be catching as we soon get treated to more comedy moments at the opposite end from a cross and then a shot that are just awful. Louth do look in control, so unless Dinnington can find some quality when it matters the three points will be leaving Yorkshire. On 65 minutes, a Louth clearance results in the ball actually going inside the tea bar which doesn't half give the lady a fright. I know how she feels when I learn Forest have gone 3-1 up on my mobile phone. But then I get 3 texts all at once that turns the score to 3-4! It looks like, in between keeping my eye on the ball to avoid it taking my head off, Leeds were level at 3-3 for a minute. My signal tonight isn't as good as the game I have missed. Reporting on 4 goals in 5 minutes here would, however, be a nice problem to have. I should be so lucky as Dinnington balloon another cross into the next field. By the time the ball lands, Forest have a fifth!

It suddenly occurs to me that there are a staggering 6 people around me all wearing headphones to listen to other matches on the radio. I am clearly not alone. I am also losing focus on the game in front of me, which is now all blood and guts but not a great deal of skill on show. I start to pay more attention to the others discussing their other games around me. In addition to them finding the score from Leeds amusing, it is getting exciting for the two Sheffield league sides. In particular, the Blades are hammering Notts County back in

Nottingham. The six listeners soon turn into seven, eight and then nine! It is similar to buying a new car in an unusual colour, but you then notice afterwards that every other car on the road matches yours. The singing is even drying up, so I now feel that very few people on the touchline are actually interested in this game. There is a lot of possession for Louth whilst the locals around me are cheering the goal feast at Meadow Lane. My phone kindly updates me that there has been a 6th and then 7th goal for Forest, which I don't find as amusing at all. I really didn't expect a ten goal thriller at Elland Road tonight when I was driving south earlier. I've seen a competitive match here, a surprisingly lively crowd, but at least this result won't ruin my evening. I start a mad sprint back to the car on the sound of the whistle. If I'm quick I may just catch something of interest on the radio!

Dinnington Town 0 Louth Town 1

Attendance 40
Admission £4
Ground Address 131 Laughton Road, Dinnington, S Yorkshire. S25 2PP
Club website www.pitchero.com/clubs/dinningtontown
Twitter @DTFCinfo

55

The Eastenders

Easington United FC v Dronfield Town

Low Farm

BARIS League Challenge Cup Quarter Final

Saturday 24th March 2012. Kick off 3pm

Today I am basking in the Spring sun on the Hull Riviera, a part of Britain that I didn't even know existed before the map at Yorkshire Main caught my eye last month. I wasn't aware that there was anything other than sea to the east of Hull. George couldn't resist a day at the seaside but Lucas' best friend's party was always going to win the day for him. The weather since leaving Hull has turned warm and sunny, but soft play looked a wise decision earlier. The fog was so thick on the M62 that I couldn't show off the Humber Bridge to my passenger. Our first stop was the seaside resort of Withernsea which has a nice beach for a game of football but the town itself has seen better days, or I certainly hope that it has! The Lifeboat cafe served a good chip meal but, unfortunately, not on the same level as Whitby, although this is an unfair comparison, particularly as it was almost half the price. The next stop was Spurn Point which is a couple of miles past our eventual destination of Easington. The long straight roads that cross the flat open farmland felt similar to my last drive to the Lincolnshire coast. I love maps and once I discovered that there was a 3 mile narrow strip of land that went out to the sea, walking this became almost as important as seeing the match itself. I wasn't put off by the latest 'WARNING!' sign, but this time it is the Brown-tail moth caterpillars that we must avoid all contact with. The view, from both sides, as you walk further away from the mainland is simply stunning. We didn't quite make it to the end due to a certain small boy's aching legs. I hope George is feeling stronger tomorrow when he does his Sport Relief Mile! I feel the need to return on another day to finish the walk but for now I am happy to be in the nearby village of Kilnsea. I have found a fine place to dwell awhile, sat outside the Crown & Anchor pub with a pint of Timothy Taylor's watching the large tankers going out to sea. This is also a good opportunity to pause and contemplate the world."I won't be long George!" Ground 55 feels special, despite George's efforts to rush me and the modest facilities of a Step 7 field that no doubt awaits me. I'm not going to let that possibility bring me down to earth just yet.

We head back to the village of Easington which is a strange mix of a rural farming community and the industrial gas terminals that dominate the landscape beyond the houses. The gas fields are around 70 km off this part of the East Yorkshire coast. The whole site consists of three plants, two run by BP and the other by Centrica. George likes the men walking around in their hard hats, but I'm too busy looking for a football ground to notice. Last night's reading up on the area should really have stretched to seeing where the Easington Recreation & Sports Ground is! Even Google maps can't help me without a mobile signal so we go back to the old fashioned method of asking a stranger for directions. Once we find one that is. We eventually see a man walking his dog, but he's "just caravanning pal" and is from Wales by the sound of his accent. We then discover where the word stranger originates from as we stumble upon a very strange man. In fact, he is so strange George laughs out aloud every time he speaks. I'm not quite sure what he is saying, but it doesn't appear he can help when he starts to shout "mam, mam". An elderly lady appears, with a striking dog print fleece on that George also finds amusing. It is all feeling a bit like an episode of the TV series, A League of Gentlemen, but she does enough pointing for us to understand that we are not far from the ground. We drive behind the village pub and find a lot of cars all parked on the grass verge, so decide this is a good place for us to also abandon our vehicle. The hand painted 'SPORTS FIELD' sign confirms that our comedy tour is over and we have found the football ground.

Easington United is the home team of Richard Lusmore, the General Manager of the club and also one of my favourite followers on

Twitter. Before we go in search of Richard, I take some photos of the open space in front of me. I am, unusually, using my ipod today as my camera battery appears to be flat, or broken from over use. This gadget waving draws attention to me, so Richard soon finds us. He greets me with a complimentary programme and a pin badge. Nice touch! I learn that the programme is priced at the higher amount of £2 because there is no admission cost. They don't own their ground so are not allowed to charge. We chat about the ground and club at the touchline as the players are warming up behind us. There is just the one sheltered area, named 'The North West Ryvita Stand Total Gross Weight'. This is a bit of a mouth full, but I expect the home fans can just arrange to meet in 'the stand'. They should find each other! Richard is starting to look distracted as we get closer to the kick off, so we let him get back to the team. I am drawn to the bench behind the goal and take the opportunity to make some notes of my day. George starts to play football with some other children in the open space behind me so everyone appears to be happy.

The teams come out, which grabs my attention, but the children continue to be lost in their own game. Dronfield Town have travelled from Derbyshire, although there is a twisted logic to claiming that they are also from Yorkshire if Sheffield FC have a chapter in my book. The visitors are in red and black striped shirts, black shorts and red socks. Easington have their green and yellow quarter shirts on with black shorts and socks. Richard said earlier that they have a "tough game" today and this looks true from the first kick. Dronfield look very lively and waste two decent chances in just the first five minutes. George's new friends appear to have left him, so he retrieves these stray shots to resume the role of ball boy. He is wearing his Leeds shirt, so he probably needs to earn his keep in these Hull City supporting parts. With a quarter of an hour gone some plastic chairs are placed at our end, which Dronfield are attacking. The home supporters have already come to the conclusion where the goals are likely to come from this afternoon. Both teams play in the same division, Step 7 of the Black Dragon North Division, but the away side are fourth in the table and 28 points above Easington. The home team's defence are starting to panic and one clearance puts the ball into the tree. My cry of "no George!" raises a few eye brows around me. I feel the need to tell everyone around me that "He likes fetching balls". The replacement ball soon goes flat so a third ball is introduced. I do hope Richard has not given too many programmes away today. With two balls out of action they might ask me for my badge back at this rate. Dronfield Town continue to put pressure on Easington, but most of the chances result in the parked cars seeing more of the ball than the net. George is also getting his fair share of the ball. Finally, on 41 minutes, we see some neat play and Trev Roberts heads the ball cleanly to give the away side the lead.

We use the goal for a toilet stop and then to slowly make our way to explore the little house at the side of the pitch in time for the break. The whistle blows for half time and once the players have left the field we are invited in. Once inside the mini clubhouse, George finds the complimentary biscuits and I admire the picture of Jack Chalton. This was taken in June 2007 when he was a speaker at the club's diamond celebration; the club was established sixty years earlier in 1947. I am kindly given a cup of tea but, once again, my request for no milk or sugar generates some strange looks. Is black tea so weird? My mug advertises the joys of 'Bringing Norwegian gas to you' and George is also promoting how 7 year olds love chocolate, particularly when it is on the house. Richard is confident that his team will get through this tie without the need for a replay but I have seen very little evidence so far to back this up.

The second half starts just as we arrive back to our bench. George, however, now appears to be redundant with no balls coming this way. I reassure him, based on Richard's earlier confidence, that things will soon pick up. He doesn't believe it either and eventually sits down next to me. George finds his role again when Easington manage a wayward shot to send him back to the ditch again. This enthusiasm is short lived. With only 5 minutes played, Dronfield go two goals up with a great volley from Nick Tilley. The goal triggers more chances for them, but the ball usually ends up in the opposite ditch. There is clearly a vacancy at that end, but we stay put in loyalty to Easington and, as George's friends have returned, he wouldn't do it anyway, even if I let him. The game is getting more scrappy with desperation now creeping in for Easington. In the 75th minute, Dronfield grab two goals in just 4 minutes to secure their place in the next round. Firstly, Aidan Ashton puts away a penalty and, minutes later, a very good shot by George Colley improves the score thanks to a deflection from an Easington player. The keeper manages to get his fingers to it but can't keep it out.

At 4-0 even Richard would admit it is game over for his side. Earlier, he did sound concerned with the build up of fixtures that his team faced, but doesn't look like he is now bothered about this. We wander towards him and then spot that the tree no longer has the ball there. I compliment him on his tree climbing skills and offer our thanks for the hospitality but, despite there being less than 5 minutes remaining, and the one sided score line, I'm not sure he has even noticed us standing next to him. His enthusiasm for every Easington touch is incredible, a total dedication to his club. In the dying minutes, Easington have a decent shout for a penalty that we can just hear above Richard's voice. The referee doesn't agree and the player is actually booked for diving. A supporter shouts, "You've been watching too much telly referee". In this fine weather, it is easy to say that we all probably watch too much TV. I have been given such a warm welcome in one of the most unusual places in Yorkshire. I know which version of Eastenders I would choose to watch. Unlike the BBC licence fee, this drama is free and, on a sunny day, this East End is much less depressing. I am very happy that there is a world East of Hull but think that I will only return on a sunny day. I can then protect that Riviera mirage.

Easington United 0 Dronfield Town 4

Attendance 51
Admission Free
Ground Address Beck Street, Easington, Hull. HU12 0TT

Club website www.clubwebsite.co.uk/easingtonunited
Twitter Non found but follow @RichLusmore

56

Tyke Travels

Barnoldswick Town FC v Ramsbottom United

Silentnight Beds's Stadium
The North West Counties Football League
Tuesday 27th March 2012. Kick off 7.45pm

On my travels I have been labelled as the "new Steve Penny" and, courtesy of Eric the Viking, I finally discovered his superb Tyke Travels. He wrote and self published six editions, with the final one being for the 2004/05 season. Eventually, thanks to social media, we found each other and have recently enjoyed many a late night email conversation. We discussed my list of clubs and soon arrived at the question of why Barnoldswick Town was missing. That will be because it's in Lancashire – or is it? I did, however, listen to his argument to include them and it was so strong, I agreed to include them. I then felt it was very fitting to invite him to join me tonight and told him to bring his notepad and pen. Can the real Steve Penny please stand up...

Nine years on and how times change. Barnoldswick Town were in the West Lancashire League in 2003 for my trip to see their 8-1 win over Lower Hopton in the West Riding County Challenge Cup on my furthest journey west for the Soap Stars and Burst Bubbles book. That was a narrative account of the 2002/03 season across Yorkshire and covered just 40-or-so matches – unlike Michael Mowbray's mammoth Route 66 project. Since then, 'Barlick' have progressed up the non-League pyramid to the cusp of promotion to the EvoStik (Northern Premier) League. They still boast a tidy ground, now with additional turnstiles, car parking and floodlights to secure their place at the higher level. It's also now the Silentnight Beds Stadium, in deference to their sponsors, rather than its former West Close or Victory Park title.The debate still goes on over whether the town is in Yorkshire or Lancashire. While it is definitely Lancastrian as far as local government is concerned, the White Rose still blooms proudly with the older generation and the football administrators. The historic, geographic county boundaries have not changed since the 11th Century, no matter what 1970s planners and the Post Office might have decided when it comes to the administrative boundaries – who can forget the Humberside debacle across the other side of the county?

My own journey has also seen change. I'm now living just 15 miles down the road from Barlick in Haworth, having moved there from York via Norfolk and Suffolk. The annual Tyke Travels yearbooks have stopped, but I keep busy covering local football on the www.keighleykicks.co.uk website. What's more, perhaps those strange folk from the 'wrong' side of the Pennines aren't so bad after all. Family history research has revealed half my ancestors fought for t'other lot in the War of the Roses, so I probably qualify for dual-nationality! My own Yorkshire Route 66 now numbers 83 senior grounds across the Broad Acres and that's without the elusive Bradford City and Sheffield Wednesday grounds I've still not got round to ticking off. I also need to revisit Doncaster Rovers and Rotherham United for their new grounds as well as newcomers such as Hemsworth, Westella & Willerby and Phoenix, which should take me towards the century mark.

Since my early days visiting the county's clubs, York RI, Pilkington Recs, Collingham, Rowntrees and, sadly for me, Scarborough, amongst others have disappeared from the senior scene, so it's another reason to ensure Barnoldswick is confirmed as a Yorkshire club.They do seem to have taken the right decision to go west though. One of their forerunners did have a short spell in the Yorkshire League but since then it has been leagues from the Irish Sea side of the Pennines where their fortunes have fallen. There are about a dozen North West Counties League clubs within a 25-mile radius of their Silentnight Stadium. If they'd joined the Northern Counties East League with their Yorkshire neighbours, the nearest 'derby' would be 25 miles away in Thackley. The present club was formed in 1972 when Firemasters and Barnoldswick Sports joined forces to become Barnoldswick United. The Town suffix was adopted fairly recently.

Tonight's game was a biggie for Barlick and attracted a season's best league gate of 316 to see the visit of the league leaders. A win for Barlick would see them keep up the promotion pace, but defeat would bring an end to any hopes of further progress up the non-League ladder, at least for another year. Barlick defended the aromatically named Sewer End and, for most of the first half, Ramsbottom were all over them like flies round, erm... a sewer. After only seven minutes, a scramble in the home area saw a loose ball fall to Dominic Smalley and he fired across goal for Ian Flannery but the tall central defender scuffed his point-blank shot straight at goalkeeper Billy Carrington. Ramsbottom's Lee Gaskell and Grant Spencer tore apart the home defence at will with tricky twists and turns but the final ball was lacking. The league leaders' combination of 'six-foot-seven' man mountains down the spine of their team with 'five-foot-nowt' speedy wingmen looked more suited to rugby union, but was extremely effective – if a daunting challenge for any team photos.Gaskell's diving header looked goalbound but Carrington scrambled the ball away just in time to see the striker collide with a post. Spencer's tricky run between two defenders was halted with a hefty hand in his back and referee Natalie Walker pointed to the spot, but Gaskell fired wide.

The one-way traffic was finally reversed after 33 minutes when a pair of Rammy defenders tripped each other up on the halfway line and a swift exchange of passes put Paul Fildes clear for the hosts, but his rasping drive pulled a spectacular diving save from Grant Shenton – the only time he was called into action during the entire 90 minutes. Captain Andrew Dawson had a glorious opportunity to finally get Ramsbottom on the score sheet when, unmarked at the back post, he somehow managed to steer a free header wide. But, after 42 minutes, at last, a goal. A cross eluded the despairing lunges of two

Rammy strikers but Jon Robinson mopped up at the far post to score. The second half failed to live up to the sparkle of the first as Barlick came more into the game, but play was held in midfield with the teams cancelling out each other.

The points were secured three minutes after the break when a deep cross saw Robinson beat Carrington to the ball to send a header looping into the net. Gary Stopforth should have added a third when he shot well wide from the edge of the area when he had time to take the ball on further. Rammy substitute Phil Dean got to the byline in the closing stages and pulled a superb ball back for Gaskell. A fantastic reaction save by Carrington kept the ball out but the rebound hit Gaskell on the head and was diverted towards the unguarded goal before a desperate lunge saw a defender hack the ball off the line. And that was it. Ramsbottom stayed ahead of the pack with Runcorn Town to challenge for the league title and promotion. For Barlick, they'll have to see what next season brings – continuing to fly the White Rose flag on the west side of the Pennines.

Steve Penny

Barnoldswick Town 0 Ramsbottom United 2

Attendance 316
Admission £4
Ground Address Greenberfield Lane, Barnoldwick, Lancashire. BB18 5LJ
Club website www.pitchero.com/clubs/barnoldswicktown
Twitter None found

57

Land of the giants

Sheffield Wednesday FC v Preston North End

Hillsborough

nPOWER League One

Saturday 31st March 2012. Kick off 12.45pm

I have been to lots of football matches, involving a wide range of teams at most levels, over the last 25 years. None, however, have been as memorable as my visit to Hillsborough on Saturday 15th April 1989. On that day, 96 supporters didn't return home after the FA Cup semi-final between Liverpool and Nottingham Forest. I'm not even going to attempt to summarise the awful events on that day, let alone try to explain why this was allowed to happen. I felt the need to visit the memorial stone this morning and spend a few minutes in silence. This is situated at the main entrance to the ground and reads, "In memory of the 96 men, woman and children who tragically died and the countless people whose lives were changed forever". I think life changed for everyone at Hillsborough on that afternoon, but we were the lucky ones. The long queues at every telephone box (no mobiles then) is an image that I still remember when I stop at a service station today. Locking myself in my bedroom every night for two weeks to watch every single news programme on the disaster is a luxury that some didn't have. Sometimes I feel guilty for thinking at the time that I had suffered in the disaster.

Sheffield Wednesday Football Club is one of the oldest professional clubs in the world and the fifth oldest in the English league. The Wednesday, as they were named until 1929, were founding members of The Football Alliance in 1889 and champions in that inaugural season. They joined The Football League three years later when various leagues merged. Sheffield Wednesday were also one of the founding members of The Premier League in 1992. The Owls, as they are known, have spent the majority of their history in the top flight of English football since joining the Football League. In their rich history they have won four League titles, three FA Cups and, most recently, one League Cup in 1991. This was their only major trophy since 1935, but they did reach both domestic cup finals in 1993. They lost to Arsenal at Wembley on both occasions, but will now look back on that season as a high point. The club now find themselves stuck in the third tier of English football. However, there is a feeling that they are finally moving in the right direction. The Premier League would benefit from having a club like Sheffield Wednesday in it. I'm sure their supporters get fed up of hearing the words 'sleeping giant'.

Hillsborough is a north-western suburb of Sheffield, so is much easier for me to get to from the M1 than their Steel City rivals, Sheffield United. Finding the stadium is also simpler for visitors who really can't miss the roof tops of the stands as they approach on the A61. The Hillsborough stadium has the largest capacity of the Yorkshire football grounds at 39,732. It has been the club's home since 1899 and, in 1934, 72,841 fans watched the FA Cup tie against Manchester City. I have chosen the kop that "houses the loudest and most partisan section of Wednesday supporters" according to the club's website. When the roof was put on in 1986 it became the largest covered standing area in Europe with a capacity of 22,000. The area is now seated and holds just over half this number at 11,210. You would need to visit the ground, or see an aerial shot of Hillsborough, to fully appreciate just how big this stand is. I enter one of the many turnstiles to find a maze of winding paths and entrances to get inside. I climb the steps up to the top and enter the kop from the height of entrance V. I am rewarded with a mouth watering view down the kop towards the pitch and of the other three stands. Wow! I had forgotten how fantastic this stadium is!

I make my way to my seat trying to keep my eyes on every step. I settle down and listen to the supporters around me discussing the game and their chances of getting into the Championship. There is a nervy feel to their predictions with Wednesday currently sitting third in the table. They are just two points behind the automatic promotion place, which just happens to be held by their fierce rivals Sheffield United. Charlton Athletic are still top of the league and it is probably beyond either of them to catch them. A win in this earlier kick off, for Sky TV cameras, would put pressure on the Blades who are away at Hartlepool United at 3pm.

To my left is the South Stand that was constructed by my favourite football ground architect, Archibald Leitch. Today, it is almost unrecognisable from his initial design after a major £7m facelift for hosting matches in Euro '96. The clock-face and filial are still there though for us to admire. They have done a very good job of modernising the stand with an extra tier yet preserving the traditional look. To the right is the very impressive North Stand which was described in Simon Inglis' classic book, 'The Football Grounds of Great Britain', as the "Dream stand of the future". The metal construction at the rear still looks as impressive today as it did when it opened in 1961. It was then the first cantilever stand in English football to run the entire length of the pitch. White seats spell out the letters S W F C, which I can just about see with fifteen minutes to kick off. Behind the opposite goal is the West Stand, or sometimes known as the Leppings Lane End, where the Preston fans are sat. It is a huge away end holding over 7,000 people so the 1,000 or so who have travelled from Lancashire look dwarfed by their surroundings.

The teams come out and the drum of the kop starts to beat. Wednesday are in their traditional blue and white striped kit. Preston have an all black away strip, so the referee is in yellow. I would show my age if I go on a rant about how officials should stay in black, so I won't. The home side will be attacking the opposite end first, but I have a great view of the entire pitch from up here. Usually placing seats onto an existing terrace is a problem, but the steep steps of the kop gives everyone a good vantage point, unless you are behind one of the large posts of course. The PA system gets the majority of spectators to sing along to, "Hi ho Sheffield Wednesday", which I may now hum for the rest of the day. Despite the drop in the temperate today, I can spot at least three bare chested fans, one of which doesn't have the figure for this bravery, but I'm not the man to point this out to him.

The game kicks off and the drum starts the "barmy army" chants. I can now hear that the beat is just one part of a full brass band at the back of the kop. Wednesday attack from the whistle and get a good shot in on goal after just three minutes. The ball goes just wide of the top corner, but is enough to increase the noise at this end. Every single song is started by the band and they fire off tune after tune. Despite their imagination, the game itself is not as entertaining. I think Preston are partly to blame as the players appear to be wasting time after only 15 minutes! The edginess of the Wednesday players is passed onto the crowd, or this could well be the other way around. We finally get a good chance for the Yorkshire side when Reda Johnson nearly catches out Preston's goalkeeper, Thorsten Stuckmann. His cross, come shot, lands on the roof of the net and almost fools all of us, including Thorsten. The referee is having a terrible game and lets the Preston players get away with their negative game plan. Their tactics of more time wasting, play acting and bad tackles is killing this game without a strong official. For once, the kop don't rely on the band for a couple of choice songs aimed at the referee. We get one further strike from Wednesday on goal, but it is hit straight at the keeper. The whistle follows and the referee gets all of the attention as he leaves the pitch. Unusually, I stay in my seat for half time as don't fancy queuing for a, no doubt, expensive Bovril. I am amused by the Under 16 players doing a lap of honour, some dancing girls and playing with my new phone.

The second half looks more positive from the first kick, which is helped by Wednesday taking the lead after only four minutes of the restart. They are now attacking the goal at this end so we get the perfect view. Chris Lines plays in Madine and the striker turns to fire his 16th goal of the season into the top right-hand corner. It was a fantastic move and almost three sides of the ground follow the trumpet leading their regular "Gary Madine, goal machine" chant.

The goal has clearly settled nerves in the stand and the players are now attacking the Preston goal every time they win possession. On 63 minutes that goal machine song goes to his head with a second strike. Madine doubles his side's lead with a header from Antonio's long throw from the right. The simplicity of this goal was its beauty and you can hear the huge sigh of relief around Hillsborough above the sound of the band. "The city is ours, the city is ours, **** off United, the city is ours" confirms that they have done enough to leap frog their rivals into second spot. I almost bought a pin badge with the 'The city is ours' slogan on earlier but opted for a more traditional design, complete with an owl. The football has been much better this half with the players looking more relaxed and confident on the ball. With that thought, the play declines and becomes scrappy again for the final twenty minutes. Everyone else's thoughts are now in Teeside hoping their team can stay in the automatic promotion place longer than two hours.

The final whistle blows and Sheffield Wednesday have stretched their unbeaten run to eight games with this 2-0 win. Preston got exactly what they deserved from this game today - nothing. I head back to my car and take one final look back at the North Stand. Apart from my recent trip to Glasgow, is there a better stand in Britain? Hillsborough is, in my opinion, one of the finest football grounds in the country. It is admittedly showing its age in places, but it oozes character. If this club can return to the top flight, the cash may allow them to put their plans into place for the next development phase. Yorkshire will then have its own Ibrox. Both stadiums have an amazing history, which has unfortunately, included some awful moments, but they still very much, have a future. It is possible to have a stadium with four distinct stands that look very good together if the roofs converge. This giant is defiantly awakening. My only regret, I should have bought a Wednesday mug!

Sheffield Wednesday 2 Preston NE 0

Attendance 18,069

Admission £20
Ground Address Hillsborough Stadium, Sheffield. S6 1SW
Club website www.swfc.co.uk
Twitter @swfc or @wednesdayite

58, 59, 60 & 61. #easterbunnyhop

In January someone tweeted about the BARIS Northern Counties East Football League's plans to stagger some of the kick off times over Easter. Their motivation was to encourage ground hoppers, or 'normal' fans, to attend more than one game in a day. I am obviously not a man who needs any encouragement to watch two games in a day so this news was music to my ears, particularly at a time when I was worried how I was going to get around all of the grounds before the curtain comes down on the season. Excitedly, I picked three unvisited South Yorkshire clubs with kick off times of 10.30am, 4.45pm and 7.45pm. I wasn't sure what to do with myself for three hours in the middle of the day so slotted in a fourth, 1.30pm at Derbyshire's Staveley Miners Welfare. I unashamedly tweeted of my insanity and I even found a couple of victims to come with me. This was the obvious ground hop to do and I soon discovered that this is, in fact, the official hopping schedule today for the tour organiser Groundhop UK.

A couple of weeks ago, whilst knocking my head against the wall trying the crack the Route 66 code on a spreadsheet, this perfect day turned messy. With the big picture in mind, I have no option but to swap Staveley for a visit to Handsworth FC. The complication to this tactical move is that this is a 3pm kick off so I will need to miss some of the play to get to Hallam, or miss the start of the game at Sandygate. I am not sure yet what I'll do and will probably just go with the flow. It will be fun I tell myself! Yesterday's matches also had the kick off times staggered which generated gates above their average. There were 253 at Eccleshill United, 317 at Liversedge and 327 at Thackley which are all very good crowds for Step 5 and 6 of the Non League pyramid. I am not sure if this is due to other hoppers flocking to South Yorkshire or it being a bank holiday. I will count the rucksacks today and we will soon know the answer. Easter Saturday has never been so action packed. Oh, and a final detail, it can all be followed for the next 12 hours on Twitter...

58

Maltby Main FC v Parkgate

Muglet Lane
BARIS Northern Counties East League Premier
Saturday 7th April 2012. Kick off 10.30am

8.40 The Easter Bunny Hop is here! First stop Maltby Main FC at 10.30am kick off #route66 #easterbunnyhop

10.11 This could possibly be the world's first live chapter in a book, or certainly one about the football grounds of Yorkshire! #easterbunnyhop

10.13 Follow grounds 58, 59, 60 & 61 here today on the #easterbunnyhop Your replies may just end up in this chapter too if they are printable

10.14 Arrived at Maltby Main and there are cars everywhere! The hopper next to us has travelled from Margate! Now he is more insane than me surely

10.17 @TonyCSGreenall Enjoy the delights of Maltby. Last year v Farsley,I saw a delayed 2nd half after the ref was locked in the dressing room

10.20 It is appropriate that it is raining for our southern tourists #easterbunnyhop #route66

10.22 Didn't know we could buy advanced tickets! They have a special turnstile for these hoppers. £5 cash is exchanged

10.28 The first programme and pin badge of the day. That's why most people here have got rucksacks. At least I'm not the only one with a camera

10.30 Teams are out. Maltby in are red shirts with white sleeves like the Arsenal of old. Parkgate are Celtic in this fantasy

10.33 2 stands to choose from on the same touchline. One is seated but now full. We join the busy terrace for the shelter from the rain

10.34 This is a very long warm up. Suspect the players are enjoying the larger crowd #easterbunnyhop

10.39 I see from the programme that badges are usually 50p cheaper. They could probably sell them for a tenner today so can't blame them #route66

10.39 @GrahamYapp Green woolly hat and blue rucksack level w/ 18yd line on left of stand side as MM attack if any tweeters want to say hello

10.40 we will look out for you. Just so I can borrow your hat. Mines in the boot of my car #easterbunnyhop

10.41 Game slowly warming up. Unlike my hands. Gloves in the car

10.42 George happy at the touchline. Let's see how enthusiastic he is on ground number 4 #easterbunnyhop

10.42 @leedeetee Made it! Can't believe the crowd! (Or the slope on the pitch!)

10.43 welcome! Where are you? We will find you later

10.47 @leedeetee currently stood directly behind Maltby's goal!

10.47 1-0 to Maltby Main. The big number 10 ran onto a through ball and calmly slotted it in for the lead #easterbunnyhop

10.48 Maltby are 19th in the table and just one place off the bottom. Parkgate are 6th. Even if the home side win they don't move up the table.

10.52 George wants to be a ball boy so we are moving behind the goal that Parkgate are attacking. I have found my hat! #Easterbunnyhop

10.53 Why have I put on my spring jacket?! Bitter cold and may chase some balls myself to keep warm

10.56 Goal alerts only now until I get a warm drink on my fingers at half time

11.04 According to the white board the Maltby number 10 is Tom Folyton Brown. I now have my hot gravy

11.10 Should be 1-1 but Maltby keeper tipped a header over the bar. George retrieved the ball but the corner was wasted

11.17 Now 1-1. Own goal. Number 2 heads into his own net from a corner #easterbunnyhop #route66

11.18 @ParkgateFC GOAL: Maltby Main 1 - 1 Parkgate '42 Griffin #NCEL

11.23. Duncan next to me is now on ground 283. Travelled from London to do 9 this weekend & will do another 3 on Monday

11.25 Half time 1-1. Just seen a fan in a Partick Thistle shirt. Surely not?

11.35 @Glasgow_Red and me! I came all the way from Glasgow. 103 for me today.

11.29 Dave has come on the organised coach from Wakefield. Train from Wycombe on Thursday. Ground number 1,109! Wow! #easterbunnyhop

11.32 Nice chatting to Dave. He was a Wycombe Wanders season ticket holder but didn't renew this season to concentrate on his hopping

11.41 "150 ish" from the man next to me now. He really needs to know the exact number?! His 2 year old is in the twenties

11.47 Talking to strangers is definitely more interesting than the game on the pitch

11.51 2-1 to Maltby Main! Number 9 hit a beautiful shot in the top corner from the edge of the box

11.57 The man in the Partick shirt is called Chris. He organised the trip as Groundhop UK. He even has his name on his fleece. Really nice guy

11.59 Chris is from Swansea but now living in Long Eaton. Only 800 grounds "I'm nothing"

12.00 @8chrisOKeeffe8 Keep up good work, loving the updates from the village I was brought up in #MaltbyMain

12.01 Chris introduces me to Jens from Germany. He is here for 8 games. Wait for it... almost 5,400!!! #beyondyorkshire

12.03 Jens has watched football in 78 countries! He is only 46 so has plenty of grounds left in him apparently #easterbunnyhop #route66

12.05 There is a Karl back in Germany who has been to over 8,000 grounds. He is in his 70's so Jens may beat this

12.06 Jens wants to introduce me to his German friend Boris

12.09 Boris "less than 2,000" but in 151 countries!! Double wow

12.09 @LUFCDanish and where's Fritz in all this? Joking aside, those are amazing statistics

12.12 Malty Main score a third but miss it as Boris has got my full attention

12.14 Boris has plans to watch a football game in every single country in the world! I have only known him for minutes but believe him

12.19 2 go down in this league so this win gives Maltby Main a chance now. They still have to play Lincoln Moorlands who are one place above them

12.22 Bottom 2 go down. Selby are bottom & relegated who they have got to play on the last day. Chairman says they need 3 wins from the last 4

12.25 Come on whistle my fingers are numb. "Always cold here" I'm told

12.26 Final score of ground 58 is Maltby Main 3 Parkgate 1. Back to the car to get the heater on #easterbunnyhop #route66

12.34 Everyone appears to be jumping in their cars to race off to Derbyshire. We will join the hoppers later but we are staying in Yorkshire

Maltby Main 3 Parkgate 1

Attendance 253
Admission £5
Ground Address Muglet Lane, Maltby, Rotherham. S66 7JQ

Club website www.maltbymainfc.f9.co.uk
Twitter None found

13.00 Now at Meadowhall for some lunch. I wonder if there is a german here who collects shopping centres?! #easterbunnyhop #route66

13.07 Number 7 is now the most important number to me. The stairway where we have parked our car. That was my 150th ground by the way. Small beer

13.23 The shoppers at Meadowhall would think Boris is strange. He probably is a bit but flocking here every week is stranger #easterbunnyhop

13.28 @jonnyc68 there sooo sad, i have to work there everyday!!!! #poorpoorme!!!!!

13.29 Someone asked me when we left if I would hit 5,000 grounds. I said my wife would leave me. "Mine already has at only 1,000!". Priceless

13.48 Leaving Meadowhell for ground number 59. Rather be a hopper than a serial shopper

59

Handsworth FC v Appleby Frodingham

Olivers Mount

BARIS Northern Counties East League Division One

Saturday 7th April 2012. Kick off 3pm

14.06 In Handsworth FC car park with 55 minutes to spare. Going to chill out in the car for a bit knowing that there is a mad rush on the horizon

14.09 Think if I'm going to miss some of this game anyway I should leave early enough to not miss anything of the next one. Then only one suffers

14.11 Sorry Handsworth FC. The other option was to miss you off #route66 completely. Spent weeks studying the fixtures trying the crack the code

14.13 I mentioned Handsworth to some of the other hoppers. They were not impressed "The club trying to derail the hopping day"

14.15 Handsworth FC have greeted my visit warmly with a tweet "ask at the bar for Dave Wragg Club Secretary. He'll look after you for your visit"

14.17 The crime appears to be offering free admission to attract hoppers in the area to Handsworth FC. Therefore "not supporting the hopping day"

14.24 Follow @leedeetee who is at Staveley MW on the official hopping tour. We will meet Lee hopefully at Hallam #easterbunnyhop

14.30 @HandsworthFC the free entry is about rewarding the 100 or so whom we are so grateful visit us every week- we fully support #groundhop

14.31 @Risto1980 you definitely need to do a full write up on the Worlds oldest ground! So definitely leave early and get up to @HallamFC1!

14.56 Met Dave & Steve (tweeter for the club) in the bar. Could not be more friendly. Discuss the plans they have for the club

14.58 Dashing from the clubhouse to the pitch. Need to make kick off as we are ditching them later! #easterbunnyhop

15.01 Handsworth are top of the league but they could be kicked out in a NCEL meeting next Thursday due to their ground facilities #route66

15.03 Arrive just as the game is starting. Club have plans to improve their facilities but may need to ground share next season if that is agreed

15.05 I have been given a programme, pin badge, bottle opener & scarf which is a very kind gesture. I can now identify the home side immediately

15.07 Handsworth play in yellow (perhaps gold?) & black stripes. Appleby Frodingham are wearing a Blackburn Rovers style blue & white kit #route66

15.09 This is a top v bottom game so would expect to see some goals and to miss some when I am charging at speed to Hallam

15.11 Average attendance is around 100 but doesn't look any higher despite the free admission & the hoppers that have flooded South Yorkshire

15.13 One nil to Handsworth! Easy header from a floating cross. Looks like the number 5 but his number is peeling off his back

15.16 Its all Handsworth now so can see an easy and possibly cricket score win. George is Man City on his PSP so hasn't noticed this

15.17 Penalty to Handsworth!

15.19 A yellow card to the offending fouler and the number 9 calmly slots in the spot kick. 2-0 to Handsworth so good value at free admission

15.21 The facilities are modest admittedly. We have one small seated stand & a pitch that has a perimeter fence that is Olivers Mount

15.23 Appleby now have a -88 goal difference compared to Handsworth's +48!!

15.27 Anyone tell me where Appleby Frodingham is? If it's in Yorkshire I will find a good use for this scarf and a nearby tree branch #route66

15.28 Handsworth hit the cross bar. This may get embarrassing #easterbunnyhop

15.28 @LeeWest1865 deepest darkest Scunthorpe

15.29 thanks Lee! I'm sure I'll go there one day and find a German there too

15.33 I'm told that I need to leave at 4.15pm to miss the traffic from Sheffield United. I owe them a full 90 minutes & will come back next season

15.35 Handsworth FC Can you please tweet me a final score with goal scorers? I can then RT this from Hallam #panicking already

15.36 @HandsworthFC no worries

15.38 George scores his first headed goal on the PSP. He shows me the replay whilst Handsworth take 3 corners in a row. Not sure how its still 2-0

15.43 There are 3 people with rucksacks, one with a notepad. I smell hoppers! #easterbunnyhop

15.43 @samWBAmarley Just walked past two guys in Kiveton to here the conversation "who's sorting us with our sniff tonight?" Oh I love the village I live in

15.44 looking forward to coming to Kiveton Park FC on Easter Monday then! #route66

15.47 Half time in game two, #route66 ground 59. Handsworth 2 Frodingham 0. Battery flat. Turning off until Hallam. The journey will charge it up

16.24 And the hare is on the move..... #easterbunnyhop A57, A61 and A57 again towards Glossop. I know it in my sleep by now

Handsworth 4 Appleby Frodingham 0

Attendance 84
Admission Free
Ground Address Olivers Mount, Handsworth, Sheffield. S9 4PA
Club website www.pitchero.com/clubs/handsworthfc
Twitter @HandsworthFC

60

Hallam FC v Teversal

Sandygate

BARIS Northern Counties East League Division One

Saturday 7th April 2012. Kick off 4.45pm

16.45 At the oldest football ground in the world just as the players are lining up. Hallam FC is ground number 3 today but number 60 #route66

16.48 Hallam are all in blue and kicking up the slope this half. The ball strikes the brand new club house & it is still standing #easterbunnyhop

16.51 The club house was opened today in time for the hoppers. I can see the Germans enjoying the Yorkshire sun rather than the new facilities

16.53 Another record is £5 for my badge. Although it is special. Commemorates Boxing Day 2010 for the oldest derby in the world v Sheffield FC

16.55 Match lost again with conversations around me of the grounds people have visited. 2 southern men next to me discuss their German grounds

16.57 This is a lovely ground in nice surroundings. The green hills in the distance still have lines of snow on them. Its cold but clearer skies

16.57 @HandsworthFC 4-0 Sam Smith 2 (29 + 30th of the season) , Gareth Giffiths + Lee Hill with the goals - thanks for visiting us today

16.58 thanks! I hope the 4th goal was a modest tap in. I will return for a full 90 minutes very soon #route66

17.01 The main stand on the half way line is modern like the entire ground. It has character yes but nothing to show off the grounds age

17.07 Sandygate has been acknowledged by the Guiness Book of Records as the Worlds first & oldest ground. Had their 150th anniversary in 2010

17.09 @Risto1980 trust me the old stand is not particularly sorely missed! No modern ground would have this slope or setting though!

17.10 They are the 2nd oldest club in world though. Sheffield FC have that claim to fame. We are definitely in the city where football was born

17.14 The vision for the future includes a history of football museum to attract visitors from around the world. They are already here!!

17.17 Not sure this game has quite lived up to the bumper crowd yet. Hallam have the edge so far #easterbunnyhop

17.21 Hallam almost got a goal with a decent shot. I have also spotted someone in sandals who must be an overseas visitor

17.24 Today's visitors Teversal have travelled from Nottinghamshire. They are wearing red shirts with black shorts & socks. They have a stall too!

17.34 George is getting a bit bored but in his defence he is doing well for 7 year old. The warmth of the clubhouse calls. Half time whistle blows

17.36 No score so far in game number 3 of the day. Perhaps the players are as tired as my legs. It's definitely Red Bull time! Very nice clubhouse

17.41 Hallam started the day in 14th in the NCEL Div 1 3 points & 2 places behind Teversal. Has that mid table feel. This bar stool feels good!

17.44 Both stalls are doing good business today in souvenirs. The crowd feels higher too than the 85 that were here last Tuesday against Worksop

17.51 The game has restarted & I am now wide awake. I have wings as the advert says! I also have a Hallam FC mug to go with my Whitby Town one

17.59 I have finally found @leedeetee. He is also still in the clubhouse watching the game from the window. The door is open!!

18.03 The conversation soon turns to the Germans statistics. 5,400 divided by 21 adult years = 257 a year! He can't be married we all agree

18.06 We are all hoppers but agree we will see a doctor before we want to do those sort of numbers #easterbunnyhop

18.08 Still goalless in the game by the way which we are all watching from behind glass. I blame George who says he is cold #easterbunnyhop

18.11 The serious hoppers will now all burn my book in disgust that we have broken the rules by leaving a game early. Don't we all make our own rules up in ground hopping

18.16 Some hoppers only count grounds where they have touched the ball. Some feel the need to touch every corner flag. Says the man with a mug

18.18 We leave the warmth to watch the final 20 minutes. Come on Hallam let's have a goal!

18.26 The hoppers are already getting itchy feet for the whistle. Some are gathering by the corner flag nearest the exit. The game is poor I admit

18.28 We move to the small terrace behind the goal that has the sign 'Gentlemen No Swearing Please'. Women have all the fun

18.30 Fantastic. Number 8 for Hallam smashes the ball into the roof of the net. 1-0. I didn't think it would ever happen in this game! #route66

18.30 @TeversalFC GOAL!!! 88mins and @HallamFC1 take the lead - 1-0. Shot from edge of area high into roof of net. Bugger!

18.33 The area by the exit is getting busier since that goal. The whistle will be like a starter gun

18.34 @LeeWest1865 aim carefully!

18.35 There we go. Let's get back to the car to head north on the A61 in convoy. Ground 60 of #route66 ended in a win for the Yorkshire team

18.36 are you the other Lee I am trying to meet?

Hallam 1 Teversal 0

Attendance 212
Admission £5
Ground Address Sandygate Road, Crosspool, Sheffield. S10 5SE
Club website www.hallamfc.co.uk
Twitter @HallamFC1

18.42 @GrahamYapp I have paused at the McDonald's healthfood emporium on the A61

18.53 Just passed Hillsborough! Wow again #route66

18.57 @BridgetteG68 was that 'wow' look at all that rust?

61

Worsbrough Bridge Athletic FC v Rossington Main

Park Road

BARIS Northern Counties East League Division One

Saturday 7th April 2012. Kick off 7.45pm

19.13 A small housing estate in Worsborough has been invaded by hoppers parking everywhere. Not a night to pop out for a takeaway #easterbunnyhop

19.17 Our 5,400 ground German has just parked in front of us with a lady. The perfect couple? Reassuring that he arrives in a VW #easterbunnyhop

19.21 Jens has a 'Distillery FC Marching On Together' car sticker. I may have blown his cover now. I need a drink too! Great fun but tiring

19.24 Picnic tea in the car before that final souvenir hunt. Hoping for some goals to end on a high. Ground looked nice when we passed it though

19.35 Inside the clubhouse which has become a hopping heaven. Stalls selling badges, programmes & books. Love the whiteboard with the teams on

19.43 Now this is a nice ground. Helped by the surrounding countryside & one very old stand that Hallam needed #easterbunnyhop #route66

19.48 Teams are out for our final game today. There is only one place to sit tonight! The bricks & metal look like they belong on a Victorian house

19.50 Great being able to photograph a stand without drawing attention to yourself or feeling like a potential serial killer. I am not alone!

19.51 George wants to find @leedeetee who is "cool". I have a flat cap just like him which he once told me looked stupid #easterbunnyhop

19.53 Worsbrough Bridge Athletic FC is #route66 ground number 61 for those not following everyone of my 10,000+ tweets #easterbunnyhop

19.54 Worsbrough are wearing red & white striped shirts with black shorts & socks. Rossington Main are in their usual blue & white home strip

19.55 The home side have made the better start who the majority of the crowd are cheering for based on that shot #route66

19.56 @simonjcope nice ground? Seriously? Shocking pitch that wouldn't be out of place at the Somme. Terrible trouble with floods too

19.56 @leedeetee George, you da man! Never been called cool in my life.

19.56 well done Lee. How much for the flat cap? Lol

19.57 although in the company you are keeping tonight Lee....

19.58 @bertyowls come on rossington #blue and white stripes

19.59 @leedeetee Ha! I had to order it from the internet because the circumference from my head is 62cm. #cannonball

20.01 We are behind the dug outs & the stand is quite full to create a decent atmosphere #easterbunnyhop

20.02 @TonyCSGreenall Come on,Rosso! It's the only way we can bring 3 points back to Doncaster these days

20.04 come on anyone Tony. We need some goals at this stage in our day #easterbunnyhop

20.04 @RossingtonMain Blue with wite sleeves... but near enough. Stick with us. You know it makes sense

20.06 The Rossington number 7's shorts are so low it looks like he is wearing a skirt #weneedagoalatthisstageintheday #easterbunnyhop

20.06 @TonyCSGreenall Rossington have had regular high scoring games this year,so hopefully you get a few goals tonight

20.08 @RossingtonMain Tony has just daubed 0-0 all over this game in a big fat marker pen

20.09 Worsbrough are 8th the table at the start of the day. Just one place & 2 points below Rossington. A 9 all thriller for sure? #route66

20.10 I am optimistic though. I went shopping for Mrs Mowbray's birthday present on Thursday in North Shields....

20.11 @TonyCSGreenall I only mentioned it once, under the Beetlejuice rule it has to be said 3 times.We're safe yet!

20.15 Opposite touchline has a covered terrace & rest is open space. We arrived in the light so can appreciate how nice this part of Yorkshire is

20.17 That tackle made such a noise 3 woman squealed. Fair but hard. Welcome to Yorkshire he should of shouted for the sake of our tourists

20.21 Boris has been spotted. He is in the clubhouse watching the game through the window. He is human!!! #easterbunnyhop

20.28 A couple of minutes left until half time. Still goalless and need a Bovril to warm up. There is a beer in my fridge awaiting my return

20.34 Boris has ordered some chilli. Not that I am stalking him or anything. Although I wouldn't half bag some grounds if I did start

20.35 He's chosen to sit next to us. He may be stalking me now. After all this is my 154th ground tonight. Let's see if he is at Kiveton on Monday

20.42 Follow @groundhopuk Could just change your life! Teams will be out soon so heading back to the touchline for the final push #easterbunnyhop

20.51 I have finally met the other Lee known as @LeeWest1865 Not as cool in George's opinion as @leedeetee but 1,500 grounds to his name

20.55 @leedeetee 1500 grounds takes a lot more effort and skill than simply purchasing an XXXL flat cap. :)

20.55 A goal! Someone at the far end hit a good shot to give Worsbrough the lead. They announce the scorer but the speaker must be under water

20.55 Oh and we have found the dog who has apparently visited all 6 games during the last 48 hours. Woof!

20.58 The game has returned to its midfield battle of swear words and tackles. George has found a big fishing net & my battery is being murdered

20.59 The net is for fishing out the ball when it lands in the river. No George I tell him! #route66

21.01 I say well done to the dog as we start our lap. His owner corrects us. He has done 10 matches just in the last 5 days #easterbunnyhop

21.05 Should be 1-1. Rossington miss a sitter. The ball is still travelling towards Barnsley when it really deserved a goal

21.09 2-0! Corner and a sweet header. I think by number 7. The lad next to me says it was the number 2 and the speaker again gives no clues at all

21.11 A third opinion is it was the number 2 that scores. A photo of the white board doesn't help but Dean Jones wins the vote of our end

21.12 3-0! Another header and again we all disagree on the scorer. @leedeetee says the speaker says Scott Ruthven

21.18 4-0 now! Free kick from the number 3 which may have got a touch. Speaker says Robert which we can't find in our programme. Blame exhaustion

21.19 At half time this did not look like a 4-0 score was possible. Worsbrough are now running through the defence like a hot knife through butter

21.33 Waiting for the final whistle now. Happy with 4-0 as the curtain on the #easterbunnyhop

21.35 Final score on #route66 Ground 61 is Worsbrough Bridge 4 Rossington Main 0 Slow walk back to the car to accept this #easterbunnyhop is over

21.35 @stainedglassme Finished 4-0 to Worsbrough Bridge Atheltic. Rossington heads dropped after the first goal. Had the pleasure to stand with @MowbrayRoute66

Worsbrough Bridge 4 Rossington Main 0

Attendance 273
Admission £5
Ground Address Park Road, Worsbrough Bridge, Barnsley. S70 5LJ
Club website www.pitchero.com/clubs/worsbroughbridgeathletic
Twitter None found

23.06 Back in Ilkley after 152 miles, 8 badges, 4 programmes, 3 Bovrils and I've seen 12 of the 13 goals to produce 4 home wins #easterbunnyhop

23.09 Met some very interesting people & been part of a new community for just 11 hours. Most importantly I have visited 4 more #route66 grounds

23.13 @RobGrillo There's a nice ground in Ilkley too. Might be a bit dark to go lookin' for it now though :)

23.13 Time for a beer courtesy of my new Handsworth Junior Sporting Club bottle opener. If I have any followers left, goodnight! #Easterbunnyhop

Revisited...

Handsworth FC v Glasshoughton Welfare

Olivers Mounts

BARIS Northern Counties East Football League Division One

Friday 20th April 2012. Kick off 7.45pm

17.33 2 weeks tomorrow #route66 will conclude at Rotherham United. After 10 months & over 100 oxo cubes I won't know whether to laugh or cry

17.44 @TonyCSGreenall Normally I'd say laugh,but it's at Don Valley which is enough to make the most hardened fan burst into tears!

18.57 Ground 59 @HandsworthFC revisited! Leaving so early on Easter Saturday has been niggling away at me. I've arrived at Olivers Mount #route66

19.45 "Olivers army is here to stay" plays as a busier ground awaits the arrival of the players. 1 point will give @HandsworthFC a top 2 finish

19.51 The last of the programmes are sold & the game kicks off. Glasshoughton are 3rd so a win for them will keep their promotion hopes alive

19.54 More complicated for @HandsworthFC as there is a NCEL meeting soon to discuss their status due to their facilities not being up to scratch

20.08 Both teams clearly are playing for the win. The tackles are flying in! Decent game so far but a goal would really get things going #route66

20.15 Red card! Glasshoughton down to 10 and @HandsworthFC have a free kick on the edge of the box. Good decision by the referee!

20.17 Chance wasted but should hopefully help @HandsworthFC get the draw they need. It was a bad tackle from behind so no complaints

20.25 Some serious rain is heading this way. Not sure everyone will fit into the 1 small stand! It would almost be funny if it got abandoned

20.38 Half time and 0-0. Handsworth finished the stronger side so get the carva on ice

20.57 Second half kicks off as I head to the Railway End. I now remember seeing the On Tour flag on that windy night in Askern #route66

20.59 The Railway End is at one end & by a railway but just flat grass, not the kop this fine flag deserves!

21.11 Half chances at both ends & the rain has missed this part of Sheffield. Starting to look like a goalless draw. The best type in this case!

21.27 Fans & players both relaxed about the score staying level. The children rolling down the grass bank has been my highlight of the 2nd half

21.39 Not sure how @HandsworthFC are not ahead. At least 3 shots blocked from close range. Should have been a penalty too a few minutes later

21.43 Great shot by Glasshougton and they take the lead against the run of play

21.45 Come on @HandsworthFC They so deserve the point to take them to the Premier!

21.50 The whistle blows & the promotion race is now wide open with this defeat for Handsworth. Glasshoughton are just a point behind Worksop

23.23 Arrived home. Very tired but need a beer and a study of the league table to unwind

23.32 Gosh. Handsworth's remaining game is away at Worksop Parramore! Worksop will be top of the league by then if they win tomorrow #route66

23.39 NCEL Division 1 Table 1. Handsworth P 37 Pts 79, 2. Worksop P 36 Pts 77, 3. Glasshoughton P 37 Pts 76 Set up for a great finish next weekend

23.44 So no promotion party tonight for @HandsworthFC Glad I've seen a full 90 minutes - biggest in their short history so far! Ground 59... Tick

Handsworth 0 Glasshoughton Welfare 1

Attendance 286
Admission£3

62

Easy Street

Kiveton Park FC v Easington United

Hard Lane

Windsor Foodservice Central Midlands Football League

Black Dragon Division North

Easter Monday 9th April 2012. Kick off 3pm

It is a Bank Holiday so, predictably, it is wet and windy. I am also very predictable, so I'm parked outside another Yorkshire football ground. I think I have found Kiveton Park FC, but it is not obvious from the view from this piece of wasteland. Finding the village of Kiveton Park was easy from junction 31 of the M1. Although returning to South Yorkshire so soon after Saturday's hopperathon wasn't really what I wanted to do when I first looked out the window this morning. George hasn't been put off and proudly held in the car the sheet of paper with the directions to the ground. Their website directs visitors to an empty car park that has a distant view of the pitch but the tall irons gates are firmly locked. Perhaps it is a trap to round up ground hoppers and then ship them overseas to Germany after dark. We got out alive and eventually found the correct street after five attempts. We decide that we will stay in the car as long as possible as the rain is now torrential. We have everything we need in here which includes our Easter Egg chocolate. Poor Lucas has come down with chicken pox so a wet field isn't what he needs today, although he would allow us to skip the queue for our refreshments!

Kiveton Park has had a football club ever since the former colliery opened in the 19th century. They played in the old Yorkshire League and were founder members of the Northern Counties East League. Relegation saw them join the Central Midlands League at the start of the 1990s. When the colliery closed in 1994, Kiveton lost its football club and major financier. The following season, the current chairman David Carswell got a team of young lads together to play football in the Sheffield Sports and Athletic League. They were called 'The Waleswood' and in their first season won the League cup and were runners up in the league. In the 1999/00 season they were approached by Worksop Town to become their A side playing in the Central Midlands Reserve League. The 2000/01 season saw Kiveton Park Football Club re-emerge and join the Central Midlands Premier Division. They have remained at Step 7 of the Non League pyramid and currently sit 9th in the table. Today's visitors, Easington United, are in 12th after 3 consecutive wins and, of course, are not strangers to George and I after visiting the East End a couple of weeks ago. I contacted their General Manager, Richard, again last night after the club website listed the kick off as 12 noon. The news of a 3pm start was very welcome to give a much more relaxed pre match build up. Apparently, the kick off time was only confirmed yesterday so I can be excused for asking him for clarification.

It is now 2.50pm, so we leave our steamed up car in search of a game of football and hopefully a warm drink. We find a building and the first door leads us to a counter in front of a kitchen area. Again, I am offered black pepper with my Bovril which is served in a mug. I spot the admission prices written on the wall so, after no prompting, offer to pay more than the 50p I am asked for. They have sold today's programmes and have also run out of pin badges. Their loss. I would have happily increased my £3.50 investment to over £10. We walk slowly around the corner, so not to spill my drink, to find the players and officials leaving the changing rooms that are at the back of the building. We hang back and follow them towards the pitch that is in the distance. A large covered stand is a welcome sight as we are already quite wet. The ground is a bit run down and is one of the worst pitches I have encountered so far. The one stand is, however, well above average for this level and looks like it has been recently repainted black and white. It looks old in the nicest possible way. We make our way inside where the entire crowd has congregated to get shelter from the elements. There are no dugouts, so a small group of coaches stand on the touch line in front of us. I recall reading recently that they had built some dugouts, but unfortunately they were vandalised. The substitutes have more sense, although they do look strange standing on our terrace in their football boots. The ground doesn't have any floodlights but there is a solid perimeter fence. Some parts of the ground have the benefit of a concrete path. That completes my description of this ground!

Kiveton Town are in navy blue shirts with black socks, or it may have been light blue when dry. Easington United have their away strip on which consists of white shirts with green shorts and socks. I climb the steps further up the stand to avoid the drips of water from the roof as the game kicks off. It looks like there may have once been seats here, but I am happy with what we have today. The steep steps and solid construction offers a great view of play and, importantly, shelter from the downpour that continues outside. I say hello to Richard who is also in the stand with his clipboard and shouting words of encouragement at every pass his team makes. The rain is pouring off the roof, but the passing is good considering how wet the pitch must now be.

The noise of the rain and warmth of my hot Bovril gives me another nice moment, similar to the cider in a thunder storm. It may be helped by the mug, rather than the usual disposable cup, which improves the taste. Watching George, who is watching every pass, also makes me feel all smiley. This is something he wouldn't have been capable of at the start of the season, but now look at him. Grass roots football in the pouring rain! We have had such good father and son quality time this weekend from Route 66. Life feels good at this moment in time, an emotion I wasn't really expecting at a wet Hard Lane.

I get talking to the man next to me and within a couple of minutes discover that we follow each other on twitter. Karl, or @footysphere, lives in Kiveton and, when he is not ground hopping, watches his local side. He tells me that this ground has had a lot of problems from vandals. The dugouts were, in fact, burnt down and the paint job on the stand was to cover the graffiti. He shows me the 'before photo' on his mobile. They have also improved the fences in an attempt to "keep the chavs out". I have enjoyed Karl's tweets so it is good, and a little strange, to talk to him for real. I now wonder if his description of being a 'Bladesman from the Lane' refers to Bramall or Hard Lane? I suspect the latter as he shares my disillusionment on the modern top flight game. Karl's favourite ground is Belper Town due to the backdrop of an old mill and the beautiful Peak District countryside. He is definitely my kind of fan! I once broke into that ground in my suit, complete with briefcase, to have a look at the pitch; but that is a story for another day...

After 11 minutes the Kiveton number 9 runs onto a good through ball. He shows great composure to round the keeper and score in the now open net. The home side probably just about deserve the lead but the ball looked like it was going to stop in the long grass before the line, although, from up here, I can't even see that the pitch is marked out. There is no distinction between where the pitch starts or ends so I'm not sure when it was last painted. After 20 minutes the Easington number 10 taps in the equaliser after a good cross from the left found him on his own, unmarked. Richard tells me the scorer's name, but at the same time as George asks me if he can be a ball boy again. I agree, despite the rain getting heavier every minute, but still don't know the name of the Easington striker. The roof is now leaking in places but nobody is getting as wet as George. He is ignoring my calls to come back but does at least put his hood up; the hood from his top rather than the waterproofed one on his coat, but it's progress I suppose. After 33 minutes the home goal scorer grabs another goal under similar circumstances. The number 9 skips through the Easington defence and calmly places the ball in the net. A couple of minutes later I can see that George's trousers have changed colour so I order him to come back into the stand. He is soaked but happy. A couple of minutes before half time, Easington almost grab an equaliser, but the number 10's chip goes just wide of the post.

Half time arrives but, unusually, we, like everyone around us, stay put. It is a long walk to the tea bar and the rain is creating lines in the sky. Even with my 'burglar hat' on I would be soaked. I am told that I don't look as cool as hopper Lee, but I like it. We all discuss the half time scores and play with our phones until the players are spotted returning in the distance. Someone is armed with a large brush and, to our amusement, uses it to sweep some of the water from the penalty area that Kiveton will now be attacking. I have to move again, this time a few steps to the left, as the roof above me has decided to leak. The puddles around me are getting bigger so I am not the only person who needs to search for a drier place to stand.

The game, like the weather, also gets worse. There are even less clear cut chances now and the only action has involved each keeper gathering the ball on the edge of the box. I hope the referee knows where the box starts and finishes, although he is getting so wet he may have lost interest in such small details.

The rain appears to be easing so I stupidly send George back out to retrieve some balls on the strict instructions that the correct hood is used. Most of the play is from the home side, but the strikers are struggling to control the ball in the mud bath the penalty area has become. Didn't we have a drought yesterday? So how can the ground be so wet after just one day of rain? It is getting harder to control the midfield area too and the rain gets worse as I recall George. The players are struggling to stay on their feet which is causing mistakes in the defences but no goals. Kiveton Park look in control with them having most of the play, but Easington remind us that they are still in this game with every break they make. It is, therefore, no surprise when Easington equalise with around five minutes left of normal time. Jamie Cousins crosses the ball into the box which takes a slight defection from a Kiveton defender and ends up in the net. It is now 2-2 and few in the ground, or our stand, would argue that it hasn't been coming.

The whistle eventually blows and we all dash back to our cars in an attempt to keep as dry as possible. I am told by some of the locals that the attendance isn't recorded and wouldn't be accurate anyway as a couple of men around me proudly boast that they haven't paid this afternoon. A man with a tin is clearly needed at this ground. Perhaps they do have one and he just didn't fancy getting drenched today. I have a quick count myself, ignoring the handful of officials and players sheltering, and arrive at the number 30. I think we have been rewarded this afternoon for bravely leaving our homes. The beauty of today has been in its simplicity. It was so easy. There wasn't the need for any planning and it didn't involve any rushing around to get here. I have enjoyed watching a game of football with my son despite, or perhaps even because of, the conditions. It has only cost me £3.50 and some petrol. Simple! I now have just 4 grounds left to complete my journey around Yorkshire, but, like any groundhopper, I would be lying if I didn't admit that I have also got pleasure from the fact that I have today visited my 154th ground. I may well be the only one counting, but in my world it's important.

Kiveton Park 2 Easington United 2

Attendance Not recorded
Admission Price £2 Adults and 50p Children
Ground Address Stone Close, Kiveton Park, South Yorkshire. S26 6NB
Club website www.kivetonparkfc.co.uk
Twitter None found

63

A life more ordinary

Wakefield FC v Cammell Laird

Stade France

Evo-Stik League Northern Premier First Division North

Saturday 21st April 2012. Kick off 3pm

It would be a real shame to allow a portion of bad (ok, really bad) chips to put me off a ground but I haven't exactly been excited about returning to the Stade France. Thankfully, Mrs Mowbray has fed Lucas and I well, so snack bars don't interest me today. The truth is that visiting new grounds is always going to be more fun than going back to somewhere I left in November with stomach ache. Wakefield FC probably don't want to be here either after they were evicted from their previous home, College Grove, at the end of the 2010/11 season. The Wakefield Sports Club preferred to allow the Japanese hockey team to train there for the Olympic Games. Nice. The club started this season sharing a ground with their Division 1 rivals, Ossett Town. Their financial difficulties of last November, which forced the club to go amateur, were just the start of their problems.

The club's history intertwines with chapter 16 as they were originally formed in 1903 as Emley FC. In 2000, the club left Emley for Belle View in Wakefield to support their ambitions to move up the Non League pyramid. They finished their first season there with 101 points, but missed out on promotion to the Conference by a single point. They lost 3-2 to the team that pipped them, Stalybridge Celtic, in the final game of the season in front of a bumper home crowd of 3,708. They have struggled to reach these heights over the following years. This period has included relegation from the newly formed Conference North. Off the pitch, they have changed their name to Wakefield & Emley FC, Wakefield - Emley AFC and eventually

Wakefield FC. In 2008 the club went through a complete re-branding with new kits, badge and nickname as the Bears.

The club's vision of promotion to the Premier Division has been clouded by their current plight of staring relegation in the face. I had the tension of promotion last night when I revisited Handsworth to get a full ninety minutes of Olivers Mount under my belt. Today is quite a contrast. It is the last game of the season and Wakefield need to draw to guarantee their survival. They are third from bottom, one place above relegation. Today's visitors, Cammell Laird, are bottom and already down. Two points below Wakefield are Harrogate Railway who have a considerably worse goal difference. Wakefield won at Railway 1-0 last weekend to put them in the driving seat to retain their Step 4 status in the Non League pyramid. At the other end of the table, AFC Fylde have won the title this week. I was very impressed with them when they played at the other ground in this area, Ossett Albion .

Whatever my experience from my last visit, I do recall that it is quite a child friendly ground, provided they bring their own food of course. Therefore, I have brought Lucas with me today to say his fair well to his Route 66. I feel like I have spent a lot of time recently in the Sheffield area with the last 6 grounds all being in South Yorkshire, so the shorter drive to West Yorkshire is very welcome. It is also nice when you don't need directions. We arrive at the ground but, this time park in the pay and display car park because of the daytime restrictions on the nearby street. We enter the ground just in time to see the players lining up for battle. Wakefield are in blue and Cammell have a black kit with red stripes on the front of their shirts. Lucas wants us to go in the "big red stand" and we arrive at our chosen seat just as Cammell score a goal in front of our noses. With just a minute played this is a terrible start for Wakefield in such a crutial game. It is a very soft goal to concede; a tap in from Aaron Bowen to open the scoring for a side that is already relegated. The game restarts and the ball then spends a lot of time stuck in midfield or in the air. This gives me an opportunity to study the ground in the light. It is actually ok, even with all the Ossett Town red around us for a team that is blue, but, like most Non League grounds, needs a lick of paint. Lucas likes it just how it is and finds a section of the stand to store his sweets. I quickly tell him the boundaries for his running game with the finger puppets that have made the trip too.

The Wakefield defenders don't look quite as happy as my son as they spend most of the first quarter of an hour swearing at each other. At least they are communicating I suppose. Cammell are looking much more relaxed on the ball and, despite there still being 75 minutes remaining, I will make a brave statement - if Harrogate Railway win today then Wakefield are down. I don't particularly want to see a club relegated for the sake of my book but someone from Yorkshire will follow Cammell today. In response to my defeatist thoughts, Wakefield fire a header just over the bar when an equaliser looked likely. The quality of the football in front of me, on the whole, is poor but understandable when you study the league table statistics. Lucas is trying to help by providing some entertainment to the seven other people in the stand with some dancing from the swan and parrot. I have Twitter, which rewards me with news that Railway are also a goal down at home to Mossley.

Wakefield appear to be getting back into this game with more possession and less arguing from their players. They may have heard the news from Station View that Mossley have now taken a two goal lead. After 32 minutes, confusion in the Cammell defence almost produces an equaliser courtesy of an own goal. The high pitched scouse sounding complaints suggests that they have travelled from the North West. A quick flick through the programme confirms the exact location is Birkenhead. It is now time for our first toilet stop, once we find some that are not locked. We return to the game in time to see Cammell attacking but the move is halted by the linesman's flag. Lucas has found a friend, so I now have to keep one eye on the game and the other on them, thanks to a game of pebble throwing. The big red stand has lost its appeal and a section of the terracing on the side becomes a playground. Three corners for

Wakefield in succession gets the home fans excited just before the referee spoils the mood to blow for half time.
The Wakefield players can relax for fifteen minutes; and probably for the next three months if they hear about the 0-2 half time score from Harrogate. I fancy a quick pint in the club house bar but after four failed attempts to get my son back it is easier to just give up on that idea. I am happy that he is happy at a game of football, unlike most of the others around me. There is, however, a spring in the step for those that head towards the bar. I have a view of a fried chicken takeaway, a fire station and some wet clothes hanging out to dry, which is not quite as inspiring as some of the previous 62 grounds. Perhaps this reflects the real Yorkshire more accurately, or just normal life wherever in Britain you have chosen to live your life. Watching boats on the sea or lambs skipping in the fields from a football stand is great but not really the norm. I have a scene from my spot on the terrace that is much more real or, dare I say, ordinary.

The teams return to the pitch just as I discover that Railway did in fact pull a goal back with a penalty just before half time. Wakefield may need a draw after all, more than my book needs the tale of a dramatic fight back in North Yorkshire that results in a dancing beaver. Most fans make their way to the stand behind the goal that their team are now attacking, or should be attacking anyway. With ten minutes of the second half gone, the ball has not come anywhere near this end. If Cammell could finish better they would be 2-0 ahead; and probably not bottom of the league of course. A minute later Wakefield get a good chance after their striker runs onto a ball into the box, but the resulting dive doesn't fool me or the referee.

Lucas' friend has a scooter so may now be a friend for life, or at least for the next 30 minutes, as he is very good at sharing his wheels. They don't take any notice of the action on the pitch in the 62nd minute when Cammell's Stephen Ferrigan scores a goal with a simple header. At 2-0 this relegation battle is now all over, so the events in Harrogate have more relevance. Wakefield are really poor and will only stay up if Railway also self destruct. I am not the only spectator who has reached this simple conclusion with everyone around me now playing with their phones. I get distracted by some clapping that is followed by the chant, "Mossley, Mossley...". My phone confirms what I already know, it is now Harrogate Railway 1 Mossley 3 with around 20 minutes left of the season. Within a couple of minutes I see a tweet giving news of a fifth goal for Mossley - I didn't know they had scored a fourth. I hope that the Wakefield players are listening to the cheers around them. They have shown exactly why they could quite easily have been relegated today. Getting a ground of their own, let alone getting to the heights of the Conference, would then have been even harder. It will be hard enough for them next season.

The sound of a "6-1, 6-1" chant by the same group of teenagers and then immediately the final whistle starts a small celebration around me. Alternatively, it could just be a release of the relief that it is all over for another season. I find myself just staring down at the programme, or the same sentence - 'the fate of some clubs who have finished higher up the league is likely to mean a reprieve from relegation for those sides occupying the bottom two places'. Oh. The beaver may well be dancing tonight after all, along with the younger Wakefield fans hitting the pubs. In contrast, I wonder if it is a good night for a takeaway. This is what ordinary people, of my age, do on a Saturday night. I am very happy to join in such traditions by sending Mrs Mowbray to Silsden. I am glad that I didn't read the programme earlier though. This is thanks to bringing a certain four year old boy with me. Otherwise this exciting fixture would have become very ordinary. With just three games remaining of my Yorkshire tour, it is anything but for me!

Wakefield 0 Cammell Laird 2

Attendance 89
Admission £7 (Children £1)
Ground Address Ingfield, Prospect Road, Ossett, W Yorkshire, WF5 9HA
Club website www.wakefieldfc.com
Twitter @WakefieldFC

63 ½

The North Ridings

Guisborough Town FC v Dunston UTS

The King George V Stadium
Northern League Division One
Tuesday 24th April 2012. Kick off 7.45pm

I was born in Leicestershire so can obviously never claim to be a Yorkshire man, even after 7 years of living enthusiastically in this fine county. I will have to settle for my 'new Yorkshire' tag and leave Lucas, and my unborn son, to take the glory. It was therefore only natural that my list of clubs was based on the present Yorkshire borders. I have, however, discovered during the last 10 months that this subject can be controversial with some people. This first came to my attention when a Guisborough Town fan on Twitter appeared to be offended that his club was not on my list. The town is situated in The North Riding of Yorkshire, one of the three historic subdivisions, or ridings, of the county of Yorkshire. Alongside the East and West Ridings, the three ridings were treated as three counties for many purposes.

An administrative county was created with a county council in 1889 under the Local Government Act 1888 on the historic boundaries. Many years later, in 1968, a new county borough of Teesside was created. This took in Middlesbrough and parts of the administrative counties of Durham and The North Riding. From The North Riding came the boroughs of Redcar and Thornaby-on-Tees, the urban district of Eston, and part of Stokesley rural district. The entirety of Teesside, including the parts north of the River Tees historically in Durham, was associated with The North Riding for lieutenancy and other purposes. In 1974 The North Riding was abolished as both an administrative county and a Lieutenancy. The majority of its former area became part of the new non-metropolitan county of North

Yorkshire. Middlesbrough and Redcar became part of Cleveland and are now in independent unitary authorities which became part of North Yorkshire for ceremonial purposes. Confused? I was. So, after seeking guidance from The Yorkshire Ridings Society's website, I decided to contact their chairman for some help. Roger's kind and swift email response to me read:

Hello Michael,

The orders which created the new administrative areas which came into being on 1st April 1974 stated that, 'The new boundaries were not intended to replace the boundaries of the existing counties or the allegiance of the people who lived within them'. This statement has been repeated in orders which have changed some of the 1974 boundaries, eg. when Humberside was abolished on about 1994.

Therefore any team which is within the county boundary which largely has been intact for hundreds of years and is still intact, is a Yorkshire team. The map on our website is probably sufficiently accurate for the most of your research. If you visit the website of The Association of British Counties and go to their Gazetteer, you can input the name of a settlement and it will show which county the place is in.

I hope you will make reference to your use of the county boundary in your work as this is the foundation of all the work which YRS and other county organisations undertake. Presently, county organisations are working towards county boundaries being shown on maps and marked by road signs.

Please get back to me if you need further clarification. I can, probably, supply the full text of the quote above should you ever need it to support your work.

I hope this is helpful and wish you well with your project.

Best Wishes, Roger Sewell, Chairman.

That sounds straightforward then... Although, upon reflection, getting an opinion from someone who heads up a campaign to maintain the old borders is always going to be a little biased. Using the maps on the Society's website would add another eight clubs to my Club Route 66. From the Football League down to Step 7, includes the clubs Middlesbrough, tonight's Guisborough Town, Marske United, Stokesley Sports Club, Thornaby, New Marske, Redcar Athletic and Stockton Town.

I used the above debate as my excuse for coming to Guisborough Town FC tonight. I was in fact 'passing'; well it was just a slight detour from my day in Newcastle. I have really enjoyed my visit to the home of 'The Priorymen' with the bonus of watching a very good game of football. The two sides were very evenly matched, so it was never going to be a goal feast. A draw would have probably been a fairer result, but Dunston's Terry Galbraith goal late in the first half was enough to give the away side the points. The ground's facilities are well above average for my travels. They have two modern, but interesting, stands, one seated and the other terraced. They also have a very friendly clubhouse that can sell visitors a choice of three Non League books to accompany their pint. The accents inside sounded more similar to the people of the North Yorkshire town of Thirsk than the North East that I spent the day in. I didn't really need a room full of people wearing flat caps and white roses to tell me that we are in Yorkshire or not. After all, Yorkshire is a very diverse county and would only become more interesting with the inclusion of the North Ridings. However, none of this is relevant to this argument. Including them simply because they would bring something to the party would be wrong.

My decision is actually relatively simple. I agree, admittedly after many months of pondering, with Roger's view. These borders have existed for hundreds of years, so why use boundaries that are younger than me? My future list will include any football club at Step 7 or above located in the original three Ridings. Yorkshire is England's largest county and its boundary, over 600 miles long, was established more than 1100 years ago. I really can't argue against history. I will produce my Club Route 66 list each season on the 1st August every year, an appropriate date being Yorkshire Day just before the new season begins. Although, there is now one slight problem - I now have six additional grounds to get in if I am going to become a fully fledged member. It would be an awful shame if I didn't qualify for my own club!

Guisborough Town 0 Dunston UTS 1

Attendance Not recorded
Admission £5
Ground Address Howlbeck Road, Guisborough, Cleveland, TS14 6LE
Club website www.clubwebsite.co.uk/guisboroughtownfc
Twitter @guistownfc

64

It must be love

Leeds United AFC v Leicester City

Elland Road

nPOWER Championship.

Saturday 28th April 2012. Kick off 12.30pm

This season has been hugely disappointing for Leeds United supporters. The team's failings have been overshadowed by events off the pitch to provide me with enough material to write an entire book. One of the positives to come out of this rocky period has been the birth of LUST, the Leeds United Supporters Trust. They have flourished from the widespread unhappiness of many fans with regard to the way the current owner, Ken Bates, is running the club. Selling some of their best players, such as the fans' favourite Max Gradel and club captain Jonny Howson, may be the reality for a Championship club, but the cash generated hasn't been invested beyond the usual bunch of loan signings. This lack of ambition was highlighted by the sacking of manager Simon Grayson hours after the transfer window shut. His replacement, Neil Warnock, is viewed by most as a step in the right direction, but results have declined since his arrival to further expose the inadequacies of the squad. Bates treats Leeds United purely as a business, but what other businesses go out of their way to alienate their customers? He has branded some of his customers as "morons" and "sickpots" but has now gone a step further as he doesn't share my enthusiasm for LUST. Gary Cooper, chairman of LUST, was surprised to find that his, and other board members', ticket-purchasing accounts had been stopped. Leeds' chief executive Shaun Harvey's explanation of, "In simple terms we are exercising our right to only sell tickets to those who we wish to do so" is at least honest, but worrying. If that is not enough, Bates has used his match day programme notes and Yorkshire Radio to attack

LUST, which includes, according to Cooper, the disclosure of personal information.

The club has competed at the top level of English football for the majority of its existence, following the disbanding of predecessor Leeds City in 1919. Under Don Revie's management during the 1960s and 1970s, Leeds won two First Division titles, the FA Cup, the League Cup and the Inter-Cities Fairs Cup twice. Eight years after Revie's departure to manage the England team, they were relegated to the Second Division in 1982. They didn't return to the top flight until 1990, when they were managed by Howard Wilkinson. Wilkinson's Leeds were league champions two seasons later. During the 1990s and early 2000s Leeds competed for places in Europe, reaching the semi-finals of the UEFA Cup and the UEFA Champions League in consecutive seasons. Shortly after, the club got into serious financial problems caused by living beyond their means and gambling on securing Champions League football, which they failed to do for the 2002/03 season. The following season, Leeds were relegated from the Premier League and then from the Championship three years later. After three seasons in the third tier of English football, they were promoted back to the Championship on the last day of the 2009/10 season with a dramatic win against Bristol Rovers. Last season the team over achieved in my opinion by finishing 7th, just one place off a play-off position. Expectations were then raised towards securing automatic promotion this season. Admittedly, it doesn't take much for this happen!

When I originally chose today's fixture last August, I had hoped it would be the final curtain on my travels and also include a promotion winning party to finish the book with a bang. Perhaps the team's poor form is due to me taking advantage of the extra week that the League Two season gave me; and then Wednesday's match at Albion Sports was postponed to make Elland Road ground number 64. There really isn't a lot to celebrate today. However, LUST don't agree and emailed their 5,000 members with an invitation to join them to say goodbye to season 2011/12 in the "most appropriate way we can think of: by having a bloody good party". The venue for the party is very appropriate, a section of the East Stand Upper tier. There is, after all, much disapproval on the reportedly £7m, secured against two years of season ticket sales, that was lavished last summer on new corporate facilities in this stand. Where LUST is strong is in their organisation and the professional way that they have conducted themselves, such as the publishing of a Vision Statement and holding a peaceful march attended by over 1,000 fans to a home game. It is then much harder, with credibility anyway, to slate these fans. A disillusioned lone supporter doesn't have much of a voice, but LUST is now one of the largest supporters' trusts in the country according to Supporters Direct. As their latest email states, 'The response from those in charge of the club has been to dismiss those on the protest march as "kids"; to claim that the Trust represents nobody; to claim that the Trust are having no effect on anybody, while at the same time claiming that the Trust are putting off potential investors; and finally to prevent the Trust board from buying any more tickets to Leeds' games'. I can confirm that my son George was actually one of the few kids on the march that day!

I recognise that there needs to be a balance between investment on and off the pitch in the modern game. This does, however, feel very one sided at the moment, but it is only fair to say that the East Stand development does look good from the outside. Ken Bates argues that, "We'll have a much better stand and much better facilities for the fans whether they be corporates or ordinary fans ... It's going to be a magnificent stand when it's finished. We won't have the biggest ground in the country but I think we might have the best. One of the best, if not the best as far as facilities for fans are concerned whatever size of the pocket." I decided to transfer our season tickets today to the upper tier to join in with the fun and it would also be a treat for George. I took him to the Etihad Stadium earlier in the month and he really liked the height of his seat. We may not have Aguero and Tevez but hope that if we are high enough up he may not notice the difference. I was warned by LUST that there would be an 'admin fee' for transferring our seat. I was also happy with the explanation by the ticket office that we would have to pay the difference for moving to a more expensive area of the ground. I knew that tickets in the Upper tier are priced at £40 so £11 for me seemed as reasonable as it could be when charging a ridiculous amount of money for a mid table Championship game. However, paying an extra £27 to transfer George's ticket is nothing short of disgraceful. I just can't accept the "there are no concessions in that stand" explanation, particularly when this is an area that is always a mass of empty seats. Is this the way to treat a seven year old season ticket holder? He is surely the lifeblood of this club. I was so annoyed I paid the extra, (this logic makes sense to me anyway). I think that my son, with his small pockets of an 'ordinary fan', deserves a chance to watch a game from the flagship stand.

We enter our usual turnstile, but today take a sharp right towards the upper tier. We climb a lot of stairs! I am reasonably fit but I'm out of breath by the top. I would love to say that it was worth the effort but feel very disappointed by my surroundings. We have bought the most expensive seats, but have the luxury of a small bar in a drafty concrete space, similar to standing in a multi storey car park to drink some overpriced cider. So how have we, non corporate fans, benefited from this revamp? I would go as far to say that the facilities up here are actually worse that my usual area below us.
A couple of pints later, we go to our seat just to warm up. The view is very good at least, but exactly the same view that has been there since the stand was built. Or am I missing something? The teams soon kick off to start a rendition of every anti-Bates song there is from the couple of hundred party goers. Some revellers get carried away and their standing up, not usually a crime on Route 66, is attracting a lot of attention from the army of stewards that have arrived. After ten minutes, a fan is removed from the party for having the words Bates Out on his t-shirt! I can't help myself and feel the need to argue his case to the steward, but George's concerned face stops me in my tracks. Five minutes later, the ejected fan is eventually let back to a hero's welcome because he has agreed to cover up the "offensive t-shirt". Nobody will be offended now thanks to the thoughtful

stewards. The "you're the scum of Elland Road" chant can only help their job satisfaction. The LUST branded balloons are not only spreading around the stadium but some have entered the pitch to risk getting a life ban. A wad of false notes are also thrown into the air to accompany the "where's all our money gone?" cry. The stewards are watching our every move whilst the couple of police officers are watching the game.

At half time I make the most of the sparse crowd in this area and head back to my concrete lounge for another apple juice. The really vicious steward, who I recognise from my kop days as the "he's got bird shit in his hair" man, patrols the concourse. We should feel honoured that we have warranted his presence up here. He does have the biggest ear piece on show in addition to his naturally streaked hair. He must have been bullied at school and now enjoys this power for two hours every fortnight. The stewarding of Elland Road is nothing short of diabolical in truth. Why do they have to be so aggressive? I am of the school where I do genuinely believe that if you treat people like animals they will behave like them. I beat my chest and decide that I have had enough fruit for today.

George and I return to our seats to find even more stewards watching our every move. More supporters are disciplined like naughty children and another person is removed. The offence this time was for standing up too long after a Leeds attack. One teenager is actually warned for waving a balloon. I really do wish that I was joking. The protesters think on their feet (sorry, I meant sitting down nicely) and come up with the rare football song of "thrown out, for having a balloon, thrown out...." that generates a smile from the friendlier police officers. The next 45 minutes are just a repeat of the first 45 minutes so stop making notes. The final whistle blows to end this party and Leeds United's season. We are told on the tannoy system, which is crystal clear up here, that the players will come back out for their traditional lap of honour if we all behave by staying off the pitch. They look as embarrassed as we are for still being here when they do arrive. I use the time to have a chat with one of the police officers.

I ask him why a Bates Out t-shirt was such a problem today. "It's not a problem to us. We are not allowed to get involved though. The stewards are in charge up here. If I took the t-shirt off him I would keep it for myself". Clearly, the stewards are the law, which I think is slightly worrying. We eventually drag ourselves away from the waving players and return to our old life of roughing it on the bus.

Ken Bates has been in the courts this week for remarks he has made in his programme to a more powerful individual than the chairman of a supporters trust. Bates has used freedom of speech as his defence, but doesn't feel that his own ticket buying customers, the supporters of the club that he is privileged to 'own', deserve the same rights. There was, of course, a match also going on today which I'm afraid was irrelevant. Leeds have finished 14th in the table and I can't really look beyond this fact. Next season is an important period for this club. The big question of whether the current owner will back the manager with funds to strengthen the team will be answered before a ball is kicked. I fear the worst but hope that I am proven wrong. George tells me that this has been a good party, but it's a shame more people didn't come. I'm not so sure myself. £40 a ticket, whatever your age and pocket size, to watch a poor Championship game whilst being harassed is not really great value for money. This blatant disinterest in the next generation of supporters, despite an empty stand, says everything about the current state that this once proud club is in. There is a very good reason, or many reasons in fact, that there is very little love lost between the club and their supporters. LUST may help, or may actually drive them even further apart. As for Route 66, I'm not sure you will ever be able to buy this book in the club shop now that I have bravely criticised the chairman. I can definitely live with this fact. This is called freedom of speech, just my personal views but what do I know? I just hope that by moving my seat to L37 today on the ticket office computer we are not now blacklisted for coming back next season. Nothing would surprise me after today.

Leeds United 1 Leicester City 2

Attendance 25,660

Admission £40 (Children £40)

Ground Address Elland Road, Leeds, LS11 0ES.

Club website www.leedsunited.com

Twitter @LUFCLeedsUnited @OfficialLUFC @lufctrust

65

Above us only sky

Albion Sports FC v Shirebrook Town

Throstle Nest

Baris Northern Counties East League Division One

Thursday 3rd May 2012. Kick off 7.45pm

Albion Sports were not included on my original list of Yorkshire clubs. On the opening day of Route 66 at Eccleshill United I heard that they had been elected to join Step 6. The club was founded in 1974 and initially played in the Bradford Amateur Sunday League. After a brief spell in the lower divisions, they gained promotions on a regular basis. They also won some silverware along the way in the Amateur District and Senior cups. Albion Sports won the Premier league title in 1996 for the first time and then won a further five league titles, two County Cups, three District Cups and seven Senior Cups. Albion Sports have been honoured by receiving three civic receptions from the City of Bradford as well as beating Star Trek's Patrick Stewart to the award of 'Ambassadors of West Yorkshire' (this has no relevance to this chapter but it impressed me). The club resigned from Sunday football in 2007 in order to progress up through the pyramid. In 2007 Albion Sports joined the Telegraph and Argus league and won promotion in their first season as well as winning the League Cup. Albion Sports were elected to the WRCAFC in 2008, gained promotion in their first season and also won the District Cup. In 2009/10, Albion Sports finished runners-up in the Premiership and won the Divisional Cup. In the 2010/11 season, the team again finished runners-up and were then successfully elected to join the NCEL last August.

I was due to return to the Horsall Stadium last week as Albion Sports share Bradford Park Avenue's ground. Based on my experience on that cold evening in January watching Avenue, I am not really a fan of this venue. It could well be perfect for watching a 100 metre sprint, but it doesn't create the unique atmosphere of a Non League football match. However, the postponement of their match due to a waterlogged pitch didn't trigger any celebration from me. Once I had got over how we appear to have moved from a drought to floods in a couple of days, this news actually made me feel physically sick. The scenario that repeatedly went around my head, for over 5 hours until I found out the rearranged date, was simple - if the rearranged game was to be played on the same day as the Leeds or Rotherham matches then I could not complete Route 66! All the spreadsheets in the world, and despite ten months of dashing around Yorkshire, could not save me from this doomsday scenario.

The news that the game would be played tonight was very good indeed. Thursdays are usually free and, from memory, the first game I ever attended on a Thursday. The following day I received a tweet asking me if the fact that the game is now going to be played at Eccleshill United was a problem or not for my mission. This would only be an issue if their own ground hadn't already been visited. They can play anywhere provided I'm there and it felt quite fitting to return to the opening venue where Albion Sports' existence was discovered. Yesterday, however, after a quick check on the website, the venue has moved again. I am now going back to Farsley! At least I know how to get there and, importantly, it hasn't rained to put any doubts on whether ground 65 will happen.

I enter an eerie Throstle Nest as there appears to be even less people here than when Mrs Mowbray's Farsley Ladies played. The usual club shop, selling Farsley AFC goodies, is understandably closed but, in anticipation of a low attendance, they have also decided not to open the tea bar. I fear it could possibly be one of the smallest of Route 66. A Bradford team are playing in Leeds and there is not a lot, or I could go as far as saying nothing, to play for. This is the final game in the Division 1 season and Handsworth were crowned champions last weekend at Worksop Parramore. Albion are 4th and Shirebrook are 13th but they will both stay in these positions regardless of the score tonight. I am therefore, pleasantly surprised to count at least 20 other people here. I didn't think Thursday nights on TV were that bad. There is, however, a programme to buy, complete with the date on the front cover changed with the help of some Tipex. Unfortunately, the pin badges "didn't travel" which is a mistake harder to correct in my opinion. Albion Sports play in yellow and blue, but I'll never know how that would have looked on metal. The visitors from Derbyshire are in all white.

The game kicks off without me really noticing. Within minutes Albion get my attention by almost taking the lead with a shot from close range. The Shirebrook keeper makes a very good reflex save. A minute later, the 'home' side almost find the net again to suggest that this meaningless game is not so meaningless after all to the players. I have chosen to stand behind the goal that Albion Sports are defending. I am all alone so I must look like a solitary away fan, although of course, we are all away tonight. All of the play is at the other end so I may be switching my position soon. After 15 minutes, the Albion number 10 hits a volley in the box that just goes wide of the post. It is definitely time to stretch my legs!

I stand alone again, but this time at the opposite end. The other spectators are all huddled together in or around Farsley's main stand. The play has, annoyingly, now moved to the opposite end and Shirebrook almost score on 25 minutes. Albion react to that scare, (and to reward my walk), with a couple of chances, but their finishing is poor again. I may not see another goal this season is my sobering thought as Albion embarrass themselves by side footing a cross wide when hitting the goal was the easier option. With 10 minutes left to half time, the floodlights are switched on to take away the possible excuse of bad light for the goalless score line. I decide to take a walk again to edge closer to the clubhouse ready for the dash to the bar. The Shirebrook players follow me down the pitch and start to put some pressure on Albion with an attack. They should have left more defenders back though as I watch Aron Heywood in the distance turn and fire the ball into the roof of the net. He certainly made no mistake with that finish!

A quick cider at half time feels appropriate and I'm pleased to find that Cardiff verses West Ham in the Championship play-offs is showing on the big screen. I'm not bitter, but I have no interest who wins the play offs. If Leeds were playing West Ham tonight this would have given me a huge dilemma! I remember the days when 15 minutes gave me more than enough time to sink a pint. The men beside me are discussing the "2-0" score at this game. After the fun of finding a signal, the internet confirms that Aron Heywood actually gave Albion the lead in the 18th minute! How could I have missed that? I didn't go anywhere. Despite all of these matches giving me a lot of practice, I appear to still be utterly useless at concentrating on a game of football. Perhaps I blinked for too long in the 18th minute or am suffering from a rare disease. I'm also suffering with this pint, but decide that my excuse with this poor performance is because of my sensitive teeth to the cold.

I return to the pitch but the game has already started. I ask someone if "it's still 2-0?" in the hope that someone tells me that I am crazy as it is 1-0. No, it is in fact 2-0, but I catch the number 14 tapping the ball into the net for 3-0. At least I saw that one. Adam Jones is the scorer according to the fan next to me. His friend missed it but his excuse of "it's rude not to look at the person you are talking to" is credible. I agree under normal circumstances, but football matches..? I'm not rude, it's just that occasionally I lose my concentration at critical times. When I do finally see a goal, particularly at this level of football, I don't always know who the player is. This knowledge must take years. I have been brought up on the loud cheers that greet goals and the electronic score boards in the Football League. I can clearly see that it is now one way traffic in front of me. Albion are attacking constantly so keep watching very carefully. On 70 minutes the post is struck which halts, for a second or two, the men's conversation on horse racing, pubs and how everyone is skint. They really should pay more attention as another shot flies wide. The fourth goal soon arrives from Heywood who now has a hat trick. He confidently hits a shot from the edge of the box to make my earlier concerns about seeing a goal look rather silly.

With five minutes of the game remaining, Alex Cusack makes it five goals for Albion Sports, or he may well have made it 15-0 as I did visit the toilet earlier. The whistle blows to put me out of my misery and I say goodbye to Non League football. Well for Route 66 anyway. I still have Guiseley's involvement in the play-offs to keep me at grass roots for a couple of weeks more. Two more trips to Nethermoor in the next ten days could see Guiseley start next season in the Conference. Promotion would result in bigger crowds, singing on the terraces and the segregation of fans. Perhaps this is not what I want at all, although they may then have the funds to build a score board to help me keep track. I am getting all confused. It is all that swapping of ends that has made me dizzy and watching a 'home' team play away at a ground that has already featured this season. But saying that, it was the ladies who played then and I didn't write that chapter. Or dear. My jibbering nonsense could actually be because I am now standing on the top of Route 66 heaven with nothing above me but a dark sky and a trip to Sheffield. Heading south on the M1 will never feel this good! "Here we go, here we go, here we go..."

Albion Sports 5 Shirebrook Town 0

Attendence 18
Admission £5
Ground Address Horsfall Stadium, Cemetery Rd, Bradford, BD6 2NG
Club website www.albionsports.co.uk
Twitter @AlbionSportsAFC

66

Empire State of Mind

Rotherham United FC v Northampton Town

The Don Valley Stadium
nPOWER League Two
Saturday 5th May 2012. Kick off 3pm

Hey, look at me. In a few hours time the football grounds of Yorkshire will be all mine. It has been very easy to be swept up in the momentum of ticking the grounds off. The months soon pass and the seasons just changed without me really noticing. Other than the stresses caused by the threat of failure, I have been completely blinkered. I can now finally open my eyes to take in this moment and reflect on my own personal achievement. During the last 24 hours I have come to terms with the fact that I have actually done it! I had told myself that failure was not an option but looking back now it could quite easily have happened. My state of mind could not be better today as I travel to Sheffield in the sunshine. I am prepared to bask in my glory, for a few hours anyway, by choosing the comfort of the train. This will allow me to have a couple of pints. I have my favourite gourmet jelly beans for half time and we have some Champagne in the fridge for my return. In my eyes, I have had one of the best years of my life so it's worth recognising my achievement. Well, it is a good excuse to drink too much!

You don't have to go back far in Rotherham United FC's history for it to be eventful. In 2006, the club faced an uncertain future. They needed to fund a gap of around £140,000 per month. Their ground had already been sold in order to clear a previous debt of £3m, so they had no tangible assets. Despite the huge "Save The Millers" campaign and some new investment, the club entered a Company Voluntary Arrangement. Their administration resulted in them being docked ten points at the start of the 2006/07 season. This handicap, and having a skeleton first team squad, resulted in their relegation to League Two. In March 2008, the club again went into administration and were deducted ten points. Local businessman

Tony Stewart bought the club and was advised not to exit administration via a CVA. On 6th August 2008, days before the new season, the Football League threatened to block their participation in League Two due to their continued administration. Rotherham had no choice but to start the campaign at minus 17 points. In addition, they were forced to leave Millmoor, that had been their home for over 100 years, over a dispute with the landlord. They had also sold their training ground at Hooten Roberts so trained in Doncaster Rover's Keepmoat Stadium. The Football League demanded a £750,000 bond for playing outside of the town's boundaries for a maximum of 4 years. If they failed to move back to Rotherham by 2012 they would risk losing their league status.

The club are now entering a new era with chairman Tony Stewart leading the charge to their new £20m landmark venue, the New York stadium. The name New York is the historic name for the area. The old Guest and Chrimes Foundry made the distinctive fire hydrants there that were dotted around the streets of New York. The company exported metal infrastructure to the growing cities on the other side of the Atlantic. Stewart described the name of the stadium as the perfect link between the history of the area and the bright new era which awaits the club.

On the pitch, manager Steve Evans joined them this year following a successful spell at his former club, Crawley Town. Evans appears to be very unpopular in the football world, at least based on my twiter followers' comments, from his shady past. Rotherham are currently 10th in League Two but five points adrift from a play-off place. Northampton Town are 19th but have a six point cushion from relegation to the non league. No one can go up or down, so is this another end of season meaningless fixture? Not at all! For the majority present today, they can finally say goodbye to playing football in Sheffield and go home to Rotherham. Without their new stadium, the club would have been thrown out of the Football League, so today will become a hugely significant date in its history.

I have high hopes of finally eating a Pukka pie today as the pie man from Rotherham, who you have previously read about, has kindly organised the day for me. Mathew Twigg, of Eric Twigg Foods, has got me a ticket in the Executive Lounge and the hospitality even extends to meeting me at Sheffield train station. I recognise his photo from twitter so can ignore the advice of not getting into a strangers car. Matthew then takes me on a tour of Rotherham to visit both the new and the old. The lonely image of Millmoor that looks, from a distance, ready to open its gates would have been even sadder if it wasn't for the excitement of seeing her replacement. The New York stadium is an example of how a new ground can be a step forward. A bowl, rather than four plain rectangular stands, with a roof construction designed by an architect with an imagination. The sensible 12,000 capacity and steep stands that close in on the pitch offer the potential of a great atmosphere being created. Certain areas of the ground will include some retail outlets to help the club generate revenue on non match days and hopefully avoid their previous financial problems. I can now see why manager Steve Evans has seen the benefit of showing their new ground to their potential signings.

My tourist trip of Sheffield ends as we arrive at the Don Valley, park up and enter the VIP area via the lift. This doesn't feel right, similar to how I felt going up an escalator in the new Wembley. We make our way to the bar, but I am refused entry for wearing jeans. This would be very ironic if I can't get in! The world stops for a few minutes, but Matthew works his magic, again, and I am soon holding a pint of cider watching Rangers v Motherwell on the big screen. One of Matthew's friends comments to me that watching 66 games in a season is a "colossal achievement". After a few seconds to digest his compliment, I reply, "I've been to Ibrox too this season" pointing at the TV. This gets me thinking. 66 minus Hutton Cranswick, plus 25-ish Leeds games and add a few extra trips on those Tuesday nights without a fixture in Yorkshire... "Good lord. I think I have been to at least 100 games this season". Is this something to boast about or keep a secret?

The day keeps improving with the news that Matthew has arranged for me to visit the changing rooms to meet the players and manager! I am given a Rotherham shirt and wander around with a permanent marker pen. I just smile, a lot. Like the months, time passes and I am soon heading back to the bar with a shirt covered in signatures. Steve Evans, who came across well to me in our 60 second chat, has written 'Route 66' on the bottom in a thick pen. It looks great, so I make a very quick decision, without consulting the others that live with me. This shirt just has to be framed to become my trophy of the season! Even the news that today's hospitality does not include a Pukka pie, instead the strange combination of gammon steaks and rice, will not dampen my mood. I just keep smiling. I smile when Matthew's friend tells me that leaving the Don Valley will be mixture of happiness and sadness. I am introduced to the club chairman and again I continue to smile. I only get happier when Matthew's father, the Eric of Eric Twigg Foods, promises me a Pukka pie when I am invited to visit the New York stadium in pre season. It would be rude to say no.

The room starts to empty around me to remind me that there is also a game of football here today. I am led to my seat which is one of the best in the ground, although I am still at least 3 miles away from the pitch. For those that have not had the privilege to visit the Don Valley stadium, it is a huge athletics stadium and putting a football pitch in the middle of it doesn't change this fact. We would be quite a distance from the inside lane to watch the two teams compete in the 800 metres relay. The far touchline could well be in another county. Today, it doesn't matter though as this is ground number 66. To the supporters around me, it doesn't matter. They have put up with this view for four seasons but are now finally leaving! The chairman makes a speech over the PA system and there are a few watery eyes in the posh seats. So posh in fact, he then takes his seat immediately in front of me.
Rotherham are in red shirts and socks with white sleeves. Northampton are in their away strip of claret and yellow. Many of the travelling supporters have chosen to wear fancy dress and based on the position of the away end, in the distant corner, also have

something to celebrate today as they will not miss the Don Valley stadium either. The playing surface looks good to give me something positive to write about the ground. The game kicks off on the horizon and I decide to make a special effort to only write nice things for the next 90 minutes... Many minutes pass. Rotherham hit the post after 9 minutes which results in the chairman jumping off the ground. The song "Sheffield's a shit hole, I want to go home" makes me smile again and after 32 minutes Alex Revell sweetly hits the ball on the half volley to give Rotherham the lead. That really is about it for the first 45 minutes, but I am conscious that my smile may have developed into a weird grin that may be scaring the junior fans.

At half time I excel myself, drinking my complimentary coffee and another pint of cider. We discuss the FA Cup final that is kicking off today at 5.15pm. I politely remark that I will be on the train home then without the luxury of a portable television. I really want to start a rant. The biggest domestic football cup final in the world is now just a sideshow to anyone who actually supports a team. The majority of fans who have attended a game today will be stuck in traffic. This is nothing short of appalling and shows that the people that now govern our national sport do not understand the game that provides them with a high standard of living. I hope it's a rubbish game! I enter the prize draw to win a signed shirt, even though I have one in my bag, just to show that I am not the grumpy old man that I am feeling like.

The second half begins as I am finishing another pint, but I eventually make my way back to the game as I realise that I am all alone in the bar. The achievement of Route 66 has clearly gone to my head, literally. I go back to my seat and nothing much has changed in front of me. I am not sure I have been missed either. Rotherham continue to create more good chances to extend their lead but lack the final ball. The same songs continue about Sheffield which readers from the city should not take personally. The Millers' fans just want to go home and in a strange way so do I. As I think this thought it sounds totally crazy. It has been the perfect day in so many ways, but I am now simply looking forward to returning to Ilkley. I want to get home in time for my sons' bedtime story, perhaps wave my prize shirt in the air and drink my sparkly with Mrs Mowbray on the sofa. Northampton equalise with seconds left, but it doesn't matter. Nobody cares and the final whistle is greeted with a roar fit for a cup final. Despite the warning to not enter the playing surface, a small pitch invasion begins. I just have to join them! I shake Matthews hand, say thank you and find myself running down the steps towards the turf. I hurdle the advertising board, like the athlete this stadium deserves, dodge a steward, young enough to be my son, and run across the grass with my arms in the air. This is my moment. I'm now being selfish I know. This city is mine. Yorkshire is mine!

I didn't unfortunately ever get the chance to visit Millmoor, but I have now bagged the Don Valley with just hours to spare. The New York stadium, like for the majority of people travelling back to Rotherham from Sheffield, excites me. The club hope that the name of their new stadium could open up doors for commercial opportunities and possibly to set up links with New York in the USA. Provided that they keep those sponge hands for baseball in the States, I am sure they will be very happy with their move. I am now the first member of Club Route 66, or, to the average man on the street, the nutter who has been to every football ground in Yorkshire. Has this been a mid life crisis? Perhaps it has. If so, this is my half time moment on this world. Tonight I will have my Bovril, but with bubbles. I can't wait for the second half of my life to begin. I search my iPod on the tram and find the song that has been going around my head all day. "New York, these dreams will make you feel brand new, these lights will inspire you" could have been written for the Millers.

As I write my final chapter of this book, Rotherham United are entering a new chapter in their history. It won't all be bright lights, but it will at least be home. On that note, I am also pleased to be going home. Despite spending so much time on Route 66, I actually quite like the place, a surprise to those who may have questioned my priorities during the last ten months. I can still remember how good my bed felt after my mammoth day watching the Seadogs. Or the relief of sinking into my warm sofa after manoeuvring through the packed snow on the Harrogate ring road. I can now finally smile at how nice tucking my boys up in their beds felt after returning from Northallerton. Football to me is good because life itself is good. Football is clearly a huge part of my life and it is a relief that I am not alone. If you are an armchair fan reading this book, I hope it inspires you to taste the live action. It could just change your life!

Rotherham United 1 Northampton Town 1

Attendance 4,729
Admission Free
Ground Address Worksop Road, Sheffield, S9 3TL.
Club website www.themillers.co.uk
Twitter @rotherhamunited @OfficialRUFC

Brand new

Rotherham United FC *Revisited* v Doncaster Rovers

The New York Stadium
Pre Season Friendly
Tuesday 24th July 2012. Kick off 7.45pm

Despite attending over a 100 football games last season, I now feel refreshed and itching to get back on my travels just ten weeks later. If we didn't have a baby due in a few days time, that will no doubt turn our lives upside down for a good chunk of the new season, I may now be planning my next adventure. I have been busy, of course, finishing my book and designing my new website, which will be up and running by the time you read these words. Fans with addictive personalities need to stay clear of www.clubroute66.co.uk!

In an attempt to get my pre-season fix, this is my fourth game in the last two weeks. I have already welcomed Knaresborough Town to Club Route 66 since their promotion to Step 6, returned to Nethermoor (at the very first opportunity!) and, last week, discovered Chorley's magnificent Victoria Park. Gold membership of Club Route 66 appears to be getting harder with the news filtering through that more leagues have been awarded Step 7 status. This would take the total number of clubs past the 100 mark. Many of these new open spaces, closer to a children's park than a stadium in some cases, will be pram friendly, so allow the task of regaining membership to my own club to start immediately.

Continuing where I left off in May, and with Alicia Keys' chorus still inside my head, I am not the only one feeling brand new. I am outside the new home of Rotherham United – The New York Stadium. I am waiting for my pie man, Matthew Twigg, and I am hoping to finally get a Pukka Pie this evening. The signs are good; two huge signs, in fact, of his family business complete with the Pukka logo above my head. Eric Twigg Foods has sponsored one of the new stands and

Matthew continued his generosity by kindly inviting me to see inside for this pre season friendly. My excitement, and hunger, are helping me to forget how hot it is this evening. My temperature gauge read 31 degrees Celsius as I parked my car earlier, which is almost identical to the weather across the Atlantic in New York. The stadium doesn't quite look finished cosmetically, very visible inside the various empty retail outlets. I am told that the ground almost didn't get the Fire Brigade's approval days earlier for their opening game. It was a relief to everyone involved that the game did take place with a reduced 50% capacity and rewarded by a victory over local Championship side Barnsley. Tonight the club have made 75% of the seats available and on Saturday they play Hearts when the restrictions will be lifted completely. The match on the 28th July against the Scottish side was more appealing, but falls on Mrs Mowbray's actual due date. Without a crystal ball, tonight's match felt like the best option.

Once inside, I can see for myself exactly why Matthew and the other Rotherham fans have been so excited about their new home. It really is perfect for them! An imaginative design, a roof that changes height, a sensible capacity and steep sides leading right up to the touchline. It could not be more different that the Don Valley Stadium that they left behind in May. The Millers are wearing their brand new commemorative amber and black away kit. The club's motivation may well be to boost sales but will allow everyone to be sentimental this season. I am close to tears myself with emotion as I tuck into my steak and kidney Pukka pie. The game itself is less appetising, a typical pre season encounter where I think you probably need to support one of these teams to actually enjoy. Lots of effort and a few half chances, but the score stays goalless.

The half time interval is an opportunity for me to play text tennis with my wife. She is probably fed up with me asking how she is when she can't tell me what I am really asking her. Babies come when they are ready apparently. There are no labour pains back in Ilkley, but I detect, or over analyse, less certainly that tonight is not the night. This makes me a little nervous being in Rotherham and my thoughts are not really on tonight's game as the players return for the second half. The game does improve with a goal. Doncaster take the lead when David Cotterill scores a stunning goal, hitting a shot from the edge of the penalty box. It was a good strike that takes my mind off calculating my journey time home and my remaining mobile phone battery life.

In the 64th minute, the Millers get the equaliser that they deserve with a clean finish from Mark Bradley. It is not just the drama on the pitch that has increased as the texts from home are unsettling me. The latest message, "I am feeling a bit strange", is followed by a notification that I now have less than 5% battery power remaining on my phone. I am a good hour and a half from home and even further away from Airedale hospital. My phone will struggle to see out the second half and I make a very quick decision that I won't be either. Tonight isn't the night to take risks and I have seen enough of the New York Stadium to know that I will return on many occasions. I quickly thank Matthew, again, and slip away into the night. Not that I need to. None of the other 5,966 people inside will notice my departure, or care. Life goes on and will do for years to come. People come to our football grounds and then go again without anyone noticing. Babies are born into their over-priced mini football kits and fans pass away leaving their ashes to be scattered on the turf. Rotherham United Football Club has started its new life and I will soon be welcoming my new son to start his life. A steward lets me out of the gate just as I hear the roar of the home supporters celebrating another goal without me. There we go - I told you they really don't need me!

Rotherham United 2 Doncaster Rovers 1

Attendance: 5,967

James Mowbray was born at 4.55am on Saturday 28th July 2012 on his due date. I could have just about made the Hearts game after all...

ACKNOWLEDGEMENTS

I would like to thank...

John Beevers for some much needed inspiration when this book was just a silly idea,
My Twitter followers for confirming that Route 66 was an adventure worth taking... and then not blocking me for my jibber jabber ,
Author Tom Palmer for his time and good advice at the Ilkley Literature Festival .
Blackline Press for backing me from day one.
Eccleshill United's Adrian Benson and Nick Hird for giving me the start I needed.
Jonathan Stittle for an amazing evening in Sheffield and putting so much into his club.
Bob Main for the pint.
Dan Moylan for not eating my spare ribs.
Matthew Twigg for being a genuine and decent person.
Lee Thurston for being a fashion role model for George and reinventing the flat cap.
Tony Greenall for always being there at the touch of a button.
Michael Vaughan for giving my life a moment of credibility.
Alan Davies for his patience and personal time to proof read my book. Route 66 would still be a rough draft without our meetings at the banks of the river Aire to exchange brown envelopes.
My children for actually liking the fact that their father is insane

And most of all THANK YOU to my wife Susan who has proven that happy husbands can achieve anything

M J Mowbray

Twitter @MowbrayRoute66

www.clubroute66.co.uk

Thank you for buying my book and your interest in the last year of my life. Can I ask you one final thing? Please read this page. Only then have I really achieved something. I am keen to raise greater awareness of MND, which is always the first step.

Michael
(M J Mowbray)

About motor neurone disease (MND)

• Motor neurone disease (MND) is a fatal, neurological disease for which there is no effective treatment and no cure.
• MND kills five people in the UK every day.
• Today there are 5,000 people living with MND in the UK.
• Life expectancy from diagnosis is two to five years, and around half of those die within 14 months.
• It can affect any adult at any age.
• There is no cure and we do not know the cause of MND in 95% of cases.
• Imagine being trapped inside a body that can't move. That's the devastating reality of MND.
• MND attacks the nerves that control movement; people with MND can still think and feel, but their muscles refuse to work. As these nerves die the muscles weaken and waste, leaving people locked in a failing body, unable to move, walk or talk.
• MND is a complex disease and the symptoms of MND are unique to each person.
• Its often rapid progression and wide range of symptoms requires a proactive and multi-disciplinary approach to care. People with MND may require up to 18 different health specialists to help manage their condition.

About the Motor Neurone Disease (MND) Association

• The MND Association is the only national charity in England, Wales and Northern Ireland dedicated to people affected by MND.

• The MND Association funds and promotes research to bring about an end to MND. Until then we will strive to enable everyone with MND to receive the best care, achieve the highest quality of life possible and die with dignity. We will also do all that we can to support the families and carers of people with MND.

• The MND Association is a leader in the funding of cutting-edge MND research both within the UK and across the world. We only fund research of the highest scientific excellence and greatest relevance to MND and help to kick-start exciting new areas of scientific investigation into MND.

• The leading reputation of the MND Association means that for every £1 committed to collaborative MND research, another £2 to £3is attracted from other major funding bodies.

• The MND Association currently fund ground-breaking projects in a number of various world-class research institutes in Edinburgh, London, Oxford, Sheffield and New York, among others. This flexible approach allows us to fund the best and most promising research regardless of the geographical location.

• The MND Association was founded in 1979 by a group of volunteers determined to provide support for people affected by MND and fund research into effective treatments.

For more information on the MND Association please visit their website www.mndassociation.org.
Registered Charity Number 294354.

mnda
motor neurone disease
association

www.ossett-brewery.co.uk